**SAGE** was founded in 1965 by Sara Miller McCune to support the dissemination of usable knowledge by publishing innovative and high-quality research and teaching content. Today, we publish over 900 journals, including those of more than 400 learned societies, more than 800 new books per year, and a growing range of library products including archives, data, case studies, reports, and video. SAGE remains majority-owned by our founder, and after Sara's lifetime will become owned by a charitable trust that secures our continued independence.

Los Angeles | London | New Delhi | Singapore | Washington DC | Melbourne

# Migrants, Refugees and the Stateless in South Asia

## Bulk Sales

SAGE India offers special discounts
for purchase of books in bulk.
We also make available special imprints
and excerpts from our books on demand.

*For orders and enquiries, write to us at*

Marketing Department
SAGE Publications India Pvt Ltd
B1/I-1, Mohan Cooperative Industrial Area
Mathura Road, Post Bag 7
New Delhi 110044, India

*E-mail us at* **marketing@sagepub.in**

## Get to know more about SAGE

Be invited to SAGE events, get on our mailing list.
*Write today to* **marketing@sagepub.in**

This book is also available as an e-book.

# Migrants, Refugees and the Stateless in South Asia

## Partha S. Ghosh

Los Angeles | London | New Delhi
Singapore | Washington DC | Melbourne

*First published in 2016 by*

 **SAGE Publications India Pvt Ltd**
B1/I-1 Mohan Cooperative Industrial Area
Mathura Road, New Delhi 110 044, India
*www.sagepub.in*

**SAGE Publications Inc**
2455 Teller Road
Thousand Oaks, California 91320, USA

**SAGE Publications Ltd**
1 Oliver's Yard, 55 City Road
London EC1Y 1SP, United Kingdom

**SAGE Publications Asia-Pacific Pte Ltd**
3 Church Street
#10-04 Samsung Hub
Singapore 049483

Published by Vivek Mehra for SAGE Publications India Pvt Ltd, typeset in Minion Pro 10/12.5 pt by Zaza Eunice, Hosur, Tamil Nadu and printed at Saurabh Printers Pvt Ltd, Greater Noida.

Library of Congress Cataloging-in-Publication Data Available

**ISBN:** 978-93-515-0854-0 (HB)

**The SAGE Team:** N. Unni Nayar, Vandana Gupta and Vinitha Nair

*Dedicated to*
*Professor Dietmar Rothermund with affection and gratitude*

*Panchhi nadiya pawan ke jhonke, koi sarhad na inhe roke.*

(No border can prevent birds, rivers and wind from crossing it.)

Song from the Bollywood flick *Refugee* (2000)

*Lyrics*: Javed Akhtar; *Composer*: Anu Malik

# Contents

# Contents

# List of Tables

# Preface

Two things have majorly contributed to writing this book, one my teaching responsibility at Jawaharlal Nehru University (JNU) and the other my stint as a senior fellow at the Nehru Memorial Museum and Library (NMML). In both places, I could concentrate on the subjects that constitute this book. At JNU's School of International Studies (SIS), the M. Phil. course on cross-border population movements that I offered (2007–12) sharpened my understanding of various issues involved in migration research in general and its South Asian context in particular. My interactions with students were most helpful. At NMML, I worked on a project that dealt once again with these issues. The vibrant academic atmosphere of the place where one gets to interact with all kinds of best brains provided me with the idea of thinking beyond my shibboleth, that is, political and security-centric debates over migrations. Out of my box, I started digging into such other areas as migration of culture, migration of music, migration of disease, impact of violence and displacement on memory and vice versa and other related areas. I also noted how historians, literary writers and other social scientists were revisiting the Partition and its aftermath, even the Bangladesh liberation war and its social reverbera-tions, and coming out with cutting-edge research studies based on archi-val, literary and oral sources. I took as much advantage as possible of this new knowledge revolution to enrich my perspectives. I almost entirely owe Chapter 6, 'Cultural and Psychological Dimensions', to this body of knowledge. There has also been a flood of scholarly writings in Bengali or by Bengali scholars that looked into the caste dynamics of the Bengali refugee phenomenon and its impact on the subsequent West Bengal poli-tics, which again refined my understanding of migration politics interface. While my entire study has benefited from these scholarly interventions, three completely new chapters (Chapters 4–6) owe their inclusion in my book primary to these new arrivals. All in all, it helped me fulfil my self-imposed commitment to make my book as comprehensive as possible.

I am aware that many gaps still remain that deserve scholarly attention. For example, while I could look into the impact of Partition refugees
on Hindi and Bengali cinema, I could not do any justice to the impact
of Sri Lankan Tamil refugees on Tamil cinema and other art forms. My
linguistic handicap came in the way. A motivated Tamil scholar can
certainly fill the gap. Another area which warrants closer scrutiny is the
issue of undocumented Bangladeshis in India. It is a subject on which
everybody seems to be knowing so much, still they know so little, largely
because of the unavailability of hard data. Expert opinions are often
formed on the basis of non-governmental organization (NGO) reports
or newspaper dispatches. While researching on the Bangladeshi factor
in Delhi politics, I realized this problem. I came across just one scholarly
paper which is now two decades old. Recently, a Ph.D. dissertation of the
University of Delhi has made some efforts in this direction, but much
more remains to be done.

This book has eight chapters, including the Introduction. The following
narrative summarizes them to explain the logic of my organization. Since
definitional issues must figure at the outset and so also the relevant theories of migration, the introductory chapter, 'Introduction: Definitional
and Theoretical Issues', is devoted to them. The three categories—
migrants, refugees and the stateless persons—which are the warps and
woofs of my study have been defined as they are available in scholarly
literature and United Nations (UN) documents with an advisory that
in South Asia these definitions do not necessarily operate as per their
texts on account of political, social and historical reasons. For the same
reasons, they tend to overlap or get used interchangeably, even in policy
documents. The remaining part of the chapter focuses upon various theories of migration which are available in the voluminous academic literature. They explain the circumstances under which one migrates across
borders or becomes a refugee. Since this literature has primarily been
generated in the West, it has somehow bypassed the South Asian experience. South Asia figures only in respect of subcontinental indentured
labour migrations during the colonial times or skilled or semi-skilled
labour migrations to the Gulf countries in recent times. Post-Partition
and other refugee movements that I have discussed in this book have
virtually been ignored by Western migration researchers, leaving the job
primarily to their historians of modern India or a handful of cultural
anthropologists. There are some efforts in the present study to compensate for this gap by highlighting which particular theories can be seen as
relevant for our understanding of the South Asian categories. In writing
this portion, my JNU lecture notes have come handy.

In Chapter 1 (Mapping the South Asian Scene) we have done a stock-taking of who the 50 million migrants, refugees and the stateless are, where they are located, what forced them to cross the border, how to end their statelessness, if any, and can all these processes be put under one category or the other to serve as a ready reckoner. Here too, my readers have been warned against seeing these categories in exclusive terms, for overlapping is inherent in South Asia's circumstances. It may be highlighted, as my research has revealed, that even an otherwise liberal state like India was unnecessarily vindictive in the aftermath of the India–China war of 1962 to evict scores of ethnic Chinese settled in Kolkata for more than a century. Their resettlement blues in China or other parts of India make a sad reading.

Chapter 2 (The Political Connection) underlines the umbilical connection between migration and politics for, as the theory goes, wherever there are people there is politics. Refugees and migrants add to the stimuli. As Augustus Comte has told us that 'demography is destiny', politics and migration go hand in glove. As soon as the initial sympathy for refugees and migrants dries up in the host society, nativist suspicions about their continued presence start surfacing. Each South Asian state has been grappling with this problem, though an unsuspecting analyst may overlook it. Whether they are Punjabi Hindu/Sikh refugees in Delhi, Bengali Scheduled Caste refugees in West Bengal, Muhajirin in Sindh, Punjabi Muslim refugees in Pakistan's Punjab, Pashtoon refugees in Khyber Pakhtoonkhwa, Bihari Muslims or Rohingya refugees in Bangladesh, they all have provided fodder to the local and national politics of these states in terms of ethnic, linguistic and sectarian divides. Even religious militancy in these countries has a complex link with these processes. Following the transfer of enclaves between India and Bangladesh, the political parties of both the states are active in these areas to influence these so-called 'new citizens'.

The migration–security interconnection is the focus of Chapter 3 (The Security Variable). Of the several causes of interstate migrations and refugee movements, one important factor is civil war in which a neighbouring state invariably gets sucked in. This creates security-related tensions between the two. Since insurgencies and ethnic and/ or religious persecutions are almost always linked, the security–migration connection becomes inevitable. Sometimes the very presence of refugees affects the relationship between the sending and the host countries. It may be underlined that the very first document that defined a refugee, the 1951 UN Refugee Convention, was the direct outcome of security-related considerations. Likewise the creation of Bangladesh can also be explained through the unprecedented refugee arrivals from East Pakistan into bordering India, which the latter took full advantage of in its war with Pakistan, both in military and in diplomatic terms. One of the doyens of migration research, Myron Weiner, had tellingly stated that it was the migration of East Germans in massive numbers that destroyed the East German state and not any invasion. In the post-Cold War world, this connection has become even more palpable. New kinds of South–South conflicts have arisen, leading to fresh flows of refugees. As more and more barriers are being built to prevent refugees from entering their chosen destinations, new forms of social strife are rising. The rise and fall of the Taliban and its prospective rise once again is pregnant with consequences for Pakistan's security, which has implications for India's security.

Issues pertaining to relief and rehabilitation of refugees have been discussed in Chapter 4 (Relief and Rehabilitation). South Asia as a region that has experienced hosting millions of refugees, that too without any legal framework, has accomplished the commendable job of providing relief and, quite often, rehabilitation as well with rather limited resources. Largely, these efforts have been state-centric, though at times the cooperation of private individuals and organizations was also available. Sometimes the two concerned states have coordinated their efforts, but seldom it was multilateral, and certainly never at the regional level. We have discussed four national relief and rehabilitation efforts, namely those of India, Pakistan, Bangladesh and Nepal. The remaining four states, namely Afghanistan, Bhutan, Maldives and Sri Lanka, are not relevant in this context as none of them has been a refugee-receiving country. Similarly, we have not found it useful to discuss state mechanisms to deal with migrants, particularly the undocumented ones, for the remaining any way have managed to become the so-called 'paper citizens'. So far as undocumented citizens are concerned, they would be happy if the concerned state is indifferent to their illegal existence. They prefer to remain faceless and gradually melt into the population before becoming 'paper citizens'.

Chapter 5 (The Legal Dynamics) addresses the question whether it is desirable to have a regional refugee regime to replace the existing system of handling the problem through national legal mechanisms. We have seen in this chapter why regional efforts towards building a regional refugee regime have not made any headway. It has been explained why and how the South Asian states have made use of their own national laws to deal with their refugee/migrant/stateless issues and why they have consciously avoided signing the international refugee covenants of 1951 and 1967. Afghanistan is an exception, for it has signed these documents but since it does not host any refugees, its membership in these conventions effectively means little. An important part of this chapter is the discourse in the South Asian states, most notably India, over the legal rights of refugee/migrant/stateless and why there is a case for a South Asian regional convention as the issues are often not strictly state-centric. It must be, however, confessed that our analysis is largely drawn from the Indian experience and only wherever relevant other experiences have been taken into account.

Cultural and psychological aspects involved in the phenomenon of South Asian migrations have been discussed in Chapter 6 (Cultural and Psychological Dimensions). It is a theme which migration researchers have generally neglected, though social anthropologists and literary writers have given much importance to them. Cultural and psychological impacts work both ways. Migrants influence the society and culture of the places they move in. Likewise the host societies too influence the migrants culturally. While these two-way interactions found reflection in music, poetry/lyrics, painting, drama, architecture and even in culinary habits, it is not always benign. Sometimes social tensions develop which may not always take violent turns, but their presence is felt in individual and collective psychology. These aspects of migration research are as important as other more palpable and mundane ones, and in South Asia they are increasingly drawing scholarly attention. To write on these aspects, particular efforts were made to draw from the field of memory research. Is it not intriguing that even after almost seven decades, the Partition of India is still recalled in the subcontinent almost on a daily basis? Not only literary writings are pouring in, even new doctoral dissertations are being written on the period. There is no dearth of Bollywood flicks on the event. They prove that Partition was not only a narrative of death, destruction and displacement, but it also galvanized human creativity in the long run. The South Asian migration saga shows how cultural forms and productions move alongside migrating humans.

The essence of my concluding chapter, Chapter 7 (Conclusion: Making Sense), is that in spite of South Asia being a witness to one of the most massive human flows starting with the Partition of India, that in spite of its being one of the most populous and culturally diverse regions, that in spite of its being politically noisy and at times faltering, and that in spite of its being a witness to massive societal upheavals, its humanitarian spirit has not been dented. Each nation has displayed an unusual empathy towards the refuge-seeking people or unauthorized settlers in its midst. If not through direct actions, such sympathies are often expressed through benign indifference, somewhat on the pattern of benevolent neutrality in diplomatic parlance. This benign indifference is embedded in South Asia's shared history and societal similarity. Even in the teeth of much animosity displayed through public posturing, to the extent of going to wars, Indians and Pakistanis still feel at home in each other's lands. Anand Patwardhan's anti-nuke documentary/film, *War and Peace*, produced right after the back-to-back nuclear tests by India and Pakistan in May 1998, was hugely appreciated in both countries at the popular level, in spite of all the hurdles that the dominant political forces there could put up. The runaway success of the 2015 Bollywood flick, *Bajrangi Bhaijan*, in both countries tells the same story.

In writing this book, I have taken help from all kinds of people including the common man on the street through routine conversations. My students figured prominently in my efforts as they constantly encouraged me to develop my class lectures into a book. Moreover, wherever I have spoken on the theme I have found incisive and informative responses from my audience. This book is the result of this aggregate reassurance. My former student, and subsequently my colleague as Associate Editor of the *India Quarterly* which I edited, Dr Vikash Kumar, deserves special mention in this regard. He is my 'research assistant 24/7' in every practical sense in the traditional *guru–shishya parampara* (teacher–student bond) of India where the service is free and always with love.

Professor Dietmar Rothermund of Heidelberg University has been my pillar of strength ever since he hosted me in his university as a Humboldt Fellow 30 years ago. Not only have I gained so much from him academically, but I have also learnt how one should maintain one's friendship through all ups and downs. As a token of my cherished association with him and with a deep sense of gratitude, I have dedicated this book to him.

Among my professional friends who deserve my thanks, Ranabir Samaddar figures most prominently. I owe my interest in migration research largely to him. At the institutional level, I have no words to thank the Director of the NMML, Professor Mahesh Rangarajan, who hosted me as a Senior Fellow during 2012–14. The way he formalized regular seminars and talks in the institute helped all fellows like me, and others as well, to take advantage of a variety of subjects and research methodologies. The library of the institute is not only well stocked, but is also well served by its dedicated staff. My thanks goes to all of them.

I would not have been able to complete this study without such holistic support of the NMML.

My family's support and encouragement should generally go without saying. But it was with a difference. All three of them, my wife Indira, son Arunabh and daughter Suparna, have listened to me speaking on some aspect or the other of this book at various places and also at home, and dissected them later on the dining table, giving me valuable advice as to how to improve my communication skills. It was always so helpful!

**Partha S. Ghosh**
New Delhi
January 2016

# Introduction: Definitional and Theoretical Issues

*It isn't that they can't see the solution. It is that they can't see the problem.*

—G.K. Chesterton (Cohen and Cohen 1971)

## Introduction

Seven out of eight South Asian states, namely, Afghanistan, Bangladesh, Bhutan, India, Nepal, Pakistan and Sri Lanka, which account for almost the entire region's space and population, are both refugee/migrant-receiving and -sending countries. The only exception is the Maldives. Against the region's 1.5 billion population, its tiny population of 300,000 is of little consequence. Moreover, its strictly Sunni social order does not permit any non-Sunni settlement anywhere in its 1,100 islets, not even as spouses of its own citizens. Afghanistan is primarily a refugee-sending country, particularly since the 1970s when its politics entered into an uncertain phase following the ouster of its king, Mohammad Zahir Shah. Bangladesh, which was earlier East Pakistan, has a long history of both receiving and sending migrants in which both India and Pakistan are involved. Lately, it has been hosting refugees from Myanmar.[1] Bhutan has received migrants from India's Nepalese-majority areas as well as from Sikkim (now a state in the Indian Union, was till 1975 an independent monarchy) and sent refugees to Nepal, and to India as well. Being centrally located, India has received refugees/migrants from Afghanistan, Bangladesh, Bhutan, Nepal, Pakistan and Sri Lanka and has sent refugees/migrants to Nepal and undivided Pakistan. Nepal has received migrants from India and Bhutan and sent migrants to India. Pakistan has received migrants from India and Afghanistan and, to some extent, even from

Bangladesh. During the Partition, it sent refugees to India. Sri Lanka has sent both Indian Tamils and Sri Lankan Tamils to India as two distinct categories, first as unwelcome setters in their country and second as refugees in search of security from the Sri Lankan state oppression.

In spite of this massive experience, the region has the unique distinction of having no legal regime to guide its refugee/migrant policies. Barring Afghanistan, no South Asian state has signed the UN Refugee Convention of 1951. But, law or no law, no South Asian state has been ever unwilling to provide shelter and relief to its refugee/migrant guests, even though their resources are limited. This is the region's yet another unique distinction. However, because of the absence of legal regimes, quite often the categories get mixed up and migrants, refugees, illegal settlers or stateless persons become one and the same. Sometimes even the nomenclature of a single category changes over time, say, from refugee to new refugee to new entrants; from illegal settlers to undocumented migrants to infiltrators. Whatever the merits of these ambiguities, for the sake of clarity, it is necessary to know how the international literature has defined these categories for they constitute the warp and woof of this study. In Part I of this chapter, we provide the definitions, in Part II we briefly address the theories that are relevant for our understanding of the refugee/migrant phenomenon in general, in Part III we see to what extent these theories are relevant for understanding the South Asian scene, and in Part IV we refer to the role of memory in violence for most of South Asia's migratory/refugee movements are violence driven.

# I

# Refugee

The United Nations (UN) Convention Relating to the Status of Refugees held on 28 July 1951 defined a 'refugee' as any person who

> as a result of events occurring before 1 January 1951 and owing to well-founded fear of being persecuted for reasons of race, religion, nationality, membership of a particular social group or political opinion, is outside the country of his nationality and is unable or, owing to such fear, is unwilling to avail himself of the protection of that country; or who, not having a nationality and being outside the country of his former habitual residence as a result of such events, is unable or, owing to such fear, is unwilling to return to it.

In 1967, there were some amendments to this definition. The UN Protocol of 31 January 1967 went further and omitted the phrases 'as a result of events occurring before 1 January 1951 and ...' and '...as a result of such events' from its own definition.

Later, at the Organisation of African Unity (OAU) Convention held on 10 September 1969, the African states revised the definition further. This definition came into force on 20 June 1974. It was decided that in addition to the UN definition

> [T]he term 'refugee' shall apply to every person who, owing to external aggression, occupation, foreign domination or events seriously disturbing public order in either part or the whole of his country of origin or nationality, is compelled to leave his place of habitual residence in order to seek refuge in another place outside his country of origin or nationality.

It added:

> [I]n the case of a person who has several nationalities, the term 'a country of which he is a national' shall mean each of the countries of which he is a national, and a person shall not be deemed to be lacking the protection of the country of which he is a national if, without any valid reasons based on the well-founded fear, he has not availed himself of the protection of one of the countries of which he is a national.

In the 1980s the concept was further revised. On 22 November 1984, the Cartagena Declaration on Refugees reiterated:

> [I]n view of the experience gained from the massive flows of refugees in the Central American area, it is necessary to consider enlarging the concept of a refugee, bearing in mind, as far as appropriate and in the light of the situation prevailing in the region, the precedent of the OAU Convention and the doctrine employed in the reports of the Inter-American Commission on Human Rights. Hence the definition of concept of a refugee to be recommended for use in the region is one which, in addition to containing the elements of the 1951 Convention and the 1967 Protocol, includes among refugees persons who have fled their country because their lives, safety or freedom have been threatened by generalized violence, foreign aggression, internal conflicts, massive violation of human rights or other circumstances which have seriously disturbed public order.

The Declaration further reiterated:

> [T]he importance and meaning of the principle of *non-refoulement*[2] (including the prohibition or rejection at the frontier) as a corner-stone of the international protection of refugees. This principle is imperative in

regard to refugees and in the present state of international law should be acknowledged and observed as a rule of '*jus cogens*'.

The debate is, however, unending. Over the years, drawing from the Universal Declaration of Human Rights (1946), which had proclaimed that 'everyone has the right to leave any country, including his own, and to return to his country' and that 'everyone has the right to seek and enjoy in other countries asylum from persecution', as well as several other international conventions, considerable progress has been registered in the discourse that includes now environmental concerns as well. Within specific regions, voices have been articulated for working out region-specific refugee conventions. In Chapter 5 we have discussed the South Asian discourse in this regard.

## Migrant

Migration is generally defined as 'a permanent change in place of residence by the crossing of specified administrative or political boundaries. The persons who fulfil these two criteria are regarded as migrants' (Nabi & Krishnan 1993: 83). Clearly, this definition has its limits, for it does not take into account the nomadic or wandering people, seasonal migrants, and movements back and forth of people having more than one residence. Moreover, it does not address questions such as what should be the length of one's stay in his second abode to qualify him as a migrant. The UN's *Multilingual Demographic Dictionary* suggests that the expressions 'move' and 'migration' on the one hand and 'internal migration' and 'international migration' on the other should be distinguished.

> A move is a change of residence within the same political or administrative boundary. Migration is a change of residence and also a crossing of the political or administrative boundary. While internal migration is a change in the place of residence from one administrative boundary to another within the same country, international migration is a move over a national boundary. (Nabi & Krishnan 1993: 83)

## Stateless

It was in 1954 that the term 'stateless person' was first defined. The Convention relating to the Status of Stateless Persons, adopted on 28 September 1954 by a Conference of Plenipotentiaries convened by the

UN Economic and Social Council Resolution 526A (XVII) of 26 April 1954, defined it as 'a person who is not considered as a national by any State under the operation of its law'. Among the general obligations, 'every stateless person has duties to the country in which he finds himself, which require in particular that he conforms to its laws and regulations as well as to measures taken for the maintenance of public order'. But what about those cases where the state fails to honour its duty? Are they not stateless also in every practical sense, say, the India–Bangladesh enclave people, or, broadly speaking, the undocumented Bangladeshis in India?

There are two categories of stateless persons: de jure and de facto. The de jure stateless persons are those who are not nationals of any state, either because at birth or subsequently they were not given any nationality or because during their lifetime they lost their own nationality and did not acquire a new one. The de facto stateless persons are those who, having left the country of which they were nationals, no longer enjoy the protection and assistance of their national authorities, either because these authorities refuse to grant them protection or assistance or because they themselves renounce the protection and assistance of the countries of which they were nationals. A stateless person, in short, is one who is unable or unwilling to avail himself of the protection of the government of his country of nationality or former nationality (Lawson 1996: 1076). The UN High Commissioner for Refugees' (UNHCR) Expert Meeting held in Prato, Italy, on 27–28 May 2010 had the following to say about de facto stateless persons in its conclusion:

> The extent to which de facto stateless persons who do not fall within its refugee mandate qualify for the Office's protection and assistance in largely determined by UNHCR's mandate to prevent statelessness. It was noted that unresolved situations of de facto statelessness, in particular over two or more generations, may lead to de jure statelessness.

The above definitions, though important, are not always adequate for our purpose as our approach is comprehensive, and we are dealing here with a complex region. Since we would be dealing with the impact of migrations also on politics and security the number of migrants would be critical for our analysis. Moreover, there is a huge humanitarian dimension. The emphasis on the humanitarian question was highlighted rightly by Ursula Berge, an adviser to the Swedish Integration Minister Ulrica Messing. She suggested an alternative nomenclature, that is, 'person of foreign background' in the place of the word 'immigrant'. Since the label 'immigrant' was connected with many negative aspects, such as unemployment and social exclusion, her suggestion made sense. After the 9/11 terrorist attacks on the World Trade Center and the Pentagon, the scene has drastically changed. It is no longer only the large number of immigrants that matter for national security, sometimes even small numbers equally matter. It depends on circumstances. We have taken note of this dimension in our chapter on security (Chapter 3). The crux of the matter is, therefore, whether large or small, migrants matter for any society because their presence has all kinds of ramifications (political, security, legal and cultural) for the receiving state.

# II

# Theoretical Concerns in Migration Research

Migration research has attracted the attention of scholars from almost all social science fields, resulting in several approaches to study the phenomenon. Since migrants often include the refugees, refugee research too has benefitted from this multidisciplinary methodology. Had it not been the case, refugee research would have continued to suffer from the partial interpretations presented by nation-centric historians, social and human rights activists, and law scholars.

Migration research has a long history. It was in the 18th century that the system of collecting empirical evidence to study migration started. The exercise was largely an offshoot of the processes of urbanization as well as increasing mobility within the European states. In the 19th century, as the European migratory hordes crossed the Atlantic, the subject got further boost. In the 20th century, migration researchers found yet another empirical set to enrich their knowledge, the northern Chinese migrations to Manchuria. But while these migratory processes encouraged economic growth in the receiving societies, they also became causes of anxiety for the political elites and the middle classes there, notwithstanding that they benefited from the contribution made by the migrants to economic development. In their apprehension from the new entrants, these middle classes often lumped the poorly paid migrants with the local poor people, viewing both as social evils. The migrants were often looked down upon as criminals or potential criminals who should not be entitled to full membership of the nation, meaning citizenship (Harzig & Hoerder 2009: 54–56).

In the colonized world, there was hardly any migration research, arguably because the 'colonizer rule retarded independent academic activity' (Harzig & Hoerder 2009: 60). The first evidence of data collection on migration in the non-Atlantic world was the exercise done by the Japanese-owned South Manchuria Railway Company in the 1920s and 1930s. They had hired social scientists to assess the labour demand in Manchuria. Otherwise, the migration of tens of millions of northern Chinese to Manchuria during the 1890s and in 1937, that included the establishment of the Manchukuo regime in 1932, did not evoke any interest among the educated elites to study the phenomenon. Later, the Nankai Institute of Economic Research in Tianjin in China, which was established by He Lian (or Franklin Ho), a PhD from the Yale University, started research in the field but the Communist takeover in 1949 put an end to the efforts. The interesting part of the research conducted by this institute was that unlike the US portrayal of the migrants as pioneers and tough,[3] these Chinese migrants were seen merely as simple and hardworking people living in difficult conditions (Harzig & Hoerder 2009: 60–61).[4]

Since most of the migration-related research was done in the receiving countries, it was often couched in terms of immigrants as social and political problems for reasons explained above. The concept of White Man's Burden might have had its origin in this pattern of thinking. As it has been noted:

> In the imperial British 'Empire Settlement' program, bureaucrats sent such 'white' migrants to the 'coloured' segments of the empire to improve or 'whiten' them. In Germany, sociologist and political economist Max Weber understood the demand for East European, especially Polish, migrant workers but pronounced them to be racially inferior. The attitudes of respective nations' scholars to Italians in France, Czechs in Vienna, or East European Jews in many societies were similarly skewed. This 'scientific' racism deeply affected migrants' chances of inserting themselves into receiving societies, since academic pronouncements and stateside migration policies were often linked. (Harzig & Hoerder 2009: 56)

By and large, the West European approach to immigration was racist (Harzig & Hoerder 2009: 56).[5] But in spite of this angularity, over the years several theories emerged to study the phenomenon from various perspectives, of which some of the major ones are discussed below.

## World-Systems Approach

The argument is that from the 16th century onwards, world markets expanded from powerful capitalist core countries first to the semi-

periphery and then to the periphery. This led to inter-peripheral migrations—European indentured labourers to Americas and Indian indentured labourers to the Caribbean, Sri Lanka, Malay, Fiji and South
Africa. From the same perspective, the dependency theory became popular—migration is induced by the penetration of capitalist markets and
production methods into peripheral societies. In the post-colonial phase,
migration is directed from ex-colonies to former colonizer countries. The
world-systems perspectives thus provide a frame for a global approach
to the economics of migration. Andre Gunder Frank's *Capitalism and
Underdevelopment in Latin America* (1967) and Immanuel Wallerstein's
*The Modern World System* (1976) are the most eminent formative texts
in world systems and dependency theory. In his later career Frank wrote
*ReOrient: Global Economy in the Asian Age* (1998) and, with Barry Gills,
*The World System: Five Hundred Years or Five Thousand* (1993). His theories centred on the idea that a nation's economic strength was largely
determined by its historical circumstances and geography, which determined its place in the global hierarchy of power. Frank is particularly
known for his theory that purely export-oriented solutions to development create imbalances which are detrimental for the poor countries.
According to Frank, numerous world systems are a misnomer. If there
are many world systems in the world, then they simply do not deserve to
be called world systems.

## Labour Market and Push/Pull Approach

The basic premise in this approach is that there is a three-layer labour
market in any state. The state sector is primarily reserved for native-
born workers, and the wages and facilities are the best in this sector.[6]
A competitive secondary sector provides irregular employment and this
is the second sector. In the third sector, we have the tertiary, marginal
and the ghetto economy. Insofar as their connection with migration is
concerned, it is premised that less-developed national economies push
people out while those with higher wages and standards of living pull
them in, and this rule is valid particularly for the third sector. The labour
market approach can as well be called the disequilibrium approach. In
this regard, though both economists and political scientists subscribe
to the disequilibrium theory, they view it differently. In explaining the
cross-border migrations, economists argue that there is a disequilibrium
between the sending and the receiving countries. Compared with the

receiving countries, wages in the sending countries are low, employment opportunities are fewer and agricultural land use is poor. Therefore, the so-called push factor is in operation, resulting in outmigration from the sending countries.

Political scientists, however, emphasize the disequilibrium within the sending country itself and not between the sending and the receiving countries. Since there are regional and other kinds of disparities within the sending countries, the disadvantaged people migrate to other countries to escape from their miseries and eventually contribute to the disequilibrium in the receiving countries as well. Thus,

> [W]hile economic explanations of migration induce one to think about ways to reduce economic differences between sending and receiving countries in order to reduce unwanted international population movements, political explanations for migration induce one to think about ways to resolve political differences among ethnic groups within the sending countries or between a people and their government. (Weiner 1993: 1745–46)

On account of this perceptual hiatus, 'a politically driven model of international migration is a highly conflictual one, both for sending and receiving countries' (Weiner 1993: 1745–46). The explanation supplied by political scientists also is not foolproof. Historically, barring the indentured workers, mostly prosperous communities from India, such as the Punjabis and Gujaratis, have migrated to the West. In that sense, the sociological argument is also important. The familial and community networks have played a major role in these migrations compared with other Indian communities.

While the migrants leave their country in search of better wages, prospective employers in the receiving countries welcome them for the cheaper services they provide compared with the native workers. What should logically follow from this is that there should be opposition from the local labour unions or labour markets to the entry of cheap labour. But this theory does not hold water always as empirical evidence suggests. If we take India's case vis-a-vis Bangladeshi migrants, we see nothing like that has happened. The opposition to these entries has primarily been led by some political parties in Assam and at the national level by the Bharatiya Janata Party (BJP), both having latent ethnic or communal agendas which have been politically and economically articulated. But even if we disregard Bangladeshi clandestine migrations to India to serve as a good example, for they in any case do not pose threats to organized labour as they are mostly unskilled and are engaged in unorganized sectors as menial workers, the American example does not tell any different story either. In the United States the illegal immigrants from Mexico do pose an economic challenge to poor African Americans, but there too no evidence exists of any serious opposition to the illegal Mexican labour force (Fuchs 1993: 174–77). This tends to suggest that immigration as such does not invoke any nativist reaction unless it is projected as a racial, communal or ethnic threat. The opposition of Indian Tamil plantation labour in Sri Lanka falls in the same category. The economic determinism contained in this approach has been questioned from other angles as well. For example, family, caste and village connections too matter in people's decision to migrate, which we may call the non-measurable emotional factors or chain-and-network concepts (Harzig & Hoerder 2009: 75–76, 80). The last mentioned is particularly relevant for Gujarati migrations to the United States and earlier to East Africa.

## Demographic Approach

Significant demographic changes taking place in several parts of the world may impact global migratory patterns. While China's population growth rate has fallen largely because of its one-child policy since the early 1970s, even in other countries such as Brazil, Indonesia, Iran and some parts of India, fertility rates are falling fast. India's annual population growth is now 1.3 per cent, which by 2025 will fall to 1.1. At the global level, over 80 countries have fewer births than that required to replace the number of individuals who die each year. They need large flow of immigrants each year just to prevent their population from peaking then declining. These low-birth countries contain over 40 per cent of the world population, including every country in Western Europe, China, Japan, Russia, Poland and Canada, to name just a few. Birth rates in many other countries, including the United States, Mexico and Iran, are only little above the level necessary to replace the number of deaths. According to world population data, India will be one of the prime countries which will reap demographic dividends until 2035. Interestingly, in some developed countries, such as France, Italy and Sweden, fertility rates are rising again to reach the replacement rate, but it appears to be a short-term phenomenon. Since South–North migration is facing some problems, South–South migration, which has already been high and contributing hugely to expatriate remittances, may pick up. Developing countries have been establishing new economic links through trade, aid and investment as well as outsourcing, and these processes would further help the flow of migrants from developing countries to the industrialized world. This trend is very much evident in spite of recent visa restrictions in several developed countries. Indian software companies, such as Infosys, WIPRO, Cogent and TCS, have now more than 80,000 Indian and non-Indian employees in South and North America and Europe. Against this backdrop, the Indian government has prepared a proposal for the General Agreement on Trade in Services. The Doha round of trade negotiations is to be concluded. The immigration proposals are encountering opposition from the developed countries. However, the ageing population problem may enable developing countries to obtain some benefits on this issue.

# Political Approach

Political approach is closely related to the demographic approach discussed above. According to this theory, there is a continuing, dynamic and intricate relationship between the issues pertaining to population on the one hand and those pertaining to society and politics on the other. In India, however, the population issues have largely been the forte of demographers, who did not pay enough attention to these interactions until recently. The sociologists, however, have recognized these interactions, as reflected in their argument that ecological demography, which is a combination of demography and human ecology, promises the most systematic and comprehensive treatment of the core of sociology—the study of societies and social systems and vice versa (Namboodiri 1992: 321–49). Of all the kinds of demographic factors impinging upon politics, however, the most complex are probably the ones having religious or ethnonationalistic roots. Since both religious nationalism and ethnonationalism draw their sustenance from human emotions, which are often irrational, the interstate conflicts rooted in ethnic and religious discords are the most intractable and most violence-prone of all the issues relating to international conflict. Compared to them, issues related to resources, for example, seem to be much more concrete and hence conducive to compromise, if not solution (Mandel 1980: 435). As has been noted by one scholar:

> Population size may function as a political parameter when, for example, it generates population pressures upon resources that lead to expansionist tendencies. Population composition may be a parameter of a conflict when it sets the cleavages in a society, generating tensions that result in ethnic

or religious conflict. So, too, the population distribution may be a political parameter when, for instance, tribal allegiance crosses national boundaries and generates overt conflict, or when the migration of population changes the ethnic composition of the receiving community and results in nativist reaction. (Choukri 1978: 30–31)

So far as the interaction between the demographic issues and politics is concerned, it has been both theoretically and empirically proved that the demographic characteristics of a society invariably influence the politics of that society. It has been argued that

[M]any problems, which are viewed as strictly political, have, in fact, demographic roots. Conversely, policy interventions that are proposed with demographic intents often result in distinctly political consequences. It is this dual interaction between population and politics that has contributed to the increasing politicisation of the demographic issues in the world today. (Choukri 1974: 1–29)

Demographic variations as a factor influencing politics, however, could be of various types: internal migrations, increased birth rate and/or reduced mortality rate, cross-national migrations or the dismemberment of a country. The Partition of India, for instance, turned the Hindus into a minority in Pakistan overnight. Similarly, the secession of Bangladesh instantly turned the Punjabis into a majority in the linguistically and ethnically plural Pakistan.

During the 1970s, when the North–South dialogue was high on the intellectual agenda of the world, many in the developing countries tended to undermine the danger of the burgeoning population growth in the Third World on the ground that, after all, world resources, if pooled equitably, were good enough to feed many more millions. It was argued that the real problem lay with the skewed distribution system (Ghosh 1982; 131–38). But as years rolled by, it became increasingly evident that there was hardly any global approach to societal problems, and nation-states were still parochial in their thinking. As has been noted:

We can speculate about how the world might get organized, but individual nation-states, as Karl Deutsch was fond of pointing out, face a condition, not a theory. This condition dictates action. To be sure, an appropriate policy for one country, given its resources, social values, and ability to organize and carry out policies, may or may not be appropriate for another country. (Merritt 1995: 412–13)

Since any country has hardly had any population policy worth the name (China's one-child policy or India's forced sterilization drive during the Emergency created many problems), the easiest escape from an impending population explosion has been to migrate to greener pastures, as happened during the 19th century.

On the face of it, the number of people should matter in migration research. But there is an alternative view as well. Ranabir Samaddar argues that by assigning too much importance to this variable in our migration discourse, we tend to miss the human factor, which should be the real issue. The more we give emphasis to the numbers, the more it is inevitable that statistical data would be manipulated for political purposes. In support of his argument, Samaddar shows that more Hindus than Muslims have migrated to India from Bangladesh, more of them have overstayed and even more percentage of illegal overstayers are Hindus. Still the Indian state apprehends more number of Muslims as illegal migrants than their Hindu counterparts. He strongly argues that the whole business of finding how many Muslims or Hindus have migrated is itself skewed. Not that numbers are unimportant, but by putting too much emphasis on this factor, one 'ignores the history of migration, its economics and most importantly … the migrant him/herself, his/her subjectivity and also the universe of South Asia where such transborder migration has become such an overwhelming phenomenon'. The numbers game 'creates its own history, constructs a world where observers are enchanted into entering, arguing and counter-arguing in a closed circle' (Samaddar 1999: 201–3).

So long as politics would be nation-state oriented, the reasons of state would operate. In that situation, it is bound to happen that in search of the woods we will miss the tree. In other words, it is the age-old dichotomy between scholars and their subjects. Historians, sociologists and economists study the agrarian system while the peasant is left out. What is needed, therefore, as Samaddar argues, is to go 'beyond the received disciplinary boundaries for opening up the massive, still unwritten, biography of moving populations across the borders in South Asia. It will result in a discussion of their rights, justice to them, a transcending of the juridical–political framework of state sovereignty, territoriality and frontiers, in short, a displacement of the core of the study' (Samaddar 1999: 211). Samaddar's concern cannot be overlooked. But the problem is that the enormity of numbers involved makes the task as proposed by him desirable yet unachievable. It amounts to undertaking massive oral history projects which neither the states concerned nor the possible private agencies have the necessary funds or willingness to undertake. The result is an unfulfillable wishful thinking and, at the end of the day, taking recourse, once again, to the numbers game and drawing conclusions.

Even Samaddar admits of the ambivalence, being caught between the conflicting parts of structure and subjectivity (Samaddar 1999: 211).

# Geographical/Ecological/Developmental Approach

Ideally, each of these three approaches deserves individual treatment, but since they are closely interconnected one may study them under one category. For example, the way river Ganga changed its course so massively in the 13th–18th centuries, contributing to the conversion of a forested East Bengal region into a paddy-yielding plain, inviting people from other parts of Bengal and elsewhere, and the way it led to the peopling of the area with the encouragement from the ruling Mughals, tells about this connection. Richard Eaton's *The Rise of Islam and the Bengal Frontier, 1204–1760* (1994) narrates this history in detail (also see Ghosh 2011).[7] Climate change has been used as an approach to study migrations because this has been a massive factor in human migrations historically. For example, the Indian Oceanic migrations in the latter half of the 19th century that we have mentioned above have been linked to the failure of monsoons in the region. The portent of El Nino, the warming of surface waters in the equatorial Pacific, has links with migratory phenomena.[8] In developmental approach to migration research, we see how dams, firing ranges, bridges and resettlement schemes have direct connection with displacements that often lead to permanent human movements in search of livelihood. The best example is the construction of the Kaptai/Karnaphuli dam in the Chittagong area of East Pakistan in the 1960s, that made thousands of Chakmas, Marmas and other tribes move to India in massive numbers. A large number of them are now in Arunachal Pradesh, having been granted Indian citizenship to the antipathy of the locals (discussed in Chapters 2 and 5).

# Integration/Assimilation Approach

Migration research has often been absorbed by the controversy whether 'integration' or 'assimilation' would be the right policy for the receiving country to follow in respect of its immigrants. It is widely believed that the term 'integration' conveys the meaning better than 'assimilation', for it is a mutual rather than a one-way process. There can be a cultural variety within a growing social unity. This view was well articulated by the Canadian department of citizenship and immigration: 'Integration … is used in Canada to express a theory which contains unity and diversity. The unity is sought in common citizenship. The diversity is maintained by reciprocal appreciation of diverse cultural contributions'. In the American and Indian contexts, the salad bowl thesis has gained more currency: let every ethnic group maintain its specificity yet enrich the overall cultural fabric. Yet, earlier the melting pot ideology seemed to appeal the Americans the most. But even at the height of its popularity and that of Americanization, such a public intellectual as Randolph S. Bourne had said: 'America is coming to be, not a nationality but a trans-nationality, a weaving back and forth, with the other lands, of many threads of all sizes and colors'. Democratic societies have no reason to panic, the moment migrants ask for self-determination or freedom of cultural expressions. Horace Kallen has conceptualized cultural pluralism as states being federations of nationalities rather than monocultural nationalities. Still, racist views, as expressed in Madison Grant's *The Passing of the Great Race* (1916), seemed more appealing. In 1917, the American government imposed exclusion measures on migrants from Europe (Harzig & Hoerder 2009: 64).

With regard to the idea of assimilation, Robert E. Park and his colleagues at the Chicago School of Sociology had conceptualized assimilation as fusion and interpenetration by which individuals and groups would achieve a common culture. But the problem was that this school took the absorptive power of established institutions for granted and saw ethnic groups or races as less developed. Still, Park was not a rabid white supremacist, as was evidenced by his editorial role for the Carnegie Corporation's *Americanization* series where he was influential far beyond his own research. The concept of assimilation, which was meant to imply a surrender of the original cultural traits to become part of the new majority society, has since the 1980s been replaced by such notions as acculturation, accommodation, insertion and adjustment (Harzig & Hoerder 2009: 57–58).

# Feminist or Gendered Approach

Until recently, migration research was generally silent on the issue of gender, but it is not so any longer. A volume of literature has emerged on the subject, the focus of which is to have a gendered view of the processes involved in the human flows. There are several ways in which women suffer more than their male counterparts. For example, it has been argued that in the case of migrants by choice, the decision to migrate is generally a male decision. The female migration that follows is largely due to the requirements of family reunion. The fact that female migrants are less in number globally, and in the case of South Asian migrants particularly, because of its additional cultural reasons, underscores the point. In 2010, the global percentage of female migrants was 49, but in South Asia it was 44.4 (see http://www.ucis.pitt.edu/global/sites/www.ucis.pitt.edu.global/files/migration_women_southasia_gulf.pdf, accessed on 8 January 2016, and Thapan and Chadha-Behera 2006: 9). Besides, women migrants are always discriminately paid, what is worse is that their physical vulnerability exposes them to sexual abuse and maltreatment at workplaces. At home, the real burden of resettling in new abodes primarily falls on women. Whether it is the Afghan, Bangladeshi, Indian or Pakistani experience, the story is the same.

Since patriarchy dominates almost all societies in the world, it will be tautological to say that women are greater sufferers as refugees, forced migrants or displaced persons. This pattern was noticeable even during the Partition exodus when millions of humans were involved. Women were not only killed but were often raped and abused before that. They were also abducted in large numbers. Brothels of Delhi and Mumbai were full of refugee women. The efforts that were made, quite seriously, by both Indian and Pakistani governments, to restore many of the abducted women had little success because of sociocultural reasons. Ramchandra Guha writes:

> By May 1948 some 12,500 women had been found and restored to their families. Ironically, and tragically, many of the women did not want to be rescued at all. For after their seizure they had made some kind of peace with their surroundings. Now, as they were being reclaimed, these women were deeply unsure about how their original families would receive them. They had been 'defiled' and, in a further complication, many were pregnant. These women knew that even if they were accepted their children—born out of a union with the 'enemy'—would never be. (Guha 2007: 95)

The argument that migration is generally a male decision, however, is questionable. Although it may be generally the case, but in most South Asian families, such decisions are often taken in consultation with others in the family, for ultimately all are going to benefit from the expatriate money. Irudaya Rajan, a noted scholar in the field, found the argument flawed at least from the experience of migrations from Kerala to the Gulf countries. In a seminar held at the NMML on 9–10 October 2014, he said that the sufferings too are equal for both the females and the males. The gendered argument in that sense was flawed as both the benefits and pains of migration were equally shared by all in the family as the Kerala experience showed, he argued.

## Social/Cultural Approach

Oscar Handlin's pioneering work *The Uprooted* (1951) highlighted this connection through his painstaking research on the Irish immigrants in Boston area. Similarly, Alex Haley's *Roots* (1976) talked about the search of African Americans about their African origin and what impact this African connection had left on American life. In recent times, Homi Bhabha's theory of 'third space' or that of Arjun Appadorai on 'spaces' discusses how migrants carry with them their cultures to their new lands of residence. At one level, it is a sense of being uprooted and at another, the desire to re-root in a new land. The experience of the people of the Bhojpuri-speaking areas of Bihar and eastern UP as indentured workers in the Caribbean tells this story. Even after about 150 years of their arrival in the Caribbean, these Bhojpuri-speaking people have still retained their culture partially and enriched it with borrowings from that of the locals. We have referred to this phenomenon in our discussion above and have further discussed it in Chapter 6 in greater detail keeping in view the South Asian experiences.

## Other Approaches

Besides the above approaches, there are many other approaches that one can take into account depending upon the specific issue one is studying. Some of these may also overlap. Some of these approaches are: security approach (discussed in Chapter 3), transcontinental historical approach, globalization approach, decision-making approach (who decides to migrate; if it is the man, then does he worry about his wife's or children's concerns in this connection, an issue that we have discussed above in the 'Feminist or Gendered Approach' section), caste and family network approach, the diaspora approach and religious persecution approach (the 'vested property' laws of Bangladesh silently pushed many Hindus to India, discussed in Chapters 1 and 2).

# III

# The South Asian Context

Many of the theories discussed above have gone into our understanding of the South Asian migration scene. But since the approach of this book is primarily empirical, the theoretical dimensions have figured largely circumstantially. It may, however, be underlined that in two significant ways, the West-inspired migration research has limited usefulness for our understanding of the South Asian scene. One, since the region figures marginally in the Western migration literature, the evidence and examples cited there are seldom drawn from the South Asian experience, although it is vast, and two, collective violence, so critical to explain cross-border migrations in South Asia, finds little mention in the Western migration theories.[9] With regard to the first factor, the explanation can be as follows. While the Western scholarship is essentially concerned with intra-European migrations in the medieval times and inter-oceanic migrations during the colonial times, including the Asian and African migrations to other colonized nations, South Asian migration scholarship is concerned with cross-border land-based movements of people in the post-colonial period. Even in the colonial time, intra-regional migrations like India to Sri Lanka, an island nation, were not oceanic in the real sense. The water body (Palk Strait) that the South Indian plantation workers had to cross to reach the island was barely 25 km wide and easily crossable. On account of this dichotomy, one oceanic and the other territorial, the racial element that figured in some Western theories is absent in the South Asian migration scene. There are religious, ethnic and linguistic components in South Asian research, but seldom racial. Even in the case of South Indians working on Sri Lanka's coffee, tea and rubber plantations there was no race factor, although they differed from the local Sinhalese in religious and linguistic terms, and probably, even racially. In any case, because of the very nature of the Sri Lankan plantation economy, the Indian Tamil and other south Indian workers barely interacted with the Sinhalese community at large.

With regard to the second factor, the most important element to study migrations in their South Asian context is collective violence. This factor finds little space in Western migration literature, although religious persecutions were at the core of early migrations of several European communities to the North American continent. Since collective violence has much to do with collective memories of the South

Asian communities, our understanding of the South Asian migration scene would be incomplete unless we pay adequate attention to these factors and their interconnection. Although these two concerns run through the entire book, they warrant a special theoretical treatment which we have attempted below.

## Collective Violence

Collective violence is the prime factor causing migrations in South Asia. Table I.1 highlights the point. As the table shows, there have been massive flows of refugees in South Asia, primarily in search of security for life and honour (details given in Chapter 1). As such, it must prominently figure in the theoretical literature on migration. Like wars, which have underlying and immediate causes, societal violence too has immediate (failure of politics) and underlying (deeply embedded inter-communal suspicions) causes. The task of nation-building in South Asia is not only incomplete, the future is not promising either. The institutional democracy that works in almost the entire region now may be a facilitating factor but not a comprehensive instrument to ensure nation-building. Otherwise, South Asia's oldest democracy, Sri Lanka (universal adult suffrage was introduced in the country as early as in 1931), and the world's largest and secular democracy, India, would not have witnessed recurring ethnic and communal riots. If this is the case with relatively successful polities, one can well imagine what can be expected from some of the other nations that are still struggling to sustain even their rudimentary democratic institutions. The societal conflicts in South Asia in most cases result in displacement and massive refugee creations, which often spill over across the international borders.

The larger challenge, however, is to understand why this violent temper persists and why it routinely produces communal riots. Simultaneously, it is equally challenging to explain the parallel phenomenon of inter-communal coexistence reflected in every sphere of South Asian life. Paradoxically, the region has created millions of refugees, but at the same time it has also taken care of millions of them with abundant sympathy, a point we have discussed in Chapters 2 and 5. The methodological tool that can partially explain this contradictory phenomenon is memory research, which is increasingly drawing the attention of social scientists all over. In South Asia, it explains the region's societal illogicalities, more so the alternate outbursts of communal violence and communal coexistence.

**Table I.1**

*Violence-triggered migrations in South Asia*

| Year | Victims of Violence | Countries Involved | Number of Migrants | Political Impact |
|------|--------------------|--------------------|--------------------|------------------|
| 1947 | Hindus, Muslims and Sikhs | India and Pakistan | 15–20 million | Still politically relevant, more so in India |
| 1959 | Tibetan Buddhists | India and China (Tibet) | 100,000 | Irritant for India–China relations |
| 1971 | Hindu and Bengali Muslims | Bangladesh and India | 10 million | Divisive issue in Bangladesh politics and a tension point for Bangladesh–Pakistan relations |
| 1977 | Rohingyas (a section of Bengali-speaking Muslims of Myanmar) | Myanmar and Bangladesh | 260,000 | Tension point for Bangladesh–Myanmar relations and a divisive issue in Bangladesh politics as well |
| 1979 | Pashtuns and other Afghans | Afghanistan and Pakistan | 3.5 million | Pakistan–Afghan tensions and cause of regional insecurity |
| 1983 | Sri Lankan Tamils | Sri Lanka and India | 100,000 | Tension point for India–Sri Lanka relations, Tamil Nadu politics and New Delhi–Chennai political equations |

| 1989 | Bhutanese-origin ethnic Nepalis | Bhutan and Nepal | 100,000 | Nepal–Bhutan political tensions but now dormant |
| 2001 | Pashtuns and other Afghans | Afghanistan and Pakistan | 3.5 million (they keep coming and going ever since their first migration in 1979) | Pakistan–Afghan tensions and cause of regional insecurity |

*Source*: Author.

*Notes*:

1. The 'year' column gives only the commencement year of the violence. In most cases, the violence continued for several years thereafter with varying intensity.

2. The figures shown are approximations.

3. Small-scale migrations caused by sudden violent incidents have not been included, for example, Hindu and Sikh asylum seekers in India following violence in Afghanistan and Pakistan perpetrated by Islamic militants, clandestine migrations of Hindus from Bangladesh following anti-Hindu riots there and migration of Sri Lankan Tamil refugee movements to Tamil Nadu following deterioration of ethnic relations in the country. Also not included in the table are the Chakma migrations from East Pakistan/Bangladesh during the 1960s through 1980s as they were mostly on account of their displacement by the dams constructed on the Kaptai/Karnafuli river. There was some violence too unleashed by the East Pakistani/Bangladeshi security forces.

# IV

# Theory of Collective Memory

Memory research has generally concentrated on unpleasant memories of individual victims of traumatic experiences which because of historical and other circumstances, have taken the shape of collective memory over the years. The central theoretical question is: Does historical amnesia lead to reconciliation? Or, is the acknowledgement of past error a means to inter-ethnic, inter-religious or interstate conflict resolution? Therefore, if reconciliation is the goal, is 'the truth' at all germane to that goal? The focus of the memory discourse all over the world is on collective memories: *Who* remembers *what*—what is selected, highlighted, amplified, modified, or, just not mentioned. It has been argued that sometimes even 'silence' could be a memory statement and even a resolve for future action.[10] For any country, its memory project is closely linked to its present circumstances based on ideology as well as the texture of politics and statecraft. Against this background historical truth has often the chance of getting distorted, thereby the memories themselves get subjected to manipulation.[11] In the context of historical encounters between peoples, cultures and nation-states, memory recollections range freely over unrestrained time and space. At times they can be cohesive, at other points in time, disruptive.

# The Memory Question in South Asia

The history of the Indian subcontinent, at least for the last 150 years, has seen three political trends vying for pre-eminence—Hindu nationalism, Muslim nationalism and the composite Hindu–Muslim societal coexistence, if not national syncretism. Each trend has a base in respective communal memories. While in India, and to a lesser extent in Bangladesh, these memories are mixed, leading to some kind of Hindu–Muslim syncretism which breaks down at slightest provocations in Pakistan, the memory factor is largely state created, which gives little chance for syncretism to have a popular space. While the Muslim factor in India and the Hindu factor in Bangladesh are a social reality, the Hindu factor is virtually non-existent in Pakistan so far as its social reality is concerned. Hindus in Pakistan are very small in number, and their existence is at the margins of the society. They matter only if blasphemy cases are to be registered against them. But in Pakistan's national political memory, the Hindu factor matters, thanks to the unresolved problem of Kashmir and the persistence of Army's role in politics, for which its hate-India trump is a crucial force multiplier. These nuances apart, in all these three countries, violent expressions have been seen in their religious conflicts which have sent people across the borders, though the latter trend is less of late. The pattern is different now. While Bangladeshi and Pakistani Hindus still leave their countries and arrive in India for physical safety, Muslims in India do not leave for Pakistan or Bangladesh, although anti-Muslim riots are more violent in India compared to those against Hindus in Bangladesh or Pakistan. There are explanations for this, but this is not the occasion to labour the question.

Where does memory research figure in this narrative? It is difficult to say when did Hindu–Muslim distrust of one another start. My earlier research had convinced me that it all started towards the end of the 19th century, broadly speaking after the end of the East India Company rule and the establishment of the British rule. In this suspicion building, both the communities contributed equally and the process was evolutionary, brick by brick (Ghosh 2000: 52–77). In recent times, the memory of Partition has the most enduring influence since Partition was both the consequence and the cause of the Hindu–Muslim distrust. It is not that Hindu–Muslim riots did not occur before 1947, but their frequency has measurably increased in the post-Partition phase. In spite of the fact that the generation of Partition is almost gone, still the trauma lingers in the nation's memory. Even after more than six decades, new books and research papers are being produced in large numbers in several Indian languages, such as Bengali, Hindi, Punjabi and Urdu. Such fictional writers who lived the generation and wrote on the events around them in the form of short stories and novels, like Saadat Hasan Manto, Amrita Pritam and Bhisham Sahani, continue to be popular and their writings are being translated in other languages. They have been subject of academic research, and Ph.D. dissertations are being written on them. Their works are increasingly being used by historians to understand the then human dimensions of the tragedy.

The more seamy side of the situation is that a sizeable section of India's Hindus even today consider the Partition as a case of Muslim perfidy, refusing to believe that only a small section of India's Muslims had actually demanded for Pakistan and an even smaller section had actually left for that country after its creation. These Hindus also believed that the beginning of Muslim rule in India heralded India's dark chapter in an otherwise glorious history. No less a leader than India's Prime Minister Narendra Modi also tends to think like that. Addressing a massive gathering of Indian Americans at New York's Madison Square Garden auditorium on 28 September 2014, he referred to India's thousand years of servitude, by which he obviously meant the Muslim rule. Hindu–Muslim riots take place in various parts of India at regular intervals, in most of which the Muslim casualty is more. They indeed do not send refugees to bordering countries but they do cause displacement and subsequent ghettoization. Once again, most of these displaced people belong to the Muslim community, with the exception of Kashmiri Hindus who had to flee the valley in the early 1990s under the shadow of majoritarian (Muslim) imperiousness, although nothing like Muslim–Hindu riots had taken place. All this tend to suggest that what political scientist Gopal Krishna wrote about four decades ago probably holds good even today:

> The inescapable truth seems to be that Hindu India cannot escape the consequences of its medieval defeat, however much it might try, and Indian Islam cannot overcome the consequences of the failure of its mission of conquest in India whatever it might do. The result has been on both sides frustration, hatred, and apparent powerlessness to alter the situation. (Krishna 1974)

The above, however, is not the whole story. Alongside Hindu-Muslim contestation there is also the phenomenon of a syncretic inter-communal culture which run through the veins of all South Asians at large. India, being the largest country provides the best example and it is conceivable it has its ripples all over the region. The way some of India's neighbours try to obliterate these syncretistic memories proves that their relevance is not over at the societal levels and hence their earnestness to disparage the pluralistic concepts. A detailed discussion on the subject is not necessary as there is enough literature on it (for a short narrative, see Ghosh 2000: 404–7). Suffice it would here to use a quotation from one of Ramchandra Gandhi's writings, which drives home the point succinctly:

> Let us look at the situations where the conditions of tolerance do obtain, but we do not recognize them and become intolerant: in the field of religion, for instance. Take Islam and Hinduism, these great actors on the field of religion, a field of both battle and creativity. Now, anyone who looks at the presence together of Hindus and Muslims in this subcontinent should be struck by the sheer scale of this togetherness; by the fact that Hinduism has endured and not lost all its members to Islam; by the fact that Islam has endured and expanded, and not been assimilated, and

in that way overwhelmed, by Hinduism. This is a most miraculous happening, and I think it should encourage Hindus and Muslims to give each other the benefit of theological doubt, doubt regarding whether the 'other' religion is acceptable to God or not. Quite clearly, Allah is not displeased with Hinduism. Quite clearly, Ishvara is not displeased with Islam. This simple knowledge about one another is the discovery that tolerance is not error or weakness. Because of the way theology and history are understood and taught, however, Hindus and Muslims are encouraged to mistrust one another, provoked to doubt their intentions regarding one another. And yet at the ground level, as human beings, Hindus and Muslims know that the fact of their historical coexistence are proof—that their traditions are worthy of mutual tolerance. (Gandhi 2007: 148–49)

For demographic and political reasons, India's case is most important to understand. The next country to understand is Bangladesh, also for the same reasons, because in some respects it is the mirror image of India. The argument that the Bangladeshi society is divided between the 'Bengali nationalists' and the 'Bangladeshi nationalists' is not completely valid. There is a fairly large cusp zone between the two, otherwise the Awami League and the Bangladesh Nationalist Party (BNP) would not have alternated in power. At the core of the 2013–14 controversy over the issue of dealing with the criminals of the 1971 liberation war is the question of punishment and forgiveness. Did Bangladesh forgive the war criminals all these years, and suddenly woke up to punish them? Though efforts were made in the initial years of Bangladesh to punish those who collaborated with Pakistani military junta to suppress the Bengali freedom struggle, nothing happened in the post-Mujib era to bring them to book. Evidence, however, suggests that at the subcutaneous levels the traumatic memory of 1971 remained in public consciousness, though Jamaat-i-Islami and BNP succeed in considerable measure to obfuscate the discourse by injecting into it the controversy over secularism versus Islam. In the same context, questions were raised as to what extent India mattered in the collective memory of Bangladesh. Has the political divide between 'Muslim Bengal' and 'Hindu Bengal', which had its first expression in the 1905 Partition of Bengal, been a matter of the past or it has remained as a constant fixture in the politics of East Bengal, which neither the Partition of India in 1947 nor the creation of Bangladesh in 1971, in which India had a substantive role to play, could do away with? In what way would Bangladesh be able to reconcile itself to the baggage of this multifaceted memory?

In Bangladesh, it is a clash of three memories, the memory of 1905, the memory of 1947, and the memory of 1971. The first relates to its memory of domination by the Hindu upper castes, which at the village level meant the oppression by Hindu zamindars. This dichotomy led to several Muslim–Hindu riots prior to the Partition. It may be noted that although the Partition riots were much more sanguinary in the Punjab region, the latter did not have experience of riots prior to Partition. Against the background of a deteriorating communal life in East Bengal even before the Partition, many upper caste Hindus had migrated to West Bengal. During the days of Partition, therefore, when the riots started touching even the lower caste Hindus, it was their turn now to migrate to West Bengal, Assam and Tripura. The liberation movement of 1971 was of a different kind. It was not Muslim–Hindu this time, it became a clash between Bengalis (both Muslim and Hindu) on the one hand and the Punjabis, Biharis and pro-Pakistan Bengalis on the other.[12] Unlike the earlier communal clashes, which had made the Hindus flee to West Bengal and other neighbouring areas, this time it was both Hindu and Muslim East Bengalis who came to India in droves as refugees. This memory has left the most lasting image in Bangladesh psyche, though the earlier anti-Hindu memories too have existed side by side, which the Shahbag incidents of February 2013 brought to the fore.

The controversy over the Shahbag agitation hovered around three questions—punishment, justification and pardon. Who did what during the liberation war of Bangladesh and why not those responsible for suppressing the freedom struggle in collaboration with the Pakistani military junta be brought to book? While the Awami League argued that such criminal elements who had organized the massacres of 1971 should be punished, the forces supporting the Islamists, most notably the BNP and the Jamaat-i-Islami, tried to whitewash their crimes as most of them formed the core of these parties. Since the politics of Bangladesh is polarized, arguably, between secularists and Islamists, the issue assumed political colour. In the late 1980s too, it was a big issue when Jahanara Imam had become a household name in the country for her forceful tirade against some of the war criminals of 1971 (for details, see Ghosh 1993: 697–710).

Pakistan's national memory experience is different from that of both India and Bangladesh in three significant regards. In the first place, the way the Pakistan movement was conducted from the 1930s onwards and the way its constitution was drafted in the 1950s, it had become necessary for the ruling elites to obliterate the memories of its pre-Muslim Indian past as well as India's nationalist movement past, which under the leadership of Mahatma Gandhi had made secularism its mainstay. This is reflected in Pakistan's social science, particularly history, textbooks and the Islamic thrust of its constitution. Textbook writing in any case is a political project in many new countries. In India too, the Hindu nationalists have always tried to rewrite the school textbooks whenever they are in power. In Pakistan, there is no controversy as such because whoever has ruled Pakistan, it has subscribed to the nation's Islamist ideology ingrained in its constitution. To propagate that ideology, there is no scope for any reference to its Hindu past and therefore its history textbooks gloss over its ancient Hindu heritage. In school books, Pakistan's history starts straightaway from the Muslim rule in India with emphasis on the Mughals. Second, as an extension of the first reason, for Pakistan, unlike India, Partition is not to be remembered as a loss but more as a victory celebration. Barring a very few Pakistani academics, mostly located in the West, I rarely come across Pakistanis who regret the Partition. Third, following from the second, if at all there is real regret about anything it is about the dismemberment of the country following the creation of Bangladesh in 1971 and the India's central and controversial role therein. Neither Bangladesh, therefore, has to be pardoned for this impertinence nor its agent, the 'Hindu' India.

Against this background, who would care what Hamid Mir, the Chief of the Geo TV of Pakistan, had to say about Pakistan seeking apology from Bangladesh. On the contrary, he should be punished. Mir had written:

> I am sure that Pakistan is changing fast. A day will come very soon when the government of Pakistan will officially say sorry to Bengalis and March 26th will become an apology day for patriotic Pakistanis. I want this apology because Bengalis created Pakistan. I want this apology because Bengalis supported the sister of Jinnah against General Ayub Khan. I want this apology because I want to make a new relationship with the people of Bangladesh. I don't want to live with my dirty past. I want to live in a neat and clean future. I want a bright future not only for Pakistan but also for Bangladesh. I want this apology because I love Pakistan and I love Bangladesh. Happy Independence Day to my Bangladeshi brothers and sisters. (Mir 2010)

Leave aside any taker for Mir's advice, he was outrightly ridiculed in Pakistan and even physically attacked (see Mir 2014).

Earlier, Pakistan had reacted sharply against the Dhaka trials to bring to book the Bangladeshis who had served as conduits to the Pakistani military actions against the civilians in the Bangladesh Liberation War in 1971. The execution of Abdul Quader Mollah, one of the accused in the trial, was protested at the highest political level in Pakistan, that is, its

National Assembly. The latter passed a resolution condemning the act. The Bangladesh government retaliated in equal measure at this interference in their domestic affairs. Prime Minister Sheikh Hasina Wajed said clearly 'Pakistan has proved that it never accepted the victory of Bangladesh in the Liberation War of 1971, and they still have allies in Bangladesh' (*Strategic Digest*, New Delhi, January 2014: 46).

The memory discourse in Sri Lanka hovers not around religion but around ethnicity, Sinhalese versus Tamil. The ethnic conflict between the majority Sinhalese and the minority Sri Lankan Tamils is at the core of Sri Lanka's politics, which has deep-seated historical memories of suspicion of each other. It is interesting to note that while there is so much historical evidence to prove that both Sinhalese and Tamil kings depended on the other community to serve in their respective armies, still there was the virtual mythical notion of who overpowered whom, the Sinhalese king Dutthugamini or the Tamil king Elara. During the British rule, when English education was introduced it was the minority Tamils who took greater advantage of the situation at the cost of the dominant Buddhist educational institutions. The mutual suspicion kept on growing as British started introducing political reforms. The climax came when as an independent country it mass based its politics, and the policy of 'Sinhala only' was introduced in 1956. This was the beginning of the end. The first major communal clash of 1983, in which thousands of Tamils were killed, was a watershed in Sri Lanka's history and the nation is still struggling to extricate itself from its fallout. The first mass Tamil refugee arrival in India was the direct result of this anti-Tamil communal riot in which for the first time that even middle-class Tamils were not spared (for details about the evolution of the Sinhala–Tamil cleavage, see Ghosh 2003: 35–146).

## Memory–Violence–Migration Cycle

The above discussion is meant to show that in South Asia, there are deep-seated historical suspicions amongst the communities, which often result in violent clashes. Since all the nations of South Asia share borders with one or the other and in most cases they have intimate shared historical experience, they find it most convenient to run away from that violence by taking shelter in the neighbouring country, which inevitably has its co-ethnics living there. As a result, even if the state machinery does not come to immediate relief, the very fact that co-ethnics are around it is a reason good enough to feel secure. This sort of reality must also be there in Africa, but international migration theories for reasons explained above have not done justice to them as well. In the migration literature, therefore, the role of inter-communal violence, which has its real origin in memory-based suspicion, must necessarily find its legitimate place.

# Notes

1. The country was known as Burma until 1989 when the ruling State Law and Order Restoration Council (SLORC) regime changed its name to Myanmar.
2. The principle of non-refoulement is often referred to as the cornerstone of international refugee law. No State shall expel or return ('refouler') a refugee in any manner whatsoever to the frontiers of territories where his life or freedom would be threatened on account of his race, religion, nationality, membership of a particular social group or political opinion. The only possible exception is the case when someone who is seen as a risk to the security of the country, or who has been convicted of a 'particularly serious crime'.
3. The idea here is to relate it to way American historian Frederick Jackson Turner in his 1893 essay 'The Significance of the Frontier in American History' had attributed the essential American character of toughness and risk-taking adventures to the changing frontier of the United States. Before Turner, the essentials of American psyche were understood to have been influenced by their European 'germs', the so-called germ theory in American history. In his subsequent publications Turner further elaborated on his theory. For more on the point, see Partha S. Ghosh (2011).
4. On Franklin Ho, one can consult the dissertation of Arunabh Ghosh, 'Making It Count: Statistics and State Society Relations in Early People's Republic of China, 1949–1959', Columbia University, New York: 136–38.
5. It was the 19th-century nationalist historians and ethnographers who had invented the primitive–civilized binary. Later, when white scholars read more carefully the travel accounts of early Dutch and Portuguese traders in West Africa or of Jesuits in China, it was found how much these travellers had been impressed by the sophistication of these societies and their level of scholarship.
6. In the age of globalization, this is not completely true. There is a vast corporate sector which is open to foreigners at the higher level in developing economies and at the lower level as well in developed economies.
7. Even now the Ganga near the India–Bangladesh border is changing its course, partly because of natural reasons and partly because of Farakka barrage causing displacement, statelessness and impoverishment. A dispatch from Malda, in *Times of India*, 21 April 2014.

8. Fear has been expressed that because of global warming and the resultant rise in the sea level people in low-lying countries may be forced to migrate to high-lying countries. In this context the potential Bangladeshi and Maldivian migrations to India are cited. But there is an alternative view which argues that this apprehension of sea level rise has been overplayed. See Hugh Brammer, 'Climate Refugees: A Rejoinder', *Economic and Political Weekly* (Mumbai), 44(29), 18 July 2009: 87.

9. For example, Harzig and Hoerder's book (2009: 54–85), which mentions all kinds of reasons that caused migrations through ages, does not mention violence as one of the factors responsible for the process.

10. Italian historian Nicola Labanca (2015) has discussed this at some length (2015: 123–27). Semanti Ghosh's book in Bengali (see Bibliography) uses the word in its title itself. Sometimes silence can be deafening. After visiting the camps in Ahmedabad where the Muslim victims of 2002 Gujarat riots were sheltered, Mumbai police chief Julio Rebeiro sensed the pent-up anger among many of the inmates. Their silence spoke more than their expected statements. He wrote: 'I visited the Shah Alam camp where nearly 10,000 Muslims had been accommodated after their homes were burnt and looted and their relatives raped and killed. I had expected histrionics and wailing but I was astounded at the matter of fact manner in which young boys and girls recounted the sordid details of what they had seen and experienced. It gave me an uneasy feeling that these young people were not going to forget the injustices heaped on them. I do not know if the VHP and the Bajrang Dal, who had been gloating over their "success" in Gujarat, visualised the danger to which they are exposing their innocent co-religionists somewhere, sometime in the future.' See Julio Ribeiro, 'Lost Middle Ground: A Community Loses Hope in Gujarat', *Times of India* (New Delhi), 24 April 2002. The rise of the Indian Mujahedeen and other militant Muslim groups in India and the news about some Muslim youth joining the Jihad launched by the Islamic State in Syria and Iraq may point to some uncanny connection between what Ribeiro feared and what has been seemingly happening.

11. The debate over what really happened when the Indian Army flushed out the Sikh militants from the revered Sikh shrine, the Golden Temple, in 1984 (the Operation Bluestar), in the context of a documentary telecast in early June 2013 on a Punjab-based TV channel on the event showed how memories could be manipulated/contested. The controversy was over why Balwant Singh Ramoowalia, then a Member of Parliament (MP) and with the Shiromani Akali Dal (SAD), a party opposed to Congress now, did not reveal the facts all these 29 years. Was not he making political capital out of his 'questionable' memory? *The Hindu* (New Delhi), 10 June 2010, and subsequent TV programmes.

12. The oral historical narrative of Sayeeda Saikia provides some significant insights in this regard (Saikia 2004).

# 1
# Mapping the South Asian Scene

*Mil hi jayega raftagan ka suragh*
*Aur kuch din phiro udaas udaas*

You are bound to find a trace of the departed
Keep up this melancholy wandering for a few more days.

—Nasir Kazmi (Nauman 2012)

## Introduction

In the last six decades, South Asia has witnessed massive interstate migrations and refugee movements as no other region of the world has. About 50 million people have been involved in the process. It is not easy to put them into categories. From a strict methodological standpoint, based on theories of nation-building, probably all human traffic in South Asia may be put into two or three categories. For example, the Hindu/Sikh–Muslim migrations after the Partition of India, the Bengali refugee influx into India in the wake of the Bangladesh liberation war, or the Sri Lankan Tamil refugee arrivals in India in the 1980s onwards can all be attributed to the failure of nation-building. But can it not as well be argued that the role of the imperial British masters was central to the massive Hindu/Sikh–Muslim migration, which was certainly not there in the case of either Bangladeshi or Sri Lankan Tamil refugee flows? Moreover, while in the post-Partition years the Hindu refugees from Pakistan indirectly contributed to the rise of Hindu chauvinistic politics in India, in the case of East Pakistan refugees both Hindu nationalists and their Indian critics closed their ranks. The fact that the majority of these refugees were Hindus made little difference. It is, therefore, not easy to categorize the 50 million people who have intra-regionally crossed the borders in tight compartments. Still for the purposes of making things simpler for my readers, let us divide them into eight categories, particularly in keeping with the circumstances that have contributed to their decision to cross the borders and settle in a neighbouring state. These categories cannot be exclusive. Because of South Asia's inherent circumstances they have to overlap. Here are the categories in causal terms:

1. Partition-related uncertainties,
2. Failure in nation-building,
3. Inter-ethnic conflict,
4. Open or virtually open borders,
5. War-related qualms,
6. Developmental and environmental effects,
7. Statelessness or virtual statelessness, and
8. Intra-regional and extra-regional military interventions.

# Partition-related Uncertainties

## The Pre-Partition Riots

The Partition of India resulted in untold misery in terms of human casualty, displacement and dishonour. In the Partition-related riots, about two million people perished, tens of thousands of women raped and ravaged, and about 15 million rendered homeless. In dishonouring women, the communal divides collapsed: the Hindu, Muslim and Sikh men as if competed with one another to rape the women belonging to the other community to demonstrate their masculine prowess. In this connection, a passage from Ayesha Jalal is worth quoting:

> [T]he commonality of masculinity was stronger than the bond of religion. Men of all three communities delighted in their momentary sense of power over vulnerable women; such was the courage of these citizens of newly independent states. Gender eroded the barriers that religion had been forced to create. Whatever women may have accomplished by aligning their interests with nationalist organisations it was more as abstractions appended to the religious community seeking sovereign statehood than as substantive subjects constituting the nation. (Jalal 1998: 2189–90)

India had witnessed many communal riots in the past, more so in Bengal, but the catalyst in this case of was the Muslim League's 16 August Direct Action Day, resulting in The Great Calcutta Killings of 16–19 August 1946, which was just a year ahead of the Partition. S.P.G. Taylor, the Inspector General of Police of Bengal, reported:

> The situation was seriously aggravated by the action of the Chief Minister of the Provincial Government [Huseyn Shaheed Suhrawardy], who personally organized and addressed a mass meeting of his Muslim followers, several thousands in number in Calcutta. In a highly inflammatory speech he impressed upon his audience that they must oppose to the utmost limit any plan to allow the Hindu community to assume control. ... [His] attitude to rioting was reprehensible to a degree. At the height of the disturbances he drove round Calcutta with the local army commander to assess the situation. The commander said: 'This is all extraordinary; in the Army Hindus and Mohammedans live and work very happily together.' Then the Chief Minister replied: 'We shall soon put an end to all that'. (Taylor 2003: 247–48)

An English official maintained that the 1946 Calcutta riot was a 'new order in communal rioting', describing it as a 'cross between the worst of London air raids and the Great Plague' (Talbot & Singh 2009: 69). The exact number of casualty was not known, and depending upon one's political persuasion it varied. Between the Congress and the Muslim League, it ranged from 5,000 to 50,000, respectively. Viceroy Lord Wavell's guess was that it was between 5,000 and 10,000 (Ghosh 2007: 2–3). According to a Bangladeshi scholar, about 5,000 Muslims and Hindus lost their lives and about 25,000 were injured in the riots. Among the dead the majority belonged to the Muslim community, most of whom were the labourers working in the Khidirpur Dock. Most of these labourers belonged to Noakhali and Tippera (Anisuzzaman 2011: 43–44). The massacre of the Noakhali and Tippera Muslims in Khidirpur was soon avenged. In October 1946, massive anti-Hindu riots broke out in the districts of Noakhali and Tippera in East Bengal, in which the Hindu minority in 350 villages had to suffer large-scale violence.

The cycle of riots did not halt there. Noakhali was soon avenged in Bihar. In many districts, from Saran to Patna, and in Gaya and Munger 10 to 20 thousand people lost their lives. Ever since the time the British had arrived in India these riots were the worst. The Bihar riots were soon followed by those in Garhmukteshwar in the Meerut district of western Uttar Pradesh (UP) engineered by well-organized Hindu toughs (Hindu militant groups). That riots served significant political purpose was amply clear from the way Muslim League and the local Congress organizations responded to the situation. While visiting the Muslim refugee camps in Bihar, Jinnah greeted the inmates for their sacrifice which, he declared, had 'certainly brought the goal of Pakistan nearer and shown out [Muslims'] readiness to make any sacrifice for its attainment'. In similar vein, the then Congress government of Bihar and the province's landed aristocracy took advantage of the Noakhali riots to fan the violence. On the one hand, the Bihar government called a Noakhali Protest day to 'remember' the Hindu victims while, on the other hand, the local zamindars encouraged its impoverished Hindu *ryots* (peasants or tenant farmers) to loot Muslim properties so as to divert their wrath aimed at them. In the case of Garhmukteshwar, the former Indian National Army's Major General Shah Nawaz Khan said: 'Had the police acted more vigorously and promptly, much of the destruction of life and property could have been prevented' (Talbot & Singh 2009: 70–74).

All these riots resulted in displacement and migrations. Around 50,000 Hindu victims of the Noakhali riots were temporarily sheltered in relief camps before they were transferred to Guwahati in Assam. Similarly, many Muslim victims seeing the generally deteriorated atmosphere decided to move to Muslim-majority future provinces of Pakistan. By March 1947, there were 1,000 Bihari refugees in the Sind province and by April 1947 some 60,000 refugees who were in West Bengal camps left for East Bengal (many of them went to West Pakistan after the creation of Bangladesh in 1971). Following the creation of Pakistan, the Sind government, in September 1947, allocated 10,000 acres of land to set up a Bihari colony in Golimar, Karachi (Talbot & Singh 2009: 70–73). But compared to the Punjab violence and the resultant displacements, all the riots discussed above pale to insignificance both in terms of numbers fallen prey to them and the associated cruelties. To understand the magnitude of the problem, it would be instructive to refer to the Radcliffe Award, which demarcated the borders between India and Pakistan.

## The Radcliffe Award

On 22 March 1947, Lord Louis Mountbatten arrived in India to become the British government's last Viceroy to India. It was soon clear to him that Partition was the only option as all his efforts to resurrect the Cabinet Mission proposal failed. The Partition idea was indeed not imposed by him on 'unsuspecting Indian leaders' nor was it 'a "parting gift" of the outgoing imperial masters: it was self-consciously willed by the All-India Congress and Muslim League leaders and, above all, reflected their fears and mistrusts, as well as hopes, that a "right-sized" state would deliver to them the power to construct a new political, economic and social order in a free subcontinent' (Talbot & Singh 2009: 41). Even M.K. Gandhi seemed to have been overtaken by events. The overall inter-communal distrust had reached such nadir that even for him the situation was irretrievable, making him take no steps such as fasting or convince the Congress to rescind the decision (Mahajan 2012: 243–55). From mid-April 1947, the Partition plan was underway, and on 3 June it was announced in a series of radio broadcasts, though Jinnah was not very happy as it involved the partition of Punjab and Bengal. He wanted both the provinces in full. Later, the Indian Independence Bill was drafted for a transfer of power on 14/15 August 1947. Interestingly, the date chosen was not 26 January 1948, which the Congress-minded Indians had celebrated every year since 1930 as India's Independence Day. What was so special about 15 August 1947 that Mountbatten could not wait for another five months to have the independence on 26 January 1948? The date, 15 August, was the second anniversary of the Japanese surrender to the Allied Forces in the Second World War. According to Ramchandra Guha, 'so freedom finally came on a day that resonated with imperial pride rather than nationalist sentiment' (Guha 2007: 4–5).

The task of partitioning Punjab and Bengal was entrusted to a British lawyer named Sir Cyril Radcliffe, who arrived in India on 8 July 1947. His name was suggested by Jinnah. He had no prior knowledge of India nor had any experience of border demarcation. This was considered to be an advantage by all parties concerned for it would make him impartial. He had barely five weeks to accomplish his job of drawing the lines in both east and west with the help of some outdated maps and undependable census data. He was instructed to demarcate the international boundaries on the basis of 'contiguous majority areas' and also by taking into account 'other factors'. But neither these factors nor the unit of the area to be divided was clarified: whether it was the district, or smaller sub-units like the *tehsil, zail*[1] or village, where the populations of Hindus and Muslims were to be taken into account (Khilnani 2004: 200–201). No wonder then that the seemingly intelligent man that Radcliffe was, he realized the mess his Award would result in. A day before India became independent, he wrote to his stepson:

> I thought you would like a get a letter from India with a crown on the envelope. After tomorrow evening nobody will ever again be allowed to use such stationery and after 150 years British rule will be over in India – Down comes the Union Jack on Friday morning and up goes – for the moment I rather forget what, but it has a spinning wheel or a spider's web in the

middle. I am going to see Mountbatten sworn as the first Governor-General of the Indian Union at the Viceroy's House in the morning and then I station myself firmly on the Delhi airport until an aeroplane from England comes along. Nobody in India will love me for the award about the Punjab and Bengal and there will be roughly 80 million people with a grievance who will begin looking for me. I do not want them to find me. I have worked and travelled and sweated – oh I have sweated the whole time. (Khilnani 2004: 201)

Before Radcliffe left India he burnt all his notes and never thereafter did he write anything about his experience in India. Poet W.H. Auden portrayed the deep pathos in this whole exercise in the following words (quoted by Khilnani 2004: 200):

> Shut up in a lone mansion, with police night and day
> Patrolling the gardens to keep assassins away,
> He got down to work, to the task of settling the fate
> Of millions. The maps at his disposal were out of date
> And the Census Returns almost certainly incorrect,
> But there was no time to check them, nor time to inspect
> Contested areas. The weather was frightfully hot,
> And a bout of dysentery kept him constantly on the trot,
> But in seven weeks it was done, the frontiers decided,
> A continent for better or worse divided.
> The next day he sailed for England, where he quickly forgot
> The case, as a good lawyer must. Return he would not,
> Afraid, as he told his Club, that he might get shot.

Radcliffe, however, cannot be entirely faulted for his deed for he was ignorant of the Indian realities and that is the reason that he was chosen for the job. Besides the bickering among the Indian members in the commission on communal lines, they did not care to 'do their home-work', which had surprised Radcliffe (Bandyopadhayay 1997: 62–63).[2] More importantly, one may question as to how could such tall leaders like Jawaharlal Nehru, Mohammad Ali Jinnah or Lord Mountbatten be so myopic not to anticipate that the Partition would result in the massa-cre and displacement of millions of people who would become refugees if they survived. So much so that neither Nehru nor Jinnah had even insisted upon seeing the report of the Radcliffe Boundary Commission before the day of independence. Mountbatten's contentment was appall-ing. He managed that these demarcations were kept secret until after the inauguration of the two dominions. Perhaps he considered it prudent that 'by conducting the operation under anaesthetic the patient would get over it more easily, and by the time he awoke he would be reconciled to what had happened'. In fact, Mountbatten was so assured of this that he went on a holiday to the hills after the inaugurations and was taken aback when a tempest of violence swept the Punjab once the demarcating line became known (Kulke & Rothermund 2004: 322).

But whether or not Radcliffe was responsible, or why was he chosen, which may be matters for academic scrutiny, for those who really suffered, particularly in eastern India where it was impossible to demarcate the undemarcatable terrain, people were not at all willing to give Radcliffe the benefit of doubt. If popular jokes speak a ton about an existing reality, here is one prevalent on the India–Bangladesh border. Urvasi Butalia narrates it from her experience there:

> In Berubari village in India, Jagadishbabu, walk me through the BSF checkpost to one edge of the village. 'Look there,' he says, pointing to one side, 'that is Bangladesh, and where we are, that's India.' We move a little further and stand by a tree at one edge of a small, winding road. 'This tree is in India,' says Jadadishbabu, 'and the one across the road, the banana tree, is in Bangladesh.' We get into a car and drive down the small road. Some distance away, a thin cycle path cuts across the road—you can barely see it in the dust. 'That,' says Jagadishbabu, 'is the boundary that demarcates Bangladesh and India.' He laughs and tells me a tale that the villagers of Berubari enjoy telling. 'You see how this border curls and winds,' he says? 'Which person in his sane mind would draw a boundary like that? You know that Radcliffe? What did he know about anything? He was so confused by what he had to do that he decided, forget it. I'll just get drunk! The bastard drank all night, and then in the morning he woke up and picked up is pen, and naturally he couldn't draw a straight line! So he went this way and that—and botched the whole thing up. And of course we have to live with the consequences!' (Butalia 2003: 117–18)

## The Punjab Riots

From the beginning of 1947 the communal situation in Punjab was getting violent because of the murky political developments there. Ishtiaq Ahmed's detailed district-wise description of the events in the state during 1947 in his book *The Punjab: Bloodied, Partitioned and Cleansed* (2011) tells the story of how communal temper was getting built up, which was inevitably preparing the ground for the communal carnage that would soon be witnessed during and after the Partition. There was an almost total genocide of Hindus and Sikhs in

West Punjab and that of the Muslims in East Punjab. They resulted in millions belonging to these communities to cross over to the newly created nations where their co-religionists were in majority. The communal riots and exodus of Hindus, Sikhs and Muslims was so massive that the newly formed state machineries were overwhelmed. In any case, as noted above, the national leaders had hardly anticipated the magnitude of this chaos. To stem the tide, on 17 July 1947 the Punjab Boundary Force (PBF) was formed, which became operational on 1 August. But it was soon realized that this 15,000 strong unit was hardly adequate to meeting the challenge it had to face. Initially, the districts that were considered disturbed were Sialkot, Gujranwalla, Shiekhpura, Lyallpur, Montgomery, Lahore, Amritsar, Gurdaspur, Hoshiarpur, Jullundur and Ferozepur, to which other districts were later added. After independence, the PBF was disbanded. Already there were allegations against its cadres for being communal. Moreover, the PBF had no jurisdiction over the Sikh princely states of East Punjab, where Muslims were being massacred. After the force was disbanded, the newly created Indian and Pakistani governments decided to manage the riots and the resultant refugee problem through the coordinated efforts of their respective armies, which too, in the given circumstances, were hardly of any efficacy (Ahmed 2011: 320–22, 398).

The unprecedented communal riots in Punjab and the massive migrations of Hindus, Muslims and Sikhs resulted in the total breakdown of societal harmony, though there were stray Good Samaritan experiences across the communities. For the Sikhs it was their second migration. Earlier, taking advantage of the canal land rehabilitation schemes in West Punjab, scores of Sikhs had migrated from East Punjab to West Punjab. Following the Partition, the Sikh refugees were mostly resettled in Delhi and Kurukshetra (now in Haryana, but then in Punjab).[3] The Hindu refugees in general were mostly resettled in Delhi and its vicinities, while the Hindu Sindhis in Mumbai. So far as the Punjabi Muslim refugees were concerned, they were mostly resettled in West Punjab and Sind, while those from north India in general, in Sind, particularly in Karachi. It is estimated that about 13 million people were involved in these two-way migratory processes during the first few months before and after the Partition. During the 1950s, another four million each of Hindus/Sikhs and Muslims migrated to their forced destinations. Though an exact estimate of the refugee inflow during these years is difficult to draw, the above figures should be more or less accurate (Davis 1949: 254–64, Prasad 2009: 559, Spate 1957: 119).

## Jammu and Poonch Riots?

There have been reports, though not fully substantiated, of anti-Muslim riots in Jammu and Poonch districts of Jammu and Kashmir (J&K) immediately after Partition which led to the 'massacre' of about 200,000 Muslims in these districts, largely perpetrated by forces let loose by the Hindu Maharaja and the Rashtriya Swayamsevak Sangh (RSS). The latter had a strong presence in the Jammu province as against the Muslim Conference which was pro-Pakistan. Whether such mass murders took place exactly the way they were rumoured about or not, probably there was some truth in these reports. Otherwise neither the anti-Maharaja and pro-Pakistan Azad Kashmir movement would have been launched in Poonch in September 1947, leading to the creation of Azad Kashmir on 24 October 1947 (two days before the accession of Kashmir to India on 26 October), nor 200,000 to 250,000 Muslims would have fled from the province to Azad Kashmir and other parts of Pakistan.[4] A comparative reading of the 1941 and 1961 census reports would tend to suggest that there were extermination of Muslims in large numbers. It may be noted that in the 1941 census, Jammu province was a Muslim-majority province the religious break-up of which was as follows: Muslims 61.19 per cent, Hindus 37.19 per cent, Sikhs 1.41 per cent and 0.21 per cent accounted for by Jains, Christians, Buddhists and others.[5] The 1961 census tends to suggest that indeed Muslims were reduced to a minority in the region without mentioning about the riots. Had they gone voluntarily the same should have happened with the Valley Muslims as well, which was not the case! The 1961 census said:

> ... a large number of villages which were well inhabited till 1947 were completely depopulated consequent upon the migration of their populations to West Pakistan and to the State territory on the other side of the Cease-Fire Line [i.e. Azad Kashmir] .... There was a phenomenal fall in the rural population of [the] Muslim community in Jammu district during the last two decades as a result of mass migration to Pakistan of most of the Muslims [which] is about one-third of what it was in 1941 ....

It was estimated that about 500,000 Muslims went to Azad Kashmir or to West Pakistan as refugees from the state (Snedden 2001: 116, 127, Snedden 2013: 48; also see Hassan 2006: 58).

Likewise, thousands of Hindus and Sikh refugees from Pakistan too arrived in the state of J&K. The fact that certain areas in the state fell on the way to India for the fleeing Hindus and Sikhs from Pakistan aided the process. According to the 1961 census, 48,856 Pakistan-born people belonging to these communities migrated to J&K, of which as many as 46,836, that is 96 per cent, settled in Jammu. By September 1947, there were about 70,000 such refugees in the state (Snedden 2001: 128, Snedden 2013: 48). Probably the process continued as reports suggest that in the wake of India–Pakistan wars in 1965 and 1971, just like the one in 1947, many migrated. The total number of such refugees from West Pakistan and Pakistan-occupied Kashmir (POK) arriving in J&K (mostly in Jammu) is estimated to be about 100,000. Since many of these refugees did not have Kashmiri domicile, they could not become J&K state subjects, though they became Indian citizens.[6] In the parliamentary elections held in mid-2014 and in the J&K assembly elections held later that year, one anomalous thing that surfaced was that while as Indian citizens they were entitled to vote in the general elections, but as not being state subjects of J&K they were not entitled to vote in the assembly elections. For the same reason, they have not been able to own property in the state and cannot apply for state government jobs which are meant for J&K state subjects only (*The Hindu*, 9 April 2014).

## The Delhi Scene

Delhi was both the refugee-sending and refugee-receiving city, though it received much more than it sent. In 1947 Delhi's population was 900,000, to which were added 470,000 Hindu, Sikh and Sindhi refugees from West Pakistan. Of course, it also lost a large section of its Muslim population: 320,000 Delhi Muslims left for Pakistan. The overall situation was that while Delhi's population in 1941 was 700,000, it rose to 1.4 million in 1951 (Kumar 2013: 16). Most of the West Pakistan refugees were sheltered in seven camps located at Kingsway, Karol Bagh, Shahadra, Purana Qila (Old Fort), Anand Parbat, Tis Hazari and Bela Road. All these camps were not state-run. For example, the Purana Qila camp was a self-supporting camp where 5,500 refugees lived. Many refugees stayed with their relatives and friends or in forcibly occupied houses abandoned by fleeing Muslims. Soon several refugee associations emerged to work as lobbies or to serve as bridges between the refugees and the state functionaries. Some such associations were the Homeless Provinces Refuge Association, the Refugee Teachers Association, the Railway Vendors Association, the Free India Sikh League, the Arya Samajist Refugees, the Hawkers and Vendors Association, the Western Punjab Protection Board, the Refugee Association, the Refugee Lawyers, Evacuee Press Association, All India Refugee Students' Committee, Delhi Sindhi Association, Dera Ghazi Khan Refugee Relief Society, Anand Parbat Refugee Association and so on (Kumari 2013: 63–65).

## Refugees from Sind

The Hindu–Muslim riots that engulfed Punjab did not touch Sind in the beginning. Rather, both the Pakistan and the Sind provincial governments boasted that under strict administrative vigilance no such riots were permitted in the province as a rigid curfew had been imposed. But the communal incident of 6 January 1948, in which a *gurdwara* was attacked, where Sikhs from other parts of Pakistan had arrived on way to Bombay by sea changed the situation altogether. The communal situation deteriorated fast, in which the incoming *Muhajirin* contributed massively. Soon riots broke out in the province, forcing a large number of Hindu Sindhis to migrate to India. About 1,250,000 Sindhis migrated, mostly to Bombay by ships, but also to Rajputana (present Rajasthan) by crossing the deserts that bordered the provinces. Later, these refugees were dispersed in various parts of India, and since they were mostly urban people having interest in small business and other urban activities they got absorbed into their host societies, though to the disadvantage of the local traders who could not compete with the superior business skills of the Sindhi refugees (Alexander 1951: 59–62, Zamindar 2008: 48–49).

## The Bengal Scene

Between India and East Pakistan the volume of human flow was not as massive as the western part of India. Also, unlike the latter, it was not confined to only a few months. Besides, again unlike Punjab, Bengal had a tradition of Hindu–Muslim riots (Das 1990, Batabyal 2005), making the Partition events as something already experienced. But the communal temper worsened leaps and bounds in the wake of Partition. The riots of Calcutta, Noakhali, Bihar (in Tarapur) and Garhmukteshwar in UP, as we have noted above, aggravated the Hindu–Muslim conflict as never before. The continued communal tensions routinely led to cross-border refugee movements for years to come. The Hindu refugees from East Bengal mostly settled in three Indian states, namely, West Bengal, Assam and Tripura. In the beginning, most refugees came from the urban areas, but later the pattern changed. With the systematic deterioration of inter-communal relations in East Bengal, even poor farmers, otherwise reluctant to leave their homesteads, felt the heat and, by early 1950, massively migrated to West Bengal. During the police action in Hyderabad in September 1948 (discussed below), communal tensions once again flared up in East Bengal, leading to another spate of Hindu refugee movements.

For some time, there was a bit of hope that the Nehru–Liaquat Pact would discourage the refugee flows. Even prior to the pact, which did indeed encourage many Bengali Hindu refugees to return to East Bengal, many Muhajirin were returning to India seeing Gandhi's sacrifice and the Indian government's resolute decision to protect the minorities. But the exact number of such returnees was probably fewer than what some contemporary reports suggested. For example, in a report submitted to the Commonwealth Relations Office in May 1948, the United Kingdom High Commission in Delhi noted that 100,000 to 250,000 Muslims had returned to India, of which 40,000 to Delhi alone. Zamindar's study, however, found that the number of returnees to Delhi did not exceed 12,000 (Zamindar 2008: 86–87, 256).

The introduction of the passport system in October 1952, first by Pakistan and then by India, further fuelled fear amongst the potential migrants, more so for the Hindus of East Bengal, leading to their movement towards India (Mandal 2011: 120–22). The introduction of the passport system in place of earlier permit system was not without controversy. While Pakistan was keen for its introduction to stem the flow of Muslims from India, the latter was opposed to it, particularly for the eastern sector where it argued that the system would stop the flow, thereby creating a panic amongst the Hindus of East Bengal who should be given a chance to migrate to India if the situation worsened. Even many Pakistanis opposed it, because while the permit system was simpler by which one permit was good enough for the entire family, passport was issued to individuals. In any case these passports, which were India–Pakistan-specific and not universal, could not stop the flow of refugees either in the west or in the east (Zamindar 2008: 180–3).

The flow continued well into the 1960s, which was particularly triggered by the 1964 anti-Hindu riots in East Pakistan. According to the Indian Commission of Jurists' report of 1965, an estimated 5.5 million refugees had moved into India by then (pp. 309–12; also Bhattacharya 1978: 19–20). A micro study done by an American sociologist of a Hindu–Muslim riot in an East Pakistani village in the 1950s has shown that even after riots subsided and normality returned, there was a tendency among the minorities (meaning Hindus) to feel insecure and look for a safer abode which was India (Roy 1996: 112–16, see also Chakrabarty 1996: 2143–52).

We are presenting here three tables (Tables 1.1–1.3) which would give a fairly clear picture of the migratory pattern from East Bengal to some of India's eastern states along with its religious dimension. The

**Table 1.1**

*Migration between East Bengal and West Bengal, Assam and Tripura*

|  | Hindus | Muslims |
|---|---|---|
| **To India before the Indo-Pakistan Agreement of 8 April 1950** | | |
| From East to West Bengal (7 February–8 April 1950) | 547,049 | 6,847 |
| From East Bengal to Assam (7 February–8 April 1950) | 190,350 | Negligible |
| From East Bengal to Tripura | 120,000 | n.a. |
| Total | 857,579 | 6,847 |
| *To India after the Indo-Pakistan Agreement* | | |
| From East to West Bengal (9 April–25 July 1950) | 999,290 | 218,708 |
| From East Bengal to Assam (9 April–27 July 1950) | 191,751 | 46,617 |
| From East Bengal to Tripura (9 April–18 July 1950) | 93,582 | 32,083 |
| Total | 1,284,623 | 297,408 |
| Grand Total | 2,142,202 | 304,255 |
| *From India before the Agreement* | | |
| From West to East Bengal (7 February–8 April 1950) | 65,537 | 254,715 |
| From Assam to East Bengal (7 February–8 April 1950) | Negligible | 124,063 |
| From Tripura to East Bengal | Negligible | n.a. |
| Total | 65,537 | 378,778 |
| *From India after the Agreement* | | |
| From West to East Bengal (9 April–25 July 1950) | 503,273 | 409,741 |
| From Assam to East Bengal (9 April–25 July 1950) | 32,561 | 37,578 |
| From Tripura to East Bengal | 5,417 | 2,649 |
| Total | 541,251 | 449,968 |
| Grand Total | 606,824 | 828,746 |

*Table 1.1 continued*

*Table 1.1 continued*

|  | Hindus | Muslims |
|---|---|---|
| **Migrations after the Agreement (9 April 1950–25 July 1950)** | | |
| *From East Bengal to India* | | |
| Hindus | | 1,284,623 |
| Muslims | | 297,408 |
| Total | | 1,582,031 |
| *From India to East Bengal* | | |
| Hindus | | 541,251 |
| Muslims | | 449,968 |
| Total | | 991,219 |

*Source:* Hasan (1997: 170–71).

**Table 1.2**
*State-wise break-up of Bengali refugees, until 1957*

| State | Number |
|---|---|
| West Bengal | 316,000 |
| Assam | 487,000 |
| Tripura | 374,000 |
| Bihar | 67,000 |
| Uttar Pradesh | 16,000 |
| Orissa | 12,000 |
| Manipur | 2,000 |
| Madhya Pradesh | 1,000 |
| Andamans | 4,000 |
| Total | 4,313,000 |

*Source:* Das (2000: 16).

total period covered in these tables is from 1946 to 1970, after which the pattern assumed a different form in the wake of the Bangladesh liberation movement.

Of all the three states of eastern India that received East Bengali refugees, the case of Tripura was unique in the sense that the migrations changed the demographic character of the state altogether. The Bengali settlers now outnumbered the local tribes who were in majority hereto-fore. This process of migration of non-tribal population, however, had its

**Table 1.3**
*Refugee arrivals from East Pakistan, 1946–70*

| Year | Reasons for Leaving East Pakistan | Total |
|------|-----------------------------------|-------|
| 1946 | Noakhali riots | 19,000 |
| 1947 | Partition of India | 334,000 |
| 1948 | Police Action in Hyderabad | 786,000 |
| 1949 | Khulna and Barishal riots | 213,000 |
| 1950 | Khulna and Barishal riots | 1,575,000 |
| 1951 | Agitation over Kashmir | 187,000 |
| 1952 | Economic conditions, passport scare | 227,000 |
| 1953 | | 76,000 |
| 1954 | | 118,000 |
| 1955 | Unrest over Urdu in East Pakistan | 240,000 |
| 1956 | Pakistan's Islamic constitution | 320,000 |
| 1957 | | 11,000 |
| 1958 | | 1,000 |
| 1959 | | 10,000 |
| 1960 | | 10,000 |
| 1961 | | 11,000 |
| 1962 | | 14,000 |
| 1963 | | 16,000 |
| 1964 | Hazrat Bal incident in Kashmir | 693,000 |
| 1965 | | 108,000 |
| 1966 | | 8,000 |
| 1967 | | 24,000 |
| 1968 | | 12,000 |
| 1969 | | 10,000 |
| 1970 | Elections in Pakistan | 250,000 |
| Total | | 5,283,000 |

*Source:* Chatterjee (n.d.: 5).

origin much earlier. It had started in the beginning of the 20th century when both Muslim and Hindu Bengali migrants had started arriving in the princely state of Tripura in large numbers, threatening the numerical dominance of the tribal population. At the end of the 19th century, the tribal population constituted 64 per cent of the population, but by the time India became independent they were not more than 60 per cent of the population. The post-Partition Hindu migrations further marginalized them. Due to this Hindu demographic invasion, even many Muslims settled in Tripura decided to move to East Pakistan. By 1961 the tribal and Muslim populations were mere 31.5 per cent and 5 per cent, respectively (Sen 2003: 123–25).[7]

## The Muhajirin of Pakistan

A large number of Muslims from eastern Punjab, UP, Bihar, West Bengal, Assam and other parts of India migrated to West and East Pakistan in the wake of Partition and in the subsequent years. Barring the east Punjabi Muslims the remaining who went to Pakistan came to be collectively called Muhajirin in West Pakistan, though the inclusion of Bihari Muslims among them caused some consternation among the dominant UP-origin Muslims and the local Sindhi leadership at some later stage. Many of them raised the bogey of a 'sinking boat'—the provincial economy would not be able to sustain so many people from outside. Some of the leaders even argued that Pakistan should ask India to provide additional territory to accommodate these refugees (Zamindar 2008: 176–78). The east Punjabi Muslims were all settled in West Punjab and the leaders of the latter saw to it that other Muslims did not settle there (Bose 2004: 144). Of the total number of refugees in West Punjab, 97.5 per cent (71.2 per cent of the total number of refugees in Pakistan) came from East Punjab, including some from the princely states of Rajasthan and J&K. Only 2 per cent came from UP (Waseem 1994: 103–6). Until 1950, on an average 4,000 UP Muslims left for Pakistan everyday to settle mostly in Sind. The latter had prepared the ground for their reception. Karachi became their coveted destination, which at that time was sparsely populated, besides being the hub of Pakistan's commercial activity. By the end of 1951, roughly 6,597,000 Indian Muslim refugees had moved to West Pakistan and 794,127 to East Pakistan. Of the 464,000 strong UP Muslim migrants, 60 per cent went to Sind (Ghosh 2007: 11–12). Compared with UP, the number of refugees from central and eastern regions of India was fewer, though proportionately they were more from the professional classes. From Delhi, UP and Bihar government servants formed the core. There was such an exodus from the Delhi police department that it suffered a severe personnel crunch (Hasan 1997b: 50).

## The Bihari Muslims

During 1947–48, about 96 per cent of Muslim migrants from Assam, Bihar and West Bengal, collectively called Bihari Muslims in Pakistan/ Bangladesh, migrated to East Pakistan. Only a small section, about 3 per cent, went to Karachi. According to the 1951 census of Pakistan, 66.69 per cent of the refugees in East Pakistan belonged to West Bengal, 14.50 per cent to Bihar, 11.84 per cent to Assam and 6.79 per cent to other parts of India. In the pre-Partition communal riots in Calcutta and Bihar, Muslims were largely on the receiving end. When Noakhali was revenged in Bihar, the first migration of Bihari Muslims took place. Between 30 October and 7 November 1946, some 30,000 of them left for East Bengal. After the Partition another 1,300,000 did so (Whitaker 1977: 7). Even in India a large number of refugee camps were set up for the riot victims in Bihar and West Bengal (Ghosh 2007: 12–13). Against the general atmosphere of fear the factor that contributed the most in making the Bihari Muslims flee to East Pakistan, besides riots, was proximity. The other related factors were frequent searches of Muslim homes by the police, acute food shortages in Muslim areas and the Muslim bureaucratic elite's lack of trust in India's political leadership. By July 1947, 90 per cent of the Muslim employees in Central Government departments in Bihar had expressed their desire to leave for Pakistan. This included all the Indian Civil Service (ICS) officers serving in Bihar, almost all postal and military accounts functionaries, about 2,000 telegraphists and ticket collectors in the East Indian Railway's Danapur division, and the majority of drivers and fitters (Ghosh 2007: 12–13, see also Jha & Jha 2012: 124–25).

The Indian Muslim refugees, however, soon realized that in the Indian subcontinent provincial identities had a much greater appeal than the supra-religious identity of Islam. In both East Bengal and Sind they had to face the ire of the locals in some form or the other. Jinnah considered it a 'curse' that Indian Muslims thought of being Sindhi, Punjabi, Pashtoon and Delhi Muslims. In a speech in Dhaka in March 1948, he ranted against the 'poison of provincialism' and reminded his audience that 1,300 years ago they had been taught that all Muslims were one (Ghosh 2007: 20). The fact was that many Muslims who decided to move to Pakistan had no real idea what it meant for them. According to Mushirul Hasan:

[T]he fact is that millions were unwittingly caught up in the cross-fire of religious hatred and were indeed hapless victims of a triangular game-plan worked out by the British, the Congress and the League. They were indifferent to the colonial as well as the League's definition of a 'commu-nity' or a 'nation'.... They had no sense of the newly demarcated frontiers, little knowledge of how Mountbatten's Plan or the Radcliffe Award would change their destinies and tear them apart from their families, friends and neighbours. (*The Sunday Times of India*, 13 August 1995)

## Migrations from Hyderabad

From South India also, a good number of Muslims from the erstwhile princely state of Hyderabad migrated to Pakistan. From the day of India's independence on 15 August 1947 till 13 September 1948, the day when the armed forces of India moved into the state 'in response to the call of the people', a large number of Muslims from both urban and rural areas had migrated to Hyderabad. Being a princely state, still not a part of either India or Pakistan, it was yet another possible home for these Muslims other than East or West Pakistan. But India's armed intervention to integrate the state into India against the wishes of its Nizam, Osman Ali Khan, Asaf Jah VII, who wanted to remain inde-pendent, fast deteriorated the communal situation there. Fearing that India might force the state to accede to India, a private militia called Razakars was organized by Qasim Rizvi, who wanted the Nizam first to resist the Indian prodding and then join Pakistan. Razakars unleashed a reign of terror against the Hindus, particularly in the Telangana region, which had an ongoing Leftist movement. The Indian state had a dual challenge: one, the spectre of Hyderabad joining Pakistan, and two, the rise of a Leftist insurgency. The result was the so-called 'Police Action'. Codenamed 'Operation Polo', it was actually an army intervention. What followed was large-scale killing of Muslims and the loot of their properties in which along with some rightist Hindu groups even many army personnel participated. This was revealed by the Sundarlal Report.[8]

These anti-Muslim riots made many Muslims from Hyderabad leave for Pakistan. Ever since the revolt of 1857 there was a constant flow of Muslims from other parts of India to Nizam's Hyderabad. After 1947 the phenomenon had picked up momentum as the new migrants con-sidered Hyderabad as yet another choice besides Pakistan, as we have noted above. If one looks at the population figures of Hyderabad during 1931–61, it would be seen that while between 1931 and 1941 the city registered a 61 per cent growth and between 1941 and 1951 a 43 per cent growth, between 1951 and 1961 it was as small as 9 per cent. Both these trends are largely attributable, in the first two decades, to in-migration of Muslims from other parts of India, and in the last mentioned decade to their outmigration to Pakistan and other parts of India (Weiner 1978: 224). It is difficult to figure out how many Muslims of Hyderabad left for Pakistan and how many returned to their original homes in other parts of India. According to historian Mushirul Hasan:

> In Hyderabad, Muslims constituted 10 per cent of the population before 1947–48. Muslim government servants held, as in UP, a much higher percentage of posts. But their fortunes dwindled following Hyderabad's merger with the Indian Union. Urdu ceased to be the official language. The abolition of *jagirdari* affected over 11 per cent of the Muslim population, three-quarters of whom inhabited about a dozen of urban centres. Smaller *jagirdars*, in particular, faced a bleak future due to retrenchment in government departments, recession in industry after 1951, and a sharp fall in agricultural prices. The old nobles and the absentee landowners started selling their remaining lands and spacious houses to make ends meet. The dissolution of Princely States impoverished a large percentage, if not the majority, of the upper classes and the bourgeoisie as well as a large number of peasants, artisans and retainers who lost the patronage networks. Nearly half the population of Hyderabad depended on the Nizam for their livelihood, and thus with sources of patronage rapidly drying up this section was worse off. (Hasan 1997b: 51–52)

As a conclusion to this section, it may be mentioned that about 20 million people were involved in the two-way refugee traffic during the first two decades of independence. Of this, 15 million were in the India–West Pakistan sector and 5 million in the India–East Bengal/Pakistan sector. Both India and Pakistan had to deal with this huge influx of refugees with their limited resources and fledgling administrative machineries. How did they fare, what political controversies did they generate, will be discussed in our subsequent chapters. They would deal with such questions as India's and Pakistan's overall relief and rehabilitation schemes as well as the controversy in India over the Union Government's differentiated approach to Punjab and Bengal refugees, making many Bengali intellectuals and politicians levelling allegations against the Union Government for its stepmotherly treatment of the Bengali refugees.

## Failure in Nation-building

Unlike the European experience, in large parts of the decolonized world, state formation has preceded nation formation. This has resulted in all kinds of inter-communal and inter-ethnic tensions, of which South Asia has a good share. These tensions often have led to violent conflicts resulting in state repression or the vice versa, which then have resulted in migrations of people across the borders, in most cases into the neighbouring states. In this section, we will discuss six such cases, namely, the East Pakistan refugees in India following the failure of Pakistan to contain political disaffection in its eastern wing, the Lhotshampa[9] refugees in Nepal, the disgruntled Bhutan political refugees in Nepal, the Indian repatriates from Myanmar, the Rohingya refugees from Myanmar in Bangladesh (there are some Rohingya refugees in India also, though they are often mistaken as Bangladeshis) and the Chin Burmese refugees in India.

## Bangladeshi Refugees and Illegal Migrants

The exodus of millions of East Pakistani Bengali refugees to India during the Bangladesh liberation war of 1970–71 falls in this category. The creation of Pakistan in 1947 on religious lines did not address the problem of nation-building beyond the Islamic label. The denial of democratic rights to the East Pakistan–based Awami League to form the government following its victory in the general election of 1970 sharpened the already-existing political divide between the East and West wings of Pakistan. The people of East Pakistan, claiming a distinctive linguistic–cultural identity of their own, around which developed the phenomenon of Bengali nationalism, came in conflict with West Pakistani, or more precisely, Punjabi, nationalism. The Bangladesh liberation movement invited an unprecedented repression by the Pakistani military junta led by General Yahya Khan, which caused a massive exodus of East Pakistani Bengalis to India. About 10,000,000 refugees arrived in India, which was five times the number of people displaced in Bosnia in the 1990s. Here is a state-wise break up of these refugee arrivals (Table 1.4).

It may be noted that the migrants or refugees from East Pakistan, including those during the liberation struggle, consisted mostly of Hindus. The pattern changed only after the creation of Bangladesh, when Muslim migrants too were large in number. It is difficult to suggest what was exactly the percentage of Hindu migrants in the earlier phase, but Table 1.5 might give a fairly good idea, though the term 'Hindu' has been camouflaged here as non-Muslims.

By the end of May 1971, the refugee flow had assumed the proportion of a flood, 71 refugees entering India every minute (Raghavan 2013: 74).

The creation of Bangladesh, however, did not solve the problem of outmigration. In the beginning it was felt that the thrust of political strategy of the newly formed Awami League would be progressive,

**Table 1.4**
*Percentage distribution of East Pakistani refugees in different Indian states (until November 1971)*

| State | Number of Refugees | Percentage of the Total |
|---|---|---|
| West Bengal | 7,500,000 | 76 |
| Tripura | 1,400,000 | 15 |
| Meghalaya | 700,000 | 6 |
| Assam | 300,000 | 3 |
| Total | 9,900,000 | 100 |

*Source:* Bandyopadhyay (2000: 35).

**Table 1.5**
*Non-Muslim refugees from East Pakistan to India, 1947–August 1970*

| Year | Number of Refugees |
|---|---|
| Partition to 31 December 1961 | 4,078,000 |
| 1962 | 13,894 |
| 1963 | 18,243 |
| 1964 | 693,142 |
| 1965 | 107,906 |
| 1966 | 7,565 |
| 1967 | 24,527 |
| 1968 | 11,649 |
| 1969 | 9,768 |
| 1970 (until August 1970) | 159,390 |
| Total | 5,124,084 |

*Source:* Brief for the Parliamentary Consultative Committee, P/125/82/70, MEA, 1970, National Archives of India, New Delhi; cited in Raghavan (2013: 75).

which would accommodate the interests of average Bangladeshis, including those belonging to the minority ethnic and religious groups. But it developed snags before long. The Bihari Muslims, Chakmas and the Hindus started finding it difficult to fully identify their interests with the new ruling elites. Although the 1972 constitution, by making democracy, nationalism, secularism and socialism the four pillars to build the

Bangladeshi nationalism, had instilled confidence amongst all these minority sections, yet even before the assassination of the Awami League supremo Sheikh Mujibur Rahman on 15 August 1975, it was clear to them that communal politics had not outlived its political utility. The Vested Property Act of the early Pakistan days, which had been reinforced in the aftermath of the India–Pakistan war of 1965 through the promulgation of Enemy Property (Custody and Registration) Order of 1965, was given a new lease of life by the Mujib government through the Bangladesh Vesting of Property and Assets Order, 1972 (Order 29 of 1972). The provisions of the order and their prejudiced interpretations seriously disadvantaged the minority communities, particularly the Hindus. During the period 1974–81, the extent of missing Hindu population was estimated around 1,220,000 and about 1,730,000 during the inter-census period of 1981–91. On the basis of this, it was calculated that about 475 Hindus disappeared every day from the soil of Bangladesh between 1974 and 1996 (Mukherjee 1996). The same happened to the Christians as well, although they were very small in number, not even 1 per cent of the country's population. Constituting a better-educated lot, they mostly migrated to Kolkata (for more on Bangladeshi Christians, see Timm 2002: 53–69).

## Lhotshampas of Bhutan

There is a long history of Nepali migration to Bhutan, which started following the 1865 Treaty of Sinchula, making the British Indian government encourage settlements of Nepalis in Darjeeling and Sikkim. Many such settlers gradually moved to southern Bhutan, which provided good agricultural land. The process continued for more than a century until the conflict between the Lhotshampas and the Bhutan government put an end to the process that was catalysed by the forcible eviction of Nepalis from Manipur, Meghalaya and Nagaland in the mid-1980s to which New Delhi had not objected (Rose 1994: 110–11). As a result of this migratory process, Bhutan came to be composed of two major ethnic groups—Drukpas and Lhotshampas. Drukpas are further subdivided into Ngalongs and Sarchops. Drukpas are ethnic Bhutanese occupying northern and central regions—Ngalongs in the northern districts and Sarchops in the central and eastern districts. Historically, the political power is in the hands of the Ngalongs. The Lhotshampas, who are of Nepali ethnic origin, live mostly in the southern districts. In the early 1980s, Bhutan followed a policy of inter-ethnic assimilation. The National Council for Social and Cultural Promotion, which was established in

1980, tried to ensure that Drukpa and Lhotshampa children studied together in schools, and there were inter-ethnic marriages for which even cash incentives were provided by the government. But these policies were soon supplanted by a majoritarian approach when in 1985–86 the National Council for Social and Cultural Promotion was replaced by the Special Commission for Cultural Affairs. It not only made the citizenship laws stricter but it also tried to streamline the Bhutanese people on the lines of Drupka cultural norms. Bhutan's new cultural policy that was enshrined in Driglam Namzha, lay at the heart of the country's distinctive national identity. All Lhotshampas were made to wear the traditional Bhutanese dress, Gho and Kira, in all public places and Dzongkha language was made compulsory for all. In 1999, a 260-page bilingual (Dzongkha/English) manual of Driglam Namzha enumerated in detail the prescribed cultural norms (Hutt 2003: 145–67).

The deterioration of Drukpa–Lhotshampa relations had been on the cards from the early 1980s. There were various reasons for this, which have been discussed in some earlier studies (Ghosh 1998: 213–25, also Hutt 2003: 160–230, Evans 2013: 121–24). As a result of this friction, the Lhotshampas were forced by circumstances to leave Bhutan and take shelter in Nepal. It is difficult to say who was really responsible for the exodus of the Lhotshampas to Nepal. While the nationalistic policies were indeed responsible for threatening the cultural identity of these people, leading to their sense of fear, the rise of the Bhutan People's Party (BPP) and its atrocities against them to boost their cadre and support base was no less responsible (Evans 2013: 128–33). What served the catalytic role is the same old story, which came first, chicken or the egg. The answer depends on who the interpreter is, the Bhutanese state or the refugees and the BPP. But the real point is the inability of small border communities to negotiate with the state, which is true in almost all parts of the world (Evans 2013: 138–40).

The first group of Lhotshampa refugees to arrive in Nepal was towards the end of 1990, and during the next few years it was a constant flow. In mid-1994 the flow peaked, with 600 refugees arriving every day, raising their number to about 84,000. Soon the UNHCR was involved in the refugee care. By 1995, according to the UNHCR and the Government of Nepal, there were about 90,000 Bhutanese refugees in Nepal, particularly in Jhapa and Morang districts, besides about 15,000 not living in camps. In India they were about 20,000 in number, scattered in Arunachal Pradesh, Assam, Sikkim and West Bengal. Of this, 7,000 in the Bomdila region of Arunachal Pradesh were at one point of time under threat of deportation because of the anti-foreigner campaign launched by the All Arunachal Pradesh Students' Union (AAPSU; *The Times of India*, 12 February 1996). With the natural rise in their numbers due to births in the camps, a 2007 census put the figure at 107,923 who largely depended on international aid as they were not allowed to work, own land, leave the camps or engage in political activities (Evans 2013: 134).

### Bhutanese Political Refugees

The absence of democracy in Bhutan until recently had also resulted in many Drukpa Bhutanese leaving the country and seeking refuge in Nepal and India. These exiles mostly belonged to the Sarchop community. From the conversations this author had in Kathmandu in late November 1996 with Rinzin Dorji, an active member of the Druk National Congress, and the editor of the Kathmandu-based Dzongkha publication called *Lhoyi Khuju*, it was revealed that the publication was printed by the Indian embassy in Kathmandu, a fact which could not be authenticated for obvious reasons. The Druk National Congress operated from Kathmandu and fought for the democratic rights of the Bhutanese people. The organization claimed to have 32 active workers in Nepal, besides 977 'registered' members in Bhutan. Following the introduction of electoral democracy in Bhutan in 2008, the activities of such exile groups have come to an end.

## Indian Repatriates from Myanmar

In Myanmar, the strategy of nation-building through ethno-centric drive aimed at indigenising the society caused exodus of a large number of ethnic Indians, mostly Tamils, but also many Bengalis and Sikhs, to India in the 1940s through 1960s. Indian migration to Myanmar had started on a regular basis after 1852, when the British rule was firmly established there. Before 1937 when Myanmar was part of the British Indian empire, there were about 900,000 Indians in the country holding important commercial and professional positions.[10] After Myanmar's independence in January 1948, the citizenship laws were strictly enforced, which entailed proof of ancestry in Myanmar from before 1823 and residence for the last 8 out of 10 years. The government also made Burmese language the official language, and civil servants were to be none other than Myanmarese citizens. All this made many Indians to return to India. The naturalization rules were strict, and of the 150,000 applications for citizenship only 28,683 were granted between 1949 and 1961. In 1949–50, the number of returnees to India was 21,198. In 1962, when the military government of

General Ne Win nationalized trade, industry, banking and commerce, the Indian community was badly affected as majority of them were gainfully employed in these sectors. The result was that a large number of Indians were forced to return to India. The process started on 1 June 1963 and continued up to 1989. It was expected that about 230,000 such Indians would repatriate, but the actual figure as per the Department of Rehabilitation of the Tamil Nadu government did not exceed 144, 445 (GOTN 2010).

Evidently, many continued to remain there as virtually stateless, which we discuss in the Statelessness or Virtual Statelessness section below. Since about 90 per cent of the Indian returnees consisted of Tamil Chettiars, they either arrived in Tamil Nadu, where many of them were rehabilitated, or continued to manage their business and trade out of the Manipuri town of Moreh, situated on the Manipur–Myanmar border (Weiner 1993: 1738, Hellmann-Rajanayagam 2013: 3). The Burma Bazaar is now a thriving market in Chennai's Parry's Corner. Located just outside the Chennai beach railway station, in the old financial districts of Chennai city, the bazaar was set up in 1969. It was possible because the state government had set aside land for the Tamil refugees returning from Burma during the 1960s. The bazaar is run by Burma Tamizhar Marumalarchi Sangam, an association that was set up in 1966 to look after the interests of the traders. In all, the Tamil Nadu government rehabilitated 144,445 refugees from Myanmar till March 2001 (Bhaumik 2003: 189–92).

## Rohingya (?) Refugees

My readers must have noted the question mark in the subheading. It needs some clarification. In Myanmar, the term Rohingya has a significant political connotation which is different from just Bengali-speaking Muslims. In the next chapter, we have discussed this in detail. For the purposes of the present chapter, it is important to understand the way people from the present Bangladesh, earlier East Pakistan, and, still earlier, East Bengal in the undivided Bengal during the British rule migrated to the present Rakhine province (earlier name was Arakan) of Myanmar, which till 1937 was part of the British Indian empire (at that time Myanmar was called Burma, a name which remained in use till 1989).

There are historical records to suggest that there was a constant flow of Bengali-speaking Muslims from Bengal, particularly Chittagong, into Rakhine in search of greener pastures. According to Dutch and British sources, the origin of the Muslims in Rakhine is traced back to

16th through 18th centuries. It is possible that many of them were the descendants of the Bengali slaves. At that time the mutual exclusivity between the Bengalis and locals was not pronounced, though the former retained their Bengali mother tongue. Following the British occupation of Rakhine in 1825 and the treaty of Yandabo signed next year, many people from Rakhine who had fled to Chittagong returned home. Along with them many new Chittagonians also entered Rakhine who were particularly attracted, one, by the commercialization of rice cultivation, and two, by work opportunities in the development of the Akyab port by the British. The process continued for more than a century till the British decided to separate Burma from its Indian empire in 1937. It did not stop even thereafter (Leider 2013: 226–27). The Partition of India added a new dimension to this immigration question. The number of these Bengalis was fairly large, and since the majority of them were located in the Rakhine province, they even demanded a separate status for them either as part of Pakistan or as an independent nation. Their Pakistan dream, however, did not fructify as Jinnah and his Burmese counterpart, Aung San, entered into an agreement even prior to the Partition, in July 1947, not to tamper with their international border at the Naf river (Leider 2013: 240).

The 1963–64 census had revealed that the Rakhine Muslims had spread to the Yangon (Rangoon) and Delta areas. This alarmed the Bhama Buddhist authorities. To arrest the trend, the government of General Ne Win prohibited the movement of Muslims beyond the Akyab district towards the east. The military rulers of Myanmar took away the citizenship rights of the Rohingyas on the ground that they were economic refugees who had migrated to their country during the British rule. A policy of state repression followed. Still, they did not lead to large-scale migrations as it happened later. In any case, the policy of preventing the Bengalis from going beyond the Akyab district towards the east did not work. It not only impoverished the region badly, giving rise to youth unrest and insurgencies, it could also not prevent them from settling in the area. The 1974 census revealed the hard reality of these people spreading to the eastern border and commercially important areas such as Mandalay, Pegu, Prome, Moulmein and Bassein (Maung 1989: 61–62).

In the 1970s, under deteriorating communal circumstances the Rakhine Muslims started fleeing to Bangladesh in large numbers. From 1977 the process started, and about 260,000 such refugees arrived in Bangladesh, culminating in 1984 when the exodus became massive. However, by the expedience of a tripartite arrangement among Bangladesh, Myanmar and the UNHCR, many of them were repatriated to Myanmar. But the situation once again worsened in 1992, leading to another exodus of about 250,000 refugees, though by June 1996, 200,000 of them were repatriated. The refugee movement, however, continued with varying degree of intensity (Bhattacharya 1995: 69, Murshid 2012: 106).

There is no immediate hope of an end of the Rohingya migrations to Bangladesh. In 2014 the Government of Myanmar undertook its first census exercise since 1983. But the Rohingyas were kept outside its scope because the government insisted that they should identify themselves as 'Bengalis' and not 'Rohingyas'. While the former identity is linguistic the latter religious and given the nature of Buddhist–Muslim conflict in the country this nuance is significant. Religious riots since June 2012 have resulted in 237 deaths and 140,000 displacements. Although contrary to the fear that during Myanmar's 2015 presidential election there could be a rise in the ultra-Buddhist nationalism (Bhatia 2014: 64–65) which actually did not happen still the Rohingya issue is far from being solved. Much would depend upon the way the military agrees to pass on the political mantle to the civilian leaders. In spite of Aung Ssan Suu Kyi's National League for Democracy's (NLD) massive victory (80 per cent seats won from among the 75 per cent seats open for civilian contest) this question is still begging an answer. Once that is done there would be the question of political rules in the regions and states wherein would lie the catch of the Rohingya problem. Unless this transition is handled properly there could be yet another possibility of anti-Rohingya riots leading to their exodus to Bangladesh as refugees.

## Myanmarese Political Refugees

The repressive military rule in Myanmar has forced a large number of political refugees from the country to take shelter in India for security and for continuing their activism from a safer soil. The phenomenon picked up momentum in the late 1980s, when a democracy movement was unleashed in Myanmar under the leadership of Aung San Suu Kyi, daughter of the country's great independence hero Marshal Aung San. Massive state repression followed, which resulted either in the formation of rebel armies like the Karen National Union (KNU) or in escapes to India and Thailand. Several thousands of democracy activists arrived in India, where they were welcomed. The Government of

Myanmar alleged that not only India was supporting Aung San Suu Kyi's National League for Democracy (NLD), it was even funding the government-in-exile, called the National Coalition Government of the Union of Burma (NCGUB). According to the Indian government and UNHCR reports, between 1988 and 2001, 6,324 Myanmarese refugees had entered India, of which 1,245 were granted UNHCR refugee status. India's pro-democracy policy, however, started changing towards the end of the 1990s because of two reasons: one, China's growing closeness with the Myanmarese military rulers, and two, Myanmar's policy of providing shelters to several anti-India insurgent groups operating in India's north-east (Bhaumik 2003: 196–204). Though lately there have been some indications towards making Myanmar more representative, still complete civic liberty and political freedom remain a far cry. Even student protests are being ingeniously curbed by shifting educational campuses to places away from the cities. Many students are being used as secret agents to keep the government adequately informed about any danger to the military junta (Ghoshal 2013: 117–18). Against this background, it is inevitable that the flows of political refugees to India would continue. As of 2010, there were 8,541 such refugees, of which 4,484 had sought asylum (Zutshi et al. 2011: 55–58).

## Chin Burmese Refugees

Besides Myanmarese political refugees, there has been a flow of Chin Burmese to India as well. Chins are about 1,500,000 to 2,500,000 in number. Partly on account of the repressive policies followed by the State Law and Order Restoration Council (SLORC) and partly for economic reasons, Chins have left Myanmar to settle in Mizoram. Among them some are Nagas who have taken shelter in Arunachal Pradesh and Nagaland. Ever since the tri-junction of India–Myanmar–Bangladesh has become an economic corridor, the migration and settlement of Chins in India has become a continuous phenomenon. By 1996 there were 40,000 such Chins in India (Manchanda 1997: 204). In the beginning the Mizos used to welcome them as they considered the Chins as their ethnic cousins, both being Christian as well. These Chins also provided cheap labour to the Mizo middle class. But the situation changed once the Mizo political and student groups launched the 'Quit Mizoram' campaign aimed at the Chins. The insurgency situation in the region complicated matters, and the Chins found themselves becoming the targets of both the Indian and Myanmarese security forces (Bhaumik 2003: 206–7).

# Inter-ethnic Conflict

## Sinhala–Tamil Conflict

Almost all South Asian conflicts have ethnic connections. But the most conspicuous of them all is Sri Lanka's Sinhala–Tamil ethnic conflict, because unlike other cases the Tamil demand for a separate state has been the most strident. It all started after the anti-Tamil riots that rocked Colombo in July 1983. Sri Lankan Tamil refugees started arriving in neighbouring Tamil Nadu in large numbers. At least 30,000 Sri Lankan Tamils took refuge in India. Since the ethno-political situation in Sri Lanka continued to deteriorate, the flow continued with varying degree of intensity for almost three decades. As per the Department of Rehabilitation of the Government of Tamil Nadu, these refugee arrivals can be divided into four phases, as shown in Table1.6.

About 100,000 of these refugees voluntarily repatriated to Sri Lanka between 1987 and 1995 with financial assistance from the Tamil Nadu government and UNHCR (GOTN 2010). Clearly, many refugees preferred to remain in India. According to one estimate, in 1990 approximately 120,000 Sri Lankan Tamils were living in refugee camps, while about 80,000 were living outside the camps (Bastiampillai 1996: 195). It has been globally experienced that wherever the refugees have the choice to avoid state-sponsored refugee benefits they do so by using their social contacts. For them freedom of movement and freedom to select jobs of their choice is much more important than being confined to the restrictive camp life (Hovil 2007: 599–620). It was the same experience with the Bengali Hindu refugees from East Bengal after India's Partition. Whoever could avoid the refugee camps they did so even if they had to stay on railway platforms or footpaths.

**Table 1.6**
*Influx of Sri Lankan Tamil refugees to India in phases*

| Phase | Period | Inflow |
| --- | --- | --- |
| Phase I | 24 July 1983 to 31 December 1987 | 134,053 |
| Phase II | 25 August 1989 to 30 April 1991 | 122,078 |
| Phase III | 31 July 1996 to 31 August 2003 | 22,418 |
| Phase IV | 12 January 2006 to 4 January 2010 | 24,527 |
| Total | | 303,076 |

*Source:* GOTN (2010).

Following the assassination of Rajiv Gandhi in May 1991, Sri Lankan Tamils in India generally became suspect in the eyes of the Government of India. The AIADMK government in Tamil Nadu responded favourably to the Centre by withdrawing all facilities of higher education for them and by monitoring the movements of the internees of the refugee camps more stringently. Even the non-camp refugees were asked to register with the police immediately. By July 1991, more than 26,000 such persons were registered. Soon afterwards police began to apprehend those who had not registered, resulting in 1,800 arrests under the Foreigners Act (Suryanarayan 1996: 221–22). The then Tamil Nadu Chief Minister, J. Jayalalithaa, demanded immediate action: 'I appeal, rather demand, that the Centre should take immediate action so that all Sri Lankan Tamils could be sent back.... It should take place immediately' (Suryanarayan 2003: 328). A plan of repatriation was drawn, and between 21 January 1992 and 20 March 1995 arrangements were made to repatriate 54,188 people. To counter the criticism that the government was forcing the Sri Lankan Tamils to leave, the UNHCR was permitted to oversee the repatriation. Following the defeat of the Liberation Tigers of Tamil Eelam (LTTE) in Jaffna and Killinochchi in November 1995, the repatriation was halted, which once again resulted in refugee movements into India, which stood at 164,000 in 1997 (Suryanarayan 2003: 321–22).[11]

There are now four categories of Sri Lankan Tamil refugees in Tamil Nadu: (a) refugees in the camps, (b) recognized refugees outside the camps, (c) Sri Lankan nationals and (d) Tamil militants detained in special camps. In 2002, the 111 refugee camps in Tamil Nadu sheltered 63,941 refugees belonging to 16,955 families. Of the total, 39 per cent belonged to the first category, 12 per cent to the second, 48 per cent to the third and 1 per cent to the fourth category (Suryanarayan 2003: 332, 351). According to a recent report there are now 113 camps that shelter 80,000 Tamil refugees (Priyamvatha 2013: 20, see also Guha 2014).

## Open and Virtually Open Borders

In this category fall those cross-national migrations, which are caused largely by open or semi-open international borders. While India and Nepal are treaty bound to keep their borders open, the India–Bangladesh, India–Bhutan, India–Myanmar borders, though not officially open, are in many practical purposes open at several points.[12] Even portions of the India–Pakistan border in Rajasthan and Gujarat are open too in many a functional sense.

# India–Nepal

According to the India–Nepal treaty of 1950 and the exchange of letters that followed between the two countries, the border is open. According to Article 7 of the treaty: 'The governments of India and Nepal agree to grant, on a reciprocal basis, to the nationals on one country in the territories of the other the same privileges in the matter of residence, ownership of property, participation in trade and commerce, movement and other privileges of a similar nature'. Everything, however, is not so much guaranteed as the Article says. For example, Indians are not allowed to own property in Nepal or to set up a business there without a Nepali business partner. Similarly, movements of Nepalis are restricted in J&K and Arunachal Pradesh. There are other questions as well pertaining to the legal rights of the Nepali and Indian migrants, which of late are causing tensions between the two nations (Hausner & Sharma 2013: 100–101). Also, though there are specified border points at which border crossings are allowed and which are policed and patrolled, there are many such points where crossings take place routinely without any difficulty. Some of the important crossing points are: Kakarbhitta–Siliguri border that falls on the traditional trade route to Darjeeling, Sikkim, Shillong and Kolkata, the Bharahawa–Sunauli border and the Nepalganj–Rupediya border.

The Nepalis have migrated mostly to India's north-eastern states, particularly Assam, the northern districts of West Bengal, and to Uttarakhand.[13] Their migration to north-east had started with the Moamoriya Peasant Rebellion in the last quarter of the 18th century and the Burmese invasion in the first quarter of the 19th century (Thapa 1995: 80–92). During the reign of Maharaja Ranjit Singh (1780–1839), the recruitment of Nepalis in his army opened a regular economic opportunity for them, which became more institutionalized by the policy of the British Indian Army. It is difficult to find out exactly how many Nepali migrants are there in India. According to one study, in 2001, of Nepal's 23,000,000 population, 3.3 per cent, that is, 760,000 was absent from the country, of which 591,741 were in India. This was 77.6 per cent of the total number of absentees (Thieme & Wyss 2005: 61–62, also Kollmair et al. 2006).

The Indian census enumerates the Nepal-born population in the country. According to the 1971 census, there were 1.3 million Nepal-born Nepalis living in India. Migrant organizations, such as the Emigrant Nepali Association, however, claimed a much higher figure of 3,000,000. There have been various other guesses too and they range from 5,000,000 to 10,000,000 (Jha 1994: 7, Thapa 1995: 86–88, Sud 1975, Sinha 1982). It may be noted that many Indians tend to confuse Nepal-born Nepalis in India with India-born Nepalis, a distinction that is politically crucial particularly in the context of the Gorkhaland movement in Darjeeling. The 2001 Indian census that enumerated the stock of immigrants by country of last residence, gave the figure of 596,696 in its Nepal column (cited in Khadria 2009: 47).

Like the Nepalis in India, the Indian population in the Terai region of Nepal has also been allegedly growing. While part of the growth in the Terai is attributable to the migration of people from the hill regions of Nepal, it has also been caused by the Indian migrations. In 1952–54, the demographic growth rate of the Terai was 2.4 per cent. During 1971–81, it rose to 4.11 per cent. The growth rate in other regions in the corresponding period was much less. In the Mountain and Hill region, a rate of increase of only 1.42 per cent was registered in 1952/54–61. It rose to 1.65 per cent in the period 1971–81. In extreme cases, the district of Kanchanpur in the Terai registered an annual growth of 9.39 per cent, while the district of Humla in the Mountain and Hill region registered a growth of minus 2.72 per cent (Shrestha & Rayappa 1992: 296). According to the 1991 census of Nepal, there were 439,488 foreign-born people in Nepal, of which India accounted for 418,982. Nepalese press reports in the 1980s suggested that on account of the ineptitude of the Nepalese government, thousands of Indians from neighbouring districts of Katihar, Arariya and Supoul in Bihar were constructing houses on public land in Biratnagar and Morang in Nepal. According to Biratnagar municipality, there were 10,000 such migrants in 1994, which by 1999 had increased to 15,000. Many such people even obtained Nepalese citizenship with the help of local politicians (*POT; Public Opinion Trends* 1999).

## India–East Pakistan/Bangladesh

Like the Indo-Nepal open border, the border between India and Bangladesh, earlier India and East Pakistan, is also virtually open at many points. This has resulted in large-scale movements of East Pakistanis/Bangladeshis into India. Due to the hurried job of partitioning India that Cyril Radcliffe performed and on account of the inherent difficulty of trying to demarcate areas in mixed Hindu–Muslim localities which exist along the entire stretch of the border, the international boundary between the two countries hardly gives the impression of being an international border. Prior to the creation of Bangladesh, indeed since the beginning of the 20th century, a large number of Muslim Bengalis migrated to Assam. Since the phenomenon impacted local politics immensely, which culminated in the Anti-Foreigners movement in Assam in the late 1970s and early 1980s, we have reserved the discussion for the next chapter to do better justice to the subject as the chapter is specifically devoted to grapple with the political implications of migrations. In this section, we are dealing with the phenomenon that prevailed after Bangladesh was born.

Even after the creation of Bangladesh, extensive economic and social interactions between Indians and Bangladeshis continued across the borders as they were, let alone during the pre-Bangladesh days, even during the pre-Partition days. According to the India–Bangladesh treaty of 1972, neither side can erect a fence within 150 yards of the border, known as a 'no man's land'. The treaty allows farmers to till their soil in this space from 6 AM to 6 PM. About 3,500 villagers reside in this area (Datta 2004: 337). Overall, the India–Bangladesh border is unenforceable because of the nature of the terrain and cross-border character of the local communities. A 1995 field research noted as follows:

> We have drawn a line on paper, but where is that line on ground? ... The situation was illegal but not unnatural. In this convoluted milieu I soon learnt how categories changed.... (Here) illegal meant routine; infiltration was migration; smuggling was trade, these were less Indian villages, but more border villages. (Samaddar 1995)

Another observer highlighted the ground reality even more emphatically:

> Mr. Abdus Salam of Sutarkandi in Karimganj district of Assam is an Indian citizen who crosses over to Bangladesh—without passport and visa—and returns to India, scores of time a day. Reason: the international border runs right through his house, one part of it is in India and the other in Bangladesh. Mr. Salam is by no means an exception. There are many like him. These facts came to the knowledge of a group of presspersons from Guwahati who visited the Indo-Bangladesh border in Barak Valley at the invitation of Mr. Samujjwal Bhattacharyya, former general secretary and now adviser to AASU. Mr. Bhattacharyya and other AASU leaders were on a visit along with the Joint Secretary, Home (North-East), Mr. Gopal Pillai, and the Assam Home Secretary, Mr. Mrinal Barua, to see the progress made in fencing the border. (*The Hindu*, 23 August 1999)[14]

As a result many Bangladeshis have settled on the Indian side of the border without really understanding the illegality of their action. The 1981 census revealed that in the eight border districts of West Bengal, the population grew at over 30 per cent between 1971 and 1981, whereas the remaining districts reported growth rates below 20 per cent. An extreme case was that of a town in northern West Bengal where the population leaped from 10,000 to 150,000 (Biswas 1982). According to the Indian census, the number of people who migrated illegally from Bangladesh to India was 1,729,310 in 1961–71 and 559,006 in 1971–81. These figures did not include the estimated 600,000 who entered Assam between 1971 and 1981. It is possible that many of the Bangladeshi infiltrators were the so-called Biharis (Ahmed 1996: 143, 150).

Ten districts in West Bengal have borders with Bangladesh: Cooch Behar (561 km), Jalpaiguri (157 km), Darjeeling (21 km), North Dinajpur and South Dinajpur (combined 538 km), Malda (173 km), Murshidabad (125 km), Nadia (263 km), North 24 Parganas (280 km) and South 24 Parganas (63 km). Some of these districts had a growth rate higher than that of the state in 1971–81 and 1981–91. The decadal variation in the population of West Bengal in 1871–81 was +23.17 per cent. During that period, Cooch Behar (+25.28), Jalpaiguri (+26.55), West Dinajpur (+29.31), Malda (+26), Murshidabad (+26.49), Nadia (+33.29) and North 24 Parganas (+31.29) showed a noticeable upward trend than the state average. In 1981–91, the decadal variation was +24.55. Again, districts like West Dinajpur (+30.25), Malda (+29.63), Murshidabad (+28.04), Nadia (+29.82), North 24 Parganas (+31.66) and South 24 Parganas (+30.08) strayed noticeably. In one district, South 24 Parganas, the difference between the decadal growth rates of 1971–81 and 1981–91 was as high as +10.66. The natural increase of India's population, considering the gap between the birth and death rates, should be around 20 to 22 per 1,000 population, or 2.2 per cent per year, or 20 to 22 per cent per decade. Compared with this, West Bengal's growth rate was higher, that is 24.55 per cent, and it was even higher in the bordering districts (Samaddar 1995: 17–18).

This growth was largely due to migrations from Bangladesh. In the famine conditions of Bangladesh in 1974–75, outmigration was inevitable. Ranabir Samaddar, who surveyed a few villages of Bangladesh as a sample, found that outmigration loss there had more than trebled from 2,367 to 8,073 and that the net outmigration rate increased from 9 to 31 per 1,000. Contemporary newspaper reports abounded with apprehension by the Indian security forces and the police of thousands of people fleeing Bangladesh to escape hunger. Discrimination against minority Hindus also continued during this period. From 22 per cent of the total population in 1951, the Hindu population came down to 12 per cent in 1991 (Samaddar 1995: 18–19).

According to some decade-old estimates, on an average about 2,000 people were pushed back by India's Border Security Force (BSF) every month. However, the actual number of Bangladeshi nationals illegally entering India through the sparsely guarded 1,300 km long border is suspected to be at least ten times as high. According to the figures supplied by the Government of India, during the three years ending 1996, 57,391 Bangladeshi infiltrators were intercepted and 42,246 were pushed back (*The Times of India*, 7 May 1997).[15] Even the air route is not spared. According to the immigration authorities at the Calcutta airport, in 1994, 1995 and 1996, 222, 191 and 132 Bangladeshis, respectively, were pushed back (*The Asian Age*, 27 February 1997).

To these infiltrators one should also add those Bangladeshis who entered India with forged travel documents or even with valid ones, but did not return to their country after the expiration of their validity. In 1999 the West Bengal government revealed that at least 400,000 passport holders from Bangladesh who entered West Bengal during the previous decade had melted into the Indian community without trace. In January 1999, in response to a petition filed in the Supreme Court, the Government of West Bengal in its status report on illegal immigration admitted that 1,240,000 Bangladeshis who entered the state with travel documents had disappeared among the local population, while 570,000 had been pushed back into Bangladesh between 1972 and 1998. The document said that till 1997 the intercepted infiltrators were summarily pushed back, but after 1997 this practice was discontinued (Ghosh 2004: 30).

In response to Bangladeshi protests, the Government of India issued instructions that all infiltrators should be deported only after their prosecution under the Foreigners Act. The government of West Bengal said that it faced several problems in implementing the directive:

> The sheer number of such Bangladeshis believed to have entered into India after 1971 makes it humanly impossible to prosecute all of them under the Foreigners Act, get a conviction and a court order in respect of each one of them and thereafter push them back to Bangladesh.

Referring to the overstay of Bangladeshis who entered the country with travel documents, the status paper suggested that pre-verification of their Indian referees should be done before issuing visas. Inquiries conducted at the addresses of the Indian referees of 1,240,000 Bangladeshis who overstayed revealed either that a majority of these addresses were fictitious or that the Bangladeshis never visited their referees after coming to India. Efforts to trace those who overstayed 'mostly failed'. Putting the blame on the Central Government, the status paper alleged that the number of BSF personnel deployed in the West Bengal section of the Indo-Bangla border was 'absolutely inadequate'. The sanctioned strength of the BSF for the West Bengal section of the border was 34 battalions, but only 20 battalions were actually deployed at the border, it noted (*The Asian Age*, 8 February 1999).

At present, there are millions of unauthorized Bangladeshis living in various parts of India, generally doing small and menial jobs. Demographers agree that such outmigrations of people from poorer regions to neighbouring less poor ones are as natural as water seeking its own level. The density of population in Bangladesh per square kilometre is close to 1,000, as against 300 in Assam and just seven in Arunachal Pradesh. Earlier, these settlements were concentrated in states neighbouring Bangladesh, such as Assam, Tripura and West Bengal, but of late even far flung areas, such as Mumbai, Delhi, Haryana, Punjab, western UP and so on, have started getting illegal Bangladeshi migrants. Since many of them manage to procure legal papers of residency, if not Indian citizenship, it is extremely difficult to establish their status as Bangladeshi nationals, leave alone pushing them back into Bangladesh. Sometimes they possess those documents even while entering into India illegally. In October 2014, when the Indian BSF nabbed 60 such infiltrators, they found to their surprise that the trespassers had all kinds of Indian legal documents with them, such as UID, PAN, ration cards and so on (*The Hindustan Times*, 16 October 2014). Also, the Indian authorities sometimes make the mistake of identifying the Rohingyas as Bangladeshis because they too speak Bengali and look the same. As Myanmarese they have often been granted refugee status by the UNHCR. The latter had to intervene in several such cases of mistaken identity as there were about 9,000 Rohingyas in India registered with them (*The Hindu*, 20 June 2014).

## India–Pakistan

Another category of clandestine migrants is that of Pakistanis and Indians who cross the borders of Rajasthan and Gujarat in India, and Punjab and Sind in Pakistan. This border is 512 km long in Gujarat and 1,335 km in Rajasthan. People living in these bordering areas often have kinship ties across the border. Smuggling is a way of life here, and trafficking in drugs and arms, particularly after the intensification of the Punjab crisis in India and the Muhajirin crisis in Pakistan, in the 1980s, was a problem causing serious concern to both Indian and Pakistani authorities.

In the 1970s, many Rajasthan villages in the bordering districts of Barmer, Bikaner, Ganganagar and Jaisalmer registered a much higher rate of growth than in other places. Between 1971 and 1981, the population of Bandha village went up from 172 to 5,888, of Muhar village from 9 to 247, of Kuldar from 32 to 240, of Modana from 422 to 1,198, of Mota Kilon-ki-Dhani from 48 to 540 and of Madasar from 445 to 1,171 (*India Today*, 15 September 1985: 53). While part of this growth was attributed to the construction of the Rajasthan Canal (Indira Gandhi Nahar), which attracted people from other districts, part of it was due to migrations from Pakistan, leading to a rise in the number of Muslim-dominated villages along the border (Verghese 1994: 67–73). In this connection, it may be noted that in the wake of the 1965 and 1971 Indo-Pak wars, many Indian Muslims crossed over to Pakistan and settled there. They, however, managed to continue as Indian citizens, thanks to local district politics. These people had the unique status of holding a dual citizenship of both India and Pakistan and continued to cross the border with relative ease. According to the Government of India, 11,000 Pakistanis were found overstaying in India in 1996 (*The Times of India*, 7 May 1996). The 1991 census had revealed a higher rate of growth of the Muslim population in these districts than the overall rate of growth of the Muslim population in the state (Table 1.7).

Due to the Islamic thrust of the Pakistan government, minorities there increasingly found the situation not conducive to their safe existence. This resulted in their systematic migration to India without taking recourse to legal means. While in the case of East Pakistan it was largely the case of Hindu migration to India, in the case of West Pakistan, in addition to Hindus, it was also valid for poor Muslims. Though one may find it difficult to establish a clear connection between the phenomenon of Muslim population growth in the neighbouring Indian districts of Rajasthan and Punjab on the one hand and bad governance and faulty state building processes in Pakistan on the other, yet the following statement of demographer Ashish Bose may be worth recalling here. Analysing the 1981 census data pertaining to the border states (Table 1.8), Bose wrote:

> The abnormally high rate of growth of the Muslim population in Punjab and Rajasthan calls for investigation. Internal migration alone cannot explain this phenomenon. There is unmistakable evidence from the census data that there must have been considerable illegal migration from Pakistan in these border-states and also in big cities like Delhi and Bombay. Curiously enough, in Haryana the Hindu population increased by 28.9 per cent while the Muslim population increased by very much the same rate (29.0 per cent), unlike in Punjab. The growth rates of Muslims in Bihar and West Bengal are less high. Illegal migration from Bangladesh is a demographic reality. (Bose 1988: 367)

Many a time poor Pakistani Hindus who come to India on some pretext or the other refuse to return to their country of origin. For example, to attend the *Maha Kumbh* (a great Hindu festival held every 12 years on the banks of the Ganga at Allahabad in UP) in 2013, 484 Hindu pilgrims from Pakistan had arrived, of which only 92 returned. The remaining 392

**Table 1.7**

*Percentage increase of Muslim population in select districts of Rajasthan, 1981–91*

| District/ State | Total Percentage Increase | Percentage Increase (Hindu) | Percentage Increase (Muslim) |
|---|---|---|---|
| Barmer | 28.27 | 28.82 | 29.85 |
| Bikaner | 42.70 | 42.60 | 48.06 |
| Ganganagar | 29.20 | 29.01 | 40.99 |
| Jaisalmer | 41.73 | 40.10 | 47.41 |
| Rajasthan | 28.44 | 28.09 | 41.46 |

*Source:* Census of India (1991: 4–5).

**Table 1.8**

*Growth rate by religion in selected states, 1971–81 (Per cent)*

| State | Hindus | Muslims |
|---|---|---|
| Bihar | 23.3 | 30.0 |
| West Bengal | 21.8 | 29.6 |
| Rajasthan | 32.5 | 40.1 |
| Punjab | 21.9 | 46.9 |
| Himachal Pradesh | 23.3 | 38.3 |
| Delhi (Union Territory) | 52.6 | 83.2 |

*Source:* Bose (1988: 367).

settled themselves in hutments in various parts of Delhi and its neighbourhood and demanded asylum, if not Indian citizenship (*The Hindu*, 16 April 2014). According to the Ministry of Home Affairs, in 2011, 8,037 Pakistani nationals were found overstaying in India; in 2012, their number was 1,411; and in 2013, it was 4,815. The overall figure of overstaying foreigners, including Afghans, Bangladeshis, Iraqis, Pakistanis, Sri Lankans, British and Americans, was 71,035, 71,164, and 56,785, respectively, for the years 2011, 2012 and 2013 (*The Hindu*, 19 August 2014).

## Indian Migrations

So far as the migration of Indians into neighbouring Bangladesh and Pakistan is concerned, it is much smaller in scale. Except in the aftermath of Partition, when many Urdu-speaking Muslims from Bihar,

UP and other places left for Pakistan, there is no evidence of migration into Bangladesh, though migrations to Pakistan have been taking place. Taking advantage of the porous borders between, in the case of India–West Pakistan till 1965 and in the case of India–East Pakistan till 1971, there was a constant flow of Muslims from India, again mostly from Bihar and UP, to Pakistan, contributing further to Pakistan's Bihari controversy. Many a time, East Pakistani/Bangladeshi Muslims have used India as their transit route to reach Pakistan by illegally crossing the India–Pakistan border. A 1995 Pakistani police survey revealed that there were one million undocumented Bangladeshis in Karachi who had arrived there via India. Most of these migrant workers were Bangladeshis who were treated as illegal immigrants in Pakistan whose status was determined by the Foreigners Act of 1946 (Ahmed 1997: 347).

Due to the politically sensitive nature of the question with its potential fallout on the Sindhi–Muhajirin relations, the subject did not receive much scholarly attention in Pakistan. But Pakistani scholars this author interacted with in the 1990s were aware of the phenomenon. According to one of them, the number of such illegal immigrants had touched two million by the end of the 1970s. Later, Pakistan decided to fence its entire border with India to prevent the 'illegal immigration' and 'infiltration' from India. India had already fenced its borders in several sectors. It is likely that the Pakistani decision to fence the border was politically motivated to both show the government's resolve to see the Muhajirin problem in the light of unauthorized Indian immigration to Pakistan as well as its strategy to counter the Indian charge of Pakistani infiltration. It may be noted that when Pakistan mentions the border between India and Pakistan it excludes the Line of Control (LOC) in J&K, which it prefers to call as 'working border'.

## India–Bhutan

Effectively, the border between India and Bhutan is open at several points. The commercial capital of Bhutan, Phuntsholing, which houses the headquarters of the Bank of Bhutan and the Royal Insurance Corporation, is almost totally in the hands of Indian businessmen. Even the entry of Indians to this town in the district of Chukha is free. The immigration checkpost is situated only at the northern edge of the town, so only those seeking to enter into Bhutan beyond Phuntsholing are required to obtain the necessary permit. Even otherwise the terrain on the Bhutan–Assam/North Bengal border is such that it is easy to cross it. No wonder that many Assamese insurgent groups used to operate from the Bhutanese territory till they were flushed out by joint India–Bhutan military operations in the 1990s, codenamed as Operation Bajrang, Operation Rhino and Operation All Clear.

## India–Myanmar

A virtually open border situation exists between India (in Mizoram) and Myanmar. Eastern Mizoram touches Myanmar, while the western part touches Bangladesh. As a result, there are movements of people from both Bangladesh and Myanmar into the state, more so from Myanmar. Many Myanmarese nationals routinely come to the southern districts of Mizoram. During my visit to these areas in the 1990s, I found that in the Chhimtuipui district daily-wage labourers came from the bordering areas of Myanmar for shopping and medical treatment as a matter of routine. The Chins who lived across the border in Myanmar were ethnically Mizos and as such there was no suspicion attached to them when they visited Mizoram. In the Saiha sub-division of the district (now a full district), villages nearest to the border were Vawanberk, Saichang-Kawn and Lungpher, which were motorable and just a kilometre away from the border. On the Myanmar side, three to four days of walk would be required to reach the nearest motorable road. Naturally they prefer to come to Mizoram for shopping and other amenities, particularly during the Christmas season. It was difficult to say how many such Myanmarese stayed back in Mizoram. However, one could get some idea from the records by computing the figures of permanent and temporary residents. The 1991 census showed that Chhimtuipui district registered a much higher decadal growth than two other districts, Aizawl and Lunglei. While the last two districts registered a percentage increase of 40.38 and 28.79, respectively, Chhimtuipui registered a 50.37 per cent growth (Census of India 1991, Series 17, Table C-9, Mizoram: 14).

## Pakistan–Afghanistan

The Pakistan–Afghanistan border is so porous that it is virtually non-existent. Afghanistan does not even recognize the Durand Line, which is supposed to be the legal border. The cross-border Pashtun ethnic affinity actually reinforces this porosity. As a result, a large number of Pashtuns from Afghanistan routinely live in Pakistan though it is difficult to estimate the number of such Afghans in Pakistan. Besides the reasons mentioned above, international and domestic political factors make their headcount difficult. As a result, it is the case of the elephant in the room—they are large in number but their existence is virtually invisible because they cannot be counted. It was for the first time in 2005 that efforts were made to estimate the exact Afghan population in Pakistan in the teeth of violent protests by the Pashtun settlers who did not want to be deported. The general lack of law and order in the northern areas, such as Gilgit and Skardu, made the task very difficult. The idea was to count all the Afghans who arrived in Pakistan after 1 December 1979, but since it excluded those who had obtained Pakistani identity cards (PIC) the purpose was defeated at the outset because many of them had obtained the card illegally and were, therefore, potentially Pakistan nationals. Still the census of 2005 sprang many surprises. For example, it was reported that 2.3 million Afghans had gone back to their country since March 2002, but for the census 3 million confessed that they were Afghans. That means there were 5 million Afghans in Pakistan when the Taliban fell after 9/11. It was not surprising, therefore, that the 2006 Pakistan-wide registration would reveal the existence of only 220,000 Afghans, that too mostly belonging to Uzbek, Hazara and Turkmen communities. Because of their thick social connections, the Pashtuns largely remained invisible. Even the Baluch Afghans got melted into the population of Baluchistan without any trace. Karachi, known to be 'a city of illegal immigrants', added further complications to the headcount of illegal immigrants (Sadiq 2009: 51–56, 133–35, 212). Table 1.9 gives an idea of the ethnic mosaic of the city, though it enumerates only the official figures.

According to a despatch from Islamabad in *The Hindu* (15 June 2014), the capital city too hosts a large number of Afghans unofficially as there is no recognized camps there (there are 76 refugee camps in

**Table 1.9**
*Estimates of illegal immigrants in Karachi (by year)*

| Ethnic/National Group | 1989 | 1993 | 1997 | 1998 | 2002 |
|---|---|---|---|---|---|
| Afghan | 96.070 | 83,823 | 85,499 | 200,000 | 600,000 |
| Bangladeshi | 378,125 | 1,164,793 | 1,188,089 | 1,500,000 | 1,100,000 |
| Myanmarese | 26,725 | 204,448 | 208,000 | 50,000 | 200,000 |
| Iranian | 10,470 | 2,320 | 2,366 | 50,000 | 200,000 |
| Indian | NA | NA | 118,808 | NA | |
| Sri Lankan | 445 | 78 | 613 | NA | |
| Total | 511,835 | 1,455,462 | 1,603,375 | 1,800,000 | 1,900,000 |

Source: Sadiq (2009: 56).

*Note:*   NA, data not available.

Pakistan, most of which in Khyber Pakhtunkhwa, 10 in Baluchistan and one in Punjab). In any case, the headcount at the camps does not tell the whole story as we have mentioned above. Also, even if the Afghan refugees are issued new proof of registration (POR) cards by the National Database Registration Authority (NADRA) to revalidate their cards that have expired in 2012 to make them effective till 2015 the ground realities did not change much. The problem would multiply when the American troops would withdraw from Afghanistan and the latter would enter into a new phase of political uncertainty.

## Some Other Open Border Cases

In the open border category, we must as well mention two other cases which generally escape our attention, namely, those of Goa and Sikkim. Goa was a Portuguese colony till 1961, when it was annexed by India following a military operation. Similarly, Sikkim was a monarchy till 1975 when its subjects through a plebiscite decided to merge the kingdom into the Indian Union. The borders of both these states which abutted India were porous, allowing the people of these territories to either migrate to India or Indians to migrate to those territories. In the case of Goa, its musicians, who had a significant presence in the Goan society, migrated in large numbers to neighbouring Bombay, the film industry of which provided them with vast professional and economic opportunities. Besides, they were in demand in the princely courts of India and other British colonies, particularly in East Africa (discussed further in Chapter 6 in the context of migration of music). So far as Sikkim was concerned, the kingdom experienced a constant inflow of ethnic Nepalese from the pre-Partition neighbouring districts of undivided Bengal and subsequently from West Bengal. These migrations changed the ethnic composition of Sikkim in favour of the Nepalese at the cost of the indigenous Bhutia and Lepcha communities (discussed in Chapter 3).

# War-related Qualms

## Refugees due to 1947 Indo-Pak War over Kashmir

After independence of India when confusion arose over the fate of J&K, whether to be a part of India or that of Pakistan, or its remaining independent of both, some Kashmiri Muslim migration to Pakistan occurred (this was in addition to the Kashmiri migrations to Pakistan discussed in the previous chapter). The process picked up momentum after India and Pakistan entered into a war over Kashmir in November 1947 which resulted in the de facto division of the province between the India-held J&K and the Pakistan-held Azad Kashmir (India calls it POK). While many Hindus and Sikhs fled from the POK, a much larger number of J&K Muslims left for Pakistan. By January 1952 their number had reached 582,000. Their break-up was as follows: 56,000 in Azad Kashmir, 200,000 in other parts of Pakistan, 56,000 in refugee camps and the remaining 270,000 managing on their own, or living with friends and relatives, or rehabilitated. Pakistan considered their status as refugees as they had permanent domicile in J&K and they would soon return to their homes when the situation would normalize (Alexander 1951: 5, Vernant 1953: 766–67).[16] The situation, however, never normalized. Rather the persistent disturbance in Kashmir continued to result in the migration of Kashmiri Muslims to Pakistan. According to the World Refugee Survey 1997, published by the US Committee for Refugees, there were 13,000 Kashmiri Muslims living in Pakistan in 1996 (p. 129). The routine shelling across the LOC in Kashmir keeps displacing locals on both sides, but it is improbable they would cross the borders.

## Sino-Indian War of 1962

In the early 1960s, particularly in the aftermath of the Sino-Indian war of 1962, there were demands to deport the so-called 'Pakistani infiltrators', as apart from refugees, from Assam. Armed with the Prevention of Infiltration from Pakistan (PIP) scheme, the Government of Assam deported 192,079 Muslims to East Pakistan between 1961 and 1969. This had a traumatic effect on Assam's Muslim peasantry, which had migrated from East Bengal, and not East Pakistan, much before the Partition, and actually had Asamiyaized. After independence they had identified themselves with the Asamiya nationality.

## Indo-Pak War of 1971

There was some migration of Hindus from Pakistan to India in the Rajasthan sector during the 1971 Indo-Pak war. Following the Simla agreement of 1972, when the Indian troops were withdrawn from areas occupied by them across the Rajasthan border, Hindus living in those areas migrated to India along with the withdrawing Indian troops. They feared that once Pakistan's authority was restored in the area they would be subjected to persecution and violence. At least 100,000 such people belonging mainly to three communities, namely, Sodha Rajputs, Bhil tribes and Meghawat Dalits, came to India. During the 1965 war, exactly the opposite had happened but on a lesser scale. At that time, a few colonies of Muslims in Rajasthan had crossed over to the other side of the border with similar fears (Sainath 1999).

Prior to the 1971 war, it was quite common for the Hindu communities living in border areas in Pakistan to have their social contacts across the border in India. Even bridal processions (*barat*) used to be taken across the border, and in several such ceremonies the local government officers belonging to both countries also participated. The practice continued even after 1971 but on a much lesser scale. But the Punjab crisis of the late 1970s and early 1980s put an end to the practice as borders came to be strictly guarded. The fallout of this Hindu migration was the intensification of caste conflicts in these Rajasthan villages, particularly between the Rajputs and the Dalits. So long as they all were in Pakistan both the communities suffered from a common minority complex and therefore lived a subdued life.

Once in India that complex was gone, and in its place a caste consciousness developed, which the democratic competitiveness of Indian society further sharpened. One Dalit said that soon after their migration to India they realised what the upper caste oppression they would be subjected to. Their former upper caste brethren in Pakistan were learning their oppressive practices from their local counterparts (Sainath 1999).

## Developmental and Environmental Effects

Environmental refugees, according to Eassan Hinnawi, who coined the word in a report prepared for the United Nations Environment Programme in 1985, are 'those people who have been forced to leave their traditional habitat, temporarily or permanently, because of a marked environmental disruption, natural and/or triggered by people that jeopardize the existence and/or seriously affect the quality of their life'. On the basis of this definition, one may identify three categories of refugees as environmental refugees, namely, (a) those displaced temporarily because of an environmental stress, such as an earthquake or a cyclone, and who will return to their habitat once conditions normalize; (b) those who have been permanently displaced because of a permanent change caused to their habitat, such as the establishment of dams and associated man-made lakes; and (c) those who migrate permanently or temporarily in quest of an improved quality of life because their original habitat can no longer meet their basic needs. Since we are concerned here with cross-border migrations, the (b) and (c) categories are relevant.

## Bangladeshi Developmental Refugees

In this category, one may include the migration of Chakmas and other tribals of Bangladesh into parts of India's north-east and that of poor Bangladeshis, particularly from the Khulna and Rajshahi divisions, into various parts of India. The construction of the Karnafuli (Kaptai) hydroelectric project in 1962 submerged 54,000 acres of settled and cultivable land, affecting about 100,000 people, 90 per cent of whom were Chakmas.[17] Besides, the state-sponsored schemes meant to settle Muslims from the plains in the traditional 'homelands' of the Buddhist Chakmas also made the latter aliens in their own habitat. The process led to disaffection, civil strife, militancy and eventually state repression that resulted in the flight of these tribes to neighbouring India for safety and livelihood. By August 1987, there were about 33,000 such refugees spread over several camps in India's north-east.

The migrations from the Khulna and Rajshahi divisions into India have largely been attributed to the construction of the Farakka barrage in India on the Ganga near the India–Bangladesh border, which led to the impoverishment of the people of the above divisions. Khulna was traditionally a high-growth division, but during the last few decades it has registered a drastic fall, which is attributed to the Farakka dam's negative impact on its agriculture. The exact number of outmigrants from these divisions to India cannot be ascertained, but it would not be too much of an exaggeration to put the figure at about two million.

# Statelessness or Virtual Statelessness

In this section, we will consider five cases, namely, Indian Tamils of Sri Lanka, stateless Indians in Myanmar, the Biharis of Bangladesh, Chakmas of Arunachal Pradesh and the enclave people in Indian and Bangladeshi enclaves.

## Indian Tamils

According to the Sri Lankan census of 1981, Indian Tamils totalled 825,233, constituting 5.6 per cent of the island's population. According to the Shastri–Sirimavo Pact of 30 October 1964, it was decided that of the 1953 estimate of 975,000 stateless persons of Indian origin in

Sri Lanka, 300,000 (together with the natural increase in that number) would be granted Sri Lankan citizenship, while 525,000 (together with the natural increase in that number) would be granted Indian citizenship. The status and future of the remaining 150,000 people (together with the natural increase in that number) would be decided later by a separate agreement. In 1974, through another agreement between the two countries, it was decided that both the governments would grant citizenship to 150,000 persons left undecided by the 1964 pact according to a 50:50 ratio.

The agreements, however, could not be implemented for many years because of certain inherent problems. But on 9 November 1988 Sri Lanka honoured its commitment when its parliament unanimously passed the bill entitled 'Grant of Citizenship to Stateless Persons (Special Provisions) Act', which conferred Sri Lankan citizenship on all stateless persons lawfully residing in the country and those who had not applied for Indian citizenship (Sabaratnam 1990: 205). But the Indian commitment remained unfulfilled. By 31 January 1989, 1,16,000 Indian Tamil families were repatriated to India, but neither the problem of their statelessness nor that of their rehabilitation was solved (Vedavalli 1994: 38–39, 46–49, 154–55). S. Thondaman, the Sri Lankan Minister for Animal Husbandry and Rural Industries, and the president of the Ceylon Workers' Congress, in a press conference held in April 1997 alleged that while, through his efforts, Sri Lanka had granted citizenship in 1988 to all stateless Indian Tamils who had opted for Sri Lanka, India had not honoured its commitment. According to him, many repatriates to India had been denied citizenship rights. He further informed that of about 200,000 Indian Tamils who had applied for Indian citizenship most had since died but their children still remained stateless. Due to the disruption of the ferry service between Sri Lanka and India on account of the war in the Northern Province of Sri Lanka, the process had come to a standstill so far as repatriation to India was concerned. Actually the Indian Tamils were not keen to repatriate to India. According to a sample survey conducted in the early 1990s, the majority among the 250,000 such stateless people in Sri Lanka had to opt for Indian citizenship because they had no option (Vedavalli 1994: 46–47, 154–55).

In 2003, the Government of Sri Lanka by enacting yet another law called 'Grant of Citizenship to Persons of Indian Origin Act' tried to resolve the fate of the aforesaid 250,000 stateless people. The Act said that a person of Indian origin who had been a permanent resident of Sri Lanka since 30 October 1964 or a descendant of such a person, he would be granted Sri Lankan citizenship. If any such person held an Indian passport he was required to relinquish that citizenship following certain procedures. In 2009 there were certain amendments to the Act. In spite of all these efforts, the problem could not be completely solved as, which is typical to South Asia, many people could not provide the proof of their residence as provided by law, meaning thereby that many remained stateless (Basu Ray Chaudhury 2013: 99–100). The poverty of the plantation workers multiplied the problem. Many prefer to leave for cities like Colombo and Kandy to look for better jobs (see Meera Srinivasan's report in *The Hindu,* 21 November 2014).

## Stateless Indians in Myanmar

According to the High Level Committee on Indian Diaspora constituted by India's Ministry of External Affairs in 2004 (Singhvi Committee), of Myanmar's total population of 55,000,000 about 5 per cent, that is, 2,900,000, were Indians. Their break-up was: 2,500,000 Indian-origin citizens, 400,000 stateless and 2,000 Indian citizens. The stateless were mostly third- or fourth-generation residents who were like full citizens yet without proper legal documents to prove their citizenship. Although this estimate was higher than other sources which put the Indian population at 3.9 per cent of Myanmar's population, still the stateless situation of a large number of people of Indian origin in Myanmar is noteworthy (Hellmann-Rajanayagam 2013: 1).

## Biharis of Bangladesh

Many Biharis of Bangladesh were stateless for years after the creation of Bangladesh. The question of Bihari Muslims has its origin in the Partition. At that time, Muslims in Bihar were about 4,000,000 in number in a total population of 30,000,000. As a result of the Great Calcutta Killings of August 1946, the Great Bihar Killings of October–November 1946 and other riots of 1947 and 1950, thousands of Muslims were killed. In search of security, more than 1,000,000 Muslims from eastern India, mostly Bihar, migrated to East Pakistan. Unfortunately, however, they could hardly integrate themselves into the Bengali Muslim society of East Pakistan. The fact that they had Urdu as their mother tongue while Urdu as Pakistan's national language was opposed by the Bengalis, it soured the Bengali–Bihari relationship. Their respective views on the question of Pakistan's nation-building strategy were fundamentally conflicting (discussed in Chapter 2).

The conflict of interest climaxed during the Bangladesh liberation movement when the Bihari Muslims came to be viewed as conduits of the West Pakistan's military oppressors. Even before the Pakistani military crackdown on 25 March 1971 there were several instances of Bengali mob frenzy against them. Their shops and properties were frequently looted and vandalized. Thousands of them were also killed in Chittagong, Jessore, Khulna, Rangpur, Saidpur and Mymensingh (Ghosh 2004: 112). It is possible that they were in response to real or alleged arming of Biharis by the Pakistani authorities to serve as a fifth column in the impending civil war. Major Ziaur Rehman, a freedom fighter and the future president of Bangladesh, is said to have remarked in 1971: 'Those who speak Urdu are also our enemies because they support the Pakistan army. We will crush them'. On 28 March 1971 when his troops brought some Bihari prisoners before him, he said: 'Take the men out and shoot them' and with women 'you can do what you like with them' (Hashmi 1998: 402). It is explainable why the Biharis had to close their ranks with the Pakistani authorities. Having once migrated to East Pakistan and having no other place to go they had to rely on the military rulers in West Pakistan because in a democratic Pakistan it was the Bengalis who were bound to enjoy the substance of power given their numerical advantage. They were not confident that they would get equal citizenship rights if Bangladesh became independent. Already stigmatized as conspirators, they had been subjected to violence and loot triggered by wild rumours about their participation in the mass killing of Bengalis. They feared that once politically empowered the Bengali peasants, soldiers and other lumpen elements would dispossess them of their belongings, including land (Hashmi 1998: 402).

Since many Biharis had actually supported the Pakistani authorities in the liberation war, the entire community was looked upon with contempt after Bangladesh was created. Still, the Government of Bangladesh offered them Bangladeshi citizenship. But they spurned the offer and preferred to continue as Pakistani nationals. It is estimated that there were 462,000 Biharis in Bangladesh before its liberation, some of whom had left for Pakistan either during or immediately after the creation of Bangladesh. In 1974, under a tripartite agreement between Bangladesh, India, and Pakistan, the latter agreed to repatriate certain categories of Biharis who were employed in government service in East Pakistan, excluding those in the railways.

By the end of 1974, 108,000 Biharis were transferred to Pakistan. Again in 1984, about 6,000 were repatriated. In 1990, after the premature dismissal of the Government of Benazir Bhutto and the coming of Nawaz Sharif to power, the latter tried to honour the commitment made by Zia-ul Haq in this regard. But barely 2,500 had been repatriated when the issue became controversial that halted the process. Although it was decided that the repatriates would be settled in rural Punjab, still it irked the Sindhis. They feared that eventually all the Biharis would migrate to Karachi, thereby further strengthening the hands of the Muhajirin. As a result, more than 230,000 Biharis remained stranded in Bangladesh. The 1995 annual report of the Human Rights Commission of Pakistan noted the sad state of affairs of the 235,000 stranded Biharis in Bangladesh to which, it was alleged, the high officials in the Pakistani establishment paid scant attention. Till 1996 there were as many as 41,000 Bihari families consisting of 238,000 people living in 66 camps (called Geneva Camps) scattered all over Bangladesh (Khan 1997: 27).

During the visit of Pakistani Prime Minister Nawaz Sharif to Bangladesh in January 1998, Pakistan once again reiterated its commitment to repatriate them though no time frame was fixed. In an appeal jointly signed by the Secretary General of the Muslim World League and the Minister of Finance and Economic Affairs of the Government of Pakistan, Sartaj Aziz, it was stated that the 'present Government [of Pakistan] firmly renews its pledge to do all it can to bring and rehabilitate these stranded Pakistanis, numbering over 238,000 according to census [of 'Biharis'] carried out jointly in 1991–92'. On 30 January 1998, the *International Herald Tribune* published the appeal under the heading 'Appeal for Donation to the Rabita Trust for Repatriation of Stranded Pakistanis from Bangladesh'. In 2002 President Pervez Musharraf once again made a promise to repatriate the Biharis, but there was no follow up. Ultimately it was the Bangladesh government only which came to their rescue in some sense. In 2008 Bangladesh expressed its willingness to grant Bangladeshi citizenship to all Biharis or stranded Pakistanis.

In a judgment dated 19 May 2008, the Dhaka High Court granted Bangladeshi citizenship to second-generation Biharis who were born in the camps after 1971. The court ruled that all Urdu-speaking people of the country who were born in Bangladesh, or whose fathers or grandfathers were born in Bangladesh, and who were permanent residents in 1971, or who had permanently resided in Bangladesh since 1971, were citizens 'by operation of law'. The court directed the Election Commission to register the Urdu-speaking people who wanted to be voters and give them the National Identity Cards. It was estimated that around 80 per cent Biharis obtained those cards. Most of them belonged to the younger generation.

Evidently, the remaining still wanted to be repatriated to Pakistan and hence continued to remain 'stateless'. Against the background of a June 2014 massacre of several Biharis in Dhaka's Mirpur Bihari refugee camp, Haroon Habib, a senior Bangladeshi journalist, wrote that 'the legal status could not perhaps trounce the historic realities, nor trim down the psychological barriers between the local people and the Urdu-speakers. In a Bangladesh polity that is sharply polarised on pro- and anti-liberation lines, allegations are rife that the anti-liberation camp is politicising the Bihari issue for political gain'. The Bihari issue thus remains politically relevant, as we will discuss in Chapter 2 (UNHCR 2009: 3–4, *Frontline*, 25 July 2014: 58).

## Chakmas of Arunachal Pradesh

The Chakmas of Arunachal Pradesh are de facto stateless, not de jure. In 1964, the Government of India settled about 66,000 Chakma and Hajong refugees in the North East Frontier Agency (NEFA), which is now Arunachal Pradesh. While the Chakmas had migrated from the Chittagong Hill Tracts (CHT) of the erstwhile East Pakistan after the construction of the Kaptai (or Karnaphuli) Hydroelectric Project, the Hajongs had migrated from Mymensingh and Sylhet districts to escape religious persecution. According to the Assam Accord of 1985 all infiltrators who came from East Pakistan prior to its becoming Bangladesh were to be granted Indian citizenship. As such, these Chakmas and Hajongs of Arunachal Pradesh were entitled to citizenship. But due to the opposition of the AAPSU this could not be possible. Citizenship meant inclusion into the voters' list and hence a share in political power, which the AAPSU was not willing to concede. In 1994, it served a 'Quit Arunachal' notice to them (Hussain 1995: 128).

The Committee for the Citizenship Rights of the Chakmas of Arunachal Pradesh then spearheaded a citizenship movement for these ethnic groups in the state and appealed to the National Human Rights Commission (NHRC). The latter approached the Supreme Court, which gave the verdict in favour of the Chakmas and Hajongs. In its judgment dated 9 January 1996, the Supreme Court gave a clear ruling against their disenfranchisement and eviction and suggested that procedures should be followed under Section 5 of the 1955 Citizenship Act for the purposes of granting them Indian citizenship. But the Chakmas did not apply for their citizenship as they were scared. In August 1997 the Rajya Sabha Committee on Petitions recommended that they be granted citizenship with Scheduled Tribe status. But the Arunachal Pradesh government did not heed the advice. Gegong Apang, the Chief Minister of the state, continued to insist that the Chakmas should leave Arunachal Pradesh and go back to Bangladesh. The AAPSU threatened to launch 'Operation Clean' to forcefully drive the Chakmas out of the state by force if necessary. The situation has not changed much on the ground as it is wrapped up in Arunachal Pradesh's domestic politics a significant component of which is the terms of the state's inclusion into the Indian Union as a full state (discussed in Chapter 2).

## The Enclave People

In the migration context of South Asia, the India–Bangladesh enclaves issue is not a significant matter, particularly because a very small number of people (effectively stateless till recently) are involved. But howsoever small their number, since they had to opt for either Indian or Bangladeshi nationality the subject deserves mention here. Consequent upon the passage of the 119th Constitution Amendment Bill on 7 May 2015 by the Indian parliament (The 100th Constitution Amendment Act 2015) that ratified the India–Bangladesh Land Boundary Agreement of 1974 and confirmed the Additional Protocol of 2011, 162 enclaves shared between the two countries (111 Indian enclaves in Bangladesh occupying 17,160 acres and 51 Bangladeshi enclaves in India occupying 7,110 acres) were to be summarily swapped. It happened on 1 August 2015, although the whole process might take a few more months to be fully effective. People living in these enclaves, in all 51,214, were required to choose their country of nationality. All 14,214 residents in 51 Bangladeshi enclaves in India opted for Indian nationality. Of the 36,021 residents in Indian enclaves in Bangladesh, 979 opted for Indian nationality, and remaining preferred to remain where they were to become Bangladeshi nationals in effect (*The Times of India*, 1 August 2015).

# Intra-regional and Extra-regional Military Interventions

There are three cases of this variety: (a) the Tibetan refugees in India and Nepal following the Chinese annexation of Tibet, (b) the deportation and displacement of Chinese settled for generations in Kolkata and Assam in the wake of the Chinese invasion of India in 1962 and (c) the Afghan refugees in Pakistan, and also in India, following the Soviet intervention in Afghanistan in 1979.

## Tibetan Refugees

Tibetan refugees started arriving in India as early as in 1950. It was during this year that the People's Republic of China started asserting its sovereignty over Tibet. It was, however, in 1959 that a large number of Tibetans began to flee to India and Nepal in the wake of the Chinese military action in the plateau. The International Commission of Jurists in its 1959 and 1966 reports documented several cases of religious persecution, torture, forced sterilization and destruction of families that were perpetrated by the Chinese authorities, which occasioned the migrations. It was estimated that by 1966 about 80,000 to 90,000 Tibetans had taken refuge in India. The flow continued and in 1986, 2,300 Tibetans, mostly monks and nuns, arrived in India following reports of a Chinese crackdown. After the initial settlement of these refugees in Assam (at Missamari) and West Bengal (at Buxa in Cooch Behar), and later in various other parts of India, the Indian government found a more permanent place for a large section of them in the hilly town of Dharamsala in Himachal Pradesh. Besides India, Nepal hosted about 30 thousand Tibetan refugees.

## Eviction of 'Chinese Indians'

It was as early as in the 1780s that a group of about 100 Chinese arrived in Calcutta to do business. The phenomenon of Chinese migration to India, however, can be traced to the 19th century, when the British brought them to work in the tea gardens and oil fields of Assam in the 1830s. The tea gardens of Assam in the initial days of their development had decided to import Chinese coolies from Singapore as local labour was not available and Chhota Nagpur tribes were yet to emerge as an option. Chinese coolies were known for their agricultural skills, and particularly in tea plantation they were even better skilled. But the experiment did not work. En route the tea gardens from the Calcutta port they entered into brawls with the locals, leading to their eventual deportation to Singapore, barring a few expert tea growers (Weiner 1978: 89). Besides Assam, some Chinese, however, kept coming to India, primarily Calcutta, in search of better livelihood as colonial Calcutta offered good economic opportunities. The Calcutta-based Chinese soon mastered the arts of leather processing, shoe making, carpentry and shop keeping. Their yet another significant enterprise was restaurant business. The popularity of Chinese food in India may be traced to these early Chinese hotel ventures in Calcutta. Some Chinese were engaged in the clandestine trade of opium and *charas* (an intoxicant handmade from the resin of the cannabis plant). The flow of Chinese continued, which picked up during the Second World War when many Chinese fled to India as refugees, fearing a Communist takeover of China (Mazumdar & Tankha 2010).

In the 1950s as relations between India and China deteriorated after the initial bonhomie of *Hindi–Chini Bhai Bhai* (Indians and Chinese are brothers), the Chinese started becoming suspect in Indian eyes, particularly after the flight of the Dalai Lama to India in 1959. Many Chinese were accused of anti-Indian activities and were put under surveillance. Towards the end of 1959 the Foreigners Act was amended requiring the Chinese to obtain 'residential permits' and register at the local police stations. Those who failed to do so were designated as people without any nationality and were allowed to stay in India only for three months. By 1961, about 200 Calcutta-based Chinese that included principals and teachers of Chinese schools, editors and distributors of the *Chinese Review*, the managers and other officers of the Bank of China, businessmen and many others, were deported. The bank accounts of many Chinese were frozen and many shops belonging to them were subjected to mob fury. After India's war with China in 1962, the situation worsened. Under the Defence of India Act of 1962 the Indian agencies first imprisoned and then deported thousands of Chinese settled in Calcutta, Darjeeling, Kalimpong, Jamshedpur, Mumbai and certain towns of the North East more or less on the pattern of what had happened to the Japanese in America in the aftermath of the 1941 massacre of the US air base at Pearl Harbour (Hawaii) by the Japanese bombers. As a result, the once vibrant China Town of Calcutta now exists only in name. In her Sahitya Akademi Award-winning historical novel in Assamese, *Makam* (meaning Golden Horse in Chinese), its authoress Rita Chowdhury, who also teaches Political Science at Guwahati's Cotton College, has narrated the plight of the Chinese in Assam who were rounded up and taken to the Deoli internment camp in Rajasthan, where they languished for years before being deported to China. 'We were not Chinese spies. Why were we deported', they asked. They remember India as their 'Janam Jaga' (motherland; Xing 2009–10: 399–407, Mazumdar & Tankha 2010, *The Hindu*, 8 November 2010).

## Afghan Refugees

The Soviet intervention in Afghanistan in December 1979 resulted in a massive flow of Afghan refugees into Pakistan. Although many Afghans had come to Pakistan as refugees even before the Soviet intervention (by Hafizullah Amin's time, three months before the Soviets arrived, about 400,000 Afghan refugees had reached Pakistan), the intervention increased the flow, which reached up to 10,000 to 15,000 people per month. By the time the Geneva Accords were signed in 1988, the number of Afghan refugees had crossed the 3,500,000 mark. During 1991–94, 1,757,402 refugees were repatriated as against 126,026 new arrivals. Of the registered Afghan refugees in Pakistan, about 67 per cent were in the North-West Frontier Province (NWFP; now Khyber Pakhtunkhwa), about 28 per cent in Balochistan and the rest were scattered all over the country. Some of the Afghan refugees also came to India. According to the World Refugee Survey 1996 published by the United States Committee for Refugees, India hosted 19,758 Afghan refugees. By the late 1990s, many refugees had begun to return. Given the unpredictable politics of Afghanistan it was, however, not certain that the process would continue. By the beginning of 1997, 2,600,000 Afghan refugees returned, 1,900,000 of them with repatriation assistance from the UNHCR. Another 1,300,000 had returned from Iran, taking the total number of Afghan refugees who went back to Afghanistan to around 3,900,000—the largest repatriation of a single refugee group since the UNHCR came into existence in 1949.

Following the eviction of the Taliban regime in the aftermath of 9/11, there was hope that normality would return as the United States/North Atlantic Treaty Organization (NATO) forces were in control in Kabul. But before long the Taliban resurfaced, and with the tacit support of the Pakistan authorities the situation was virtually back to square one. In 2005 a census was conducted of the Afghan refugee population, and it was found that they were about 3,000,000 in number, but probably it was much more. Of this, only 1,600,000 lived in camps. There was a follow-up census in 2006–7 after which the NADRA started registering them, and 2,150,000 of them were issued POR cards. The Government of Pakistan had an Afghan Management and Repatriation Strategy in place to facilitate their voluntary repatriation. According to Duniya Aslam Khan, the public information officer of the UNHCR, 3,800,000 refugees had returned to Afghanistan by 2012, and 1,600,000 remained in Pakistan. Since their POR cards had expired in 2012, the NADRA was issuing them new POR with the help of the UNHCR. There are 76 refugee camps in Khyber Pakhtunkhwa, 10 in Balochistan and one in Punjab. On the whole, however, in spite of all efforts to help the refugees return home, the things did not look promising. The number of willing returnees was going down systematically, and in 2013 as little as 31,000 returned

(Menon 2014). According to the 2015 UNHCR Country Operations Profile for Pakistan, since 2002 the organization has facilitated the return of 3,800,000 registered Afghan refugees to their country.[18]

# Notes

1. A *tehsil* (also known as *tahsil, tahasil, taluka, taluk* or *taluq*) is a unit of government in India and Pakistan. It usually consists of a town and the villages around the town. *Zail* meant an administrative unit of two to forty villages introduced by the British.
2. For an authoritative study of the Radcliffe Award on Punjab, see Chester (2009).
3. In a somewhat different historical context, the case of Bengali Hindus of the pre-Partition Assam district of Sylhet was identical. Following the decision of the British Indian government to separate Assam from the Bengal province in 1874, the Bengali-speaking Sylhet was given to Assam to make it economically viable against the wishes of the Bengalis that included both Hindus and Muslims. As Assamese nationalism grew in the subsequent period, the caste Assamese political leadership of the Brahmaputra valley was not comfortable with the existence of a large Bengali-speaking community in the Surma valley, which consisted of Sylhet and Kachar districts. Following the Partition when it was decided to go for a referendum (held on 6–7 July 1947) to find out where the people of Sylhet wanted to go, India or Pakistan, the caste Assamese leadership wanted it to go to Pakistan to offset the Bengali influence (most importantly Hindu) in Assam politics. Thus, while for the Bengali Hindus of Assam it was the question of their religion in the referendum and, therefore, India, for the caste Assamese it was the fear of continuation of Bengali Hindu dominance. As per the referendum results, Sylhet was allotted to Pakistan. Amalendu Guha writes: 'Sylhet, "the golden calf" that was sacrificed in 1874 to usher in a new province, was now once more sacrificed at the altar of a new state' (Guha 2006: 261–62, also see 22–23).
4. Indeed the invasion by the tribal Pashtuns must have been a catalyst too. Whether or not the tribesmen were sent to Kashmir by the Pakistan government, it is difficult to say. Indians believe they were. Pakistani sources suggest that its army was actively preparing itself to take action in J&K and in that preparation the tribal support was not ruled out. But probably before anything was actually done, the tribesmen actually intervened, which Pakistan of course welcomed (Khan 1975: 1–25).
5. A detailed analysis of the 1941 census report may raise some doubts about these figures, but the overall picture would remain more or less valid (see Snedden 2001: 131–34). For a detailed study on the subject, see Snedden 2013. The overall J&K communal break-up was as follows: Muslim 77 per cent, Hindu 20 per cent, and other communities (mostly Sikhs, with a sprinkling of Buddhists) 3 per cent. See Bose (2003: 16).

6.  As per Kashmir Maharaja's The State Subject Definition Notification, No. I-L/84, dated 20 April 1927, state subjects are 'persons born and residing within the State before the commencement of the reign of His Highness the late Maharaja Ghulab Singh Sahib Bahadur, and also persons who settled the rein before the commencement of samvat year 1942, and have since been permanently residing therein....' Another notification dated 27 June 1932 said: 'Certificates of nationality of the Jammu and Kashmir State may, on application, be granted by the Minister-in Charge of the Political Department in accordance with the provisions of section I of this Notification.' For the complete texts of these notifications, see Anand (2010: 466–67). These definitions are still valid.

7.  It may be noted that the phenomenon of demographic revolution as seen in Tripura, where natives were reduced to a minority, was not unique. It had happened in Assam and the Chhota Nagpur region of Bihar also, the only difference being that in the latter case it happened gradually, while in Tripura it happened virtually overnight. In the case of Chhota Nagpur, unlike Tripura or Assam, there was outmigration of native population too to other regions in search of better economic opportunities, such as Assam, northern Bengal and the Andaman Islands (the Assamese component has been discussed in the subsection, Black Tribal People, later in this chapter).

8.  The Sundaral Report has not yet been released for which there is a demand. See Aiyar (2012). Some excerpts from the report are available in *Frontline* (Chennai), 18(5), 3–16 March 2001.

9.  Lhotshampa is the Dzongkha word for the ethnic Nepali Bhutanese, meaning 'southern border dweller' (*lho* – south, *tsham* – border, *pa* – suffix, meaning people [Evans 2013: 140]).

10. For a detailed study of this Tamil migration to Myanmar, see Mahadevan (1978).

11. Besides India, there were several other destinations for the Tamil refugees, mainly in the West. Here is a break-up: Canada (1,25,000), the United States (15,000), the UK (35,000), Holland (15,000), Germany (60,000), France (40,000), Switzerland (36,000), Australia (8,000), Denmark (8,000), Norway and Sweden (6,000), New Zealand (1,000), Belgium (1,000), Austria (3,000), Finland (200), Russia (5,000), Botswana (2,000), Indonesia (3,000), Ukraine (1,000), Thailand (5,000), Vietnam (1,000), Rumania (750), Mexico (300), Peru (300), Chile (200), Bulgaria (800), and Cambodia (500). The pain of the scattered existence of the Tamil refugees was poignantly expressed in the following poem of V.I.S. Jayapalan, a Sri Lankan Tamil expatriate poet: My son is in Jaffna/Wife in Colombo/Father in the Wanni/Mother, old and sick in Tamil Nadu,/Relatives in Frankfurt/A sister in France/And I,/Like a camel that has strayed in Alaska/Am stuck in Oslo/And our families/Cotton pillows/To be/Torn and scattered by the/Monkey fate? (Suryanarayan 2003: 321–22).

12. In many parts of India–Bangladesh or Indo-Myanmar border regions, leave alone the Indo-Nepal border, which is de jure open, or India–Bhutan border, which is semi-open, people find it convenient to look for medical

services across the border. I have seen it in the Lunglei and Champhai districts of Mizoram near Myanmar and Bangladesh borders, and Kharkongor has written about it through her experience in the Lyngkhat village in Meghalaya bordering Bangladesh (Kharkongor 2014: 181–82).

13. For a discussion on Nepali migration to Assam, see Devi (2007).

14. The complexity of demarcating the border between India and Bangladesh is unfathomable not only to common man but even at the level of India's Supreme Court. In a 70-page judgment passed by a Supreme Court Bench of Justices Ranjan Gogoi and Rohinton F. Nariman on 17 December 2014, it was said: 'We are at a loss to understand why 67 years after independence the eastern border is left porous. We have been reliably informed that the entire border with Pakistan, 3,300 km long, is not only properly fenced, but properly manned as well, and is not porous at any point.' See *The Hindu*, 18 December 2014. There is a vast difference in the topography of India's western and eastern borders, besides the nature of human habitation and bilateral relational patterns between India–Pakistan on the one hand and India–Bangladesh on the other.

15. To exactly assess the number of unauthorized Bangladeshis in India is very difficult. It raises many methodological issues, which are complicated by changing ground realities. For a study of the methodological concerns in the case of undocumented residents in the United States (see Woodrow-Lafield 1998: 145–73). According to various methods employed, the number of such residents in America could range between 2 and 4 million.

16. In a footnote, Vernant (1953) clarified that these figures were 'based on Pakistani sources'. Since he did not use any such qualification in respect of other statistics given in his book, one surmises that probably he had some doubts about the veracity of these figures. Alexander had not given any detailed statistics, although he had mentioned that J&K Muslim refugees in Azad Kashmir and Pakistan were in larger number than those of Hindu and Sikh refugees from POK to the Indian part of J&K and other parts of India.

17. For a historical background of the Chakma problem, see Bhattacharya (2001: 319–30).

18. http://www.unhcr.org/cgi-bin/texts/vtx/page?=49e487016&subm (accessed on 8 January 2016).

# 2
# The Political Connection

*Just because you do not take an interest in politics doesn't mean politics won't take an interest in you!*

—Pericles (430 BC) (de Silva 1985)

## The Connection

Where there are people, there is politics. Refugees add to the stimuli. Since 'demography is destiny', as Augustus Comte told us, politics and migration go hand in glove. As soon as tensions arising out of resettlement woes subside, the refugees/migrants start becoming demanding. Conversely, as soon as the initial sympathy for them dries up in the host society, nativist suspicions about their continued presence start surfacing. Concerns such as pressures on civic amenities, resource shortages and the rise in the crime graph tend to ruffle popular imagination. The experience of later Jewish immigrants in Israel, later European settlers in America and that of Chinese and Japanese immigrants in the United States in the latter half of the 19th and early 20th centuries all tell the same story. In Mumbai, Shiv Sena's opposition, first to Tamil settlers and later to illegal Bangladeshis, or Maharashtra Navnirman Sena's recent tirade against immigrants from Bihar and UP, are the expressions of the same phenomenon. Theoretically, these connections are well recognized. Since South Asia is poor and populous on the one hand and democratic and plural on the other hand, this dimension becomes all the more pronounced because of the region's ethno-religious mosaic. To better understand the link, four broad points need to be spelt out.

In the first place, refugees and migrants put pressure on available resources in the places of their settlement, which result in tensions between them and the locals. In the case of territorial divisions of the Partition variety, and the resultant dislocation of economic life, resource-related tensions were unavoidable. Not only did the Partition create animosity between the refugees and the locals both in Delhi and Kolkata, but the problems related to allocations of evacuee properties, compensations to be paid to the refugees for the loss of their assets, provisions for the rehabilitation of refugees and the financial burdens on respective national exchequers of India and Pakistan strained inter-societal affairs as well as India–Pakistan relationship (Rai 1965, Vakil 1950: 69–87, 527–29). An example of this kind of nativist reaction was that even the Bengali refugees fleeing the Pakistani military atrocities in 1971 had to face the ire of the local people in the bordering areas of West Bengal, Assam and Tripura (Bass 2013: 133, 189–91). Second, migrant populations affect the politics of the host society by their direct or indirect involvement in everyday affairs. One can take the examples of Hindu and Sikh refugees from Pakistan in Delhi and India's Punjab, Indian Muslim refugees in Pakistan's Punjab and Sind, Bihari and Hyderabadi refugees in East Bengal/East Pakistan/Bangladesh, the East Pakistani and Bangladeshi settlers in India's North East and West Bengal, Nepali settlers in northern and north-eastern India and West Bengal, Indian settlers from Bihar and UP in Nepal's Terai region, and the case of Sri Lankan Tamil refugees in Tamil Nadu. Third, in most cases of refugee arrivals, there is a strong underpinning of communal and ethnic sentiment which complicates local politics. For example, since many recent Bangladeshi illegal migrants in India are Muslims, it gives a chance to Hindu chauvinistic parties in India to communalize the issue for larger political gain in a Hindu-majority country, as successive elections in India have shown. Likewise, the Sri Lankan Tamil refugees in Tamil Nadu contribute to the strengthening of the Dravidian sentiment there. Fourth, since the refugee groups sometimes bring with them their militant past, they tend to contribute to militancy in the host countries. For example, it has been noticed that prior to the arrival of the Sri Lankan Tamil refugees, the political street fights in Tamil Nadu, even when they turned violent, did not go beyond cycle chains, sticks and stones. But the Jaffna 'boys' introduced guns, which changed the nature of street fights that worried both the state and the central governments (de Silva 1985).

# Refugee Factor and Hindu Nationalism

The unprecedented Hindu/Sikh–Muslim riots that greeted the news of Partition resulted in massive migration of Hindus and Sikhs from Pakistan to India, as we have noted. It was estimated that about eight million Hindu and Sikh refugees arrived in India in those days and the process continued thereafter, though with less intensity. It is inevitable that such large-scale migrations would influence the politics of the receiving country. Though faced with a massive challenge, the Indian democracy succeeded in making the country secular and liberal in its orientation. The credit largely goes to the Constituent Assembly, though it was not democratically elected. There were Muslims in the assembly, but there was no organized effort to get the community represented. Hindu communal groups per se were not there, but many Congress leaders were staunchly Hindu-minded. Strangely, though this 300-plus member assembly was 'remarkably unpresentative', and that too without any popular pressure to initiate universal adult suffrage, still a constitutional secular democracy was introduced based on adult franchise. Such a spectacular job was virtually done by only about two dozen lawyers (Khilnani 2004: 34).

But against the background of an unprecedented violence to which all major communities were subjected to, the political task was much more complicated than the constitutional task. The Hindu nationalistic politics, which had a decades-old tradition got a huge boost from the Hindu/Sikh refugee arrivals. Even numerically it was helpful for the Hindu right. According to the first Indian census held in 1951, Hindus accounted for 84.98 per cent of India's population compared to Muslims who accounted for one-tenth of the total (Jha & Jha 2012: 21). The birth of the Hindu chauvinistic Bharatiya Jana Sangh (BJS; forerunner of the present BJP) in 1951 was directly attributable to these factors. The linkages of the Jana Sangh with the Hindu nationalistic Hindu Mahasabha and the RSS are well documented (Ghosh 1999, Graham 1990). The founder of the Jana Sangh, Shyama Prasad Mukherjee, constantly emphasized the refugee factor as one of the most important compulsions behind his launching of the new party (he was getting disillusioned with the West Bengal unit of the Hindu Mahasabha, which also contributed to his launching of the Jana Sangh, which we have discussed later). No wonder that the initial cadre base of the party came from the refugee settlements, particularly in Delhi. There was probably an additional factor as well that contributed to the rise of Hindu right on the one hand and the corresponding decline of Muslim political power on the other. The abolition of zamindari in 1951, against the background of Partition, resulted in two different rural–urban migratory patterns in respect of the two communities. Muslim landlords by and large did not migrate to urban areas, but their Hindu counterparts did, in search of new economic activities. This was noticed in Kanpur, Gorakhpur and Lucknow where between 1947 and 1955 the migration of the upper caste Hindus from rural to urban areas was as high as 68 per cent. In comparison to this, the Muslim migration was as low as 16.28 per cent (Hasan 1997a: 52).

Christophe Jaffrelot's study reveals in detail the impact of Punjabi refugees on the Hindu-centric politics of Delhi in the early years of India's independence (Jaffrelot 2000). He mentions two factors in particular, one, that the RSS was already present in Delhi's political life and it had a widespread support among the Hindu aristocrats, and two, that among the Hindu Punjabi refugees, many had traditional affiliation to the Arya Samaj, the ideology of which was close to that of the RSS and the Hindu Mahasabha. These groups had always seen Gandhi as an apologist for the Muslims and had ridiculed his fasts as pro-Muslim attention grabbers. When Gandhi declared his fast in January 1948, which proved to be his last, to press for a 'peace pledge', a 50,000-strong Arya Samaj and Hindu Mahasabha members took out a procession shouting slogans such as 'blood for blood' and 'let Gandhi die'.[1] It was not surprising, therefore, that the BJS, which Shyama Prasad Mukherjee launched in 1951, would find Delhi as its most significant initial catchment. In the Delhi municipal elections held in the autumn of 1951, the party got as much as 25 per cent of votes as against 33 per cent polled by the Congress. In the 1952 parliamentary elections too, it got 22 per cent. The continued influence of the BJS/BJP in Delhi's political life indeed owes its origin to this period (Jaffrelot 2000: 181–91, also Kumari 2013: 66).

Still, the Congress, it may be noted, did not feel the Jana Sangh heat as much, primarily because many Congress leaders too were communally oriented, and at the local levels, they could convince the refugee electorates that since political power belonged to them, they could serve their interests better in terms of refugee relief and rehabilitation. Jaffrelot draws the conclusion in the following words:

> [T]he Jana Sangh cannot be considered the party of the refugees, not only because its strength in the city-capital was not purely based on refugee support, but also because there were refugees who did not vote for this party. A large number of refugees did in fact remain close to the Congress, not

least because they already saw it as a Hindu party even before Partition. Almost since its inception in the late nineteenth century, there had been a strong Hindu traditionalist current in the Punjab Congress. Lala Lajpat Rai epitomized this school of thought till his death in 1928, as did several other extremists from the Arya Samaj. One of his lieutenants, Gopichand Bhargava, took over from Rai in the 1930s, and after Partition, Gopichand's brother, Thakurdas Bhargava, became one of the main advocates of Hindu traditionalism in the Constituent Assembly. He objected to the recognition of religious minorities as 'communities' and to the granting of rights of citizenship to non-Hindu immigrants from Pakistan. He was also one of the staunchest advocates of cow protection and the promotion of Hindi as a national language. (Jaffrelot 2000: 191)

The communal temper that was created did not escape the Sikh community either. Together with the Hindus, a large number of Sikhs too had arrived as refugees. While the Sikh ethnic identity remained as before, the Punjabi Hindu ethnic identity underwent a change. The latter now tended to identify themselves more closely with Hindi language as opposed to the Sikhs who continued to emphasize their mother tongue, Punjabi, and its script Gurumukhi. The origin of the militant Sikh separatism that rocked Indian politics in the 1970s and 1980s can be, to some extent, traced to this element of communalisation of Sikh mind after Partition.[2] The Hindu–Sikh differences that surfaced over the question of language during the 1951 census were largely created by the conflicting approaches of these two communities to the issue. In that census, most of the Hindu Punjabis recorded Hindi as their mother tongue as opposed to the Sikhs for whom it was Punjabi. The bifurcation of the state of Punjab and the creation of Haryana in the 1960s was an inevitable consequence of this ethnic dichotomy (Rai 1965: 198-205).

# Growth of Leftism in West Bengal: The Refugee Factor

Unlike the Partition of the Punjab, which contributed to the growth of Hindu nationalism, although the Congress was well prepared to thwart that beyond a point, in West Bengal, where the Bengali Hindu refugees from East Pakistan were largely concentrated, it was a different story. At the time of Partition, four political forces operated in the state, namely, Hindu Mahasabha, the Congress, the Leftists, and, calling the shots from Delhi, the central government led by Pandit Nehru. Their political outlooks and strategies differed, and with changing realities there were constant readjustments. In this game, the Leftists proved to be the ultimate winners. They first outmanoeuvred the Hindu Mahasabha and then the Congress. The West Bengal unit of the latter suffered from its constant tension with the high command in Delhi. It found the central government either indifferent or not sufficiently appreciative of the local difficulties in dealing with both the refugee problem and the political challenge the Leftists posed. In due course, a strong sense of provincialism grew among its cadres, which further distanced the Bengal unit from the centre. The more the West Bengal government was beleaguered, the more the Congress high command was exasperated at its failure, thus creating a vicious circle of one feeding the other's discomfiture.

Prior to Partition, the Hindu Mahasabha had a fairly strong presence among the middle-class Hindus of East Bengal. Since the party's entire cadre had migrated to West Bengal as refugees, the party was confident of expanding its political base in West Bengal. But it missed the point that though the first wave of refugees consisted of upper castes, the subsequent waves virtually entirely comprised lower castes, among which the Hindu Mahasabha had little support. On the contrary, they had all along supported the Muslim League (discussed below). The confidence of the Mahasabha, therefore, that since the refugees had been the victims of communal hatred its communal card would do the miracle at the polls was grossly misplaced. Because of this complacency, it did not pay enough attention to relief and rehabilitation of the refugees which its Delhi unit had made one of its central concerns. It was no surprise that the party fared badly in the assembly elections, particularly where the refugee votes mattered (Chatterji 2007: 270-71).

Besides this smugness about Hindu support, there were several other problems the Hindu Mahasabha had to confront. The Bangal-Ghoti (East Bengali versus West Bengali) dichotomy had its toll on the organizational structure. The East Bengali leaders had erroneously thought that they would overwhelm their West Bengali counterparts by their sheer numerical strength. It did not happen that way. Also, the party neglected the poor refugees and tried to look after only the relatively better-offs. By the time the party realized its mistake by setting up an All-Bengal Hindu Sramik Sangha (Hindu Workers' Union), it was already too late. It lacked the necessary commitment too. Even the loyalty of the richer refugees could not be guaranteed. Soon they switched their loyalty to the Congress which, as the ruling party, commanded their source allocations and contract distributions. The Mahasabha also underestimated the worth of Muslim votes, considering that Hindu votes would be so overwhelming that it would matter little whether Muslims voted for it or not. But since Muslims had sizeable presence in specific electoral pockets, their votes did matter as the results revealed. Shyama Prasad Mukherjee was the only leader of the party who had the vision to understand the efficacy of minority votes, but he had been sidelined in the organization both at the provincial and central levels to make any meaningful contribution to the party's political strategy in West Bengal (for details, see Chatterji 2007: 261–75).

All the difficulties that Hindu Mahasabha faced could have been taken advantage of by the Congress. But it had its own set of contradictions. The foremost, as noted above, was the distance of West Bengal from Delhi and the latter's lack of appreciation of the dynamics of Bengal politics. Despite the personal rapport that B.C. Roy, the Chief Minister of West Bengal, had with Pandit Nehru, this distance handicap remained a prohibitive factor in those days of communication delays. Moreover, unlike Delhi, a sparsely populated city with vast tracts of land available in the adjacent districts of Punjab (it included Haryana then) and UP at the disposal of the government, Calcutta and its adjoining areas were densely populated with limited available land to create adequate rehabilitation facilities for the refugees. The latter, therefore, had to forcibly occupy private lands, lawns, gardens and uninhabited houses in total disregard of legal norms. This created animosities between the affected locals and the refugees. In this connection, it may also be noted that while on the western sector there was a virtual exchange of population, in the east the inflow into India was much more than the outflow. According to Meher Chand Mahajan, the Minister of Rehabilitation of the Government of India, an inflow of 4,900,000 from West Pakistan to India was matched by an outflow of 5,5000,000 from East Punjab and its adjoining states to West Pakistan (Ghosh & Dutta 2003: 221). In the east the inflow far exceeded the outflow. The more West Bengal government tried to enforce law to prevent illegal occupation of private properties, the more it was identified as interested only in protecting the rights of the rich in total disregard of the hardships of the refugees. In the words of Joya Chatterji:

> When government tried to evict the refugees, inevitably this led to ugly incidents in which the police brutally enforced the landlords' rights of access, but usually turned a blind eye when the latter unleashed their hired thugs and bully boys to oust the squatters. The galling contrast between the alacrity with which the state and its law-enforcement machinery rushed to

defend the rights of property-owners, and its failure to acknowledge that destitute refugees had any rights at all, was clear for all to see. Refugees who had initially been prepared to pay landlords for the plots they had taken over became less and less concerned to defer to the rights of private property. Confrontations between the state and the squatters, with their modest origins in the refugees' need to have a tiny space in which to live, rapidly escalated into passionate indictments of the established order and the rules of property which it supported. (2007: 294, for more details on the subject see Chakrabarti 1990: 80–85)

In this sense, the Congress was actually poaching into the constituency of the Hindu Mahasabha. The *bhadralok* Bengalis (educated middle class, which also meant the caste Hindus) from anywhere in Bengal, including East Bengal, had a tradition of coming to Kolkata for education, jobs and other social reasons. Kolkata was urbanized and secular. In contrast, Dhaka had a rural character with its population having all kinds of rural connections. As a result, the composite group of *bhadralok* Hindu Bengalis did not have to face an altogether new situation after Partition. Almost all Hindu government servants in East Bengal had opted for India. In any case, because of their financial background and social networking, they did not depend on government support for resettlement. What they wanted from the government was its support to allow them retain their privileges. It was this *bhadralok* community that was the mainstream base of Congress politics in West Bengal.

As days passed and the distance between the common man and the Congress widened, particularly because of the deteriorating economic situation of the state, the party's political future looked uncertain. Even the middle class started drifting away from the Congress because of the deteriorating law and order situation. Against this background a strong sense of provincialism grew that included Congress sentiments also. The centre was accused of entertaining anti-Bengali sentiments. There were demands even for the territorial expansion of the state at the cost of Bihar and Orissa. This was the central plank of Sarat Bose's campaign in the South Calcutta by-election held in June 1949. All anti-Congress forces rallied behind Bose, which led to the total rout of the Congress party. In its explanation for the defeat, J.N. Ganguli of the state unit of the party wrote to the high command:

I have got only one answer from the voters—i.e. they will lend their support when the [central] Congress will cease to be anti-Bengalee. In support they compared the rehabilitation work in the Punjab and Bengal, they cited the absence of any Bengalees in any Foreign [Embassy] as its head, the language controversy in Bihar… the exploitation of the I[ndian] N[ational] A[rmy] for general elections and then throwing them away as dirty rags and so forth…. Congress lost on account of provincialism. (Chatterji 2007: 303)

So much was the anger of the voters against the centre that they manhandled Mrs Sucheta Kripalani who had been sent by Nehru to help the party. They shouted the slogan: 'Agent of Nehru, clear out' (Chatterji 2007: 303).

This provincialization of the Congress did not go well with central leadership. Far from extricating its West Bengal unit from the mess, the high command piled further confusion upon a mountain of chaos it was already in. It rebuked its West Bengal unit for its failure. When the *Nikhil Vanga Bastuhara Karma Parishad* (NVBKP; All Bengal Refugee Council of Action, or ABRCA),[3] a refugee organization, went to the Jaipur Session of the Congress in 1948 to present their case, Nehru refused to give even an audience to them and taunted them as 'foreigners' who should ideally approach the government's 'Foreign Bureau'. Expectedly, when the new executive committee of NVBKP was elected in December that year, a fewer number of Congress members were found there (Chatterji 2007: 291–92). Again, in the mid-1950s when West Bengal put up its claim to take advantage of the States Reorganisation Commission, Nehru dismissed its case as 'the most unimportant problem' facing the commission. On the contrary, the central government deprived West Bengal of some areas that the commission itself had recommended for the state (Chatterji 2007: 305). In this situation, the West Bengal Congress systematically lost its ground among all sections of Bengalis and increasingly tried to compensate by depending on non-Bengali voters, at least in Calcutta. Strangely, in this case also the high command did not understand the dynamics of West Bengal politics. Nehru naively asked Atulya Ghosh in 1958 the reason as to why 'in Calcutta, the strength of the Congress, such as it is, lies more with the non-Bengali elements there' (Chatterji 2007: 231).

The situation was conducive for the Leftists to expand their base, though they did not start off with any inherent advantage. On the contrary, they had to surmount several difficulties, including the banning of the Communist Party of India (CPI) in 1948 by the West Bengal government. Since several studies have discussed this subject in detail, it is not necessary to repeat these here (Chakrabarti 1990: 405-46, Chatterji 2007: 275-309, Mandal 2011: 193-203). It may be sufficient to only mention that four main Leftist outfits mattered the most, namely, the CPI, Communist Party of India (Marxist) (CPI(M); founded in 1964 after its split from CPI), Revolutionary Socialist Party (RSP) and the Forward Bloc. Since they were on the same ideological plank, broadly speaking, their political strategy was not to poach into each other's turf but to unite as a front to put up a joint challenge to the Congress, a strategy that has lasted till today, even after its drubbing in the hands of the Trinamool Congress (TMC) in the assembly elections of 2011 and the general elections of 2014.

The task of the Left parties, however, was not easy. The refugee politics had two segments, one, of those who forcibly occupied lands and established squatter colonies, and two, of those who were kept in refugee colonies with no particular commitment from the state for their rehabilitation in West Bengal (till today some of these colonies exist). Not satisfied with the government schemes, many refugees had started taking law in their own hands by forcibly occupying central government, state government and private lands to resettle themselves. Popularly known as *jabor-dakhol* (might is right—forcibly occupied) colonies, these squatter settlements soon dotted Kolkata and its vicinities. CPI was not particularly advantaged to strengthen its mass base amongst them for whom the issue was government recognition of these colonies. For them, the Congress party was more relevant, a situation one notices now in the politics of recognition of unauthorized colonies in Delhi. The problem of colony refugees was different. One, their number was continuously swelling, making any systematic relief operation difficult, and two, the proposed rehabilitation of some of them in the Andaman and Nicobar Islands and in the Dandakaranya forests of Madhya Pradesh was against their liking. In the beginning, it was the concern of all political parties, such as the Congress, CPI, Forward Bloc and others, to think of the welfare of all the refugees, which was reflected in the multi-party membership of the NBBK, but as the squatter movements became violent, warranting state law enforcement response, the Leftists found the situation favourable to enlist greater support among the disgruntled refugees for whom violation of law proved more helpful. Still, the refugees were ambivalent; they were not sure what would benefit them, their identification with the Congress or with the Left (Mandal 2011: 203-7).

What really helped the Left to extend its base amongst the underprivileged in general, which included the refugees, was the difficult economic situation of West Bengal during the first few years of India's independence. All social indicators—purchasing power, law and order, public health and human rights in the name of security—marked dismal decline. Against this background, the banning of the West Bengal unit of CPI on 25 March 1948 by the West Bengal government, against the wishes of Nehru, was unwise. It only helped the latter to expand its base among the refugees and urban poor (Bandyopadhayay 2006). The Communists fully supported the squatter movements and, more vociferously, the reluctance of the colony refugees to be shifted from West Bengal (Kudaisya 1996: 31–32). One of the studies that has analysed this linkage has the following to say (Zagoria 1969: 115, quoted by Kudaisya 1996: 32):

> In the urban areas of West Bengal, Communist strength [did] not appear to be based on any particular caste and community. Rather, one of the main bases seem[ed] to be the several million 'declassed' Hindu refugees who fled their homes in East Bengal after partition. These refugees constitute[d] about one-fourth of the West Bengal population and a substantial portion of the Calcutta population. They apparently voted for the Communists overwhelmingly. Here, it would seem, is a classic example of uprooted and declassed individuals supporting an extremist party in accordance with the model put forth by the proponents of the concept of mass society.

Yet another factor to be noted in our explanation of the rise of leftism in West Bengal is the shifting refugee settlements from metropolitan urban centres to semi-urban and rural areas. Although originally a large number of refugees came to settle in Calcutta and the adjacent town of Howrah, gradually they moved away to peripheral small towns and villages, as was revealed in the censuses of 1951 and 1961. The 1951 census counted 686,000 and 94,000 East Pakistani refugees in Calcutta and Howrah, respectively. In 1961, the numbers had declined to 528,000 and 80,000, respectively, while the adjoining districts of 24 Parganas and Hoogly registered a significant increase in the refugee population. In the urban 24 Parganas, there were 366,000 refugees in 1951, which became 490,000 in 1961. In the rural areas, the number increased from 225,000 to 297,000 during the corresponding decade. Hoogly showed an increase from 72,000 in 1951 to 131,000 in 1961. This pattern could be attributed to the desire of the refugees to preserve a semblance of their former lifestyle. The rural base of the political left of West Bengal was partly on account of this process of migration (Mitra 1975). Table 2.1 shows how the Leftist parties systematically gained in strength in the state during the first two decades after independence.

One may observe from the above discussion that the political orientation of the migrants from West and East Pakistan represented

**Table 2.1**

*Percentage of votes polled by left parties in West Bengal Assembly Elections, 1952–69*

| Party | 1952 | 1957 | 1962 | 1967 | 1969 |
|---|---|---|---|---|---|
| Communist Party of India (CPI) | 10.60 | 17.82 | 24.96 | 6.53 | 6.78 |
| Communist Party of India (Marxist) (CPIM) (founded in 1964) | | | | 18.11 | 19.55 |
| Forward Bloc | 5.29 | 3.84 | 4.61 | 3.87 | 5.40 |
| Forward Bloc (Marxist) | – | 0.85 | 0.32 | 0.21 | 0.19 |
| Forward Bloc Ruikar (merged with PSP [Praja Socialist Party] after 1952 elections) | 1.51 | – | – | – | – |
| Revolutionary Socialist Party (RSP) | 0.86 | 1.24 | 2.56 | 2.14 | 2.75 |
| Socialist Unity Centre | – | 0.75 | 0.73 | 0.72 | 1.48 |
| Revolutionary Communist Party of India | 0.43 | 0.42 | 0.42 | 0.31 | 0.37 |
| Workers' Party of India | – | – | 0.28 | 0.34 | 0.35 |
| Total | 18.69 | 24.92 | 33.88 | 32.23 | 36.87 |

*Source:* Franda (1971:116); reproduced in Chatterji (2007: 276).

*Note:*  To understand the real gain for the Communists, one should combine the percentages of votes earned by both CPI and CPI(M) as they were one party before the split in the early 1960s.

a split political identity which was partly seethed in historical experience and partly in the day-to-day existential problems. For example, the Bengali Hindu refugees might have contributed to the expansion of the base of the Left parties for tactical reasons, but the memories of violence perpetrated against them had lingered in their minds and given the chance they could have probably provided the votes for the Hindu-oriented parties. But for historical reasons, neither the Hindu Mahasabha nor the RSS and the BJS/BJP could sufficiently exploit the situation, unlike what happened in Delhi and Punjab. But if the story of a small settlement of Bengali refugees in the district of Bijnor in UP is any indication, it tends to support the conjecture that given the political climate the Bengali refugees could have become a base of Hindu nationalistic politics. The Bengali Hindu refugees in Bijnor are now staunch supporters of BJP and have developed their political equations with the local Jats so as to pose a political challenge to the local Muslims (*The Hindu*, 1 March 2012).

## The Caste Factor in Bengal

We have noted in the previous section that there was a dichotomy between the *bhadralok* approach to the refugee issue and that of the lower castes. In the politics of West Bengal, in respect of refugee relief, this came to the fore as the Namasudras (an 'untouchable' caste), who formed a sizeable section of the refugees, did not toe the line of the CPI and rather sided with the Congress administration of B.C. Roy. But over the question of sending the refugees to Dandakaranya they opposed even the Roy government (Chakrabarti 1990: 171-74, 208). In the Hindu politics of East Bengal prior to Partition, there was a cleavage between the upper caste Hindus and the lower castes. Prior to Partition, the Namasudras and the Rajbansis, the two dominant scheduled castes of East Bengal, had the spatial advantage of being close to each other, which had given them a major political voice. But after the Partition, while the Rajbansis could still retain some of their spatial advantage as many of them migrated to Rajbansi-dominated areas of North Bengal, thus eventually creating the demand for a Kamtapur autonomous district, the Namasudras got dispersed in West Bengal as refugees, making them lose their spatial advantage held in pre-Partition Bengal.[4] Even otherwise, there was ambivalence among them about whether or not to leave the country after Partition. The two of their leaders, Jogendra Nath Mandal and Pramatha Ranjan Thakur, had held different positions on the matter. While the former sided with the Muslim League, which wanted the entire Bengal as part of Pakistan, the latter was opposed to it and, therefore, supported the Congress–Hindu Mahasabha campaign for partitioning Bengal. The Muslim League had realized their dilemma and tried to placate them to stay back. It may be underlined that when the Pakistan Constituent Assembly was inaugurated on 26 July 1947 it elected the Namasudra leader Jogendra Nath Mandal, who had started the Bengal provincial branch of B.R. Ambedkar's Scheduled Caste Federation in 1945, as the acting president of the assembly. In his presidential speech, Mandal profusely appreciated the role of the Muslim League in creating Pakistan, which was meant to safeguard the interests of all the minorities of India. He was sure that the new nation would 'never lack in the quality of doing not only justice and fairness but acts of generosity towards the people of minority communities inhabiting Pakistan, and that is my greatest satisfaction' (SARRC 2006: 30).

But scheduled caste politics in pre-Partition Bengal was as complex as the larger communal politics was. The 1935 Government of India

Act complicated the picture further because the seat allocations for the state legislature that it provided did not exactly correspond to the demographic complexion of the state. As per the Act, Muslims, who constituted 54 per cent of the population, had 48 per cent of the seats, scheduled castes, who constituted 18 per cent of the population, had 12 per cent of the seats designated as 'depressed classes', Hindus, who constituted 26 per cent of the population (excluding the 'depressed classes'), had 20 per cent of the seats designated as 'general' seats, and Europeans, who constituted a mere 0.04 per cent of the population, had as many as 10 per cent of the seats (Chatterjee 1997: 44). Notably, while on the one hand a hiatus between the caste Hindus and scheduled caste Hindus was structurally built-in, on the other hand, there was a clear possibility of a political alliance between an important segment of the scheduled castes and the Muslim League. Still, in spite of the Mandal-led Scheduled Caste Federation's alliance with the Muslim League, as we have noted above, the scheduled castes remained a heterogeneous lot, not too sure of their future under a Muslim League dispensation.

Jogendra Nath Mandal was indeed in favour of a united Bengal even if it was under the Muslim League administration, for it would at least not make his poor caste people continue to languish under the domination of the upper caste rich Hindus. Radhanath Das, another scheduled caste leader from Bengal and a member of the Indian Constituent Assembly, argued:

> Today if we say to our Namasudra brothers in Noakhali that they come to west Bengal where the government of the separate province of West and North Bengal will provide them with shelter and other economic necessities, then I am prepared to swear that Jogen Babu will not be able to keep a single one of his caste brothers in Noakhali.... [H]e will not be able to make them feel secure under Muslim League rule or Muslim League protection.... I say the backward Hindus will be better able than others to leave east Bengal, since they have few possessions besides their tiny huts. (Chatterjee 1997: 48–49)

The latter strand had the majority scheduled caste support if the voting in the Bengal Assembly was any indication. Out of 30 such members, as many as 25 voted for the Partition (Chatterjee 1997: 49). In any case, the anti-Hindu riots of 1950 in East Pakistan cast the die. In the riots the lower caste Hindus too were massively targeted, resulting in their exodus to India.[5] One may surmise whether the initial scheduled caste support for the Muslim League had come in the way of making their presence felt in West Bengal politics in later years, unlike in other parts of India. The *bhadralok* dominance of West Bengal politics has continued unabated while the rest of India has witnessed the rise of Dalit and other backward caste (OBC) politics in massive proportions (Lama-Rewal 2009: 361-92).[6] The marginalization of the lower castes and the dominance of the upper castes in West Bengal politics, which the refugee dynamics resulted in, have continued to be the case until today (Chatterjee 2012, Samaddar 2013).[7]

## Caste Dynamics on the Rajasthan Border

In the context of Hindu migrations from Pakistan to the bordering villages of Rajasthan too, we have evidence of caste dynamics playing its role. The Hindu migrations intensified the caste conflicts in these villages, particularly between the Rajputs and the Dalits. So long as these communities lived in Pakistan, they both suffered from a minority complex and therefore lived a subdued life. But after coming to India that complex was no longer there and this factor, coupled with the democratic competitiveness of the Indian society, led to the sharpening of caste cleavages. One Dalit leader put it in precise terms:

> Soon after we came to India the upper castes began learning the behaviour of their local brethren. Freedom is greater here—and so is untouchability. In Pakistan, there was much *begar* (forced labour) on the fields of the dominant Muslim landlords. There was plenty of caste among Muslims, too. There, the Rajputs were just happy that it was us, not them, being dragged into *begar*. Here, they tried doing the same thing to us. But we don't want to exchange one *rathori* (feudal overlordship) for another. So we resisted. This side, things are better, freedom-wise. That side, things were nicer caste-wise. All of us, from all groups, prefer being in India. But over here, we have learned of the Rajputs' strength. (Sainath 1999)

## Politics of Urban Redevelopment: Delhi's Experience

Unlike West Bengal, where the refugees indulged in illegal occupation of government and private lands, in Delhi the government itself was a conduit to illegally occupy Muslim Wakf lands. Partly because of the Partition violence and partly because of migrations to Pakistan, Delhi lost much of its Muslim population. From being a city with almost 50-50

Hindu-Muslim population, the number of Muslims was reduced to 10 per cent as the large-scale Hindu and Sikh migrations from West Punjab swelled the population to double compared to what it was in 1941 (Taneja 2012). Gyanendra Pandey provides the details:

> Delhi was a city of perhaps 9.5 lakh people in 1947 (9.18 lakhs at the census of 1941). Of these, 3.3 lakhs of Muslims left the city at Partition, leaving about 6 lakh people (Hindu, Muslim, Sikh and others) behind. Nearly 5 lakhs of non-Muslim refugees arrived in the city at the same time, making the balance of the new (refugee) inhabitants and the older inhabitants of the city pretty much on par. Even in 1951, by which time the city had expanded considerably (the population of 17.44 lakhs making a 90 per cent increase on the 1941 figure). Partition refugees (not including the local Muslims) still accounted for 28.4 per cent of the total population of the city. In more ways than we have been willing to acknowledge—politically, culturally and even demographically—the Delhi of the 1950s to the 1980s was a 'Partition city'. (Pandey 1997: 2263)

A large number of Muslims had been turned refugees. To escape the communal violence, many of them had first taken shelter in safe places such as mosques and the bungalows of rich and powerful Muslims, but when that did not help they moved to refugee camps in such places like Purana Qila (Old Fort) and the Humayun's Tomb. Almost 174,000 refugees took shelter there. In the beginning, government help was cosmetic and it was only after Gandhi's arrival in Delhi on 9 September 1947 and his visits to these camps that things improved with more government involvement (Pandey 1997: 2266–67).

The drop in the Muslim population and the growth in non-Muslim population against the background of violence and mutual hatred politicized the job of relief and rehabilitation. Not only was scant regard shown to Muslim graves, which were scattered all over the city, even Wakf lands were occupied by the state in total disregard of law to provide accommodation for the Hindu and Sikh refugees. So much were the illegalities associated with these policies that concerned government departments are still reluctant to make available their records for scholarly analysis, leave alone public scrutiny. Here is the experience of an American doctoral student who had after considerable efforts managed to access the records of the Archaeological Survey of India (ASI):

> Two weeks after I started accessing the archives, I was told that my use of the archives was strictly unofficial, merely a favour, and had led to some displeasure among senior officials, and that I had to stop visiting the record room. *It seemed that the ASI's archive was not an archive of authorized*

> *memory, but of authorized forgetting, where what was once consigned to dust*
> *and darkness was never meant to reappear in public, not even as diminu-*
> *tive flickers from academic footnotes.* The authorized forgetting that char-
> acterized the ASI's archive was present just not in the impenetrability of
> the bureaucracy, or in the disorder of the record room, but also in the files
> themselves. This became clear to me when reading the post-colonial files
> I found in the record room in conjunction with the colonial files I read
> in another archive, the Chief Commissioner's Office Records stored in the
> Delhi State Archives. (Taneja 2012, emphasis added)

Reconstruction of Delhi, together with refugee rehabilitation being the
prime task of the Indian state, respect for graves even if they were of ven-
erated Muslim saints was never considered important. Even Nehru was
not serious about their preservation. Here is what Taneja writes:

> The graves disappear, Delhi becomes primeval; 'virgin' territory for
> development. Qasimi tells us the anecdote of Maulana Azad (who was
> the Education Minister [at that time the ASI was under the jurisdiction of
> the Ministry of Education] at the time and the only Muslim member of the
> central cabinet) trying to intervene with Prime Minister Nehru against the
> destruction of tombs and graveyards going on in Delhi, to which Nehru is
> said to have replied, 'Maulana, half of Delhi is graveyards and mosques. Our
> schemes will fail if we don't have room to build'. (Qasimi 2001: 37)

One of the most striking accounts Qasimi gives is of a buried Tughlaq-era
mosque in the grounds of the Lalit Kala Academy in New Delhi. He was
in a car with some other Maulanas. As they approached the former location of the 14th-century Masjid that he had heard so much about, he
asked one of his older colleagues if he knew where the mosque used to
be. They stopped the car and got out. '... while indicating a mound in the
enclosure of the Sahitya Academy and the Lalit Kala Academy they said
the Tughlaq mosque is buried inside this mound and that trees have been
planted all around the mound' (2001, 44). When the plans for the Lalit
Kala Academy were drawn, the area of the mosque fell into the plans
and Delhi Development Authority (DDA) wanted to destroy it. Maulana
Azad intervened, and said that the mosque should not be destroyed at
any cost. 'After long arguments and debates it was decided that the walls
and domes of the mosque be covered with rubble and a platform be built
there' (Taneja 2012: 45).[8]

What is more important to notice is that even some lands belonging
to the Delhi Wakf Board, an otherwise government body, were illegally
occupied by the government on the pretext that that they must not fall

into unsafe hands. The Custodian (of Enemy Property) took over many tomb sites and graveyards and sold them to Hindu and Sikh refugees at throwaway prices. At times Wakf lands were massively usurped, as it happened in Lado Sarai. Later, under the Lt Governorship of Jagmohan (1980-81) wherever there was an old Muslim graveyard or empty Wakf land DDA signboards were put up declaring them as DDA properties (Taneja 2012).

The fact, however, remained that Delhi had to meet the massive challenge of providing shelters to a huge number of refugees as well as build the city as independent India's capital. In doing so it had certain advantages which Calcutta did not have. Delhi had vast spaces under government control, which could be allotted to the refugees. Moreover, the latter had arrived within the span of a few months, making the government respond to their problem in a more organized way, unlike Calcutta where the refugee flow had continued for several years in relatively smaller numbers each time. That in the process of reconstruction Delhi's history and traditional landscape would have to be sacrificed was more or less conceded by the policy makers. Nehru knew that too well as we have seen above. For him, there was a limit to bother about the city's traditional landscape and structures. It has been noted:

> Delhi was primarily viewed as a site from where national reconstruction and planning could be designed. The new rulers invested in a technocratic modernism for the city, to be produced and managed by experts and scientists. For a capital city there was little time for experiments or utopias. It was not without consequence that Nehru invested in Corbusier's Chandigarh as the dream city of nationalism free from the anxieties of managing traditional detritus…. Le Corbusier had once asked the question 'Architecture or Revolution'. (Sundaram 2010: 17-18)

On visiting the Chandigarh site in 1949, Nehru exclaimed with excitement: 'The site chosen is free from the existing encumbrances of old town and traditions. Let it be the first large expression of our creative genius flowering on our newly earned freedom' (Sundaram 2010: 30).

Under the leadership of Meher Chand Khanna, the Minister of Rehabilitation, massive construction works started to both shelter the refugees as well as to provide them with some economic opportunities. Sixty-three markets were set up first temporarily, but many of them soon became permanent. It was an era of 'chaotic expansion' because besides quick decisions on the government's part, unauthorized constructions became unavoidable. Ever since the 1930s several efforts had been made to improve Delhi's urban space, leading eventually to the institution of the Delhi Municipal Organization Enquiry Committee (DMOEC) in 1946. But the Partition completely overwhelmed the Committee as it lost all its Muslim members and the 'old elite coalition' collapsed. The G.D. Birla Enquiry Committee, which had been set up in 1950 to look into the functioning of the Delhi Improvement Trust to which the DMOEC was answerable, submitted its report in 1951. The Birla Committee recommended private partici-pation in housing and changes in the rent control regulations. More importantly, the 'report provided clear clues to the emerging elite con-sensus on the city's urban design: centralization, an acknowledgement of "social justice" and a "master-plan". There were also traces of classic colonial and bourgeois fears of urban collapse and decay caused by the 'blight' of slums. These were now transposed to the postcolonial burden of governance, confronted by claustrophobic urban space' (Sundaram 2010: 33–34, 92–93).

It has been seen by urban historians like Gupta (2000) and Menon (2000) that with the demand to take care of millions of refugees and the resultant flows of other migrants from within India (largely to be gainfully employed in the housing industry as well as to man the newly expanded government offices) what mattered the most was functional buildings under the political–bureaucratic control that started with the Ministry of Rehabilitation and culminated with the establishment of the DDA. It mattered little that these projects were done at the cost not only of architectural finesse but also loss of interest in Delhi's architectural heritage. In the words of Narayani Gupta:

> This poverty of interest is partly cultural, partly generational.... [The] students born in the 1930s and 1940s had at least some acquaintance with the town's historic architecture. Not things were different from the 1950s. The newcomers' lack of familiarity with Delhi's landmarks, the irrelevance of historic architecture to people building their lives afresh; the habit of associating monuments with rather shabby villages, the inhabitants of which had a different lifestyle from that of the urban dwellers—all these meant an alienation from the monuments. This could have been remedied if students of history and architecture could have been encouraged to take an interest in them but, unfortunately, 'art and architecture' was taught very perfunctorily even at university level, where the nationalist movement and economic history were considered the new frontiers. (Gupta 2000: 159)

# East Pakistani Refugees (1971): Challenge for Indian Politics

During the entire 1970s when the massive refugee flow from East Pakistan was causing serious humanitarian and economic concern for India there were two additional concerns also, one related to the communal question and the other to the potential ideological threat. India knew too well that increasingly more and more Hindus constituted the refugee flow, which by the end of 1971 had reached the ratio of 82:18, a fact that The Central Intelligence Agency and US Consulate at Dhaka too had reported to the Nixon government (Bass 2013: 154, 236–37, Raghavan 2013: 76, 120, 206). Had India made this information public, it would have caused serious communal tensions in India to the extent of even causing Hindu–Muslim riots. Not only did the Indira Gandhi government keep this state secret very close to its chest, it even thought it prudent to share this anxiety with the Jana Sangh leader Atal Behari Vajpayee. She requested him not to politicize the issue, for otherwise it would give Pakistan a handle to portray the problem of refugees as a Hindu–Muslim one, thereby defeating the Indian policy aimed at the probable return of the refugees to East Pakistan (Raghavan 2013: 76).

The second set of anxieties was in respect of the spectre of either a united, Left and pro-China Bengal, or, a further incentive to the ongoing Naxalite/Maoist threat to the politics of West Bengal in particular and to the Indian state in general. That both the concerns were intertwined was common knowledge. The fear was confined to not only the Jana Sangh whose leader Balraj Madhok had warned that 'East Pakistan is going to get out of Pakistan and West Bengal is going to get out of India, perhaps Assam would also get out of India... [T]he Russian and Chinese mind is working along with these lines' but also in the highest echelons of the Indian government. The only difference was that in the case of the latter, threat perception did not include the Russians. Against the background of a serious Naxalite insurgency that had rocked West Bengal since 1967, such a fear was not baseless. P.N. Haksar, Indira Gandhi's principal adviser, had noted that 'with our own difficulties in West Bengal the dangers of a link-up between the extremists in the two Bengals are real [... and the refugee problem] constitutes a grave security risk which no responsible government can allow to develop'. Even the Bangladesh government-in-exile was worried that if India delayed in the liberation of Bangladesh, popular disaffection would grow in East Pakistan, leading to the Awami League being supplanted by the revolutionaries which would receive active help from the Chinese (Bass 2013: 43–44, 188–90, Raghavan 2013: 56, 77).

# Refugees and Pakistan's Islamic Nationalism

The large-scale migration of Muslims to Pakistan massively influenced the politics of Pakistan. The impact of both the Muhajirin and the East Punjabi refugees on the politics of Pakistan was significant. In pre-Bangladesh Pakistan, the Muhajirin constituted about 10 per cent of the country's population. The circumstances under which Pakistan was created and the nature of pre-partition Muslim politics were such that it had earned for them a unique status and purpose which is otherwise denied to any immigrant community, the most notable exception being the immigrant Jews of Israel. The Muhajirin figured prominently in the Muslim League, which had spearheaded the Pakistan movement. In 1946–47, 10 out of 23 members of the party's Working Committee belonged to the future provinces of Pakistan, but in December 1947, when the council of the All India Muslim League met in Karachi, 160 out of 300 of its members were Muhajirin (Waseem 1994: 102).

Comprising relatively better-educated people, members of the ICS, members of the Indian Army, and noted businessmen, the Muhajirin constituted a political force to reckon with. About three-quarters of the so-called 'twenty-two families', which once controlled Pakistan economy, were from this community. This was largely possible, one, because of the exodus of economically influential Hindus and Sikhs to India, and two, because of migration of economically influential Muslims from India to Pakistan. In West Pakistan as a whole, 80 per cent of industrial firms were owned by them. In Karachi, they owned 80 per cent of landed property and foreign trade almost entirely. In Lahore, out of 215 factories they had owned as many as 167.[9] Insofar as the other story is concerned, one may mention the migration of Habib, Adamjee and Saigol families to Pakistan. Mohammad Ali Habib of Gujarat had founded the first Muslim-owned bank in the Indian subcontinent in 1941 called Habib Bank. He reportedly had presented a blank cheque to Jinnah to finance Pakistan's initial expenses till the time India settled its dues in which Jinnah reportedly put a figure of Rs. 80,000,000. Two other families mentioned above, Adamjees and Saigols belonged to Calcutta having huge stakes in jute and rubber industries. The Saigols built Pakistan's second textile mill (Cohen 2004: 49–50).

Muhajirin influence was not confined to the economy alone. About 60 per cent of the officialdom of new Pakistan belonged to this 10 per cent minority (Vakil 1950, Waseem 1994: 109, Wright 1975). An early 1960s survey showed that 34.5 per cent of the public servants belonged to the refugee communities, and of the 3,121 of them 1,764 belonged to UP, Delhi and East Punjab. Although the Urdu-speaking refugees constituted only 3 per cent of the total refugee population, they captured about one-fifth of all seats in the Central Superior Services examination (Waseem 1994: 109). This indirectly contributed to the bureaucrat–army nexus of the future, though with the passage of time Muhajirin-controlled officialdom became Punjabi controlled. This nexus started off with refugee relief. Since the task was stupendous, and the political leadership was not experienced enough to deal with, it largely fell on the shoulders of bureaucrats and young army officers 'which propelled them to the new state's center stage' (Cohen 2004: 47).

Besides, as the Muhajirin came mostly from urban centres of India, they contributed to the rapid urbanization of Pakistan, which was one of the fastest in the developing world. Because of this factor, their influence in Pakistan politics became all the more visible (Burki 1973: 148–67). This point, however, has been contested to some extent by Waseem, who argues that 'the refugees were far from a monolithic group. Instead, both their disparate origins in various regions of India and then the pattern of their dispersion over whole of Pakistan make them [a] highly differentiated group. A large majority among them came from East Punjab who thus shared their political experience with those from West Punjab.' But Waseem agrees that since the refugees settled mostly in urban centres they dictated the way Pakistan's politics should move. 'By 1951, Karachi, Hyderabad, Gujranwala, Faisalabad, Sargodha and Sukhar already had refugee majorities, while in Lahore, Rawalpindi, Multan and Sahiwal refugees accounted for more than 40 per cent of the population. These urban refugees emerged as the support base for the refugee leadership of Muslim League, especially in the non-electoral context of Pakistan's politics'. This 'non-electoral' politics is important to note because on the one hand it gave the Muslim League a handle to work as a pressure group without popular accountability and then on the other prevented local groups to emerge as political actors (Waseem 1994: 103, 108).

The Muhajirin, who had left their original homes in India in search of security and a better future in Pakistan, had naturally a larger stake in the viability of the state. This explains their insistence on strengthening the forces that were supposed to help build Pakistan's unity, namely, Islam, Urdu, and a strong central government. The Muslim League, on account of both its Muhajir leadership and the large following that it had in the community, represented these theories of nation-building. Another party which also strongly represented these ideas was the Jamaat-i-Islami, a party having a large following among the Muhajirin. With the relative decline of the Muslim League, it was this party which attracted the disillusioned Muslim Leaguers the most. Jamaat-i-Islami was originally opposed to the idea of division of India on religious grounds like some of the *ulema* (theologians), but once Pakistan was created it accepted the reality and moved its headquarters from India to Pakistan. It became the most vociferous champion of Islam, opposed all modernist ideas of statecraft and supported the Pakistani establishment in the eastern wing of Pakistan against what they regarded as the Hindu-tainted force of Bengali separatism (Wright 1975: 198).

## Impact on Punjab Politics

As noted in the previous chapter, West Punjab had seen to it that it hosted primarily the refugees from East Punjab and not from the other areas of India. It had two impacts: one, the number of Punjabis increased substantially in the state, which was in any case the most populous state of West Pakistan, and two, because of the vast lands vacated by the fleeing Hindus and Sikhs, the East Punjabi Muslim refugees were overcompensated, leading to their unexpected prosperity. Almost one-third of the population of Punjab now consisted of refugees. This growth in the population of Punjab had the inevitable impact on the confidence of Punjabis vis-à-vis other ethnic groups in the politics of the nation, more particularly in West Pakistan. It sharpened the ethnic divides leading to the emergence of the Punjabis as the most dominant community to the detriment of the interests of refugees from UP and Bihar, as we will see in the following section.

So far as the economic prosperity of the Punjabi refugees was concerned, the following figures will speak for themselves. The Muslim refugee lands vacated in East Punjab accounted for 3.4 million hectares, but the Hindu/Sikh lands vacated in West Punjab accounted for 6.6 million hectares, almost double. Moreover, prior to the Partition, the Hindu and Sikh communities had a large share in the urban and industrial estates. They owned 80 per cent of the industrial capital and

75 per cent of the urban immovable properties. Allotments of these evacuee properties made the refugees rich overnight. This indeed led to some tensions between the local Punjabis and the refugee Punjabis, but in overall terms it helped the Punjabis to become the most powerful community in Pakistan politics (Jalal 2014: 266–67, 278, Waseem 1994: 107). The fact that there was no dislocation in the cultural life of the Punjab and the fact that more people now spoke the language in comparison to other linguistic groups in West Punjab also helped. On the flip side, it brought them in conflict with the Bengali linguistic group, as we will discuss below.

## Impact on Sind Politics

The other group of refugees consisted of Muslims from UP, Bihar, Rajasthan, Mumbai and other parts of India. Since there was no proper exchange of properties in case of these people, and since many of them were urban-based—professionals, government servants and businessmen— they preferred to settle in urban areas, which provided better opportunities. Their natural choice was, therefore, Karachi, which was not only the commercial and financial centre of the region from even the British days, but which also had become the capital of Pakistan. The Muhajirin who settled in Karachi did not speak the local Sindhi language. Most of them spoke Urdu, although some were Gujarati, Marathi and other language-speaking people. Since Urdu became the national language of Pakistan, these refugees developed a sense of superiority vis-à-vis the local Sindhi-speaking people. This created an animosity between the Muhajirin and the Sindhis more so because Karachi was taken out of the Sind province in 1948 to be declared as a centrally administered area in the teeth of protests from the Sindhi leaders (Jalal 2014: 148–51).

As the process of the Muhajir migration was slow but steady, unlike its Punjabi counterpart, it remained a constant source of conflict emanating from the Sindhi anxiety that they were being outnumbered in their own homeland. The cumulative effect of these two different processes was that while on the one hand it created cleavages between the Muhajirin and Sindhis, on the other it made Punjabis the dominant community, which neither the Muhajirin nor the Sindhis relished. Soon the government statement that Karachi was 'full', particularly against the background the Nehru–Liaquat Pact, was interpreted as suggestion to encourage the Muhajirin to return to India; indeed 95,000 had registered to return to India. But the inflow of refugees did not stop (Zamindar 2008: 170–74).

The cumulative effect of the two processes, the Punjabi and Muhajir migrations, was that on the one hand it created a cleavage between the Muhajirin and the Sindhis, on the other hand, it made Punjabis the dominant community, which neither the Muhajirin nor the Sindhis relished. According to a Pakistani scholar:

> Punjabis in Pakistan have generally developed a strong outward-orientation in terms of identifying themselves with larger entities both present and past. For example, Punjabis have all along felt nostalgic about the Delhi-based Moghul imperium of the past, upheld the cause of Urdu and operated along concentric identities of Punjab, Pakistan and the Muslim world. Other communities of Pakistan, including the Sindhis, Baluchis and ironically, Muhajirin—who largely shared political attitudes of the Punjabis till the emergence of the MQM in 1984—have often challenged the pre-eminent position of Punjab and sought to carve out a political space for themselves through pressure, bargaining and occasionally armed struggle. Out of the land brought under irrigation by the Ghulam Mohammad Barrage, 0.87 million out of 1.48 million acres were allotted to the serving and retired civil and military officers, a vast majority of whom belonged to Punjab. Not surprisingly, the Sindhi nationalists consider the Punjabis as grabbers of vast agricultural lands along river Indus and accuse them of expansionist designs. The MQM leadership also accused Punjab of pursuing plans to turn Karachi into its satellite. (Waseem 1999)

It may be argued that one of the reasons for the failure of democracy in Pakistan was the emasculation of the Muhajir power in Pakistan's politics. After the military takeover of Pakistan under the leadership of General Ayub Khan, there was a nexus among the military, feudal, Islamic, Punjabi and Sindhi interests at the cost of the Muhajirs' political strength (Hassan 2006: 67–68).

## The Flashpoint Karachi

The impact of migrations is most visibly felt on the life of Karachi, the commercial hub of Pakistan. The city is frequently in turmoil and inter-ethnic riots are common. On account of migrations both from other parts of Pakistan and from India, Bangladesh and Afghanistan, the population of the city has increased by leaps and bounds during the last seven decades. In the 1940s, it grew by 160 per cent. The massive increase in the population, which the economy of the city has found difficult to absorb, has resulted in civil disturbances and dislocation of normal life. According to the Human Rights Commission of Pakistan, during 1995 there were 31 days of industrial strikes and 2,000 industrial units were closed down. The net loss to the economy was to the tune of ₹25,000,000 (Waseem 1998: 277–78). During the latter half of the 1990s, about 2,000 people died every year on account of social strife. In the first eight months of 2011, more than 1,400 people were killed, according to the Human Rights Commission of Pakistan (http://www.pri. org/stories/2012-01-19/2011-brings-violent-and-bloody-year-ethnic-conflict-karachi-pakistan, accessed on 8 January 2016).

The growth of both Sindhi nationalism and Muhajir militancy can be directly attributed to the refugee question. The Sindhi leader G.M. Syed, whose faction had broken away from the Muslim League, had openly espoused the cause of an independent Sindhudesh. The factors which contributed most to this separatist demand were (a) the separation of Karachi from the province of Sindh in 1948 as the capital of Pakistan, (b) the discriminatory attitude of the Punjabi-Muhajir-ruling elite in the distribution of irrigated lands, (c) the marginalization of Sindhi language and cultural heritage and (d) the centralization strategy in favour of the Punjabis enshrined in the One-Unit policy.[10] According to the 1981 census, the Sindhi population had accounted for 55.7 per cent in the province, 36.3 per cent in urban Sind and only 3.8 per cent in Karachi. The controversial 1998 census largely kept the ratio intact (Waseem 2002: 4537, also see Rahman 2002: 4556–60). According to a recent estimate, pending the results of the 2011 census Pakistan has experienced a massive population growth since 1998. By adding 62,700,000 people, it now stands at 197,400,000, of which Karachi has a large share. Between 1998 and 2011, Karachi grew from 9,800,000 to 21,200,000. No city in the world has ever grown so massively in such a short span of time (Cox 2012: 1, 4–5). This growth can largely be attributed to Pashtoon, Balochi and Punjabi migrations. The phenomenon has further marginalized the Sindhi political voice as well as blunted the edge of Muhajirin politics.

In the aftermath of the Soviet intervention in Afghanistan, a large number of Afghan refugees arrived in Karachi, which resulted in a gun culture the city politics had not experienced earlier. In the beginning, it was confined to student politics but with the launch of the Muttahida Qaumi Movement (MQM) in 1984, which grew out of the All Pakistan Mohajir Students Organization, Muhajir-Pashtoon riots became more institutionalized, as was evidenced in the riots of 1985–86. In the Karachi municipal elections of 1987, the MQM's victory was largely attributed to its capacity to take its violent politics against the Pashto-speaking

Pashtoons in the city. Some sort of 'armed clientelism' (of Latin American vintage) started ruling the roost. The situation worsened as the MQM gained its victories in municipal, provincial and national elections, which instead of injecting sanity in politics contributed to further political and ethnic polarizations. So much so that according to the 2011 report of the Human Rights Commission of Pakistan even ambulances were targeted and hospitals selectively admitted patients on ethnic considerations (Gayer 2012: 81).

# Impact on East Pakistan Politics

In our discussion in the context of Muhajirin in Pakistan's politics (see pp. 78–80), we noted how this community massively influenced the country's national politics in the formative years. To recapitulate some basic facts, many top leaders of the Muslim League belonged to this community, which included no less important leaders than Mohammad Ali Jinnah and Liaquat Ali Khan. Among the industrial leaders of Pakistan, many belonged to such business communities of western India as Memons, Khojas and Bohras. In fact, about three-quarters of the so-called 'twenty-two families' who were said to control Pakistan's economy were from outside of Pakistan. In this context, the role of Jamaat-i-Islami is relevant. As noted above, the party was originally opposed to the Pakistan movement. But post Pakistan it became the most vociferous champion of Islam and Urdu, which according to the party was the fulcrum of the new state. It fully supported the West Pakistan military establishment in suppressing the Bengali uprising in East Pakistan (Wright, Jr. 1975: 189–205, see also Ghosh 1989: 16–37).

The conflict of interest between the Bengali-speaking Muslims and their Urdu-speaking counterparts, however, did not start immediately after the creation of Pakistan. In the euphoria of Muslim victory in dividing India, there was a period of bonhomie between the two communities. Against the background of many anti-Muslim riots in Bihar in the pre-Partition days, the East Bengali leader and the future prime minister of Bangladesh, Sheikh Mujibur Rahman, toured around Bihar and encouraged Muslims to migrate to East Bengal to be safe and secure. After the Partition when the Pakistani government introduced several rehabilitation schemes for them, Bengalis welcomed them (Hashmi 1996: 4). But this honeymoon was for a short time. By 1951 their parting of the ways was clearly on the cards.

Besides the Biharis' association with the 'colonial' Muhajirin–Punjabi ruling clique in West Pakistan and their whole-hearted support to Jinnah's call to declare Urdu as the national language of the state,[11] the way the Biharis started controlling small businesses in East Pakistan and government jobs further distanced them from the Bengalis. Since the Biharis did not belong to agricultural communities, they settled in urban areas, as the Muhajirin did in Karachi and other towns in Sind, which facilitated the process.

> The Pakistani ruling and business elites successfully hegemonized the 'Bihari' mass consciousness by distributing a few favours—jobs in mills and factories, railways and postal departments and cheap housing in several 'refugee colonies' in Dhaka and elsewhere in the province, concentrating them in ghettos and isolating them from the Bengali. Pakistani elites and their Urdu-speaking junior partners in East Pakistan exploited 'Bihari' loyalty to Pakistan regarded by many as their 'promised land'. They often regarded them [the Bengali Muslims] as 'semi Hindus', pro-Indian and disloyal to Pakistan. (Hashmi 1996: 6)

The Biharis of East Pakistan played almost an identical role in the politics of the province more or less as a B Team of the Muhajirin. Their political impact expressed itself through the display of their superiority over East Bengali Muslims, though they formed a small minority in the province. This superiority complex was possible because they could identify their interests with those of the Muhajirin and Punjabis of West Pakistan, particularly through their emphasis on Urdu as the national language which the Biharis spoke as their mother tongue. The love of Bengalis for their mother tongue Bengali came in direct conflict with the Biharis on this count. The *Bhasha Andolan* (language movement) of 1952 in East Pakistan, which was the first sign of Bengali separatism (the section on nationalist movement in the National Museum of Bangladesh in Dhaka starts with pictorial memories of this *Bhasha Andolan*) highlighted this cleavage.

By the mid-1950s, certain trends in East Pakistan politics widened the cleavage. This was revealed in the provincial election of 1954. The early abolition of the zamindari system in East Pakistan had created a new class of leadership the values and outlook of which were quite different from those of the League landowners. The 1954 election brought together this new class and the League outcasts (H.S. Suhrawardy and A.K. Fazlul Huq) as the United Front, which effectively destroyed the League in East Pakistan. In order to cope with the challenge, the Muslim League in West Pakistan took recourse to a political strategy which would, on the one hand, give it a status almost interchangeable with the state, and, on the other hand, allow it to shoulder the responsibility of furthering the Islamic ideology. The party tended to propagate a complete identification with Pakistan that it branded any anti-League activity as tantamount to treason. Prime Minister Liaquat Ali Khan declared that the party carried 'more weight than the Parliament'. The existence and strength of the League were 'equal to the existence and the strength of Pakistan', he emphasized (Qureshi 1972–73: 562–63).

The Bengali–Bihari conflict in the 1950s and 1960s often turned violent, in most of which the Biharis were on the receiving end. Hashmi's essay (1996) gives details thereof, but the important thing that he mentions is that the Bengali Muslim intelligentsia, and later the Bangladesh government, often glossed over this. They instead emphasized the Bihari perfidy. He notes that the 15-volume *History of the Freedom Movement of Bangladesh*, in Bengali, and many other writings were 'either silent about the massacre of "Bihari" civilians by members of the rebel Bengali troops and civilians or else defensive about Bengalis reacting to "non-Bengali" being armed by the Pakistan army' (Hashmi 1996: 10–11).

During the Bangladesh liberation struggle and more so after the creation of Bangladesh, the Bihari question surfaced prominently. Biharis were often targeted by the Bengali liberation forces for their collusion with the Pakistani military. All these allegations were not true, but a situation of civil war was quite a possibility (Bass 2013: 84–85). As it happens in all such situations, the petty bourgeois social envy and lumpen adventurism came in play at the Bihari lives and properties (Hashmi 1996: 14). As the fall of Dhaka neared, it was feared that the Biharis who were considered to be the collaborators would be massacred by Bengalis. The only hope for both the Pakistani Prisoners of War (POWs) and the Biharis was to obtain a commitment from India that Indian troops would not allow that to happen in accordance with the Geneva Conventions. The United States, which did not shed any tears for the Bengalis when they were being massacred, was now concerned about the fate of the Biharis. Bass writes sarcastically:

> So the United States urged India to prevent retaliation against Biharis and— as India had already pledged to do—treat Pakistani troops humanely under the Geneva Conventions. Of course, Kissinger had shown no such alacrity when the Bengalis were slaughtered; since the Biharis were, in his eyes, Pakistani citizens facing peril from other Pakistani citizens, their protection should not have been an international concern; and the White House was plainly seeking to puncture India's pretence of moral superiority. (Bass 2013: 178)

Following the liberation of Bangladesh, there was a general fear that the Biharis would be targeted by Bengali mobs as they were seen as 'collaborators'. But this did not happen partly because of Mujib's conciliatory statements and partly because of the presence of the Indian Army on the soil of Bangladesh. The latter was responsible for the evacuation of West Pakistani civilians to India, along with the defeated Pakistani army. But after the withdrawal of the Indian Army on 27 January 1972 and reports of conflicts between the Biharis and the Bengalis in several places, most notably in the Bihari enclave at Mirpur, where an equal number from both communities were killed, the inter-communal situation deteriorated. Against this background, neither Mujib nor his administrative machinery were seen to be particularly concerned about the safety and security of the Biharis (Whitaker et al. 1977: 8–10).

Subsequently, through the good offices of India any serious crisis was averted. It was decided, according to the New Delhi Agreement of 28 August 1973, that 'a substantial number of non-Bengalis' in Bangladesh who had 'opted for repatriation to Pakistan' would be exchanged with stranded Bengalis in West Pakistan, if they so desired, plus the Pakistani POWs and civilian internees in India. But while Bangladesh was willing to take back all the 128,000 Bengalis in West Pakistan who wanted to repatriate, Pakistan was not willing to take back all the Biharis. Out of a total of about 700,000 Biharis, 470,000 had opted to be repatriated to Pakistan through the International Red Cross. But Pakistan agreed to repatriate only 83,000 of them, which included 58,000 military men, former civil servants and members of divided families and 25,000 'hardship cases'. This left 350,000 Biharis stranded in Bangladesh, who were technically Pakistani nationals (Whitaker et al. 1977: 16–19).

The Bihari question continued to simmer till the time Pakistan's Senate, in 1985, passed a unanimous resolution to speed up the repatriation of Biharis of Bangladesh. Later, this became one of the major points in the PPP–MQM Pact, which helped Benazir Bhutto to form her government in November 1988. But reports of the imminent arrival of the first contingent of the Biharis sparked off riots in Karachi in early 1989, which soured PPP–MQM relations and jeopardized the pact. Following the political alliance between Nawaz Sharif's Muslim League and the MQM and Sharif's coming to power, the Bihari question was reopened in 1991 (Weiner 1990: 8–9). After considerable diplomatic wrangling between Bangladesh and Pakistan, an accord was reached in 1992, according to which Pakistan agreed to accept the 'Biharis' as Pakistani citizens. But this could not be implemented due to Sindhi protest. Given the increasing tensions between the Muhajirin and the Pakistani government in later years, the Bihari question did not seem to have an early solution.

The issue of repatriation of stranded Biharis in Bangladesh to Pakistan was intricately enmeshed in the politics of Pakistan. One reason why the 1991 census could not be held was this veritable mine which could destabilize the ethnic balance between the Sindhis and the Muhajirin in Sind. While the latter were all for the immediate repatriation of the Biharis, the Sindhis were tooth and nail opposed to the idea. The MQM of the Muhajirin, headed by Altaf Hussain, did not forego any opportunity to refer to the patriotic service rendered by the Biharis during the Bangladesh war and taunted the Pakistani government for its failure to bring them back to Pakistan. In May 1998, he telephonically addressed a large meeting of Biharis in Dhaka and embarrassed the Nawaz Sharif government by mentioning that the Pakistan defence forces would acknowledge the historical fact that the Biharis fought side by side with them in East Pakistan on all fronts and several thousands of them laid down their lives to safeguard the territorial integrity of Pakistan. As opposed to this, the Sindh Taraqqi Pasand Party feared that once the Biharis were repatriated they would worsen the unemployment problem in the province. It was not willing to buy the logic that the Biharis would be rehabilitated only in the southern parts of the Punjab province. Interestingly, the party maintained that these Biharis were the butchers of innocent Bengalis and, therefore, should not have any place in Pakistan.

For political reasons, it was not possible for Pakistan to take the Biharis back whatever promises it might have made from time to time. It was not possible for Biharis to either migrate to a new land or integrate socially and culturally with the new society. An opinion survey conducted by the Young Researchers Forum in the late 1990s in the Dhaka Camps found that 59 per cent of the interviewees identified themselves as Bangladeshi, while 35 per cent saw themselves as Pakistani; only 6 per cent thought of themselves as belonging to both the nations. A later report by an organization called Stranded Pakistanis Youth Rehabilitation Movement claimed that the so-called Biharis were always bona fide Bangladeshi nationals and they should be recognized as such. Eventually in 2008 Bangladesh granted them Bangladeshi citizenship, but as we have noted in Chapter 1 about 80 per cent accepted the offer, mostly belonging to the younger generation.

The problems regarding the Biharis or 'stranded Pakistanis' in Bangladesh are certainly not over. The tragic deaths of 10 people in a Bihari camp in Dhaka's Mirpur in early June 2014 might have been an isolated incident but the core problems of their 'repatriation' to Pakistan or their actual 'rehabilitation' continue to haunt the nation. They are still living in subhuman conditions in camps across the country, and many of them still think that Pakistan is their 'homeland', despite the voting rights that they have got through a Supreme Court intervention. Pakistan, under all regimes, has dodged the Biharis in Bangladesh despite their unconditional loyalty to Pakistan to the extent of brutalizing the Bengalis during the liberation war in 1971. Even in 2013, during the violent campaign across Bangladesh by the Jamaat-i-Islami, aided by the BNP, against the Awami League government to thwart the ongoing war crimes trials, many Biharis reportedly took the side of the 'anti-liberation' elements. The divide, therefore, between the mainstream Bengalis and the Biharis continues to persist. Neither the Bengalis trust the Biharis nor the vice versa. The political use of the Biharis by the Jamaat and the BNP is a reality, and the fact that the important Bihari camps belong to the Islamists could further complicate the scenario (based on the author's correspondence with Haroon Habib, a senior journalist of Bangladesh, June 2014).

# J&K Refugees in the Politics of Azad Kashmir/Pakistan

Azad Kashmir, or POK (as it is called in India), was created on 24 October 1947, two days before the accession of the state of J&K to the Indian Union on 26 October 1947. In the Jammu province of the state, because of the volatile mixed demography of its districts, Hindu–Muslim tensions were brewing from the time the Partition of India plan was announced. It led to the so-called 'massacre' of 200,000 Muslims in the Muslim-minority districts and the resultant exodus of Poonchis and Mirpuris, which triggered the formation of Azad Kashmir. Why Pakistan did not make use of this fact that even prior to the accession there was Azad Kashmir? Christopher Snedden, the Australian politico-strategic analyst who has worked extensively on the period and on Azad Kashmir in particular (Snedden 2013), tried to answer this question during the release ceremony of his book in New Delhi:

> At the time, the Pakistan government was heavily involved trying to establish Pakistan; they didn't have the capacity to find out and report what had happened…. The government in Azad Kashmir claimed to be government of all of Kashmir, but naturally they only controlled a little area. And

Pakistan wanted all of Jammu and Kashmir and believed that by saying 'we accept Azad Kashmir government as a liberated area', it would weaken their claim to the whole area. (Bhattacharya 2013)

The issue of Kashmiri refugees continued to figure in the political discourse of Azad Kashmir in particular and that of Pakistan in general. Refugee votes were constantly manipulated by the Pakistani state to scuttle the democratic process in Azad Kashmir. Though there is no clear definition of a refugee in Pakistan, still in the context of Azad Kashmir he is a J&K state subject (for the definition of 'state subject', see Note 6 of Chapter 1) who has moved, or fled, from J&K to Pakistan since 1947. These refugees who were scattered all over Pakistan, besides of course in Azad Kashmir, were entitled to vote for the Azad Kashmir assembly, often to the disadvantage of the Azad Kashmir-based refugees, although they were in a larger number. It so happened that the scattered refugees sent a disproportionately large number of elected members to the state assembly. Being located in the federal states of Pakistan, the mainstream Pakistani politicians found it handy to influence their votes, thereby influencing the deliberations in the Azad Kashmir assembly. In the party-less election of 1961 held under the Basic Democracy scheme of Ayub Khan, voters from Azad Kashmir's population of 1,065,000, elected 1,200 Basic Democrats, while 109,000 Jammu refugees and 10,000 Kashmir Valley refugees elected 600 each, that is 1,200. Though this anomaly was to some extent removed, as was evident in the elections of 1996, 2001 and 2006, refugees from the Kashmir Valley continued to have the advantage vis-à-vis their Jammu counterparts, probably as a strategy to show solidarity with the Kashmiris in the Indian J&K (details in Snedden 2013: 121-36).

# Afghan Refugees/Migrants and Pakistan Politics

We have noted in the previous chapter the details of Afghan refugee arrivals in Pakistan following the Soviet intervention in Afghanistan in December 1979. Without reiterating those facts, it may be mentioned here that the Afghan refugees indirectly provided a major advantage to the regime of Zia-ul Haq, which already had ensured the American support for its continuation in power through the massive military and economic assistance as a frontline state in America's war in Afghanistan. On the one hand, the refugees were potential *mujahedeen* (freedom fighters) who the Americans needed, on the other hand their Islamism came handy to Zia for furthering his Islamic cause meant to perpetuate his political dominance. He had reasons, therefore, to welcome the refugees. Zia effectively used both Islam and the traditional code of Pushtunwali to justify his giving refuge to millions of Afghan refugees. In Islamic tradition, the migration of Prophet Mohammad and his companions from Mecca to Medina in 622 CE to avoid persecution known as *hijrat* (migration) has huge respectability and as such the Afghan refugee influx served as a boon to Zia's Islamic diatribe. Since most of the Afghan refugees who crossed the Durand Line were Pashtoons, the Pashtoon traditions of *melmastia* (hospitality) and *panah* (refuge) came into play to suit the situation well (Ghufran 2011: 948).

Following 9/11, which resulted in the collapse of the Taliban regime, once again there was an exodus of Afghan refugees. The US-led bombing campaign that started in October 2001 not only led thousands of Pashtoons to take refuge in Pakistan in a fresh wave but also affected the process of UNHCR-sponsored repatriation drive. For several ethnic and political reasons, the Pashtoon, Tajik, Uzbek and Hazara refugees sheltered in Pakistani and Irani camps refused to go back. Throughout the first decade of the 21st century, it was a difficult task for both the Pakistan government and the UNHCR to manage the Afghan refugee problem as all policies seemed to fail to repatriate them. Many of them went back to Afghanistan only to come back again as the situation there was not conducive for peaceful existence and also to take advantage of the financial incentive provided by the UNHCR for their return (Ghufran 2011: 948-53).

## Bangladeshi Migrants and Assam Politics

Assam has traditionally been a migrant-receiving region because of its chronic labour shortage and resource affluence, including fertility of its soil. Since the plains of Assam are fertile and hills are climatically conducive to tea plantation, labour migrations to the area have taken place even before the beginning of the 20th century. Assam, which broadly connoted the entire north-east India during the British times, traditionally served as the bridge between two regions of Asia, South and Southeast, resulting in all kinds of migratory flows which made the region ethnically diverse. There were several migratory routes, for example, the Assam-Burma in the east through Cachar-Manipur, the Patkai route from the north-east facilitating the Ahom and other Tibeto-Burmans, the hill passages of Bhutan, Tibet and Nepal, and the valleys of the Ganga and Brahmaputra allowing Aryan migrations to Pragjyotisha-Kamrupa (Goswami 2014: 52).

In the wake of the Bangladesh liberation war, millions of East Pakistanis took refuge in India, many of them in Assam. Not all of them returned to Bangladesh after its liberation. On the contrary, there was a constant inflow of Bangladeshis throughout the 1970s largely on account of the deteriorating economic and communal situation in Bangladesh. The magnitude of the flow came to sharp focus when the Indian Election Commission released the electoral lists for the state in 1979 on the eve of the 1980 parliamentary election (Baruah 1986: 201-7, Kar 1986: 285-96, Mukherji 2000: 69-73, Pathak 1986: 106-24, Weiner 1990: 157-58). The All Assam Students Union (AASU), which had already launched an agitation in 1978 against unauthorized Bangladeshi settlers, now intensified their stir. The statement of C.S. Mullan, the superintendent of census operations in Assam in 1931, was used most effectively by them. The statement was:

> Probably the most important event in the province during the last twenty-five years… has been the invasion of a vast horde of land-hungry Bengali immigrants, mostly Muslims, from the districts of Eastern Bengal and in particular from Mymehsingh…. It is said but by no means improbable that in another thirty years Sibsagar District will be the only part of Assam in which an Assamese will find himself at home.

To arrest this tendency, the Line System was first proposed in 1916 and introduced in 1920 with a view to protect local people from the so-called 'land hungry' Bengali farmers (Kimura 2013: 42). The Assam agitation vitiated the communal atmosphere in the state, which was further worsened by political uncertainties that the state experienced. The most vicious expression of communal hatred was the Nellie massacre of 1983, in which about 2,000 Muslims were killed by Tiwa tribe members, which we will discuss below.[12]

To protect Assam from migrants from even other parts of India, AASU demanded the introduction of Inner Line Permit for their state as well on the pattern of other north-eastern states. The Inner Line Permit system, which was introduced in 1873 by the British, continued to stay even after India's independence. When the Constitution of India was being framed, the Gopinath Bordoloi Subcommittee on North East Frontier (Assam Tribal and Excluded Areas) of the Constituent

Assembly had recommended its retention because the tribal regions wanted it, although he had remarked tongue-in-cheek that the system would preserve these communities 'as anthropological specimens'. Ever since, not only the system survived, it also enrolled new champions from some sections of the Assamese people, most notably the AASU and the Assam Gana Parishad (AGP). They argued that Assam too should have the system to prevent migrations form other parts of India and beyond. Similar demands were there in Meghalaya too.[13] Those states which had it in place, namely, Nagaland, Mizoram and Arunachal Pradesh, steadfastly wanted to retain the system. Politically the most powerful student organization of Mizoram, the Mizo Zirlai Pawl, even opposed any move to put the Mizo language in the Eighth Schedule of the Indian Constitution that enumerated the national languages of India because it feared that such a move could be the prelude to the erosion of the Inner Line system. Whether the system has actually prevented illegal immigration as well as encroachments into the tribal lands by people from outside the region, however, is a moot point. Taking advantage of the legal loopholes in the system, political and bureaucratic corruption, social networking and matrimonial relationships people from outside the North East have managed to settle in the Inner Line areas. Probably the only achievement of the system is that it has created 'the lines of exclusion and inclusion between communities more volatile and conflict inducing' by sharpening the insider–outsider divide (Goswami 2014: 110-12).

## The Nellie Massacre

Against the background of cut-throat politics accentuated by unprecedented electoral violence during the assembly elections as well as elections to 12 parliamentary seats that had remained vacant from the previous elections, the Nellie massacre took place. On 18 February 1983, just on that one day, the Tiwa tribes people and other scheduled castes and lower caste Assamese killed 2000 Muslims of East Bengali origin in the neighbouring village who had settled there for generations. In the post-independence India, this was the first riot that involved villagers only, which questioned the theory that riots took place only in urban and semi-urban areas (Kimura 2013: 22, 28-29, the Bhagalpur anti-Muslim riot of 1989 was the second such case). If the immediate catalysts were such rumours as Muslims had abducted the Hindu/tribal girls, the larger backdrop was the Assam anti-foreigners agitation that called for the boycott of assembly elections and the Muslims' participation therein in defiance of the boycott call. The issue of alienation of tribal land by the Muslim peasants and their success in raising the agricultural production in those lands provided the larger justification for the attacks. Nellie was a case apart because here the perpetrators of the crime and the victims continued to coexist in the area which does not normally happen. By far the most authentic study on the subject by Japanese scholar Makiko Kimura (2013) says that in the beginning Muslims were afraid to talk about what happened to them, fearing further reprisals against the backdrop of the general anti-foreigner temper, but over time they developed courage to speak out. But what they mostly preferred to talk about was regarding the meagre compensations given to them compared to other riot victims elsewhere in the country. Even the local Tiwas and other Hindu peasants who actually were the killers were benefitting more from the government aid, they alleged. The riots helped in the formation of Tiwa identity which later came in conflict with the larger Assamese identity, as reflected in the anti-foreigners agitation. The All Tiwa Students' Union, which came into being in 1989, demanded district autonomy on the lines of other such demands.

Drawing from the theories of memory reconstruction, it is argued that we use our mental images of the past to solve our present problems and in the process our conceptions of the past get influenced. Some minorities who refuse to assimilate with the majority group develop their theories of the past to highlight their separate social existence. In the case of Assam, where most of its indigenous ethnic groups fall in the minority category, the Muslims of East Bengali origin, although also a minority community, are reluctant to highlight this element because of their tenuous existence.[14] It was only lately that the Assam United Democratic Front (AUDF),[15] a Muslim political party, started asking for its political space in the state politics which many Muslims endorsed as the assembly elections of 2006 revealed. It won 10 seats (in 2011, it improved its record by winning 18 seats). One of the demands of the AUDF was the publication of the Tewary Commission Report that looked into the causes of the Nellie riot.

## Politics of IMDT, 1983

It is important to understand both the antecedents and its import of the Illegal Migrants (Determination by Tribunals) (IMDT) Act, 1983. According to the AASU, 1951 should be the cut-off date for the eviction of foreigners. It had proposed that the National Register of Citizens for Assam, a document prepared by census enumerators from the census slips of 1951, should be employed as the basis for ascertaining the identity of migrants who came to Assam after 1951. The argument of the central government was that the cut-off date for the same purpose should be 1971. Though the Constitution of India under Article 5 said that no person who did not have domicile in India at the commencement of the Constitution could be a citizen of India, thereby declaring that all persons who came to India after 26 January 1950 were not citizens of India, Article 11 had empowered the Parliament to make law for the acquisition of citizenship by birth, descent, registration or naturalization. Therefore, a person who entered India after 26 January 1950, and who did not acquire citizenship under any of the provisions of the Indian Citizenship Act, 1955, was to be considered a foreigner (Kimura 2013: 64). This was the bone of contention between the anti-foreigners movement activists and the central government.

Following the dissolution of the 1978-elected Assam government in March 1982, there was virtually political anarchy in the state. The President's rule that was imposed had to be extended for another term of six months. After the expiration of 12 months, therefore, there was no option other than holding the assembly elections, though the Election Commission knew that the situation was not conducive for the exercise. With severe restrictions to press freedom and under the general atmosphere of fear and suspicions, the elections were held in the early months of 1983. Since major political parties opposed to the Congress boycotted the elections, though the latter had brought to power a Congress (I) government led by Hiteshwar Saikia, it was hardly representative. Still, Indira Gandhi's Congress (I) in power at the centre took advantage of the situation to claim complete authority over the question of citizenship and passed the IMDT Act, 1983. The idea was to underscore the point that in the controversy over the citizenship question of so-called foreigners in Assam, it was the centre which would call the shots. The IMDT Act was a departure from the Foreigners Act of 1946 in two basic senses: (a) though a pan-national act, its applicability was restricted to Assam, which had no precedence, and (b) unlike the Foreigners Act, as per the IMDT Act the burden of proof to establish one's nationality rested not on the person concerned but with the state. This departure from the norm was critical. People sympathetic to the Assam movement suspected that the state sympathized with the Muslim immigrants. The Government argued that it was meant to safeguard Assamese Muslim citizens from unnecessary harassments by immigration authorities. In any case, the task before the state was so humongous that its failure was preordained.

In August 1985, the Assam Accord was signed between the AASU and the Government of India, which addressed the problem in more general terms. Since the AASU demand that all 'foreigners' who had arrived in India after 1951 should be evicted was considered impractical, it was decided that 25 March 1971 would be the cut-off date. All those who had arrived after that date would be repatriated. With regard to those who came between 1 January 1966 and 24 March 1971, it was provided that they would continue to stay in India but would become full citizens with voting rights only after 10 years. As expected, neither IMDT nor Assam Accord delivered results. Even after a decade, there was little evidence of illegal foreigners being actually identified and repatriated. According to information furnished by the Government of Assam, till August 1993, the progress in respect of detection of illegal migrants (those who entered Assam on or after 25 March 1971) was as follows:

| | | |
|---|---|---|
| i) | Enquiries taken up for investigation | 2,88,103 |
| ii) | Enquiries completed | 2,37,511 |
| iii) | Cases referred to Tribunals | 25,445 |
| iv) | Cases disposed of by Tribunals | 12,011 |
| v) | Persons detected to be illegal migrants | 8,871 |
| vi) | Illegal migrants expelled | 1,219 |

*Source: Muslim India (1994: 406).*

The 1991 census data (there was no census in Assam in 1981 due to the disturbed situation) tended to suggest that the foreigners' problem had been exaggerated which came to the political advantage of the then Chief Minister of Assam, Hiteshwar Saikia. As he had a strong following among the Muslims, he found the census handy to consolidate that base. Relying on the fact that Assam had registered the lowest population growth (of 5.3 per cent) during the last 20 years, which was one percentage point lower than the national average and much lower compared to the other north-eastern states (Chand & Thakur 1991: 19-23), Saikia refuted the statement of the Union Home Minister S.B. Chavan that illegal migration continued unabated in the state. He said emphatically that 'if anybody can identify a single foreigner in Assam, I am willing to quit politics forever' (*The Times of India*, 22 August 1994), a dramatic claim he himself probably was laughing after making it.

Saikia's claim was seen as an effort to pamper the Muslims for votes, which ignited communal feelings among the Bodo militants. In July 1994, the northern parts of Barpeta district in lower Assam witnessed a series of massacres of Muslim peasants of East Bengal origin, although they had largely been Asamiyaized. Shortly before that the Bodos had killed Muslims in Kokrajhar and Bongaigaon. Although there can be several sociological causes for these anti-Muslim riots, the communalization of the Assam movement was at the core. The movement was essentially controlled by upper caste Hindus. In response, there was the sectarian movement of the Bodos. Caught in between were the unorganized Muslim peasants. To add to their woes was the role played by the Asamiya high caste-dominated vernacular press which consciously wrapped up the Assamese Muslims together with Bangladeshis. Monirul Hussain, a Gauhati University political science professor, lamented:

> Such political socialization in a situation wherein the state has failed to resolve the complex nationality/ethnic question and massive popular discontent, the Muslims have become the most vulnerable social group of repeated violence. Therefore, it would be erroneous to blame the Bodo leaders alone—because wider issues and processes have conjoined in the Barpeta massacre. (Hussain 1995b: 43)

After Saikia's death in early 1996 and the return of the AGP to power, the foreigners' issue surfaced again. Although the AGP and the AASU did not subscribe to the BJP's policy of treating Hindu foreigners as refugees who should be given shelter and their Muslim counterparts as 'foreigners' who should be deported, their criticism against granting voting rights to 670,000 foreigners was enough indication that the pot was still boiling. The demand of the Prafulla Kumar Mahanta-led AGP government of Assam was that the IMDT Act of 1983 should be replaced by the Foreigners Act of 1946, according to which the onus of proving that one was not a foreigner was on the accused, unlike the IMDT Act, according to which the onus was on the state.

Soon, however, the demand was diluted under political compulsions. The AGP itself became ambivalent on the question. Since the replacement of the IMDT Act by the Foreigners Act was opposed by the Assamese Muslims, behind whom stood the Congress party, it was not easy for Mahanta to stick to his guns. Besides, the controversy had reverberations in national politics. The Congress, the CPI, the CPI(M), the Indian Union Muslim League (IMUL) and all supporters of the United Front government were opposed to any change in the situation. Home Minister Indrajit

Gupta, who belonged to the CPI, would commit himself only to the extent that the 'mechanisms for detection and deportation of illegal immigrants need to be strengthened' (Ghosh 2004: 79–80). Against this background, Mahanta found discretion the better part of valour and his favourite phrase became: 'IMDT or no IMDT, we would like to make it clear that the minorities of Assam will not be harassed.' Since the AGP itself had developed cold feet and there was no demand as such from any political quarter except sections of the AGP led by Bhrigu Kumar Phukon and Brindaban Goswami and a few other groups, there was hardly any need for the H.D. Deve Gowda government to alter the legal position with regard to the detection of illegal foreigners. On 26 November 1996, therefore, he categorically ruled out the repeal of the IMDT Act (Ghosh 2004: 80).

Following BJP's coming to power in March 1998, there were some indications that the government might be interested to repeal the IMDT Act. The Governor of Assam, S.K. Sinha, and the BJP President, Kushabhau Thakre, hinted at that. In his report to the Central Government, the Governor said that the IMDT Act was serving the interests of illegal migrants only. Admitting the fact that deportation of illegal migrants was not easy as international law did not provide for unilateral deportation, the report suggested that the IMDT Act should be replaced by another act which should be 'fair, just and transparent, taking into account the legitimate fears of the minorities' (*The Sunday Times of India*, 10 January 1999). But before anything could happen, the government fell following its failure to win a vote of confidence in Parliament in April 1999. In the general elections that were held in September 1999, the issue figured marginally in Assam. The National Democratic Alliance (NDA), which included the BJP most prominently, mentioned only about the territorial integrity of the North East. BJP's earlier promise that once in power it would repeal the IMDT Act did not find any mention in the party manifesto. It may be noted that the BJP had not issued any separate manifesto and was committed only to the NDA's National Agenda. Eventually, in 2005 the Supreme Court scrapped the act as legally untenable (discussed in Chapter 4).

# Issue of Illegal Bangladeshis in Larger National Context

Can the opposition to Bangladeshi Muslim migrations to India be understood from the theories of nativism. In his book *Sons of the Soil*, Myron Weiner (1978) has discussed the idea, which had primarily developed in the United States in the context of local opposition to various ethnic groups that kept migrating to America from various parts of Europe and eastern Asia from the mid-19th to early 20th century. He identified six main ways of explaining the notion, namely, economic competition, threats to social status, political impact, psychological frustrations resulting in aggression, demographic change and, lastly, cultural differentiation (Weiner 1978: 269-70). Of these none really applies to the Bangladeshi situation barring probably the political impact, which we discuss later in the context of Bangladeshis in Delhi.

The question of infiltration of Bangladeshi nationals into India and their penetration into many parts of the country has been used by different political parties for their own interests. It is ritualistic for Hindutva-oriented parties to raise the question during the general elections or those assembly elections where the subject is relevant like Assam, West Bengal and Delhi. The supporters of the BJP have used the issue in conjunction with the rising population of the Muslims in many of its election campaigns. We may take a sample case of Delhi.

# Delhi: A Case Study

Delhi sends seven MPs to the Indian Parliament and 70 members of legislative assembly (MLAs) to the state assembly. The electoral contest is primarily between the Congress and the BJP, though of late the Aam Aadmi Party (AAP) has emerged as a massive force.[16] Historically, the Congress was the dominant force, but since 1989 the BJP has emerged as an equal contender. At present, all the seven parliamentary seats are held by the BJP (2014 elections). In the previous general election (2009), all the seven parliamentary seats went to the Congress. In last two municipal elections, the latest held in April 2012, the BJP had defeated the Congress.

Of all the migrant communities in Delhi, the most contentious is the Bangladeshi community. The number of Bangladeshis in Delhi, however, is an enigma; no one has the correct estimates. One problem is that since Bengali-speaking Muslims from West Bengal and other parts of India get mixed up with them, it is difficult to arrive at an accurate figure, although it is commonly believed that there are about 300,000 Bangladeshis in Delhi. They live in slums and shanty towns located in such areas as Govindpuri, Nizamuddin, Yamuna Pushta, Madanpur Khadar, Okhla, New Seemapuri, Savada Ghevra resettlement colony, Meethapur, Chakkarpur (Gurgaon-Delhi NCR), Nathupur (Gurgaon-Delhi NCR) and many other slum clusters that have come up around middle-class localities which depend on domestic maids and cooks supplied by these migrants. Bangladeshis generally eke out their livelihood through small jobs like rickshaw pullers, domestic help, rag-pickers and casual daily wage earners.

With the changing demographic composition of Delhi, migrants increasingly figure in city politics. As a result, every party tries to compete with the other in identifying itself with one migrant community or the other, particularly by owning up their ethnic markers. In this political tug-of-war, Bangladeshis matter little because they are relatively small in number and often have a tenuous existence. But they matter in certain specific contexts, namely, localized vote-bank politics, Hindu–Muslim communalism and internal–external security dynamics. Had the Delhi-based Bangladeshis been mostly Hindus, probably these dynamics would have played out differently.

There are a very few scholarly studies on the theme, of which two may be mentioned. The first one published in 1995 remains by far the best on the subject, although it was a micro study (Lin & Paul 1995, Paul & Lin 1995, both publications being essentially the same). Although its data are outdated, still they give us a good idea about how to understand and study the politics of Bangladeshi migrants in Delhi. The second study is a doctoral dissertation of University of Delhi which, though recent, lacks rigour in analysing the problem. Still it has generated some useful information from government sources by using the Right to Information Act (RTI) (Nath 2013).

In the 1970s when Indian politics witnessed the Sanjay Gandhi (Indira Gandhi's younger son) phenomenon with its unprecedented activism exerted for making Indians go for sterilization so as to control the population growth of India, Bangladeshis became the softest targets in Delhi, although Muslims in general had been targeted. But unlike other Muslims who protested against the drive on religious grounds, Bangladeshis could not afford to do so as their very stay in Delhi was questionable as most of them had no legal papers. Rather, the incentive that the Delhi administration offered to these unauthorized migrants, ostensibly under political pressure, was attractive enough to agree to sterilization. Tiny plots of land were offered, which not only provided shelters to them but also legitimized their stay in a significant way. These one-time land allotments to the original Bangladeshi immigrants having 'refugee status' became the basis of subsequent authorized concrete houses in such places as New Seemapuri (Paul & Lin 1995: 471). In due course, these people either entrenched their stay in Delhi by acquiring such legitimizing documents as ration or voter cards or sold off their plots at a much higher price to resettle in the Terai region of UP (now in Uttarakhand) and Cooch Behar (West Bengal) to become agriculturists, which was their original occupation. All this was achieved largely through the good offices of Abdullah Bukhari, the Imam of Jama Masjid and one of the influential leaders of India's Muslim population (Paul & Lin 1995: 472-73). As voters Bangladeshis became an important political community which the Congress leader H.K.L. Bhagat used most effectively in his East Delhi constituency where they were in good numbers. Bhagat expanded his support base by enrolling more and more Bangladeshis as voters, resulting in greater confidence among these people. By 1990 there were three Islamic schools in Seemapuri, where one of the teachers was a legal Bangladeshi with valid papers. The pupils there learnt Bengali, Arabic and Urdu (Lin & Paul 1995: 13).

## The Communal Dimension

Bangladeshis, however, had to pay a political price for their voting rights. Soon they got entangled into the communal politics of the city. The 1980s saw the resurgence of Hindu nationalistic politics, which the BJP championed vociferously after its creation in 1984 (details in Ghosh 1989). The political controversy over the Babri Mosque in Ayodhya (UP) assumed militant proportions culminating in its demolition on 6 December 1992 by a Hindu mob spearheaded by the BJP and the RSS. The incident changed the texture of Indian politics. Against this background, the question of Muslim loyalty to the Indian nation became a poll plank for the BJP, and in that context the demand for eviction of all Bangladeshis figured as one of its central platforms. To dramatize the demand in Delhi, Madan Lal Khurana, Delhi's BJP MP, marched to the banks of the Yamuna near Okhla to physically evict the Bangladeshi setters. Though his efforts failed because of resistance from concerned individuals, yet Khurana earned his political dividends. The BJP won the Delhi assembly elections held in November 1993 and Khurana became the Chief Minister (Lin & Paul 1995: 12). He, however, realized before long that administration was a different ball game than street politics. His efforts to drive the 'infiltrators' out from Delhi failed miserably. By mid-1995, keeping an eye on the forthcoming 1996 parliamentary elections, Khurana convinced himself that he must go slow on the matter.

There is a problem in deportation of the Bangladeshis. It is difficult to distinguish between them and the Bengali-speaking Indian Muslims. Moreover, many of the immigrants have acquired all the necessary documents illegally, which prevent their eviction. The court cases of *Abu Hanif* alias *Millan Master v. Police Commissioner of Delhi and Others* and *Abu Hanif* alias *Millan Master v. Union of India and Others*, of 2000 and 2001, respectively, are cases in point. Abu Hanif was an Indian Muslim, yet he was accused of being an alien since he lived among the Bangladeshis. He faced an immediate deportation to Bangladesh. The court, however, gave the verdict in his favour. It was argued by the accused that let there be a tribunal for illegal immigrants and let the provisions of the IMDT Act of 1983 be extended to their case, meaning that the burden of proving their illegality of status should be on the state and not on the person accused of being an alien (Sadiq 2009: 101, 117).

Given the texture of Delhi's politics, Bangladeshis did not seem to have any option other than supporting the Congress both as voters and otherwise. In the late 1980s, they had decided to throw their lot with the Janata Dal, which contributed to the defeat of H.K.L. Bhagat. The coming to power of the V.P. Singh-led National Democratic Front government, however, did not prove to be of any particular benefit to the Bangladeshis. With the collapse of the V.P. Singh government in 1990 and the subsequent installation of the Congress government under the leadership of P.V. Narasimha Rao in 1991, the policy of Operation Pushback was implemented, aimed at evicting all illegal Bangladeshis. Faced with this direct danger, Bangladeshis considered it wise to return to the Congress fold, which worked. The Operation Pushback was abruptly suspended ostensibly on the advice of the Delhi unit of the Congress. Bangladeshis realized how important it was to side with the Congress even when it was in the opposition. The reason for not going ahead with the Operation Pushback was also that it was logistically impossible to deport the Bangladeshis as Bangladesh was unwilling to accept them. The logic of Bangladesh was simple: How can one say they are Bangladeshis, do they have their Bangladeshi passports with them? Also, there are so many such people in India with same tongue and appearance; how can one distinguish between them? There was also another problem. The Government of West Bengal complained that in the name of deporting the Bangladeshis the Central Government was actually dumping thousands of these people on its soil, complicating its already complex migrant/refugee predicament (Lin & Paul 1995: 18-19).

Of late, India has been issuing biometric identity cards to all Indians, called the Unique Identity Cards (UID). The popular understanding of the scheme is that it is meant to certify citizenship to only genuine Indian nationals and weed out the unauthorized ones, most notably the Bangladeshis. But the issue is much more complex. First, because of mass illiteracy, poverty and the magnitude of the task involved, the UID experiment is progressing at the snail's pace. Two, because of an endemic corruption across the board, one is not sure of the enrolments themselves. For example, what are the basic information required to obtain a UID card—proof of date of birth and proof of residence. What are the supporting documents—passport, or, ration and voter cards. Many unauthorized Bangladeshis have acquired the ration as well as voter cards. They are, therefore, potentially eligible for their UID registration. No wonder that the UID card clearly mentions that it 'is proof of identity, not of citizenship'. At the most, UID is something like the American Social Security number which can be issued even to temporary residents. But the critical difference is that in the UID system the actual place of birth can be tampered with but not in the case of Social Security cards. In short, UID is not the solution to the problem of identifying the Bangladeshis, leave alone deporting them. So long as the BJP was in the opposition, one of its constant criticisms of the Congress government was that it was not doing enough to evict the Bangladeshis. But after coming to power in 1998, 1999 and 2014, it realized that discretion was the better part of valour. One has not seen Narendra Modi talking about it.

## Deportation Issue in Larger Context

Broadly speaking, whether it is the central government or the state government, whether it is the election commission or the courts, all have one identical public posture: The illegal Bangladeshis must not figure in the electoral rolls anywhere in India. But when it comes to the play of politics, Muslim Bangladeshi illegal migrants find themselves at greater disadvantage. In the border districts of West Bengal, which have a fairly large migrant Bangladeshi population, the Hindu migrants openly defy such election commission mandates. When the high profile Chief Election Commissioner T.N. Seshan (1990-96) made the headlines by announcing his no-nonsense approach to prevent all unauthorized persons from voting, which essentially meant illegal Bangladeshis, a satirical poem published in a popular magazine in the border district town of Malda in West Bengal ridiculed the diktat in the following words:

### Flop Master Seshan
*Tor tate ki*
*Ami Jodi Bangladeshi hoi*
*Bari amar Rajshahite*
*Indiate roi*
*Jodio ami chakri kori*
*Bangladesher daftarete*
*Nam tulechi Indiate*
*Sheshan ki ar korbere!!*

(How does it matter to you if I am a Bangladeshi, if my house is in Rajshahi and I live in India? Even though I serve in an office in Bangladesh, I have enrolled myself as voter in India and what can Seshan do? [Samaddar 1999: 166]).

In the border regions of West Bengal, all political parties play the politics of vote banks and their modus operandi is often creating disturbances prior to elections, making it impossible for the district authorities to control them. Against this background, illegal migrants are illegally enrolled as voters, making it difficult to distinguish them from genuine Indian citizens. Thus, Seshan wrote in the 9 August 1998 issue of *The Week* magazine that overnight Shahul Hameed became Shailesh Kumar and the local MLA testified that he had known his family as the resident of the area for three generations, which was an act of profane dishonesty (Datta 2004: 345, 351).

In the larger national context, there are two ways of looking at the issue. One, it was the avowed policy of the Hindu nationalistic BJP that it had no problem if the illegal Hindu Bangladeshis were granted voting rights but their Muslim counterparts should have no voting rights (*The Hindu*, 4 January 2011). Two, probably there is an element of guilt complex on the part of the Indian state that emanates from the Partition of the country. A majority Hindu state can ill afford a policy that evicts illegal Hindu migrants and throws them back into the same land which they have deserted. It is not they who had asked for the partition, and then if they have chosen to come to India should not the latter be duty bound to give them shelter? Since Delhi Bangladeshis are mostly Muslims, the danger of their eviction always hangs over their heads as the Sword of Damocles.

## Election of 2014 and the Rise of Modi

Two events, during the election campaign, more or less simultaneous though different in nature and separated from one another by thousands of miles, give us some understanding of the problem of poor

Bengali-speaking Muslims outside of West Bengal getting mixed up with Bangladeshis in popular conception. The first event was when hundreds of shanties in South Delhi were gutted in a massive fire on 28 April 2014, reducing thousands of migrant Bengalis from north Bengal and other parts of West Bengal into destitution. Through my conversations with some of the victims, I found that what was most devastating for them was their loss of their ration and Aadhar cards in the fire. There is a general tendency among non-Bengalis in Delhi and other metropolitan towns to brand all such people as Bangladeshis which Bengali Muslims in such places mortally fear. The only protection they have against such allegations is to flaunt their above cards. Not that there are no Bangladeshis among them and not that some of these cards have been fraudulently earned but the fact remains that all Bengali-speaking poor Muslims in places outside of West Bengal are not necessarily Bangladeshis, a point which assumed political proportions when the Shiv Sena in Mumbai tried to evict the Bengali-speaking Muslims from the city, bringing it in direct confrontation with TMC leader, Mamata Banerjee, then the Railway Minister in the Vajpayee government at the centre. In the aftermath of the Delhi fire incident too, the TMC was in the forefront to take up the cause of rehabilitation of the fire victims. The party's Lok Sabha candidate from South Delhi, Sreerupa Mitra Chaudhury, took interest in the job with the help of the Delhi administration (*The Sunday Times of India*, 4 May 2014).

The other event concerned the massacre of dozens of Bengali-speaking Muslims in Assam's Kokrajhar district in early May 2014 by militants belonging to the Bodoland People's Front. Reportedly these Muslims had backed out from their promise to vote for a Bodo candidate in the ongoing parliamentary election. A contemporary report showed how some of these Muslims who had settled in faraway Lucknow, the capital of UP, felt blessed that they were away from these killing fields, although their living condition was no better than their counterparts in Assam. Notably, like the Bengali Muslims of Delhi discussed above, they also suffered from the same fear of being mixed up as Bangladeshis. Their only security was their vote cards. Though it cost them a lot of money they did not fail to travel to Assam to cast their votes because that was the best way they could prove their Indian nationality. The Magsaysay Award winner Sandip Pandey, who had found the fact for sure that they were Assamese by travelling to those areas, tried to convince the UP government not to evict them as Bangladeshis. The problem was that the UP government could issue them ration cards only when they surrendered their Assam ration cards, which these migrants feared to do keeping the uncertainty in mind (*The Hindu*, 4 May 2014).

It became ritualistic for the BJP to rake up the issue of Bangladeshis in India during elections, particularly in West Bengal and Assam. Speaking in Serampore in April 2014, BJP's prime ministerial candidate, Narendra Modi, dared his rival in the state, Mamata Banerjee, by declaring that the Bangladeshis had better be prepared with their belongings packed by 16 May, the day results of the election were to be declared (Bhaumik 2014). That these threats meant little is known to all who know what happened to similar threats to Bangladeshis in Delhi made by party's leader Madan Lal Khurana in 1993, as we have noted above.

In the aftermath of the 2014 parliamentary election, and keeping the 2016 West Bengal assembly elections in mind, it was also noticed that the BJP and the RSS were playing the SC, ST and OBC cards to highlight the point that ever since the Partition these communities, which were the real victims as refugees, were on the receiving end at the hands of the upper castes, a subject which we have discussed above. According to newspaper reports, the RSS registered a 25 per cent growth in the state since 2013, and it was largely attributable to the support of the backward castes. According to the RSS' South Bengal Unit publicity chief, Jishnu Basu, 'We are concentrating on the living conditions of the SC, ST and OBC people in Bengal. These communities have been most deprived, especially during the last days of the Left Front government and the first three years of the Mamata Banerjee government'. The RSS has expanded in the SC, ST and OBC-dominated areas of South and North 24 Parganas, Nadia and Murshidabad. The BJP has promised to rehabilitate Hindu refugees—especially the numerically strong Matau community, which was one of Mamata Banerjee's assured vote banks—in the border districts of the state. Notably, all this went simultaneously with BJP's tirade against Banerjee's 'Muslim appeasement' (*The Hindustan Times*, 18 and 19 August 2014).

Generally, given the ideological orientation of the BJP, there were clear indications that the Modi government would go soft towards Hindu immigrants from Afghanistan, Pakistan and Bangladesh, or, for that matter, even from a distant country like Fiji. The tone had already been set during the election campaign. Speaking in Assam in February 2014, Narendra Modi had distinguished between Hindu and Muslim refugees: 'We have a responsibility towards Hindus who are harassed and suffer in other countries. India is the only place for them … we will have to accommodate them here'. Some critics, for example, Siddharth Varadarajan of the Shiv Nadar University, picked up the point and said: 'For all the talk about putting India first, this one line shows BJP continues to think of

Hindus as primary constituents of India. Why should a Fijian Indian who happened to be Muslim have any less claim over refuge in India than a Fijian Indian who happened to be Hindu' (*The Hindu*, 9 April 2014). After coming to power, the BJP appeared to be as accommodative as possible towards Hindu refugees. For example, manual submission of citizenship forms was allowed for Hindu refugees from Afghanistan and Pakistan (otherwise only online applications are entertained), and their children were also allowed to apply for citizenship even without holding any passports (*The Times of India*, 14 November 2014).[17] Probably, the Congress government in Assam, not to lose the political game with the BJP in this regard, granted Indian citizenship to about 850,000 refugees in the state who had been living there for 43 years. The majority of them were Bengali-speaking Hindus, which included Rajbongshis and Bishnupriya Manipuris. There were also Buddhists, Garos and Adivasis (*The Times of India*, Kolkata Edition, 17 July 2014).

# The Chakma Question

In Chapter 1, we have discussed why and how a large number of Chakmas and other tribals from the Chittagong Hill Tracts of Bangladesh had to take refuge and later settle down in India's north-eastern states. In this chapter, we will assess the political fallout of these settlements, particularly in the states of Mizoram and Arunachal Pradesh.

# The Mizoram Case

In the 1990s, the question of infiltration of Chakmas into Mizoram became a political issue in the state, particularly when in 1995 the Chakmas of Mizoram submitted a petition to the Rajya Sabha claiming that there were 80,000 indigenous Chakmas in Mizoram and that they were being discriminated against by the Mizoram government. In response to the petition, the Rajya Sabha Committee on Petitions recommended as follows:

1.  In the case of Chittagong Hill Tracts, which is the homeland of the Chakmas, a historical injustice has been done and as such the Chakmas are to be treated differently from other refugees with sympathy and on a humanitarian basis.

2. The Chakma Autonomous District Council may be expanded.
3. The Autonomous District Council, after expansion, may be put under the direct control of the Centre till the time the living conditions of the Chakmas come on par with other inhabitants of the State.
4. The Chakma Autonomous District Council should be allocated more development funds.
5. Chakma refugees who came to Mizoram prior to 25 March 1971 may be granted citizenship.
6. Chakmas who are born in India should be granted citizenship.
7. The Chakmas who are granted Indian citizenship should be declared as belonging to the scheduled tribes.
8. Regarding Chakma refugees who came to the state after 25 March 1971, negotiation may be held between the Government of India and the Government of Bangladesh on the lines of the Indira–Mujib Accord.

All the major political parties of Mizoram, including the then ruling Congress, the opposition Mizo National Front (MNF) and the Mizo Peoples' Conference (MPC), reacted strongly against the recommendations of the committee. They issued statements in the press pledging their lasting opposition to the recommendations. The Young Mizo Association (YMA), which wielded considerable influence on Mizo social and political life, decided to take up the 'foreigners issue' most seriously in its meetings. The MNF(N) resolved that any proposal to set up a separate administrative unit for the Chakmas in Mizoram would be strongly opposed. It sent a telegram to the Union Home Minister in this regard. In 1997, the Government of Mizoram prepared a note to show that the Chakma population had grown at a much faster rate than the state's overall growth rate of population. It pointed out that during the period 1951–61 the decadal growth of the Chakma population in the state was 67 per cent, which was much higher than the state's overall growth rate (Ghosh 2004: 93–94).

The government of Mizoram continued to insist that the Chakma problem in Mizoram was one of illegal infiltration by foreigners and not one of refugees, as was the case in the neighbouring states, mainly Arunachal Pradesh and Tripura. It was a pity that the Rajya Sabha Committee on Petitions considered only the arguments of the Chakmas. It was argued that with all the political parties and major NGOs and student bodies opposing the move, the Chakma issue should be handled with care in order to avoid communal tensions and major law and order problem in the state. It was the constant refrain of the Mizoram government that the actual number of the bona fide Chakmas was much less than claimed by the Chakmas. To increase their bargaining strength, they were including infiltrators as lawful citizens of India in their numbers (the author's discussions with Mizoram government officials in November 1997).

# The Arunachal Pradesh Case

More than Mizoram it is Arunachal Pradesh where the Chakma question has raised a greater political controversy. Ever since the Chakma refugees were sheltered in Arunachal Pradesh (then NEFA), Assam, Meghalaya, Mizoram, Tripura and West Bengal in 1960, it has been an issue in Arunachal Pradesh politics. The Government of India's decision of 1966 could be easily implemented because as NEFA it was a Union Territory (UT) then. But once Arunachal Pradesh became a state in 1987 its identity, as guaranteed in the Constitution of India, came in conflict with the rights of the Chakmas as residents in the state. While Chakmas settled in other states were duly absorbed (with some problems in Mizoram, as we discussed above), their absorption in Arunachal Pradesh remained problematic as Arunachalis never approved of their presence in their state on a permanent basis. It was the repeat of the Assam problem on a lesser scale (Roy 2010: 92–134).

The people of Arunachal Pradesh, particularly its student associations, which matter in state politics most, were up in arms whenever the question of inclusion of these Chakmas in the electoral rolls arose. As a result, both the Government of India and the Election Commission, in spite of their best efforts, found themselves helpless to conduct the polls in the Chakma inhabited areas. In respect of their citizenship issue, Section 6A of the 1986 Amendment to the Citizenship Act of 1955 was of little help as it was Assam-specific, which the Supreme Court verdict in the case of *State of Arunachal Pradesh* v. *Khudiram Chakma* underlined. It was held that the said clause was not applicable because the Chakmas 'had stayed in Assam for a short period in 1964 and had strayed away there from in the area now within the State of Arunachal Pradesh' (Roy 2010: 123).

After having failed to invoke Section 6A of the 1986 amendment, the Chakmas took recourse to Section 5(1)(a) of the 1955 Citizenship Act that provided for citizenship by registration. They also petitioned the NHRC for its support, which took the matter to the Supreme Court. In its appeal the NHRC, besides the citizenship issue, raised the human rights concerns. The Supreme Court upheld the rights of the Chakmas to seek Indian citizenship by registration and instructed the Arunachal Pradesh government to forward all such requests to the central government for necessary action. It held that '[w]hile the application of any individual Chakma was being considered, the state government could not evict or remove the concerned person from his occupation/habitat on the ground that he was not a citizen of India' (Roy 2010: 131). Anupama Roy, in her study suggests, that if the Assam and Arunachal Pradesh situations are compared one would notice the nuanced approaches of the Indian state to the issue of citizenship in these two states. In Assam 'the articulation of citizenship as a domain of differentiated universalism ... remained elusive', while for Chakmas 'it was only as undifferentiated citizens that the markers of a "migrant/refugee" status and the luminal state of being a "no-where-people" could be erased' (Roy 2010: 132).

During the parliamentary election of 2004, the Chakma issue was on the fore. The Chief Minister, Gegong Apang, had to do some delicate tightrope walking because, on the one hand, he had a political alliance with the ruling BJP, which was leading the NDA coalition then, on the other he could not ignore the powerful student associations of the state which were up in arms against the Chakmas participating in the elections. During my interview with him when I broached the subject and reminded him of an earlier promise made by the Deputy Prime Minister L.K. Advani that all Chakmas, Hajongs and Marmas living in the state would be granted citizenship by the end of 2003, Apang reacted sharply and tried to convince me that it was virtually impossible to grant voting rights to the Chakmas settled in the state. He warned that any such step would seriously disturb peace in the state as it would meet with stiff resistance from the people who feared that they would be outnumbered by these outsiders, indeed a weird speculation (my interview with Chief Minister Gegong Apang on 12 April 2004, also see Ghosh et al. 2005).

Soon after the election, in which the Congress regained power at the centre, Apang, typical of many other chief ministers in North East, switched sides but his anti-Chakma stance continued, though once again it was at variance with the central government policy. During the October 2004 assembly elections, his main political plank became an anti-Chakma campaign. His suggestion was that let them be settled in any other state but not in Arunachal Pradesh. In 2007, the AAPSU added a new dimension to the campaign. They raised the issue of Tibetan refugees in the state and called them foreigners like the Chakmas. Soon the scope of the campaign was further enlarged to include all illegal Bangladeshis. Through their 'Operation Clean Drive' they even evicted many and pushed them into Assam inviting strong protest from the Government of Assam (Singh 2010: 107-8).

# The Hindu Question in East Pakistan/ Bangladesh

Unlike West Pakistan, where the Hindu population has been reduced to an insignificant minority, in East Pakistan, and later Bangladesh, it has remained quite sizeable, although their proportion in the population is systematically declining. The existence of this minority, coupled with the anti-India sentiment of certain political forces in the country, has subjected the minority question to all kinds of political manipulation in which the Hindus are always on the receiving end. In the earlier chapter, we have referred to frequent anti-Hindu riots in the 1950s and 1960s, resulting in the exodus of Hindus to India. The process considerably slowed after the creation of Bangladesh but did not stop. Actually it assumed a subtle form not easily visible.

During the period of Ziaur Rehman, the promulgation of the Vested and Non-Resident Property (Repeal) Ordinance offered an opportunity to government officials and land grabbers to occupy landed properties of Hindus who had left Bangladesh for India, not always with the intention of not returning. Revenue officials at the district and sub-divisional levels were not only empowered to declare any land held by the Hindus as non-resident property and allot them to Muslim citizens, these officials were even suitably rewarded for their promptness in disposing the cases. The policy continued with some modifications during the regimes of Hossain Mohammad Ershad and Begum Khaleda Zia (Samaddar 1999: 92-93).

The psychological impact of the Vested Property Act on Hindus was devastating. It has been calculated that on an average every day 538 Hindus 'vanished', although there was a downward trend through successive decades (Samaddar 1999: 93). Even the restoration of democracy was no solace. Samaddar's survey amongst the Hindu migrants explodes the myth that democracy promotes inter-communal harmony:

> Hindu migrants ... told us repeatedly that their position was better in the Pakistan era than in independent Bangladesh; that even in independent Bangladesh, the Hindus felt more secure under Army rule than under a democratically elected government, for 'attitude towards the Hindus and (therefore) India determine [sic] the fate of a political party during elections'. (Samaddar 1999: 132)

The fact of the matter is that no government in Bangladesh has been able to ensure the safety and security of Hindus there. A representative sample of Hindu insecurity is the following statement of a victim of the post-Babri mosque demolition riots in Bangladesh:

> I remember that during the Pakistan's regime, the radio used to blare that— 'the Hindus are our sacred *amanat* [asset], we have to see to the security of their lives and property'. Broadcasts came not before but only after the mass killings were gone through and the looting of Hindu properties in the Dhaka Narayanganj areas took place during the 1964 communal uprising. It was widely said that it was the Biharis who caused the riot. During the communal attacks of 1990, it was also said that Ershad had instigated it through hired hoodlums. But does the responsibilities of the government end by just bringing such charges in one sentence and doing nothing else to firmly deal with the situation? (Guhathakurta 2002: 80)

The connection between communal politics of Bangladesh and migration of Bangladeshi Hindus to India finds reflection in other spheres of government policies as well. There is evidence of officially sanctioned discrimination against Hindus living near the India–Bangladesh borders. They are debarred from applying for bank loans on the ground that they would migrate to India after availing themselves of the loans. While there is some truth in these allegations, the fact is that there are numerous Muslim defaulters too. But seldom such fear is expressed about these bad loans. In the election of 1996 and thereafter, the controversy figured as an electoral issue aimed at maligning the Hindu minority (Guhathakurta 2002: 81).

# Reshuffling Citizenship: Swapping of Enclaves

Following the ratification of the Land Boundary Agreement in July 2015, India and Bangladesh have summarily swapped their respective enclaves, as we have noted in Chapter 1. There does not seem to be any politics involved in forcing people of these enclaves to choose their preferred country of nationality. Evidently, the small number of people that are in question does not excite any party to pay too much attention to these people. But the way all Bangladeshi enclaves people (almost entirely Muslim) have opted for India and some, almost all Hindus, of Indian enclaves people in Bangladesh have decided to migrate to India proves that even a BJP-led India is a bigger attraction than secular Awami League led Bangladesh. Three explanations are possible: one, mostly people do not want to leave their homestead and venture out in a new place; two, India's secular fabric still holds water vis-à-vis the on-and-off secularism of Bangladesh; and three, India offers better economic opportunity to all. Even prior to the agreement the Bangladeshi enclave dwellers used to sneak out into Indian territory in search of livelihood and had gone all the way to Delhi and other places in north India.

# The Nepali Question

Because of the growing number of Nepalis in India and the fact that the subject is politically sensitive, data on their numbers is almost impossible to obtain. The policies followed from time to time by India to restrict the flow of Nepali immigration have served as an irritant not only to the Indo-Nepal relations but also to the Nepalis settled in India. Both the questions, of course, are intricately linked. In October 1976, the Indian government, in response to a series of demonstrations in Nepal against India's 'annexation' of Sikkim in August 1975, imposed Restricted Area Permit on all foreigners in India, including parts of Arunachal Pradesh, Assam, Manipur, Meghalaya, Nagaland, Sikkim, Tripura, Uttar Pradesh and West Bengal. Considering the fact that India and Nepal had signed a Treaty of Peace and Friendship of 1950 and were thus obliged to keep their borders open, Nepal strongly resented the decision.

Various state governments in India have taken recourse to this act to restrict the influx of Nepalis to their states to the detriment of local Nepali political interests. Indeed, the restrictions have caused difficulty not only to prospective Nepali emigrants but also to about 5,000,000 Indian nationals of Nepali ethnic origin in the aforesaid areas who had close relations living in Nepal. The Government of India, however, did not relent. Even the Janata Party government (1977–80), which was committed to improving relations with neighbouring countries, did not alter the decision. In 1980, the government introduced the system of identity cards in the state of Sikkim to control Nepalese emigration into the state to prevent distortions in the electoral rolls, a factor which was rocking Assam politics at that time.

The so-called Nepali question in Indian politics is a curious mixture of the politics of Nepali nationals on Indian soil and that of ethnic Nepalis of Indian nationality. The question found its most articulated political expression in the politics of Nar Bahadur Bhandari of Sikkim and that of Subhash Ghising, the leader of the Gorkha National Liberation Front (GNLF) of Darjeeling in West Bengal. The GNLF movement assumed international dimensions when, on 23 December 1986, Ghising wrote a letter to the King of Nepal, copies of which, sixteen in all, were forwarded to various governments and international agencies, including the then two superpowers (United States and the USSR), the UN, and many governments in South Asia. Ghising pleaded for justice for 'the unpardonable historical crimes against ... Gorkhas in the Indian Union ... as per ... the provisions of the Charter of the United Nations' and also by taking into account 'the future status of their ceded land and territories'. Gorkhas of Assam criticized Rajiv Gandhi, who had opposed granting citizenship to those Nepalis who had immigrated to India after 1950. The Assam Gorkha Sammelan and the All Assam Gorkha Students Union argued that it was unethical to brand one section of immigrants like Bangladeshis as citizens and the Nepalis as not (Baral 1990: 55). After the BJP came to power in 1998, Gorkhas hoped that the party would grant statehood to the Gorkhas because the party was in favour of smaller states wherever such demands were made (Bagchi 2012: 106-7). In the parliamentary elections of 2014, the Bimal Gurung's Gorkha Janmukti Morcha, which commanded a significant support in the Darjeeling hills aligned with the BJP candidate S.S. Ahluwalia, which ensured the victory of the latter. The expectation was that the BJP in power at the centre, which was most likely, would grant statehood to Gorkhaland. Whether the BJP would fulfil its promise would depend on how the party views its future in West Bengal, which is opposed to the idea of any bifurcation of the state. It is likely that during the West Bengal assembly elections in 2016, the subject would again gather momentum.

## Nepal's Indian Question

The Nepali question in India has a mirror image in the shape of the Indian question in Nepal. During the days of the monarchy in Nepal, it was common to highlight the problem arising out of the growing number of Indians in the Terai region. The Task Force on Migration, which was set up in 1983 under the auspices of the Nepali National Commission on Population, referred to the problem Nepal faced from the rising number of Indians in the Terai (Gurung Report 1983: 13-14, 29). The increase in the population of the Terai, coupled with the so-called 'India factor' in Nepal's politics, made the issue figure constantly. When the issue was debated in the Panchayat (parliament), several members spoke against 'India's demographic invasion of Nepal'. A survey of the *Nepal Press Digest* during the 1980s revealed the importance this issue commanded both at political and media levels. Since under the monarchy there was 'little doubt that the political orientation of the Press in Nepal, characterised by the more ostentatious shifts in loyalty, is determined by what the government has up its sleeves' (Baral 1975: 180), this attitude of the press was indicative of the mood of the ruling elites.

Following the return of democracy to Nepal in 1990, the Terai Indians claimed that they constituted 50 per cent of the population but it did not show in the nation's sociopolitical and economic fields. The Terai-based Nepal Sadbhavna Party argued that while they were 50 per cent of the population and contributed to the country's economy to the tune of 60 per cent, still their social and cultural identity was always undermined. They were not even allowed to participate in official programmes wearing *dhoti* and *kurta*, their traditional dress (Baral 1994: 97). In the elections of 1991 and 1994, the party put up their own candidates but their performance was lacklustre. The reason was that the social demography of the Terai had changed over the years due to migrations from the hill regions (Gurung 1997: 124). There is a communal angle also. The Hindu-Muslim riots in India were making many Indian Muslims to migrate to the Terai for safety. In the 1980s when the communal situation in India deteriorated, it visibly encouraged the growth of the Muslim population in the Terai. Their population increased from 399,197 in 1981 to 653,218 in 1991, meaning an increase of 38.9 per cent within a decade. The Terai accounted for 96.7 per cent of Nepal's total Muslim population, which was 7.32 per cent of the Terai population. Since these Muslims possessed diverse occupational skills, they were generally gainfully employed, particularly in the area's garment industry (Kansakar 2005: 24). It may be relevant here to refer to a discussion this author had with Dr Mohammad Mohsin, an important Muslim leader of Nepal and a former cabinet minister, in February 2006 in Kathmandu. He had feared that Muslims were safe in monarchical Nepal but in democratic Nepal when votes would matter that safety could be endangered. First, it would lead to Hindu militancy and then over time it would end up in Muslim militancy and then riots. Such a thing has not happened so far but Mohsin's fear was not misplaced given democratic experiences in general.

# Sri Lankan Tamil Refugees in Indian Politics

Sri Lankan Tamil refugees are uniquely relevant for Indian politics. They are small in number but their bearing for Tamil Nadu politics is significant. Since Tamil Nadu has a secessionist past, it assumes national importance at times. Both the contending Tamil parties, Dravid Munnetra Kazhagam (DMK) and All India Anna Dravid Munnetra Kazhagam (AIADMK), rely heavily on their capacity to project themselves as the real champions of the Tamil cause. Congress or BJP ruling at the centre keep shifting their alliances between the two, depending upon political contingencies. The intermeshing of Sri Lanka Tamil politics with that of Tamil Nadu and then with that of India at the national level found its most dramatic expression in the assassination of Rajiv Gandhi during the parliamentary election campaign of 1991. The assassination, masterminded by the suicide squad of the LTTE, took place in Tamil Nadu, bringing the ruling DMK government under severe political pressure from the central government and its local rival, the AIADMK. Many Sri Lankan refugees were subjected to arbitrary arrest, detention and coercion. In the assembly elections held in January 1992, the AIADMK routed the DMK. At present, the Sri Lanka Tamil factor has assumed a different shape in the light of LTTE's defeat and the alleged human rights violations by the Sri Lankan army at the final stages of the war. The UPA coalition government led by Manmohan Singh was under severe pressure from the AIADMK government of Jayalalithaa not to have any truck with the Sri Lankan government. After the victory of the BJP in 2014 elections, when Prime Minister Narendra Modi invited the SAARC leaders to his inaugural ceremony, Jayalalithaa strongly protested against the participation of President Mahinda Rajapaksa in the function. But Modi went ahead and Rajapaksa participated. Evidently, unlike Manmohan Singh's dependence on his political partners, Modi's BJP is free from such encumbrances as his party has absolute majority of its own in the parliament.

## The Bhutanese Experience

At present, the Nepali issue is not politically relevant in Bhutan, but since it is now a multiparty democracy and as the democratic process would growingly unfold, there is possibility that the Nepali question would reappear. But to understand the dynamics of that possibility we must refer to the past experience which would throw some light on the Drukpa-Lhotshampa dichotomy. The population of Bhutan (about 742,000 in 2014) is ethnically divided into three groups—Ngalongs, Sarchops and Lhotshampas. The Ngalongs have distinctive features of language, religion and cultural patterns of Tibetan origin. They do not form the majority of the population but constitute the dominating element of national life. The Sarchops, who form the majority, are settled in eastern and central parts of the country. Though they speak different dialects and have distinctive cultural patterns close to the Tibeto-Burmans, they are by and large akin to Ngolongs' Buddhism-derived culture. Ngalongs and the Sarchops put together are generally known as Drukpas, meaning that they belong to the Drukpa sect of Tibet's Mahayana Buddhism. The Lhotshampas, who constitute about 20 to 30 per cent of the population, are concentrated in southern Bhutan. Divided into several castes, they are ethnically Nepalese and their religion is Hinduism.

There is a deep political divide between the Drukpas and the Lhotshampas. Actually the divide had its origin in the political hiatus between the Ngalongs and the Lhotshampas, but as ethnicity was at the core of this cleavage the Sarchops have closed their ranks with the Ngalongs. The two communities have distinctive social patterns, which have ramifications for their respective approaches to the politics of the state. While the Drukpas are insular, the Lhotshampas are extraterritorial. Constituting a part of the larger Nepali community spread across the northern districts of several Indian states abutting Bhutan their extraterritoriality finds expression in their kinship relations and political behaviour beyond the borders of Bhutan into India and Nepal. Besides being an industrious people compared to the Drukpas who are less so, they have acquired lands in excess of their proportion to the population. The size of an average land holding in southern Bhutan is eight acres, while in the north it is only two acres. There are other attitudinal differences between the two communities, making the Lhotshampas more ambitious than the Drukpas (Ghosh 1998).

For historical reasons and differentiated educational attainments, the Drukpas and the Lhotshampas had developed conflicting images of the Bhutanese monarchy when it was the only source of power. To the Drukpas their king was one from amongst them and he was the symbol of Bhutanese nationalism. Their king did not derive his legitimacy from his divine rights. The institution of monarchy, although hereditary, was a popularly endorsed one. Unlike this, the Lhotshampa outlook was influenced by their concept of divine-rights-oriented monarchy of

Nepal, because of which they did not conceive of the Bhutanese royalty as part of their experience. Besides, the tradition of democratic movement in Nepal against the monarchy had made them somewhat hostile to the institution itself. There was always a connection between the democratic movement in Nepal and the same in southern Bhutan (Rahul 1983: 54-55). From the late 1980s onwards, it became a critical factor in Drukpa-Lhotshampa political conflict.

In the late 1980s, the ethnic dichotomy between the Drukpas and the Lhotshampas reached a flash point when the former alleged that due to illegal immigration from India and Nepal the population of the Lhotshampas had increased disproportionately to their natural growth, which threatened the demographic balance of the kingdom. There was truth in Bhutanese government's argument (Rose 1994: 110-11). Conceiving their nationalism in ethnic terms, the government emphasized the cultural nationalism of the Drukpas. Not only were the citizenship laws stringently enforced, causing the eviction of thousands of Lhotshampas, the government also insisted upon all nationals to adhere to the national code of conduct—the *Driglam Namzha*—forcing them all to follow a uniform dress and other codes while visiting the Dzongs, monasteries, government offices and official functions. Dzonkha was declared as the official language, and the use of Nepali in schools even in the Lhotsampa-majority areas was restricted. All subjects were made to pledge loyalty to the king and the Drukpa political system. These policies were in contrast to the earlier ones that encouraged Drukpa-Lhotshampa cultural integration. The sectarian approach to nation building led to organized Lhotshampa protest, which in due course turned into militancy. State repression followed. The end result was the large-scale exodus of Lhotshampa refugees to Nepal. Some arrived in India.

The political awareness among the Lhotshampas, however, had started as early as in the 1940s, when in the neighbouring India the anti-British agitation had peaked in the Congress-led Quit India Movement (1942). The impact of the political developments in India was felt differently by the Nepalis and the Drukpas. While the latter watched them with caution and anxiety, as I have discussed elsewhere (Ghosh 1989: 138-51), Nepalis saw in them hope to balance their equation with the monarchy. In the late 1940s, the Jai Gorkha movement agitated in favour of social reforms, which gradually expanded its scope to include political reforms at the cost of Bhutanese authoritarianism. In 1952, the Lhotshampas formed the Bhutan State Congress branches along the Bhutan-India border regions

(Evans 2013: 121). Though the impact of this movement was limited, the contemporary politics of Nepal kept influencing the Lhotshampas. As Maoism grew in strength in Nepal, the political relationship between the Lhotshampas and Nepal became more complicated, in which the BPP had a vital role to play from the late 1980s onwards. This had a direct impact in both worsening the Lhotshampa–Bhutan government relationship and encouraging more Lhotshampas leave Bhutan to take refuge in Nepal. The violence that the BPP took recourse to hardened the attitude of the Bhutanese government, resulting in their exodus to Nepal (Evans 2013: 128–32).

# East Bengali/Chittagonian/Rohingya Refugees and Myanmar Politics

In the ethno-religious politics of Myanmar, the East Bengali/ Chittagonian/Rohingya refugees have a visible presence. As long as they are identified as Bengali immigrants, the Rakhine Buddhists want it that way, it has a particular political meaning, but the moment they are seen as Rohingya, which the politically active section of the Rohingya community wants everybody to acknowledge, it assumes an altogether different meaning. To understand this dichotomy, it is important to understand Myanmar's ethnic make-up against the background of the country's history and religious politics.

During the 19th century and a large part of the 20th century, ethnicity in Myanmar was interpreted along cultural and racial lines as if they were unchangeable ethnic markers. It led to the so-called list of 135 ethnic groups which were politically stratified. Although the concept of ethnicity has undergone several changes over the years in many parts of the world, where it is no longer understood in exclusive and rigidified terms, in Myanmar it is largely the traditional notion that persists. The conflict between the Muslims and Buddhists in the Rakhine province underlines this ethnic ordering, which makes the possibility of a politically negotiated bargain difficult. Since the early 1950s a section of the Muslims in the North of the Rakhine state has identified itself as a separate ethnic group by the name Rohingya, claiming that they had lived in the region for many generations. The Buddhist majority of the state denies this characterization and argues that they are Bengali-speaking immigrants from neighbouring East Pakistan/Bangladesh and as such they have no claim over the state as other traditional ethnic groups have. The historicity of the Rohingya, therefore, is at the core of the conflict as the homeland demands in many other parts of the world have shown. The politics of this conceptual divide is evidently complex, which a mere human rights approach to the issue tends to gloss over (Leider 2013: 204-9).

There is an unending controversy in respect of the origin of the term Rohingya and its political connotation. The earliest evidence of the use of the term is found in a late 18th-century text and there were stray references thereafter, but now it connotes almost all Bengali-speaking Muslims of Myanmar, which is not a fact. The following passage from a knowledgeable source may clarify the situation:

> From a linguistic point of view, the name 'Rohingya' is derived from the Indianized form of Rakhine, i.e. Rakhnaga. Following Dr Thibaut d'Hubert, 'the rules of historical linguistics on the Indo-Aryan languages allow to easily explain the phonological derivation "Rakhanga">"Rohingya". The passage from [kh] to [h] is the rule in the passage from Sanskrit to Prakrit, which allows us to derive Rohingya from Rakhanga: Rakhanga> *Rahanga> (short "a" becomes "o" in Bengali) *Rohangga> (introduction of [y]# to indicate the germination which induces an alternative pronunciation " -gya" and influences the vowel [a] which becomes [i] thence "Rohingya".' While the scientific demonstration may look a bit awkward to the lay reader, it accounts in fact for the change of each letter and sound. In association with the paradigm 'Rakhanga>Rohingya', one should refer as well to the name 'Roshanga', 'widely spread since the beginning of Bengali literature in the Chittagong region, i.e. since the early 17th century till the end of the 18th c'. In sum, the word 'Rohingya' does not refer to, or mean anything else, but 'Rakhine' in the local Muslim language. (Leider 2013: 219)

Until the early 1990s the commonly used term for these immigrants was Bengalis. Since during the colonial period they largely came from Chittagong they were also called Chittagonians. But here lies the bone of political contention. It has been said:

> To call the Muslims in North Rakhine 'Bengalis' is not only totally rejected by those who claim a Rohingya identity, because it connects them implicitly to their historically non-Myanmar origins, but it is seen internationally as a discriminatory statement. Naming is thus not only an integral part of a debate on a contested identity, but it also has leverage with regard to the representation of their legal status. To not use the term 'Rohingya' has become tantamount to a lack of political correctness coming close to denying them basic rights. (Leider 2013: 211)

The Buddist-Rohingya politics revolves around the following lines. Buddhists view them as Bengali-speaking immigrants who must go back from where they have come, meaning Bangladesh, at least those who are of recent vintage. In contrast, the Rohingyas assert that they must be recognized as a separate ethnic community, which means that they should be entitled to regional autonomy. In its extreme form, they demand secession from Myanmar and creating their new Rohingya state. As under state repression and local hostility, many Rohingyas have taken refuge in Bangladesh. The matter has assumed international and security dimensions which we have discussed in Chapter 3. There is no indication that the Government of Myanmar is in any mood to change its stance on how it should distinguish between Bengalis and Rohingyas. In September 2014, it was reported in the Indian press that some Rohingyas had been granted the citizenship of Myanmar, but it was found that it was granted to only 209 Rohingyas and that too a section of them belonged to the Kaman community which had the recognition of the government as indigenous to Myanmar (*The Hindu*, 23 September and 1 October 2014).

# Notes

1. Here is what G.D. Khosla, one of the Punjab High Court judges who upheld the capital punishment for Gandhi's killer, Nathuram Godse, wrote about the latter's statement explaining his motivations for the murder: 'The audience was visibly and audibly moved. There was a deep silence when he ceased speaking. Many women were in tears and men were coughing and searching for their handkerchiefs. It seemed to me that I was taking part in some kind of melodrama or in a scene out of a Hollywood feature film.... I have, however, no doubt that had the audience that day been constituted into a jury and entrusted with the task of deciding Godse's appeal, they would have brought a verdict of "not guilty" by an overwhelming majority' (Mukherji 2007: 198).
2. Long before Partition, there was a section of Sikhs who chose to say that Sikhism was different from Hinduism. In 1905, the Guru Singh Sabha achieved a major victory when it succeeded in removing all Hindu images from the Golden Temple in Amritsar.
3. In different sources different spellings and abbreviations have been used of the same organization, namely, *Nikhil Vanga Bastuhara Karma Parishad* (NVBKP) and *Nikhil Banga Bastuhara Karmaparishad* (NBBK).
4. Space as a factor in the Dalit (scheduled caste) politics of India has been studied for the first time through this Bengal experience. See Bandyopadhayay and Chaudhury (2014).

5. Although Bengal had not witnessed as much violence as Punjab had, still, after the Noakhali riots of October 1946 the rumour mill was rife about the deteriorating Muslim–Hindu relationship in East Bengal creating a situation for large-scale exodus of all kinds of Hindus, which actually happened within a few years (Bandyopadhayay 1997: 66). Fear psychosis contributes as much as real violence to make people leave their homes for safety of life and honour. One may find a similarity here with the situation in Kashmir in the late 1980s and early 1990s. Although there were no anti-Hindu riots, still the uncanny fear of Jehadi violence made the Kashmiri Pandits leave the valley lock, stock and barrel virtually overnight to take shelter in Jammu, Delhi and other parts of India. They have not returned yet.

6. It was only in the assembly elections of 2011 and the parliamentary elections of 2014 that a scheduled caste upsurge was noted. Whether it would be appropriated by the age-old Bhadralok-dominated politics of West Bengal or it would pose a threat to the latter, time would tell. On this point, see Sinharay (2014: 10–12). This subject was further debated in the *Economic and Political Weekly*. See Chandra and Nielsen (2012: 59–61) and Kumar and Guha (2014: 73–74).

7. The long shadow of the problem has reached as far as Bijnor in UP The Bengali community there owes its origin to the Partition. They belong to such scheduled castes as Namasudra, Majhi and Pondkhatriya of East Bengal who have the scheduled caste status in West Bengal, but not in UP They demand their rights as scheduled castes in UP as well. To make their voice audible they have aligned with the local Jaats and show their closeness to the *Hindutva* ideology. See Smita Gupta's dispatch from Bijnor in *The Hindu*, 1 March 2012.

8. It may be noted that building permanent structures over Muslim graves is typically an Indian practice. Islamic precepts do not allow such things. In that sense, even the Taj Mahal or the Humayun's Tomb also violates Islamic principles. See Kesavan (1994: 245–46).

9. A large number of Hindu educationists too left for India which affected Pakistan's education for years to come (Cohen 2004: 236).

10. The One-Unit policy was introduced in 1954 to neutralize the domination of East Pakistan as a province in a five-province Pakistan. The idea was to merge all the four provinces of West Pakistan as One Unit vis-à-vis East Pakistan, which was another unit.

11. In March 1948, Jinnah in a speech in Dhaka emphasized that 'Urdu and Urdu alone shall be the state language of Pakistan' and whosoever opposed this was an enemy of Pakistan. The seed of East Pakistan–West Pakistan cleavage was sown then and there. In January 1952, the seed sprouted when East Pakistan's Urdu-speaking Prime Minister, Khwaza Nazimuddin, categorically endorsed the policy (see Hashmi 1996: 5).

12. For a brief but balanced view of Assam's immigrant problem and its connection with the state's politics, see Borooah (2013).

13. In October 2013, a businessman was set afire in Shillong by activists demanding Inner Line Permit system for the state. *The Hindu* (New Delhi), 27 October 2013.

14. A reference here to the 1951 census would be instructive. The 1951 census in Assam was important in three respects: (a) The Bengali Muslims declared themselves as Assamese speaking, which contributed to the cooling down of Assamese Hindu hostility against the Muslims. (b) The separation of Sylhet from Assam following a referendum, which contained 30 per cent of Assam's population 90 per cent of whom spoke Bengali, made Assam for the first time an Assamese-majority state. The percentage of the Assamese population increased from 30 per cent in 1930 to 56 per cent in 1951. (c) A new distinction emerged now in respect of Muslim immigrants from East Bengal and their Hindu counterparts. While the latter started getting recognized as 'refugees' the former as 'illegal immigrants' or 'foreigners'. It may be noted that The Immigrant (Expulsions from Assam) Act 1950 implicitly distinguished the Hindu refugees from Muslim immigrants. Although this act was repealed in 1957, there was a 1965 secret administrative order of the Government of India that authorized the district magistrate to grant Indian citizenship to those Hindu refugees from East Pakistan who had settled in Assam for six months or more (Kimura 2013: 44–45, 64). One can find similarity with the point (a) above in the case of Punjab. In the census of 1951, Hindu Punjabi refugees declared Hindi as their language, resulting eventually in a political rift between Punjabi Sikhs and the Punjabi Hindus culminating in the Khalistan movement in the late 1970s and the early 1980s.

15. In the aftermath of 2009 parliamentary elections, it became All India United Democratic Front.

16. In the 2015 assembly elections, it won 77 seats, reducing the BJP to an insignificant minority with barely three seats. The Congress could not obtain a single seat. In the 2013 assembly elections, the BJP won 32 seats, the AAP won 28 and the Congress 8 seats.

17. It is yet to be seen, however, how far the BJP would go in this regard. According to a recent report, there are hundreds of such Hindu and Sikh refugees from Pakistan in Rajasthan who have been waiting for years for Indian citizenship. Hindu Singh Sodha, president of the *Seemant Lok Sangathan* (meaning, frontier peoples' organization), has demanded their inclusion in the Person of Indian Origin (PIO) scheme (*Frontline*, 23 January 2015: 45). But there are inherent legal problems given the provisions of the Citizenship Act of 1955 and their amendments in 1986, 1992, 2003, 2005, 2011, 2013, and probably the forthcoming one in 2015. It may be noted that the PIO under the existing law cannot be a person who was at any time a citizen of Afghanistan, Bhutan, China, Nepal, Pakistan and Sri Lanka. Under Section 5(a) of the Citizenship Act of India, a person of Indian origin who is ordinarily resident in India may be registered as an Indian citizen if he or she has been resident in India for seven years

before making an application. To be considered a person of Indian origin for registration under this section, a person or his parents should have been born in undivided India or in a territory that became part of India after 15 August 1947. Yet, an explanation issued by the Ministry Home Affairs on 25 November 2014 would treat Pakistani and Bangladeshi nationals living in India on long-term visa as specific group whose facilities may be reviewed as a policy matter from time to time (Anupama Roy's interview in the *Frontline*, 23 January 2015: 44, and this author's correspondence with her, 12 January 2015). In this regard, one may as well see the Preface to the Second Impression (2014) of Roy's 2010 book. This issue has been discussed in Chapter 4.

# 3

# The Security Variable

*It was flight, not an invasion, that ultimately destroyed the East German state.*

—Myron Weiner (1992–93)

In the previous chapter, we have analysed the interconnection between migration and politics. Since foreign policy and national security are extensions of domestic politics (Ghosh 2010), it would be instructive to study the interconnection between migration and national security in this chapter. Although the subject has been studied all along, the events of 9/11 gave a new fillip to the discourse. In a well-researched article published in the eminent journal *International Security* (Adamson 2006), its author wrote: 'The ability of nineteen hijackers from overseas to enter, live, and train in the United States in preparation for carrying out attacks on the World Trade Center and the Pentagon could not but raise concerns regarding the relationship between the cross-border mobility of people and international terrorism'. The attacks precipitated the largest reorganization of the US security apparatus since the passage of the National Security Act of 1947. From 1 March 2003, immigration and border control were brought under the purview of the Department of Homeland Security and in January 2004, the department rolled out the United States Visitor and Immigrant Status Indicator Technology (US-VISIT) programme, which introduced biometric technology at all US immigration and border control points. The bombings in Madrid on 11 March 2004 and in London on 7 July 2005 further underlined the interconnection between migration and national security (Adamson 2006: 165–66).

# Migration–National Security Connection

Security is a complex construct. There have been primarily two schools of thought. One, which belongs to the conventional school, tends to view it from the military angle—threats arising either externally or internally (for example, Nye & Lynn-Jones 1988: 5–27). The other, which belongs to the post-modern school, sees the source of threats not in narrow, military terms but finds their epicentres in environmental, demographic, ecological, economic and socio-cultural domains (Ullman 1983: 125–53). For example, Huntington (1996) did not see the future threat to the United States emanating from any particular country or region, but from a religious belief system, which was globally present without having a centralized leadership or a definite pattern of assault. Added to this dimension is the element of technological advancement which has made us find the logic of security in the following five formulations: (a) commercialisation of security, (b) increasing dependence on technological solution by the providers of security, (c) following from this, there is a massive industrialization of security, (d) globalization of security and (e) the vicious circle—more security leads to more insecurity and then more insecurity leads to more security and thus it goes on (Burgess 2007).

The problem with non-military threats, however, is that these cannot be visualized in a specific time frame, which is most critical for decision makers to respond. For example, the depletion of the ozone layer, global climatic changes or population growth are such problems that the states often fail to address in clear-cut foreign-policy terms because such issues cannot be made into electoral issues which are concerned with day-to-day existential problems. Even if the developed democracies may handle these better, experience shows that even there the domestic compulsions come in the way of taking bold steps to arrest the environmental degradation. Still, there are certain aspects of non-military threats, which can be foreseen and which have identifiable foreign-policy connections. The problems of migrations and refugee movements fall in this domain.

There can be several causes for interstate migrations and refugee movements, such as civil war and insurgency, ethnic or religious persecution, environmental disaster, famine and political vendetta. Except the last point, people do not flee their governments, they flee violence, disorder and lack of resources created by a particular crisis. But when the cause is political vendetta, the refugees are small in number and they flee their governments. The consequences of the refugee problem for receiving countries include pressures on economic resources and physical infrastructure, security risks and threats to governmental authority—especially if the government is incapable of controlling the flow across its borders. Sometimes the very presence of refugees affects the relationship between the sending and the host countries (Jacobson 1996: 657). It has been argued that the very first document that defined a refugee, the 1951 Refugee Convention, was the result of security considerations.

> UNHCR was formed by resolution 428 of the United Nations General Assembly in December 1950 to respond to a specific problem: refugees in Europe after the Second World War and in the early days of the Cold War. In the geo-politics of the Cold War, Western states and their Third World allies, saw it in their best interest to respond generously to the mass migration resulting from proxy wars waged on behalf of the interests of the super-powers. Refugees fleeing Communist regimes were seen to be 'voting with their feet', and were drawn in as pawns in the global game of the Cold War. (Milner 2004: 206)

In the post-Cold War world, the problem has taken a different shape. New kinds of South–South conflicts have arisen, leading to fresh flows of refugees. As more and more barriers are being built to prevent refugees from entering their chosen destinations, new forms of social strife are rising. The rise and fall of the Taliban and its prospective rise once again against the background of the staggered US withdrawal from Afghanistan from 2014 onwards is pregnant with consequences for the security of Pakistan though it may give the appearance of better days coming for Pakistan.

The relevant literature in the field has talked about 'refugee warriors' as quite often refugees engage themselves in armed campaigns against the country of their origin. Gil Loescher has argued that 'the emergence of armed groups of exiles, the so-called "refugee warriors", symbolized for the West the popular rejection of communist governments and served to legitimize the resistant movements' (quoted by Milner 2004: 210). Throughout history migrations and foreign policy have close connections. The best example is Israel. In recent times, the reunification of Germany provides another good example. In July–August 1989, there was an exodus of East Germans to Austria through Czechoslovakia and Hungary. This precipitated the opening of East Germany's western borders, leading to massive migrations into West Germany, which in turn led to the collapse of East Germany and its absorption by the Federal Republic of Germany. 'It was flight, not an invasion, that ultimately destroyed the East German state' (Weiner 1992–93: 91). A decade later, during the Kosovo crisis, the Serbian leader Stobodan Milosevic made use of the refugee flows as a weapon of war in what was an unbalanced conflict with NATO. Often there is a connection between the creation of a new state and the phenomenon of forced migration turning state making into a 'refugee-generating process' (Adamson 2006: 172).

The relationship between international migration and national security can be studied from three perspectives: one, from the perspective of state sovereignty, that is, how much power or autonomy the state has to deal with the problem; two, in what way the balance of power among states is relevant; and three, what exactly is the nature of violent conflict in the international system. Without going into the theoretical underpinnings associated with these perspectives, we may refer to some empirical data to highlight the points. In the beginning of this century, the number of people living outside the country of their birth had more than doubled in a span of 30 years, from 80,000,000 to 180,000,000. One out of 35 persons was a migrant. If all the migrants could form a state, that state would be the fifth largest in the world. In 2000, the Western industrialized countries hosted 40 per cent of all international migrants, of which 19,000,000 lived in the European Union (EU). In some Gulf countries, about 70 per cent of their labour requirement is met by expatriate workers. Viewing from the opposite angle, many countries are heavily dependent on remittances from their people working abroad. For example, 10 per cent Moroccans and 8 per cent Tunisians live outside of their countries. Since many countries suffer from political uncertainties, the problem of political refugees is also enormous. It has been estimated that the asylum applications cost industrial nations about US$10 billion annually, which is ten times the budget of the office of the UNHCR (Adamson 2006: 167–74).

International migrations influence three core areas of state power: economic, military and diplomatic, each one of which is closely connected to national security. Each one, however, is also doubled edged; it has benefits, it has problems. While the receiving countries harness the talent of skilled workers, it can at a later stage lead to unemployment for its own citizens. For the sending countries, they cause brain drain as the African countries face it in a huge measure. In the military sector, some countries, particularly the United States, have taken advantage from the skills of its immigrant people starting from the days of Nazi Germany's anti-Jewish madness in 1930s. The expertise of scientists like Albert Einstein and Edward Teller had made America the world's first nuclear power. In 2004, the US army recruited as many as 40,000 non-citizens. In its Iraq war, when America created a separate division to fight the war, it enrolled 3,000 Iraqi expatriates and exiles known as the Free

Iraq Forces. In the field of diplomacy, the immigrant communities often work as lobbyists for their countries of origin. The lobbying done by the Armenians of Eastern European descent living in America contributed to the enlargement of NATO. Diasporas are increasingly becoming relevant in this regard as well as in providing funds for conflicts in the home countries. The World Bank has found that conflict-ridden states having significant diaspora populations are six times more vulnerable than those having no diasporas. Besides, there are huge challenges to the states emanating from organized international crime in drugs, guns and human trafficking, all of which are closely linked to the issue of migrations across borders (Adamson 2006: 185–96).

# The South Asian Context

The phenomena of migrations and refugee movements in South Asia have generated all kinds of interstate suspicions in the region. Since these are closely linked to the principles of self-determination, national integration, politics of nation-building, and the issue of minority rights, their nature and dimensions often are complicated. This complexity is evidenced in the contradictory attitudes of the states with regard to such questions as ethnic loyalties and secessionist movements within and outside their respective national boundaries. It is more a norm than an exception that a state takes one position within its borders and a diametrically different one on the same issues in respect of other states. Even in respect of other states, its position is not always uniform. It varies depending upon the nature of the relations it has with a particular country.

Within the scope of cross-national movements of people, two broad categories of international conflicts may be considered. In the first place, these conflicts can be caused by population pressure upon resources, leading to expansionist tendencies (Chandrasekhar 1954: 102–6). Second, when clandestine population movements affect the demographic balance of the host region to the detriment of the political future of the host locality the latter may be forced to enter into conflicts with the country of the migrants' origin. Jacques Chirac, the former French Premier, stirred a political storm in 1970s when he said that 'a country with 900,000 unemployed but with two million immigrant workers is not a country with an insoluble labour problem'. In 1973, there were brutal attacks on Algerians in Marseilles, prompting Algeria to temporarily cut off emigration to France (Newland 1979: 23).

Against this backdrop, we have to understand the ways in which refugees and migrants in South Asia impinge upon the issue of national security of the regional states. But since the most fundamental ingredient in the definition of a refugee or migrant is the human activity of crossing the international border, either voluntarily or under duress, it would be imperative to understand the concept of border in the first place. While the state is committed to protect its border under an international legal regime, the migrants and refugees tend to be equally committed to violate the sanctity of that border beyond the pale of any legal regime. There is an inherent dialectic here. It is the illegal crossing of a border that underscores the legality of the border. Border, therefore, is not the warp and woof of international relations alone, it is the warp and woof for any discussion on migration and refugee movement as well. A proper discourse on border, therefore, is in order to grapple with the linkage between migrations and national/regional/international security.

## Discourse on International Border

In migration research, international border study is not necessarily an essential ingredient. Many of the massive human flows have had nothing to do with border research that has gained importance of late. European migrations to the New World, Australia, New Zealand or South Africa in the 19th century or the Indian labour movements in several parts of the colonial world, both indentured or otherwise, had little to do with borders as these movements were through sea routes. In South Asia, however, which our study focuses upon, that too during the past six decades, understanding of the international border is crucial.

Borders or frontiers, throughout history, have been a controversial subject and have invoked strong emotions particularly from people and groups staying near them. International relations theorists assume the concept of border to be sacrosanct. It is the warp and woof of the entire fabric of international relations (IR) discipline. But growing interaction with other disciplines like anthropology, ethnography and sociology is forcing them to rethink their position. In the entire Third World, where state formation and nation formation have taken paths different from those followed by Europeans in the 19th century, borders have become highly controversial. After the dismantling of the Soviet empire even Central and East Europeans have faced the same problem.

In South Asia, border demarcation is a major political problem and brings in focus the imperial interests of its erstwhile British rulers. Most of India's problems with its neighbours are related to this issue. It is alleged that although Indian nationalists fought the British rulers because of their imperial policies, after independence the same nationalists steadfastly adhered to the geopolitics of the region as defined by them, which was Curzonian. J.N. Dixit, India's former Foreign Secretary and author of many books on foreign policy and diplomacy, said that 'Curzon was among the greatest of the Indian nationalists' (Raja Mohan 2006: 204). In his 1909 essay, 'The Place of India in the Empire', Lord Nathaniel Curzon had emphasized the importance of India's geo-strategic location in the following words:

> It is obvious indeed, that the master of India, must, under modern conditions, be the greatest power in the Asiatic Continent, and therefore, it may be added, in the world. The central position of India, its magnificent resources, its teeming multitude of men, its great trading harbours, its reserve of military strength, supplying an army always in a high state of efficiency and capable of being hurled at a moment's notice upon any point either of Asia or Africa—all these are assets of precious value. On the West, India must exercise a predominant influence over the destinies of Persia and Afghanistan; on the north, it can veto any rival in Tibet; on the north-east and east it can exert great pressure upon China, and it is one of the guardians of the autonomous existence of Siam. On the high seas it commands the routes to Australia and to the China Seas. (quoted in Raja Mohan 2006: 204-5)

Lord Curzon had famously said that 'frontiers were the razor's edge on which suspended the modern issues of war or peace, life or death for nations'. The problem of borders, however, is not confined to India. Thus, while the McMahon line between India and China is a matter of controversy between the two countries, the Durand line has the same effect between Afghanistan and Pakistan (though of late it is on the back-burner). Within the subcontinent the borders between India and Pakistan (in Kashmir and in Sir Creek in Gujarat), between India and Bangladesh (largely solved now), between India and Nepal (over Kalapani) and between India and Sri Lanka (over maritime boundary and over fishing rights in the Palk Straits), continually cause tensions, which sometimes become serious.

Postmodernist scholars question the very concept of international borders though throughout history, borders have played the most crucial role in building the security centric mentality of nations. They have been the markers of state system—latter's authority and control over the spatial domain. Ironically, the violations of the sacrosanctity of the border through illegal migrations across it reinforce the concept. In India's context, Ranabir Samaddar argues that borders created by Partition have created more partitions of different kinds. The by-products of these partitions are the problems of 'minorities', 'new minorities', 'sweat and destitute labour', 'gun running' and 'drug caravans', 'immigration' and 'alien', all of which make mockery of the inviolability of the border. Actually the border 'exteriorises the interior and interiorises the exterior'. Paradoxically, while on the one hand illegal migration violates the authority of the state, then on the other, it also upholds the same authority by allowing its exclusive role there (De 1997: 14–39, Samaddar 1999b: 3).

Simultaneously, there is a growing debate about the viability of international borders. These are viewed differently depending upon the disciplinary orientation of the viewers. More practically, it depends upon the differentiated interest articulation of the concerned people. Baud and van Schendel (1997) see national borders as political constructs, imagined projections of territorial power. Although in maps these appear in precise forms, their practical consequences are not precise.

> No matter how clearly borders are drawn on official maps, how many customs officials are appointed, or how many watchtowers are built, people will ignore borders whenever it suits them. In doing so, they challenge the political status quo of which borders are the ultimate symbol. People also take advantage of borders in ways that are not intended or anticipated by their creators. Revolutionaries hide behind them, seeking the protection of another sovereignty; local inhabitants cross them whenever services or products are cheaper or more attractive on the other side; and traders are quick to take advantage of price and tax differentials. Because of such unintended and often subversive consequences, border regions have their own social dynamics and historical development. (Baud & van Schendel 1997: 211–12, also see Banerjee 1998: 179–91)

Even within the nation-state framework, there can be a variety of outlooks. To quote the above scholars once again:

> The interests of the armed forces, bureaucrats, politicians, landowners, traders, captains of industry often diverged. Whether or not this 'national' struggle continued after the border had been created depended on the cohesion of the state, the strategic and economic importance of the border, and the actual presence of the state in the borderland. State employees stationed in the borderland and their superiors in the provincial or state capitals could develop

very different perspectives on their mission in the borderland. Customs officials might become involved in smuggling, school-teachers might resist assimilatory language policy, and security forces might refuse to risk their lives against well-armed separatists. (Baud & van Schendel 1997: 217)

Oscar Martinez has suggested four models to understand the importance, or absence thereof, of borders. These are alienated borderlands, coexistent borderlands, interdependent borderlands and integrated borderlands. In alienated borderlands, routine cross-border infiltrations do not take place because of enmity between the bordering states. In coexistent borderlands, some cross-border interactions exist in spite of enmity between the bordering states. In interdependent borderlands, economic and social interactions are common across the border (Martinez 1994: 5–10). In integrated borderlands, the cross-border movements are legally recognized. In South Asia, all the four models exist. To the first model belong the India–Pakistan borders in J&K and Punjab. To the second belong the India–Pakistan borders in Rajasthan and Sind and the Indo-Myanmar borders when the relations between these two countries were not good. To the third category belong the borders between India and Bangladesh, India and Sri Lanka and India and Bhutan where cross-border movements of people take place as also social and economic interactions, though they are not officially sanctioned (van Schendel 2001: 393–421). In the fourth category falls the India–Nepal border, which is legally and effectively open.

Borders do not only fix the illegality of migration but they also play the important role in determining state responses—'the practices of state craft'. In South Asia, as in many other parts of the world, the spatial imagery that border creates stands totally disrupted through cross-border migrations. The phenomenon underscores the concept of de-territorialisation of communities in the sense that territory, national identity and political community do not any more correspond with one another. In spite of this inherent dichotomy the concept of border, however, does not seem to have outlived its utility nor does any such possibility seem to be there in the foreseeable future. Everyone has developed a habitual respect for it. And 'once a process is participatory, it is naturalised [... and] mystified', it becomes value loaded. If it is natural that the refugees and migrants would try to cross the border, it is equally natural that they would be pushed back (Samaddar 1999: 4).

In various ways, scholars have studied the border and the people who live there. Anthropologists' and sociologists' concern is with the patterns of life in these border areas and how they are influenced by their neighbourhood beyond the international border. Willem van Schendel eminently falls in this category who has extensively studied the borders between India and East Pakistan/Bangladesh, particularly the enclaves that till recently dotted the region (van Schendel 2002b, 2005). There is an inherent contradiction in the attitudes towards the state of those who live in the border areas and those who live on the mainland. Who influences whom is always a question. American historian Frederick Jackson Turner propounded his theory in the late 19th century that American character was primarily shaped by its changing frontiers. In his 1893 celebrated essay, 'The Significance of the Frontier in American History', he pointed out that the frontier had been the one great determinant of American civilization. Before him historians used to attribute the essentials of American psyche to their European 'germs', the so-called germ theory in American history. Turner's subsequent publications, of 1920 and 1932, further elaborated on the theme. The essence of this interpretation of American history was that whereas religious liberty, slavery, English authoritarianism, nationalism and the rise of democracy had been of primary concern to earlier historians, Turner's emphasis was upon the impact of the so-called Wild West on the transplanted people of America. According to him, the individualism of the frontier actually promoted American democracy. Freely available land on the frontier drew Americans away from their ancestral European moorings and thereby helped build a new Americanism. Traits that are considered to be the hallmarks of American character, such as self-reliance, individualism, restless energy and exuberance were attributable to the changing frontier. At least three legendary American presidents—Thomas Jefferson, Andrew Jackson and Abraham Lincoln—were the epitomes of this frontier freedom, argued Turner (for more on this point, see Ghosh 2011).

In recent times, the works by van Schendel (2002a) and Scott (2009) have sharpened our understanding of the intricate relationship between the mainland and the border regions. They have questioned the limited approach of Area Studies as a sub-discipline of IR which ignores the hinterlands between two states. While van Schendel developed the notion of Zomia[1] to mean the huge mass of mainland South and Southeast Asia that has historically been beyond the authority of the nation-states, Scott, by drawing from the same theory, argued that while the mainland people are the people of the state the border people are those who run away from the state. One scholar who explored these ideas further argues that during the last six decades there is an increased visibility of the state in Zomia and the latter has largely come under the control of concerned governments:

Zomia may, as such, remain in isolated places far from sites of economic, strategic, and other significance. Wherever the government decides it does not need a presence—in unimportant hamlets, by the sides of little creeks, on lonely mountain passes—it can afford to withdraw. In the political systems of contemporary Zomia there is a process of hardening the state in places that matter and withdrawing from places that do not. (Farrelly 2009: 200)

In the post-9/11 world, with the growing securitization of international politics against the background of an unprecedented globalization because of technological advances, borders are becoming increasingly unpassable for human but easily passable for goods, services and investments (Diener & Hagen 2010: 10).

Of late some scholars like Hiroshi Ishii, Katsuo Nawa and David Gellner have devised a new regional concept called 'northern South Asia'. The region encompasses an area that spreads from Gujarat and Rajasthan in western India to Bengal and Orissa in the east, as well as many parts of Nepal. The argument is that 'there were interesting cultural commonalities across the region so named, despite its division into different nation-states' (Gellner 2013: 7). But such a nomenclature is debatable because if in the context of border studies even such areas are included which have no international borders but merely fall in the cusp zone of two states belonging to the same nation, the very idea of borders as theoretically understood gets sabotaged. For example, Anastasia Piliavsky's essay dealing with the small Kanjar community that lives across the Rajasthan–Uttar Pradesh border makes no sense in this regard, though the author has tried to justify its inclusion in the Gellner's edited volume that highlights the concept of 'northern South Asia'. A look at the chosen sample of this anthropological essay would support my contention (Piliavsky 2013: 24–46).

While the discourse on borders is very useful for our understanding of both interstate relations in South Asia as well as the phenomenon of cross-border movements of people, for the purposes of the present study, which deals with massive human movements in the form of refugees and migrants, this border discourse is of limited salience. As we have discussed in the previous chapters, most of the migrants in the region have come from the interiors of their countries and have settled too in the interiors of their chosen destinations. Barring some small numbers of migrants from Bangladesh who have settled in the bordering districts of West Bengal, Assam and Tripura, or the Sri Lankan Tamil refugees from Jaffna who have crossed the Palk Strait and settled in coastal districts of

Tamil Nadu or Nepalis who have settled in the border areas of Assam, Bihar and West Bengal in India, by and large they have settled in places far away from the bordering regions.

## Fluidity of South Asian Borders and the Insecurity Syndrome

The movement of millions of people across the intra-regional national boundaries in the past six decades has largely been possible because the international borders in South Asia are virtually unenforceable. Partly on account of the hurried job of border demarcation that was done on the eve of British departure from India and partly on account of the plural nature of the population of the subcontinent crossing the border in popular imagination is a natural human activity. Thanks to the India–Pakistan conflict, particularly after the 1965 war when the borders were strictly enforced, cross-border movements are difficult though not impossible, certainly not for the motivated Islamist militants entering into J&K for the purpose of spreading Jihad in the valley and to encourage the Kashmiri separatists. The 3,223 km long India–Pakistan border has three segments, namely, the International Border (the so-called Radcliffe Line, 2,300 km long), the LOC (in existence since 1948 and 1971, 778 km long) and the Actual Ground Position Line (in the Siachen Glacier extending from NJ 9842 to the Indira Col, 110 km long) (Das 2014a: 307-8). Like the LOC in the India–Pakistan case, there is the Line of Actual Control that demarcates a section of the border between India and China in Arunachal Pradesh. There is no issue of cross-border movements of people in this region barring terrorists.

Most of South Asia's bilateral conflicts have some connection with the migration variable. The India–Pakistan conflict is essentially a conflict emanating from the incongruous characters of the two states which owe their origin to the Hindu-Muslim migrations after Partition. The Islamic thrust of the Pakistan state was conceived and nurtured by the Muhajirin, who dominated Pakistan in its formative years. It came in conflict with the secular orientation of the Indian state. But even in the preservation of that secular ethos, India had to face the challenge from the Hindu-tainted anti-Muslim ethos commonly visible among a sizeable section of Hindu Punjabi refugees. Insofar as many other threats to bilateral peace in the region are concerned, namely, India-Bangladesh, India-Nepal, India-Sri Lanka, Bhutan-Nepal, Bangladesh-Myanmar,

Pakistan–Afghanistan and the overall texture of interstate relations, the phenomenon of movements of people across the borders is one of the critical components. For historical reasons, most of these tensions are exacerbated because they are loaded with ethnic and/or religious sentiments of the migrating people.

## The Ethnic/Religious Connection

Since the migratory phenomena have close connections with racial and ethnic discriminations together with ideological, religious and economic variables, there is a possibility of these migrants bringing with them their earlier political orientation. Depending upon the relationship between the sending and host countries as well as between the migrants and militants either in the country of origin or in destination, the security question becomes relevant. Being an important theatre of international terrorism, such connections in South Asia become matters of concern for many governments. The fact that six Sri Lanka Tamil registered inmates of the Chennai refugee camps were involved in the Rajiv Gandhi assassination case would underline the point. All South Asian states have faced the problem of militant politics in some form or the other, and because of historical and geographic reasons it tends to spill over the borders either with state support or independent of it. In most cases, India is a common denominator because of geographical and historical reasons. India's expanding economic clout strengthens the connection.

## Centrality of India

India figures prominently in the region because of two reasons, one, its central location, and two, its size, which dwarfs all its neighbours. India accounts for more than two-thirds of South Asia's area and more than three-fourths of the region's population, gross domestic product (GDP) and military. To illustrate the point, a comparative picture of the South Asian Association for Regional Cooperation (SAARC), African Union, Agadir (Agadir Agreement: The Arab Mediterranean Free Trade Agreement), the Union of South American Nations (UNASUR), The North American Free Trade Agreement (NAFTA; the United States, Mexico and Canada) and the Association of Southeast Asian Nations (ASEAN) is given in Table 3.1.

**Table 3.1**

*Leading country shares of regional aggregates (per cent)*

| Aggregates | SAARC (8) India | African Union (53) Nigeria | Agadir (4) Egypt | UNASUR (12) Brazil | NAFTA (3) United States | ASEAN (10) Indonesia |
|---|---|---|---|---|---|---|
| Area | 66.22 | 3.40 | 58.69 | 48.02 | 44.40 | 42.71 |
| Population | 76.41 | 18.05 | 61.30 | 49.79 | 71.4 | 67.37 |
| GDP | 79.65 | 16.40 | 63.17 | 16.54 | 83.99 | 37.73 |
| Military Spending | 82.24 | 22.90 | 19.81 | 47.12 | 99.02 | 39.18 |

*Sources:* Computed from the country chapters of *The New Encyclopaedia Britannica* 2011; GlobalSecurity.org. For the GDP and military spending figures of Nigeria, it was difficult to compute the figures from the above sources, as a result we depended on somewhat old data available in Rudolph and Rudolph (1987: 5).

*Note:* Figures in the parentheses mean the number of constituent countries.

As could be seen in Table 3.1, barring NAFTA, in no other grouping is one particular country predominant. In NAFTA, the United States towers over Canada and Mexico in population, GDP and military strength; only in respect of area its relative command is not as striking. But NAFTA has worked better than SAARC because, unlike latter, there is no major disagreement over security issues.

In South Asia, ever since the days of the Cold War, the divide between India and Pakistan has been near total. In the 1950s, Pakistan was an active conduit for America's anti-Soviet strategy. And from the late 1960s onwards, against the background of a growing rift between the Soviets and the Chinese, Pakistan played a critical role in bringing rapprochement between the Americans and the Chinese. In contrast, India was non-aligned, which, let alone America, even Pakistan ridiculed. Its first Foreign Minister, Chaudhry Sir Muhammad Zafarullah Khan (1947–54), famously sneered at the idea of non-alignment by noting that 0+0+0+0=0, each zero representing a non-aligned country. Later, the Indo-Pak divide became much wider when India moved closer to the Soviets. The strategic shift came in handy for India when it subsequently succeeded in dismembering Pakistan and helped create the nation-state of Bangladesh. In the aftermath, the Pakistan–China friendship became firmer and the strategic divide in South Asia was manifestly obvious.

The growth of international Islamist terrorism, with Pakistan as one of its epicentres, and India as one of its major targets, completed the divide. If this situation is compared with NAFTA, one would see that even though Mexico's presence in the group is not appreciated by several of its Latin American neighbours, such as Venezuela, Bolivia and Uruguay, economic advantages of a partnership with America clearly trump these concerns. Even after 9/11 when border movements between the United States and Canada and between United States and Mexico were restricted to prevent the entry of potential terrorists, the countries worked out the idea of smart borders not to allow their trade relations to suffer (Andreas 2003: 93–96, for recent developments in this regard, refer to Hataley 2014: 143–52). But, Pakistan's perception of any economic advantage to be gained from a partnership with India is insignificant compared to the strategic and political advantage it gains by keeping the India-pot boiling.

## The Regional Scene

Before attempting an analysis of the connection between cross-border migrations and security in South Asia, some broad parameters of the security relationship in the region should be kept in mind. The triangular relationship between India, China and Pakistan is at the core of this problematic and much of the problem emanating from it is grounded in the respective circumstances and strategic perceptions and misperceptions of the respective actors. China and India have a competitive relationship since the 1950s. Although of late there are indications of a thaw, reflected particularly in their mutual decision to not allow the border dispute to come in the way of normalisation of relations (China is India's biggest trading partner now), on macro terms there is likelihood that the undercurrents of suspicion will continue. China's nuclear doctrine commits itself to a no-first-use of nuclear weapons against a nuclear weapon state or a non-nuclear weapon state or in any nuclear free zone. Still, strategic experts in India argue that any nuclear state which has declared no-first-use policy like China, which has rationalized the possibility of local war in her periphery, may well be compelled to use theatre nuclear weapons in tactical battles once it is under adverse conditions. Chinese nuclear capability concerns India, although it itself has become a nuclear power.

# Partition Refugees: The Security Connection

In South Asia, there are several cases where one can identify the connection between migration and security. It started with the Partition of India and Hindu/Sikh-Muslim migrations across the borders in large numbers. So far as India was concerned, the Hindu migrants from Punjab contributed to the rise of the Hindu-oriented BJS, which tended to view India's foreign policy in communal terms, as was reflected by its founder's, Shyama Prasad Mukherjee, views on Pakistan and how India should deal with this danger.[2] Since the party did not succeed electorally for almost four decades, that connection remained largely theoretic. But it was not the case with Pakistan. Since the Muslim refugees from India (Muhajirin) mattered most in Pakistan's politics (discussed in Chapter 2), they dictated the nation's anti-India stance, which became a permanent fixture of the country's foreign policy.

Three kinds of refugees were created by the Partition: (a) Hindu-Sikh refugees who came to India from Pakistan, mostly West Punjab; (b) Hindu Bengalis who arrived in West Bengal, Assam and Tripura; and (c) Indian Muslims who went to Pakistan, both West and East, though mostly to West Pakistan. They were from East Punjab and other parts of India, mostly UP and Bihar. Those who were from UP and Bihar and other parts of India were collectively called Muhajirin. It is this category that was most instrumental in creating the security-centric mentality of the fledgling Pakistani state. Comprised of relatively more educated people, members of the ICS and the Indian Army, noted businessmen, and, most importantly, leaders and sympathizers of the Muslim League, which had spearheaded the Pakistan movement, the Muhajirin became a political force to reckon with. Since they had left India with the specific notion in their minds to establish Pakistan's new identity independent of India anti-Indianism had to figure most prominently in their nation-building strategy. Another party that also strongly represented this idea was Jamaat-i-Islami, which too had a large following amongst the Muhajirin.

Among the Muslim bureaucrats who migrated to Pakistan was also the important one Qurban Ali Khan, the senior-most British Indian Police officer in the Intelligence Bureau. Though the departing British had destroyed almost all the intelligence files, whatever was left were carried to Pakistan by Khan. As a result, Pakistan had a head start in covert operation skills over that of India which started such operation as late as after the 1962 China war. No wonder that India had difficulties in making sense of the Pakistani radio intercepts the analysis of which could have helped it know about Pakistan's design of attacking J&K in 1947. Qurban Ali Khan's doctrine was that given India's overall advantage in terms of military power and resources, the only way Pakistan could defend itself was through sub-conventional offensive warfare, meaning covert operations. Prime Minister Jawaharlal Nehru had to admit later that from the very start Pakistan had engaged India in 'an informal war' (Swamy 2014). Anecdotally, a story may be recalled here. Just when India and Pakistan were to become two independent nations, Yahya Khan, then a Major in the British Indian Army taking training at the Staff College, Quetta, said to his instructor Colonel S.D. Varma, a Hindu, at the 'break-up' party: 'Sir! What are we celebrating? This should be a day of mourning. As a united country, we would have been a strong and powerful nation. *Now we will be fighting one another*' (Nawaz 2009: 21, emphasis added).

In a sense even the tribal incursions into J&K before the latter's accession to India, which triggered the first India–Pakistan war over Kashmir, was a case of people's movement across the border and its security connection. Whether the tribesmen were sent to Kashmir by Pakistan is difficult to say. Indians believe they were. Pakistani sources suggest that its army was actively preparing itself to take action in Kashmir and in that preparation the tribal support was not ruled out. But probably before anything was actually done the tribesmen intervened, which Pakistan, of course, welcomed (Khan 1975: 1–25). On 23 October 1947, the tribesmen attacked, on 26 October the Maharaja fled to Jammu, on 27 October he acceded to India and the very next day Indian troops started landing in Srinagar. On 26th the tribesmen had reached Baramulla, barely 35 miles away from Srinagar. The road from Baramulla to Srinagar being on the plains they could have continued without any difficulty. But they did not, and decided to do so only after two long days, which proved to be fatal for their mission. Why so? Indian sources suggest that they were busy looting the town but Pakistani sources supply another reasoning. For example, Akbar Khan suggests that the retreating Dogra army had destroyed the buildings in the town and otherwise ransacked the town, creating a lot of debris and making the movements of tribesmen difficult. Another reason was, as 'the locals at Baramulla said, that Khurshid Anwar, who was in command, had waited for Kashmiri Leaders whom he had sent for in order to confer with regarding his own position in the future Government of Kashmir. Whatever the reason, there was no time to find out for certain as it was near midnight, and the front had yet to be reached' (Khan 1975: 37–38). But the defeat of the tribesmen was inevitable. As they reached the outskirts of Srinagar, they met with massive resistance from the Indian Army and Air Force, thereby shattering their dream of capturing the city.

# Tibetan Refugees and the 'Indian' Chinese

Unlike other refugee arrivals, the Tibetans posed a twofold challenge to the Indian state, diplomatic and humanitarian (the latter is discussed in Chapter 4). Ever since the early 1950s when Tibetans started coming to India as refugees, India had to delicately balance its humanitarian commitment with that of maintaining good relations with China. The challenge reached its peak when, following the occupation of Tibet by the Chinese in 1959, the Dalai Lama fled to India and with him came about 100,000 Tibetan refugees. While India welcomed the Dalai Lama and his people, it refused to assume an overt anti-Chinese posture which the West would have liked India to do. India did not support either the UN General Assembly resolution of 21 October 1959 or that of 20 December 1961, both of which had condemned the Chinese treatment of the Tibetans. The question of Tibet remained a sensitive issue in Sino-Indian relations and in 2000 it once again became a matter of concern when Karmapa Lama fled to India from Tibet. Keeping in mind the sensitivity of its relations with China, India confined its policy to a two-pronged approach, one, not to endorse the demand for Tibetan independence to avoid any problem with China, and two, to steadfastly adhere to its commitment to *non refoulement* in dealing with the refugees as per international customary norm (Dhavan 2004: 122–23).

Has the presence of Tibetan refugees on Indian soil contributed to India's diplomatic or military posturing? So far as diplomacy vis-à-vis China is concerned, it works indirectly. Tibetan refugees invariably protest massively on the streets of Delhi whenever an important Chinese dignitary visits India. The latter suppresses these protests to drive home the point that while India stands by its commitment to recognize Tibet as an Autonomous Region of China, it is the duty to the latter to take care of the civil rights situation in the plateau, for otherwise it would invariably spill over into India, causing tension in the bilateral relations. Viewing from the other angle, that is, whether the host country India has any inherent advantage in embarrassing the sending country China, one may draw some conclusions from global experiences. It does happen that the receiving countries sometimes score some brownie points internationally by using a section of the refugees militarily against the sending country, of course covertly. India is no exception. In the wake of the Sino-Indian border conflict of 1962, when the Indo-Tibetan Border Police Force (ITBP) was raised, the Tibetan refugees formed the bulk of the recruits (Kharat 2003: 293). India also took advantage of the presence of thousands of these refugees to raise a regiment called the Vikas regiment. This low-profile regiment was particularly suited for the defence of the Baltistan–Ladakh border. Known in the Ladakh region of J&K as the Lama Fauj (army), its services were of particular value during the Kargil crisis of May–July 1999, from guarding the strategic features such as roads and bridges to being deployed for high altitude warfare (*Outlook*, 28 June 1999: 32).

There is anxiety in China that the 110,000 strong Tibetan refugees in India because of their refusal to reconcile to their fate would give a handle to India to create difficulties for Beijing. In 2011, the Dalai Lama (14th in the lineage) announced that the next Dalai Lama need not necessarily be born in Chinese-controlled Tibetan lands, thereby suggesting that he could emanate from either the Tibetan diaspora or from traditional areas of Tibetan residence, most notably Tawang in Arunachal Pradesh. More importantly, the Dalai Lama renounced his political role as head of the Tibetan government-in-exile and paved the way for a democratically elected leader. In April 2011, Lobsang Sangay, a mid-forties Harvard-trained legal scholar and political activist, who was a refugee born in 1968 in Darjeeling in West Bengal, was elected as the chief minister (Kalon Tripa). This separation of political and spiritual roles of the Dalai Lama seemingly gave the movement permanence that was supposed to go beyond the death of the Dalai Lama. China considered the move of the Dalai Lama as Machiavellian and India as a conduit in his game plan. India, of course, argued that as a democratic country it was not in a position to control all the activities of the Tibetan refugees, particularly when it had given so many cultural and political freedoms to them to operate in India even without officially recognizing the Tibetan government-in-exile. In India's 16th general elections held in April–May 2014, there were about 40,000 Tibetans who were eligible to be enrolled as voters, but only a small number registered as such and an even less number actually voted. Probably the Tibetan activists had dissuaded the people from voting as it would blight their national cause (*The Times of India*, 8 May 2014).

There is yet another virtually unknown case of refugee creation involving the two countries. During the 1950s and 1960s, following the deterioration of India–China relations, many Chinese settled in India were accused of anti-India activities. The members of the Overseas Chinese Workers' Party in Kolkata were put under strict surveillance because of their political attitudes towards the Chinese Communist Party. Many such Chinese were forced to leave India, although they had virtually become Indian after many decades of uninterrupted stay in India (Xing 2009-10: 404-7).

## Bangladesh Liberation Refugees

In the beginning of this chapter, we have referred to a statement by Myron Weiner in which he said that it was migration and not invasion that destroyed the German state. One may use the same phrase to explain the creation of Bangladesh. The India-Pakistan war of 1971 that resulted in the defeat and dismemberment of Pakistan, was directly linked to the unprecedented refugee arrivals from East Pakistan into bordering Indian states, more specifically West Bengal. It happens in situations when the host country is more powerful than the refugee-sending country, which is relatively weak. If they are in inimical terms, the latter is at great risk. The presence of millions of East Pakistani refugees on Indian soil not only helped India launch an international campaign against the military rulers of Pakistan but also gather enough moral justification to use force to make it bend. Prime Minister Indira Gandhi had to create reasonable diplomatic support in the teeth of general international indifference, if not hostility (Raghavan 2013), by using the Bengali refugee issue. She emphasized that as a poor country like India it was not possible for it to cope with the situation any longer. Actually, the relief expenditure was becoming unbearable for India. Even if only three rupees was spent per refugee in September 1971, it would have meant US\$576,000,000 for 8,000,000 camp refugees. By then, the foreign commitment was as little as US\$153,670,000, of which only US\$20,470,000 had actually arrived. The situation worsened in the next month and so on (Bass 2013: 249, Raghavan 2013: 206-7).During her visit to the United States, she under-lined that at a time when India had attained food security and things had started looking up, the huge human tragedy at the India-East Pakistan border that was thrust upon her country strained the national resources to such an extent that it would threaten the country's 'hard-earned stability'. In the state dinner hosted by President Richard Nixon on 4 November 1971, she did not make any effort to charm her host and others present there but toasted in the most matter-of-factly way:

Can you imagine the entire population of Michigan State suddenly converging onto New York State? Imagine the strain on space, on the administration, on services such as health and communications, on resources such as food and money, and this not in condition of affluence, but in a country already battling with problems of poverty and population.... Our administration, already strained to meet the rising demands of our vast population, is stretched to the limit in looking after nine million refugees, all citizens of another country. Food stocks built against drought are being used up. Limited resources scraped together for sorely needed development works are being depleted. (Bass 2013: 251)

Then appealing to American conscience she asked: 'Has not your own society been built of people who have fled from social and economic injustices?'(Bass 2013: 251, see also Khondker 1995: 181).

Although Indira Gandhi's US sojourn did not impress the Nixon–Kissinger duo to change their pro-Pakistan stance, but it could certainly earn public and opposition Democratic sympathy, particularly that of the indomitable Democratic leader Senator Edward Kennedy(Massachusetts Democrat), for the cause of East Pakistan Bengalis over the head of their government. The deteriorating political situation in East Pakistan and the massive flow of Bengalis to India for safety might not have caused any concern to the Nixon administration, for which maintaining good relations with Pakistan was very important so as to use its good offices to establish contacts with Mao's China, but the entire American political class was not impressed by this logic. The report of Senator Kennedy to the Senate Committee on the Judiciary was a harsh indictment of the US government posture. It said:

It is time … for Americans to understand what has produced this massive human tragedy and to recognize the bankrupt response of our government. It is time for Americans to understand that we must rescue the ideals of our foreign policy from cold calculations that have not only shaken and demoralized South Asia, but many other parts of the world as well. (Kennedy 1971: v)

The report was particularly critical of the US policy of continued military assistance to the dictatorial regime of General Yahya Khan:

Nothing has come to symbolize more the intransigency of American policy of supporting Islamabad, than the shipments of military supplies. And nothing has come to symbolize more the bankruptcy of this policy—carried out in the name of 'leverage'—than the simple fact that the repression of East Bengal and the flow of refugees into India continues. And war is closer today than ever before. (Kennedy 1971: 59)

Gandhi knew the importance of public opinion in any democracy and more so in the United States. She, therefore, made it a point to spend time in New York before reaching Washington to build her popular support. Hannah Arendt, the eminent American philosopher of power and violence, breathlessly described Mrs Gandhi as '*very* good-looking, almost beautiful, very charming, flirting with every man in the room, without chichi, and entirely calm—she must have known already that she was going to make war and probably enjoyed it even in a perverse way. The toughness of these women once they have got what they wanted is really something' (Bass 2013: 250).

A huge public opinion support was built up against the Pakistani atrocities and in favour of the Bengali uprising. It was the time when America was preparing for the opening up of China, for which the presidential adviser Henry Kissinger needed the logistical support of Pakistan. The Nixon-Kissinger duo, therefore, was in no mood to listen to the voice of reason and human rights (details in Bass 2013). India was not unaware of these realities yet it was keeping its powder dry for the inevitable showdown with Pakistan. To achieve the goal, two things were necessary, one, enlisting the support of the Soviets in case of the eventuality of an India-Pakistan war which might see the United States supporting Pakistan, and two, making the military use of the refugees to whatever extent it was possible. To achieve the latter, it decided to give military training to some sections of the Bengali refugees. They were first trained as Mukti Fauz and later as Mukti Bahini whose coopera-tion during the India-Pakistan war proved vital for inflicting substantial damage to static installations and infrastructure in East Pakistan such as bridges, roads, railroads, water transportation networks, power stations, communication systems and ships in the Chittagong port. The Mukti Bahini had the full logistical support from the Indian armed forces, par-ticularly the BSF (Bass 2013: 178-88, Raghavan 2003: 310-13). Indeed, the Indian troops were on the East Pakistan soil before Yahya Khan had declared war against India on 3 December 1971. Actually, India had decided to declare war against Pakistan the next day (Bass 2013: 271).

There was a non-military security compulsion as well. India believed that behind the flow of refugees was the calculated design on the part of Pakistan to push millions of East Pakistani Hindus to India so as to neu-tralize the numerical advantage of East Pakistan vis-à-vis West Pakistan which all the US diplomats stationed in Pakistan had been constantly reporting (Bass 2013, Weiner 1992-93: 123). That was a dangerous prop-osition for India. On the one hand, it would dramatically deteriorate the fragile Hindu-Muslim relations in India which would have long-term implications for the future of Indian state the hallmark of which was secularism, and, on the other hand, it would jeopardize regional security as the Partition of India on religious lines had already shown. Knowing its political import, the top brass in the Indian decision making very assiduously downplayed this element (Bass 2013: 121–22).

Besides the indirect connection between the refugee problem and the question of promoting India's politico-strategic interests vis-à-vis Pakistan, there was a direct one as well. Among the people who had fled East Pakistan was the Awami League leadership, which had set up a Bangladesh government-in-exile in Calcutta. The Government of India and the Bangladesh government-in-exile could coordinate their political strategies to mutual benefit. India had four principal objectives in mind within the overall strategic consideration. First, to see to it that Pakistan lost its eastern province and its power reduced; second, to see that the refugees returned to Bangladesh; third, the communists, particularly the pro-Chinese variety, did not gain in political strength through the liberation movement; and fourth, the new nation accepted India's pre-eminence in the region unlike Pakistan. Except for the last point, which was to be endorsed by implication than by explicit declaration, all the rest were clearly endorsed by the Awami League. The first objective does not require any documentation. Regarding the second and third, there was clear evidence that the Bangladesh government-in-exile had endorsed them. The fact that in Bangladesh politics India has many detractors even today while the Awami League stands out as its only support base had its history in the events of these fateful days of the Bangladesh crisis (for details, see Ghosh 1989: 57–64).

The third point which had the reference to China needs some elaboration as it had an important security angle. In the previous chapter, we had seen how it had fanned the Indian anxiety about its possible repercussions for the Naxalite movement in West Bengal. In this, the China factor loomed large. In the wake of the Cultural Revolution, the Chinese not only had aided the separatists in some of India's North-Eastern states, but their Chairman Mao Zedong had even met a group of Naxalites in December 1967. Mao had expressed his complete agreement with the ideological stance of the Naxalites and had even promised them a trade-off if they succeeded in their mission, namely, the acceptance of the McMahon line as China's border and requisite guerrilla training for the Naxal cadres in the Changping Military School on the outskirts of Beijing (Raghavan 2013: 193). But in spite of such menacing possibility, Indira Gandhi tried to keep China informed about India's concern about the refugee problem and sought China's cooperation in resolving the issue. In a letter to Zhou Enlai dated 18 July 1971, she wrote: 'I am encouraged in the belief that the time may be propitious to seek an exchange of views with you on a matter of current importance'. Zhou did not respond to the letter (Raghavan 2013: 199).

One of the important foreign policy expressions for modern democracies is the use of human rights violations in other countries. Either as humanitarian intervention or as right to protect, there is an increasing tendency on behalf of Western powers to intervene in ethnic or sectarian wars in the developing world or in the erstwhile Soviet provinces. NATO's intervention in the Bosnian crisis was one such example. It may be suggested in this connection that India's Bangladesh war, behind which was the presence of millions of East Pakistani refugees in India, was probably the first such humanitarian intervention, in this case by a developing country, as a foreign-policy tool. According to the Indian scholar Pratap Bhanu Mehta:

> India's 1971 armed intervention in East Pakistan—undertaken for a mixture of reasons—is widely and fairly regarded as one of the world's most successful cases of humanitarian intervention against genocide. Indeed, India in effect applied what we would now call the 'responsibility to protect' (R2P) principle, and applied it well. (quoted by Bass 2013: 334)

As India is expected to grow as a world power, its role in the creation of Bangladesh would have to be remembered for reasons not merely confined to its victory over Pakistan. In this context, what is important to understand is the critical relevance of the politics of human rights which the West has the tendency to arrogate for itself alone. As Bass writes:

> Today at the advent of an Asian era in world politics, the future of human rights will increasingly depend on the ideologies, institutions, and cultures of ascendant Asian great powers like China and India. Thus India's democratic response to the plight of the Bengalis marks not just a pivotal moment for the history of the subcontinent, but for how the world's biggest democracy makes its foreign policy—and what weight it gives to human rights. (Bass 2013: xxii–iii)

## The Sri Lankan Refugees

In the 1980s, even before the anti-Tamil riots of 1983, Tamil separatists were supported by India, though in this game the LTTE at that time was not particularly the blue-eyed boys of the Indian intelligence agency,

Research and Analysis Wing. This was largely unknown, and most of the Indians were hostile to the actions of the Sri Lankan government and tended to support the Tamil Nadu opinion in this regard. Following the riots of 1983, when a large number of Tamil refugees took shelter in India, the latter took full advantage of the presence of these thousands of refugees in Tamil Nadu to impart military training to a section of them to enable them to wage a war against the Sri Lankan state (de Silva 1995: 160-61, de Silva 2012: 30).[3] According to Narayan Swamy, who wrote the most knowledgeable book on LTTE:

> The lack of knowledge and reliable information on the covert role of India in Sri Lanka until the 1987 accord was one of the factors which precluded an intelligent analysis of the Indian involvement. Few Indians were aware of the kind of military muscle India was providing to Tamil groups to take on the government of a neighbouring country. Most Indian commentators were taken in by New Delhi's repeated assertions that it was not involved in the arming and training of the Tamils…. It would be pertinent for Indians today to look back and see how the average Sri Lankan must have felt over the brazen patronage extended to people dubbed 'terrorists' by Colombo. Tamil groups based in Tamil Nadu openly claimed credit for attacks on government/military targets in Sri Lanka—without inviting any criticism from the Indian government. Imagine the Punjab and Sind legislature in Pakistan announcing monetary aid to Kashmiri/Khalistani militants. Yet this is precisely what the Tamil Nadu legislature did in 1987. (Narayan Swamy 2008: 31-32)

That some of these trained refugee militants eventually became an albatross around India's neck which the latter found difficult to throw off underscores the security dimensions of the refugee problem. As noted above, six of the Sri Lankan Tamil refugees in the Rajiv Gandhi assassination case, namely, Robert Pyas, Jayakumar, Shanthi (Jayakumar's wife), Vijayan, Selva Lakshmi (Vijayan's wife) and Bhaskaran (Vijayan's father-in-law), were registered refugees staying in Chennai refugee camps.

Here, the role played by M.G. Ramachandran, the film star-turned charismatic Tamil politician who was the Chief Minister of Tamil Nadu from 1977 to 1987, is of relevance. MGR, as he was popularly known, was born on a Sri Lanka tea plantation near Kandy. He was a champion of Tamil plantation workers' cause which evolved into his general campaign for the Sri Lankan Tamil demands, including a separate state for them. Though he was never consistent about his commitment to one faction or the other, at a later stage he became a staunch supporter of the LTTE. When the anti-Tamil riots broke out in July 1983, all Tamil political parties vied with one another to trumpet its pro-Sri Lanka Tamil commitment. MGR declared a week-long mourning in the state and issued a call for a state-wide strike on 2 August 1983. The strike was supported by all political parties and by the centre as well, a clear indication of how the Indira Gandhi government considered it wise to go along the Tamil mainstream opinion. It was the first time in independent India's history that the central government officially participated in a strike called by a state government. All central government offices and undertakings were closed and train services to and from the state were suspended for the day (Ghosh 1989: 171). Whatever might have been his mass politics, MGR and the central government were on the same page insofar as India's Sri Lanka policy was concerned. The Rajiv Gandhi government had to depend on him to see the India–Sri Lanka accord of 1987 sail through. Kingsley de Silva and Howard Wriggins, the biographers of J.R. Jayewardene, wrote that MGR 'was always willing to change his policies on Tamil separatism in Sri Lanka to suit the needs of New Delhi. Thus, although he was a supporter of the LTTE, he backed the Indo-Sri Lanka Peace Accord, and his support had been essential to Rajiv Gandhi in containing opposition within Tamil Nadu to the IPKF's campaigns against the LTTE in Jaffna and Eastern Province of Sri Lanka' (de Silva &Wriggins 1994: 668).

The refugee arrivals in India following the LTTE defeat in Jaffna in 1995 caused concern to India's security establishment. Both India and Sri Lanka had agreed that quite often these movements were LTTE sponsored. It was feared that since Canada, Cambodia and the UK had become cold towards the LTTE following the Switzerland anti-terrorism conference in 1996, they had little option other than garnering support from Tamil Nadu. The Tigers had other compulsions too. So long as they were running a 'liberated zone' in Jaffna with all the paraphernalia of a government, they had no reason to encourage the people to leave. But as they had to retreat to the Vanni jungles after the Sri Lankan troops recaptured Jaffna, the Tigers had no use for the people. As a result, they did not mind if the people left for India in droves.

There is another element which matters and that is the possibility of migrants indulging in espionage and other kinds of covert activities in the host countries either as hostile acts or as friendly acts. Sometimes it also happens that illegal immigrants involve themselves in the politics of the host countries which have ethnic and/or religious overtones, complicating the bilateral relationship. The narcotics and the drug connection, coupled with rampant corruption in the region, converts an already volatile mixture into a witch's brew that affects almost all South Asian nations. The way the Sikh diaspora in Canada and England came to the help of the Khalistan movement in the 1970s and 1980s, to the discomfiture of the Indian government, and similarly the way the Sri Lanka Tamil diaspora aided and abetted the LTTE in the 1980s and 1990s, which virtually made it as strong as the Sri Lankan state, can be cited as examples of this phenomenon. One of the reasons that the split in the LTTE ranks in the first decade of this century, when Colonel Vinayanamoorthi Muralidharan Karuna rebelled against his master, Vellupillai Prabhakaran, did not succeed was that he could not muster the support of the Tamil diaspora. For the same reason the Sri Lankan government also did not take him seriously to deal with. It made a huge difference to Sri Lanka government's capacity to deal with the LTTE from a position of strength only when in the aftermath of 9/11 the United States, Canada, the UK and the EU nations proscribed the organization, froze its bank accounts and kept a close watch on the activities of the pro-LTTE Tamil diasporas in these countries (Peiris 2009: 171–2, 204, 252–53, 276).

# Illegal Bangladeshis in India

In recent times, there is also an ethno-communal dimension to the security question in respect of illegal Bangladeshi settlers in India. The fact that most of the villages on the India–Bangladesh border are Muslim-majority villages, there has been the danger of Inter-Services Intelligence (ISI) operations in these areas. The Islamic connection of these migrations is evident from the growth of Madrasas. Audio cassettes propounding the cause of Worldwide Islamic Terrorism (WIT) were in circulation in West Bengal about a decade ago, particularly in the border areas. One of the additions to the list included a highly provocative one of a speech by the notorious Azhar Masood who had to be released by India in exchange for the passengers of the hijacked IC 814 in December 1999. A 32-page booklet written by him espousing the cause of Jehad was distributed in West Bengal. Two ISI-operated international telecommunication centres or secret spy exchanges, close to the Calcutta airport, were closed down by the Indian authorities.

It must, however, be underlined that the security connection of the Bangladeshi immigrants has often remained unsubstantiated. To understand the linkage between the issue of illegal Bangladeshi migrants in India and the alleged internal security threat posed by them, four interrelated factors have to be grappled with: (a) the overall Hindu–Muslim politics of India; (b) the growth of international Islamist terrorism and the jihadist threat posed to India by elements in Pakistan and Bangladesh with the help of their conduits on Indian soil; (c) the nexus between politicians, illegal migrants and traffickers of drugs, smugglers and other black money racketeers and (d) the federal structure of the security architecture. In India barring the Union Territories (UT), for example, Delhi (a quasi-state), where the police is under the central government, in other states it is under the control of the state government. It is possible to assume that along with other migrants from Bangladesh, some jihadists too are sneaking into India. But given the porous India–Bangladesh border, any motivated jihadist would not wait for this sort of cover. India does not have any noticeable problem of illegal Pakistani migrants, yet India's internal security is ever threatened by the Pakistan-based jihadists operating in India. So, the connection between Bangladeshis in India and Islamist terrorism is at best a conceptual formulation with very little substantive evidence.

For political reasons, however, this connection is always overplayed. Since at the national level the contest for power is between the Congress and the BJP and at the state level between either of them and a dominant state party, the issue of secularism versus communalism on the one hand and between the central authority and the states' rights on the other, the two ideological/political positions over which these parties contest, is ever vibrant, although whether the Congress is fully secular or whether the BJP is fully communal is contestable (Ghosh 1999: 402).[4] It is because of this ideological/political divide the Bangladeshi Muslim migrants in India have a natural ally either in the Congress at the national level or a West Bengal-based political party, say, the TMC or CPM, of course for vote-bank reasons. Unless the BJP threatens these migrants with life in riots, it will remain as their natural enemy.[5] Two case studies, first, that of West Bengal, and second, that of Delhi, would explain the point better. It is a fact of life, in West Bengal, that whether the state is ruled by the Left Front or TMC, the importance of the state's 25 per cent Muslim population can never be overlooked by these political parties. It makes sense to these parties, therefore, to add to their votes by not preventing illegal Muslim migrations from Bangladesh. Here lies the conflict of interest between the state ruling party and the BJP. The latter can electorally gain in West Bengal only if it is able to expand its Hindu vote base by whipping its fear of Bangladeshi illegal migration, which has its roots in both their social and historical experience. The controversy between the BJP-led NDA government at the centre and the TMC government in West Bengal over the incidence of a bomb blast in Bardhaman in early October 2014 that killed the makers of the bomb would illustrate the point. However, before we discuss this controversy, a reference to the centre–state battle over their respective rights over security matters within the Indian federal system calls for some analysis.

# Security in Federal Context

India being a federal state, there is a division of responsibility between the centre and the states so far as the country's security is concerned. Broadly speaking, external security is the responsibility of the centre, while internal that of the states. But this division is not very clearly demarcated, and as a result there often are tensions between the centre and the states over their respective turfs. More the politics of India has become coalitional, making the central government and several state governments belonging to different sets of parties the informal arrangements for coordination are breaking down. This was evident during the debates over the establishment of the National Counter Terrorism Centre (NCTC) in May 2012. Though theoretically there cannot be any dispute that external and internal threats are closely linked and hence they should be tackled holistically, yet the political problem is equally serious to make it work that way. For example, the Assam Rifles (almost always headed by army officers) that primarily takes care of internal security in the North Eastern states, is under the Home Ministry. It poaches into the police powers of these states. The controversy over its human rights violations under the protective umbrella of the Armed Forces Special Powers Act (AFSPA) hovers around the division of powers between the states' rights and the role of the Central Government. In spite of widespread resentment against the Act expressed by the civil society groups, the centre is steadfastly upholding its relevance by resisting all efforts to dilute the Act's premise. It is important to underline the fact that most of the North Eastern state governors have been either retired army officers or officers from other security services. The scuttling down of the NCTC idea underlined the gulf between the respective central and state approaches to the question of security.

Indeed there are several problems that beset the Indian police service. Besides the issues of corruption in the department and its politicization, there is the problem of insufficient training and unfilled vacancies in the force across the states. During the debates over the NCTC, it was argued that the state police had not outlived its utility, as the centre tended to argue and thereby justify that it should be subordinated to the Central Intelligence Bureau. The need was to revamp the state police. Ajai Sahni, Executive Director of the Delhi-based Institute for Conflict Management, said: 'You can't have first-rate counter-terrorism in a third-grade policing'. Even Prime Minister Manmohan Singh had observed in September 2006: 'Unless the "beat constable" is brought into the vortex of our counter-terrorist strategy, our capacity to pre-empt future attacks would be severely limited'. The number of vacancies in the police forces in India was staggering. About 25 per cent of their sanctioned strength, meaning 501,069 personnel in all ranks, was vacant. In April 2012, R.K. Singh, the Union Home Secretary, had informed the Indian Parliament that the actual strength of Indian Police Service in the country was 3,393 against the sanctioned strength of 4,720 (Singh 2012: 61).

The division of powers between the centre and the states is essentially political, in which each side tries to make use of the other. My discussions with army officers over the years have convinced me that it is often the case that the armed forces are reluctant to deal with civilian problems as there is always the possibility of human rights violations as the enemy is not clearly identifiable. In one such discussion, it was revealed that in 2007, it was Ebobi Singh, the Chief Minister of Manipur, needed to show to his people that he had at least done something in respect of the repeal of AFSPA, which was most unpopular in the state. He requested the central government to make AFSPA inoperative in the Imphal municipal area so that he could politically use this success to impress his electorates. The central government, which belonged to the Congress party, to which Singh also belonged, obliged the latter. In the Imphal area, AFSPA is still inoperative. Ironically, probably in 2009, when there was some serious disturbance in Imphal and the state police wanted the army to intervene with AFSPA powers one after another of the security agencies used all kinds of subterfuges not to accede to the request. The handing over of the Kangla fort back to the civilian authorities and the withdrawal of the armed contingent from there tells the same story. One may remember how the fort was ceremonially handed over by giving a huge key of the fort to the civilian authority. A proposal to remove all armed forces battalions from heritage forts was already under active consideration of the Government of India at the highest level and eventually it was decided that the Red Fort, the Kangla Fort and one in Amritsar would be vacated of all armed contingents. But the army took full advantage of the situation to make it a big news by showing that it respected the popular sentiment and vacated the fort. Indeed, it was done in connivance with the political leaders of the state.

## Bardhaman Bomb Blast

Against the above background, when one analyses the Bardhaman incidence it makes sense as to why the BJP-led Central Government and the TMC government of West Bengal have their own political axes to grind. The newspaper reports suggested that the bomb makers killed in the incident were illegal Bangladeshis who had no plan to disturb peace in West Bengal but were preparing the bombs to be used by Jamaat-ul-Mujahideen Bangladesh (JuMB) to destabilize the Sheikh Hasina government in Bangladesh. The central government wanted that its National Investigation Agency (NIA) should probe the incidence, while the state government argued that it was their job to probe the matter. The latter argued that the central government had the ulterior motive to malign the state government for its incapacity in the matter, thereby scoring political points and ultimately boosting its political presence in the state. Anybody having any understanding of Indian politics would smell the rat in both the central government's over enthusiasm to probe the event and the state government's efforts to stonewall those efforts. While the Central Government argued that the illegal infiltrations from Bangladesh were encouraged by the state government, the latter accused the Central Government for failing to prevent those infiltrations as it was the job of the BSF, a central security force, to do so and not that of any security agency of West Bengal (*The Times of India*, 8 October 2014; *The Hindu*, 12 October 2014).

## The Case of Delhi

In some sense, the Delhi experience was the mirror image of West Bengal. During the first BJP-led NDA government (1999–2004), internal security threat emanating from illegal Bangladeshi migrants figured in a big way. BJP leader L.K. Advani as the Deputy Prime Minister thundered that the government would 'locate and throw out' all Bangladeshi illegal migrants from India. Under such a diktat the Delhi Police, which is under the control of the central government, had to act. It came out with information that it had intelligence reports suggesting that under police pressure Bangladeshis had left Delhi and moved to J&K to help the jihadists operating there, mostly as carriers and messengers (*The Hindu*, 15 September 2003). Probably there was enough evidence to argue that the rise of Islamic politics in Bangladesh, particularly during the BNP regimes, had an inevitable connection with the jihadists in Pakistan, and also with the ISI of Pakistan, but to link it to Bangladeshi migrants required substantial evidence, which was not easy to lay one's hand on (discussed in Chapter 2).

Whether or not one finds any clear connection between security threats and the presence of Bangladeshis in India, the Delhi Police seemingly does not take any chance under whatever political dispensation, as was seen during the Commonwealth Games held in October 2010. Many of them were asked to vacate certain sensitive areas or were under strict surveillance. A World Bank-funded NGO survey conducted during those days, which was supposed to look into Delhi-based Bangladeshis as well, had to skip Delhi for the same reason and had to substitute it by Lucknow, because in that city 'the security threat perception from illegal migrants didn't appear to be a dominant public discourse. As a result the sample was found to be far less resistant to respond to the questionnaire (to reveal identity) as compared to the sample in Delhi' (TARU 2010).

## Migrations and the Border-Fencing Issue

One of the strategies considered by India to prevent cross-border migrations, which have the potential connection with internal security, is to fence the India–Bangladesh and India–Pakistan borders, though it is only the former which figures in popular imagination. The reason is that the illegal Bangladeshis have a visible presence in India, and since the majority of them are Muslims they have relevance for Indian politics. In contrast, so far as illegal Pakistanis are concerned that debate gets consumed by the issue of Pakistani terrorists sneaking into India for whom there is already the security apparatus in place, making it a political debate of a different kind. The Hindu or Sikh refugees who arrive from Pakistan from time to time receive due legal and moral protection from the state for whom majority sympathy is taken for granted.

The issue of fencing the borders emerged soon after the Partition. In 1955, Pakistan put up a short fence on the border facing Dinajpur in West Bengal to prevent smuggling (van Schendel & Abraham 2005: 212-36). As the issue of migrations from East Pakistan to Assam picked up political momentum, the latter demanded, in 1964, the erection of fences along its East Pakistan border. In its memorandum to the central government, the Congress Parliamentary Party of Assam highlighted that large-scale espionage networks were operating in the state, which was beyond the capacity of the state government to handle. It is necessary, therefore, to completely seal the border facing East Pakistan (Kar 1997: 120). The demand remained unchanged, and in the Assam Accord of 1985 this demand figured prominently. Clauses 9.1 and 9.2 of the accord read:

> The international border shall be made secure against the future infiltration by erection of physical barriers like barbed wire fencing and other obstacles at appropriate places. Patrolling by security forces on land and riverine routes all along the international border shall be set up. Besides the arrangements mentioned above and keeping in view security considerations, a road all along the international border shall be constructed so as to facilitate patrolling by the security forces. Land between border and roads would be kept free from human habitation, where possible.

Even before the Assam Accord the matter was receiving the attention of the central government. It had been decided in the early 1980s that fences should be constructed to cover 200 km in Dhubri in Assam and West Dinajpur in West Bengal (Bhasin 1996: 827-28). Bangladesh protested to the Indian move but India did not relent (Bhasin 1996: 846-47). In 1986, the government prepared a project to be completed in two phases, all by 2007 (MHA Annual Report 2005-06). But because of delays the dates had to be constantly extended. The date of the first phase was extended from 1996 to 1998 and then from 1998 to 2000. But even in 2003 the first phase work was still on. Till early 2006, of the sanctioned 2429.5 km, only 1275.415 km had been constructed (MHA Annual Report 2006-7:37). Though according to the 1986 decision it all had to end in 2007, the date was first extended to 2010 and then to 2012. On 8 December 2009, the Assam Accord Implementation and Revenue Minister Bhumidhar Barman told the state assembly that just a few kilometres of the 262-km land border the state shares with Bangladesh remained to be fenced, but a 10-km stretch ringed by water would continue to remain unfenced. The remaining portion would be completed by March 2010. In a written reply to a question by AGP's Alaka Sarma, Barman said: 'There are few stretches that are also disputed and in adverse possession of Bangladesh. Hence fencing work could not be taken up'.

At present, a total of 3,438 km of the fence remains to be erected (details in Ghosh 2014: 121–59). The project, however, suffers from some inherent problems besides political. The controversy over the demarcation of the border and the problem of nature complicating the issue is the other major hurdle. The problems of land acquisition and the issue of adverse possession and enclaves complicated matters.[6] As per international norms, though fences are to be erected 150 yards away from the international zero line, often the rule is flouted once again because of the terrain problem which, as some analysts say, as if the Indian state has given up its claim over its own territory (Prakash & Menon 2011: 33).

Like efforts to fence the India–Bangladesh border there have been efforts to fence the India and Pakistan border too. The only good thing about this project is that the border there is well defined and the terrain is not as problematic as in the case of India and Bangladesh. But at places, it is riverine, marshy, and in winter reaching the sub-zero temperature level. Politically speaking, unlike Bangladesh, Pakistan is India's enemy number one, which relieves India of the guilt complex, making it more confident to go ahead with its fencing scheme that includes troop reinforcements and floodlighting the borders. Like the Bangladesh border fencing, which was conceived in the 1980s, the same was true for the borders facing Pakistan, although it was in the 2000s that the work was accelerated by taking advantage of a relative thaw in the conflict. It was in the background of the 'four-step' formula that had been worked out between Prime Minister Manmohan Singh and President Pervez Musharraf (Haidar 2014). Table 3.2 would give an idea about the present state of the fencing.

## Rohingyas in Bangladesh

It is instructive in this context to discuss about the Rohingya refugees in Bangladesh and their relevance for Bangladesh's Islamist politics as well as Bangladesh's relations with Myanmar from where these refugees have come. It is alleged both by the secular forces in Bangladesh and the Government of Myanmar that these refugee camps contribute to Islamic militancy in Bangladesh to the detriment of liberal and democratic politics in Bangladesh and that of the national security of Myanmar. The latter claims that the Rohingyas are Bangladeshis who have illegally settled on their land and as such they would have to be evicted. This irks the Bangladeshis, particularly in the camps' neighbourhood areas, who

**Table 3.2**
Fencing and floodlighting of the India–Pakistan border (km)

| Name of state | Total length of border | Total length of border to be fenced | Length of border fenced so far | Remaining length of border to be fenced | Sanctioned length of border to be floodlit | Length of border floodlit so far | Remaining length of border to be floodlit |
|---|---|---|---|---|---|---|---|
| Punjab | 553 | 461.00 | 462.45* | | 460.72 | 460.72 | |
| Rajasthan | 1,037 | 1,056.63 | 1,048.27* | | 1,022.80 | 1,022.80 | |
| Jammu International Border | 210 | 186.00 | 186.00 | | 186.00 | 176.40 | 9.6 |
| Gujarat | 508 | 340.00 | 261.78 | 79.22 | 340.00 | 241.00 | 99 |
| Total | 2,308 | 2,043.63 | 1,958.5 | 79.22 | 1,900.92 | 1,900.92 | 108.6 |

*Source:* Compiled from MHA Annual Report 2012–13 by Das (2014: 314–15). It may be noted that the MHA Annual Report 2013–14 has irreconcilable discrepancies. To avoid any confusion for the readers, 2012–13 data have been used.

*Note:* *The length is at times different because of topographical factors/alignment of fencing.

insist that they should be sent back even if force will have to be used. This may have also been caused by the fact that there is a growing militancy amongst a section of the refugees under the leadership of Rohingya Solidarity Organisation (RSO), which has close links with such terrorist groups as JuMB and the Harkat-ul-Jihad-al-Islam (Huji). Because of this militancy variable, neither the Bangladesh government is sympathetic to the plight of the Rohingya refugees nor is the Myanmar government in any mood to take them back. In 2008 when the Bihari Muslims were allowed to become Bangladesh nationals, many had thought that it might mean that the government was willing to consider similar policy for the Rohingyas but nothing of that sort happened, for it would have been an unpopular move, especially in view of their terrorist links (Murshid 2012: 105-8). The way Myanmar has been witnessing the rise of militant Buddhism and the government's apartheid-like attitude towards the Rohingyas, one may merely speculate about the systematic deterioration in Bangladesh–Myanmar relations.

## Rohingyas and the Islamic Militancy

To understand the security connection between the phenomenon of Muslim migration from East Bengal to the Rakhine province in Myanmar and that of the rise of Islamic militancy in the broader Chittagong-Rakhine region several interconnected realities must be simultaneously grappled with. They are as follows: one, the Partition of India and the subsequent understanding between the Pakistani and the Myanmarese leaderships to honour the sanctity of the Pakistan–Myanmar border; two, the compulsion of the Rakhine Muslims to construct their identity independent of their East Pakistan/Bangladesh connection and the resultant consolidation of the Rohingya ethnic consciousness; three, the rise of Islamism in the politics of East Pakistan/Bangladesh; four, the trend towards growing anti-Indian ethnic insurgency in India's north-eastern region with the insurgent hideouts in Bangladesh and Myanmar; five, the flow of Arab money to promote Islamic (Wahabi) influence in many parts of the world, including this region; and lastly, but importantly, the Anglo-Japanese competition for the domination of Myanmar during the Second World War, in which Muslims were noticed to be on the side of the British while the Rakhine Buddhists were seen to be on the side of the Japanese. During this period, many confrontations took place between Muslim-armed groups and the Rakhine Buddhists. The memories of these violent interactions continued to influence the inter-communal relations even after the war as no efforts were made to undo the respective territorial dispossessions in the north. It took years for the Myanmar government to regain effective control over Rakhine, where several militant groups had entrenched themselves to fight the state (Leider 2013: 239–40).

During the rule of General Ne Win (1958–60, 1962–88), the Rohingya rebels seemed to gain their first political victory in 1960 when the Mayu Frontier District was created comprising Buthidaung, Maungdaw and a part of Rathedaung. It was an all-Muslim district. From 1961 to 1964, the army ruled it directly from Yangon and its administration was separate from that of the rest of Rakhine. Though its creation had followed the surrender of Rohingya freedom fighters to the army, still it is to be noted that the creation of Mayu Frontier District was the culmination of a process because it was in the 1950s that the ethnic nomenclature 'Rohingya' was systematically recognized by the central political leadership. For example, the formation of the Rohingya student association in Yangon had been allowed and the use of Rohingya language in radio broadcasts was permitted. Even in the speeches of the rulers, the word 'Rohingya' was often used. But this so-called Rohingya political victory was not enduring because of internal feuds which led to the rise of several militant factions and their confrontations with the state. Some such groups were the Rohingya Independent Force, Rohingya Independent Army and the Rohingya Patriotic Front. All of them, which came into being in the 1960s and the 1970s, were essentially the same, who assumed new names from time to time. But the establishment of the RSO in 1982 made a qualitative change in outlook of the Rohingyas (Leider 2013: 240–45).

Started in Bangladesh by Dr Mohammad Yunus, the RSO's original purpose was to safeguard the interests of Rohingya refugees in Bangladesh who fled from Myanmar in search of security. But gradually it became an Islamist militant movement that aimed at the 'creation of an autonomous Arakan state uniting the Rohingyas of Burma and Bangladesh'. Because of its connection with Jamaat-i-Islami and Afghan militants, it, far from being a security threat to Myanmar, became one for Bangladesh itself, which tried to suppress it. The organization also developed international links through the Organisation of Islamic Conference (OIC) and by lobbying in the United States. In 2011, under the patronage of OIC the senior Rohingya leaders founded the Arakan Rohingya Union. On the whole, however, it is difficult to say how much of mass base these movements have among the Muslims of Myanmar, a subject which is worth researching (Leider 2013: 246–47). Insofar as India is concerned, it is keeping its vigil on the developments as there are reports that Pakistan's Lashkar-e-Taiba, Jamaat-ud-Dawa and Falah-i-Insaniyat may be poaching into the Rohingya disaffection to enlist new recruits for their mission. On 3 July 2015, Pakistan embarrassed Myanmar by sponsoring a resolution at the 29th session of the UNHRC condemning 'all violations and abuses of human rights in Myanmar, in particular against Rohingya Muslims' (*The Times of India*, 28 July 2015).

## Afghan Refugees in Pakistan

Pakistan's experience vis-à-vis Afghan refugees in the post-Soviet invasion phase also highlights the connection between migration and security. Millions of Afghan Pashtoons had taken shelter in Pakistan, mostly in the NWFP (now Khyber Pakhtunkhwa). At one level their presence on Pakistan's soil was a God-send for the dictatorial regime of Zia-ul-Haq, but later they became a liability. Through them Zia-ul-Haq had bargained with the United States a new lease for his political life, besides demanding huge amounts of arms and economic aid. But before long a pernicious nexus developed between the multi-million dollar illegal trade in narcotics and arms on the one hand and the massive corruption in the politico-military–bureaucratic establishment on the other. Not only did it affect Pakistan's political development, it also dragged Pakistan into the vortex of factional ethnic conflicts of Afghanistan, which it found difficult to extricate itself from. As the Afghan situation became complicated, Pakistan's federal problems in the NWFP multiplied, for it was the home of the same ethnic groups to which the major warring factions engaged in the Afghan civil war belonged. Still, the Taliban regime that ruled Afghanistan from 1996 to 2001 following a bloody civil war was pro-Pakistan, which indeed the latter had raised from amongst the refugees. The Pakistan army had trained them for the job to Pakistan's advantage. It had been the strategic requirement of Pakistan to have a friendly regime in Afghanistan through which it could fulfil its need of strategic depth given the rivalry with India. These developments cast their shadow on India–Pakistan–Iran relations, causing complications for South Asian regional security.

While the Taliban victory was to Pakistan's advantage, insofar as India was concerned, it not only affected India–Pakistan relations but also resulted in refugee problems for India. Not only did the Hindu and

Sikh settlers in Afghanistan felt threatened and left for India, even many disgruntled Afghans opposed to the Taliban regime took shelter in India. One of the members of the first group of 80 Hindu/Sikh refugees that arrived at the Rajasansi airport in Punjab on 17 October 1996 said: 'It is not just that we are required to go out in a burqua. The general atmosphere of fear and terror that stalks the land has made our lives miserable' (*The Times of India*, 18 October 1996). Indian settlers in Afghanistan felt that the situation was becoming increasingly hostile and began to leave for India. Pakistan viewed its problems from a somewhat similar ethnic angle. The Washington-based *Pakistan Affairs* reported that Zia-ul-Haq had told Rajiv Gandhi in early 1987 that if India desired a declaration from Pakistan to the effect that the latter would not interfere in the internal affairs of India, the latter would also have to declare that it would not support the so-called 'Sindhu Desh and Pakhtoonistan' (1 March 1987: 1). In May 1987, the ruling Muslim League, in a party resolution, reiterated the proposal. Later, there were allegations that India was actively behind the militancy launched by the MQM (Altaf) that rocked Karachi. On 10 November 1998, Pakistan announced the sealing of its western borders with India to check the cross-border movement of unscrupulous elements.

The Taliban militancy, which has now spilled over into Pakistan in the form of several indigenous militant outfits, the most notable of which is the Tehrik-i-Taliban, has posed serious threat to Pakistan's political stability as never before. In the situation of a US withdrawal from Afghanistan, even if it is partial and staggered, the fear of India is that this Afghan militancy, coupled with the issue of constant Afghan migrations to Pakistan, would not leave India unaffected. The challenge for India is how to handle the paradox called Af-Pak. The paradox is this: The United States and its allies depend (pending total US withdrawal this dependence would continue) on Pakistan for access to the war theatre (General James Jones, President Obama's National Security adviser has put it, 'there are several countries, but there is one theater') and to keep the supply lines open. They must thus accept the political conditions set by Islamabad to keep the arrangement. Yet, the whole purpose of the war was to deny the safe haven provided to Al Qaeda by the Taliban regime and eradicate the forces of terrorism and fundamentalism from Afghanistan. If the latter continue to be supported and financed from Islamabad (though they also get help from elsewhere), the US–Pakistan arrangement itself becomes self-defeating. Its short-term logistical advantage is more than offset by a long-term bolstering of the very enemy Washington is fighting. In fact, there is a misalignment between Pakistan's interests in Afghanistan and those of the United States (Heine & Ghosh 2011). Still, what Ayesha Jalal writes seems to be the hard reality. She argues that it is not realistic for the America to break off ties with Pakistan and lean more heavily on Indian monetary and military help to rebuild Afghanistan: 'Most security experts on the region grudgingly concede that American success in Afghanistan depends on the Pakistani army. *Paradoxically, this army is the main obstacle as well as the key to peace in Afghanistan*' (Jalal 2014: 5, emphasis added).

# Nepali Migrants and Sikkim's Loss of Independence

The connection between Nepali migrations to Sikkim, Bhutan and India on the one hand and the security and foreign-policy approaches of these countries on the other is an important issue, although it has not received adequate academic attention. Most of the writings on the subject are related to domestic political developments and ethnicity building, while their international dimensions are often overlooked. To study the subject from foreign policy and security angles one may analyse it in three segments—first, the impact of these migrations on India's security outlook in the Himalayan region, second, their impact on that of Bhutan, and third, the impact of the above two phenomena on India-Bhutan and India-Nepal relations. All these are closely linked to India's relations with China. The migration of ethnic Nepalis from Nepal and the northern districts of India from 19th century onwards to Sikkim (till 1975 an independent kingdom) and Bhutan was a regular phenomenon. It tended to change the demographic balance between the migrants and the indigenous populations measurably, more so in the case of Sikkim where the Nepalis virtually displaced the original Bhutia and Lepcha communities. Because of politico-strategic reasons, India took advantage of the situation to become an interested party calling the shots.

Ever since the exit of Britain as the imperial power in the region, an important element in India's China problem was the spectre of its potential influence in India's Himalayan neighbourhood that included three kingdoms—Sikkim, Bhutan and Nepal. Ethnically, the common denominator across these states was the Nepali ethnicity. China's forward policy in the region had started causing anxiety to India's strategic establishment from the early days of independence exactly the way it used to bother the

British. The systematic occupation of Tibet by China from the early 1950s till it was annexed in 1959, and its war against India in 1962, had made India concerned about the future of its small Himalayan neighbours, which had traditionally served as buffers between the two Asian powers. This was amply evident in the discussions and exchange of notes between the Indian and Chinese governments in the 1950s and 1960s (details in Rao 1972: 162–76). Against this background, India's policy for Sikkim was to make use of the Nepali 'fifth column' to get the kingdom incorporated into the Indian Union because the royal family there was not playing its cards in consonance with the Indian interests. Eventually, India manipulated Sikkim's merger with the Indian Union in 1975. In achieving this, India's principal conduit in Sikkim was the militant Sikkim Youth Congress led by Nar Bahadur Khatiawada, who was also the president of the Committee on Land Reforms of the Sikkim government.

In early 1975, Khatiawada submitted a report, the communal implications of which were far-reaching. Its recommendations were meant to dispossess the influential Buddhist monasteries of their huge landholdings. Since these lands supported a sizeable portion of the kingdom's original Bhutia–Lepcha population, the report if implemented had the potential to deprive these communities of their economic and political power. It is instructive here to recall what the Calcutta-based *Statesman* had editorialized on 18 February 1975. It cautioned Kazi Lhendup Dorji, the Chief Minister of Sikkim, that he:

> must be aware that the acceptance of this report will, in time, lead to the disappearance of the indigenous community of which he is a leading representative. This has happened already in Darjeeling district where Bhutia-Lepchas were in majority before the 19th Century Nepalese influx and also, to some extent, in the southern regions of Bhutan. A similar process was arrested in Chota Nagpur, Nagaland, Mizoram and other parts of India by preventing the transfer of Adivasi and tribal holdings; and it is to be hoped that the Chief Executive of Sikkim will take adequate precautions to protect the indigenous minority community.

But exactly the opposite happened. Soon, there was a unanimous resolution in the Sikkim assembly for its merger into the Indian Union, which was approved by a state-wide referendum.

It may be noted that by the beginning of the 1970s, the inter-ethnic political rivalry had become chronic, resulting in the dramatic decline in the king's capacity to rule. Against this background, Kazi Lhendup Dorji, Nar Bahadur Khatiwada, Ram Chandra Poudyal and Krishna Chandra Pradhan emerged as leaders who mattered. It was alleged that behind these leaders were the Indian armed forces in readiness to intervene. Events moved very fast thereafter:

> ruler's refusal to compromise with the agitating politicians, invalidation of 1973 election, fresh election to the State Council in 1974, demand for associating Sikkim with India, *ruler's visit to Kathmandu against the advice of the government of India*, State Council's resolution to abolish the office of the Chogyal, referendum to decide Sikkim's future and its merger with India in May 1975. (Sinha 2006, emphasis added)

It was decided through a tripartite agreement among the king, the representative of the Government of India and leaders of the political parties in Sikkim to convert the existing State Council into State Assembly and to allow it to continue for a period of five years from its election in 1974. The Government of Sikkim Act, 1974, Clause 7, Section II stipulated:

> The Government of Sikkim may make rules for the purpose of providing that the Assembly adequately represents the various sections of the population, that is to say while fully protecting the legitimate rights and interests of Sikkimese of Lepcha or Bhutia origin and Sikkimese of Nepali origin and other Sikkimese, including Tsongs, Scheduled Castes, no single section of population is allowed to acquire a dominating position in the affairs of Sikkim mainly by its ethnic origin.

For details on Sikkim's ethnic politics, see Sinha (2006).

# Nepali Migrants and Bhutan's Sense of Insecurity

In the case of Bhutan, the use of the Nepali card by India took an altogether different form. Here, a bit of recalling the history of India–Bhutan relations since India's independence would be necessary. After the British left the subcontinent, Bhutan was worried about its future. In all the three Himalayan states—Nepal, Sikkim and Bhutan—pro-Congress forces were actively pitted against the respective monarchs, namely, the Nepal State Congress Party (since 1946), the Sikkim State Congress Party (since 1947) and the Bhutan State Congress Party (since 1948). Although Bhutan did not immediately sign any 'standstill agreement' with India like Nepal and Sikkim, for all practical purposes it too adhered to a similar arrangement, as was evident from the fact that the Bhutan Agent in India continued to function in his previous capacity and the Indian Political Officer in Gangtok continued to be accredited to Bhutan as well. On 8 August 1949, both the states signed a treaty according to which Bhutan agreed to 'be guided by the advice of the Government of India in regard to its external relations'. It was further agreed that the 'treaty shall continue in force in perpetuity unless terminated or modified by mutual consent'. Soon, China's civil war was to end in the victory of the Communists in October 1949 and China was to occupy Tibet in 1950. It has been argued that India's terms might have been harder had the negotiations taken place sometime later as by that time India had faced serious challenge from China in India's North Eastern border with Tibet. Leo Rose explained the situation in the following words:

> In contrast, when negotiating new treaty relations with both Nepal and Sikkim in 1950 the Indians were acutely disturbed by the expressed determination of the new Communist regime in China to 'reunite' Tibet with the 'Chinese motherland'. India's heightened concern over the vulnerability of its Himalayan bulwark was reflected in the secret letters attached to the 1950 Treaty of Peace and Friendship with Nepal, and in the retention of Sikkim as a 'protectorate' in the 1951 Treaty with that state. (Rose 1974: 193–94)

Subsequent events showed India and Bhutan closely coordinating their national interests in which India's border war with China worked as a catalyst. India's China war on the one hand demonstrated how vulnerable Bhutan was to the Chinese forward moves while, on the other hand, it raised the question in Bhutanese minds as to what extent their alliance with India would be effective in safeguarding their independence given the virtual walkover for the Chinese troops in dealing with their Indian counterparts. Yet, in spite of these dialectics, Bhutan decided in favour of aligning closely with India. It did not emulate the model which Nepal was in the process of developing: that is, to follow a policy of equidistance from both India and China. A significant indication of this reaffirmed trust in India was Bhutan's acceptance of an 'Indian Adviser' to assist the then Bhutanese Prime Minister, Jigme Dorji. This was attributable to the basically different Bhutanese and Nepali perceptions of China's Tibet policy. While the Nepali political elite had little sympathy for the Tibetans, the Bhutanese, in contrast, were perceptibly disturbed by the Chinese action, which tended to destroy an ancient culture with which Bhutan had so much in common. Moreover, Bhutanese considered as spurious China's justification that its actions in Tibet were based on historical claims. They feared that the same justification could someday make them meet the same fate (Rose 1974: 198).

India-Bhutan relations moved ahead smoothly with no serious tension. Against this background, when in the late 1980s and the early 1990s the question of Nepali migrations to Bhutan and their possible repercussions on Bhutanese polity and security rocked the country's politics, resulting in a state of insurgency in the Nepali-dominated southern districts of the Kingdom that made thousands of Nepalis flee to Nepal as refugees, India's policy turned out to be one of benevolent neutrality—in effect, pro-Bhutanese. It may be underlined that Bhutan's borders did not touch those of Nepal. They touched those of India, that too those areas of India's north-eastern region which hosted a large number of ethnic Nepalis. It would be logical to surmise (documentary proof is difficult to garner on such matters) that India saw to it that these Lhotshampa Nepali refugees did not take shelter in India, which would have complicated India-Bhutan relations. It suited the Bhutanese interest as well. For Bhutan dealing with Nepal on the subject was relatively easy compared to dealing with India, which was a bigger power bordering Bhutan. Many rounds of failed talks between Bhutan and Nepal on the refugee issue have shown the farsightedness of Bhutan and Indian leaderships. So far, Bhutan has not taken back a single refugee. The issue is virtually a dead one now in spite of all kinds of UN and NGO interventions. The American offer of granting immigrant visas to many of these refugees has further watered down the problem to Bhutan's satisfaction.

India could have played its Nepali card in Bhutan the way it did in Sikkim. But there were two significant differences in the situations. One, the Bhutan king threw his lot in favour of India, and two, its policy was to see to it that it continued to identify its security interests in coordination with those of India. In both cases, the presence of Nepalis was made use of, though in different forms. In Bhutan, unlike in Sikkim, it did not support the Nepali cause; it rather threw its weight in favour of the Bhutan king who represented the Drukpa interests.

# Lhotshampa Refugees and the India–Bhutan–Nepal Relations

The impact of the exodus of Lhotshampas to Nepal in the early 1990s was not confined to the domestic political domain of Bhutan and Nepal, which we have discussed in the previous chapter. Its foreign-policy impact was equally significant. The most important point to be remembered is that, though the Bhutan-India border is contiguous and the

Bhutan-Nepal border is not, still almost all the Lhotshampa refugees had to take shelter in Nepal because India saw to it that they did not settle in India, which was potentially harmful for India-Bhutan relations. Not that it has escaped the notice of the Nepalis. In a seminar on Bhutanese refugees held in Kathmandu in 2007, the former Deputy Prime Minister and Minister for Foreign Affairs K.P. Sharma Oli minced no words when he said:

> Speaking clearly, there is no cause for Nepal to be affected and to be engaged with Bhutanese refugee problem. Bhutan is neither geographically connected with Nepal nor the Druk Kingdom is Nepal's immediate neighbor. Generally, people take shelter in an immediate safe place. This is a general phenomenon of migration. Having analysed this way, Bhutanese refugees should have taken refuge in India itself. There was no reason for them to enter Nepal at that time, as there was no violence and insecurity in India. According to the international laws, moral duty and on the basis of responsibility, the task of giving asylum and managing camps should have been carried out by India. But by violating and neglecting basic values of refugees, India was hell bent on sending them to Nepal. Nepal also did not protest against such a villainous Indian role and got into quicksand of unnecessary burden. (Oli 2007: 39-40)

Even in 1995-96 when under the auspices of the Appeal Movement Coordinating Committee the camp-based refugees tried to lead a peace march to Bhutan to put back the issue on the international human rights radar, it was disrupted by India. Since the march had to pass through India, the marchers were arrested as soon as they reached India and were sent back to their camps in Nepal (Evans 2013: 133-34, 136). All this was not only because Bhutan had taken care of India's concern about China in the region, but also because in all UN votes which mattered to India it had voted on India's side. Following India's independence in 1947, and again after the annexation of Sikkim into the Indian Union in 1975, there was possibility of some misgiving between the two states, but through quiet diplomacy they were not allowed to spill over (details in Ghosh 1989: 137-51). There was yet another reason for India to be supportive of Bhutan in its dealing with the problem of the Lhotshampas. The potential link between the Nepali Maoists and the Lhotshampas was watched with caution by India, which had a tradition of thwarting Marxist/Maoist insurgency on its soil dating back to the days of Nehru when he had to quell the Telangana movement almost immediately after India's independence with ostensible Soviet support (Evans 2013: 137-38, Mehra 2008: 2).

# Nepali Migrations, the Maoist Insurgency, and India's Security Concerns

Against the background of Maoist militancy in Nepal that started in the mid-1990s, a new security dimension was added to Indo-Nepal relations as well. India was suspicious of the operations of the ISI, LTTE, Kashmiri and Punjabi terrorists on Nepali soil and feared that at critical moments they could penetrate into India to foment trouble. During the assembly elections held in August 1996 and the parliamentary elections held in October 1996 in J&K, the Indian press was rife with reports that the ISI was planning to send thousands of trained militants to disrupt the polls. Since the interest of the Indian government and the Nepalese monarchy coincided on the matter, they jointly increased the surveillance on the border and started asking for 'citizenship cards' from Nepalis travelling to India after the 2001 State of Emergency in Nepal. In 2004, both governments agreed that Maoist insurgency was a threat to them, following which India reinforced its security presence on the border between the two countries to monitor the border entries (Hausner & Sharma 2013: 102).

It was India's constant fear that the use of Nepal by international terrorists had the potential to complicate India–Nepal relations. Historically, it is the hallmark of Nepal politics to entertain strong sentiments against India's interference in Nepal's politics in which the issue of alleged growth in the number of Indians there figures prominently. The more India's security interests interfered with the politics of Nepal the more vicious these sentiments became. As one Nepalese scholar put it: '[T]he intermittent quarrel over the "people of Indian origin" (which has also become a strong point in reference to the origin of Sadbhavana Party in Nepal) could generate unwarranted ethnic turmoil in Nepal (which, in fact, has already encouraged several Jana-Jati groups to build pressure on the government)' (Kumar 1994: 83).

Nepal figures prominently in the Sino-Indian strategic question, which naturally brings into focus the Indo-Nepal treaty of 1950. Although Nepal repeatedly highlights the problem of the influx of Indians into the Terai region while demanding the re-negotiation of the treaty, there is also an element of security-related consideration in its plea. In the past, Nepal's efforts to declare itself a zone of peace had caused considerable consternation in New Delhi. The latter interpreted it as a move against Indo-Nepal strategic partnership enshrined in the treaty. The controversy over Kalapani betrayed the same hiatus. According to

India, Kalapani was inside its territory and was the source of the river Mahakali. According to Nepal, Kalapani originated at Lipu–Gad, which was within Nepalese territory. India argued that if the Nepalese claim was conceded, then the Lipu–Lekh pass, which was the gateway to Tibet and Kailash Mansarovar, would have to be handed over and security of the region, which had substantial Chinese troops in the neighbourhood, would be threatened. Considering the area to be a high-security zone, India posted a large contingent of the ITBP there. India was concerned over ISI activities in Nepal, which were believed to have been intensified and at least four camps were set up along the Indo-Nepal border to incite subversion in India. During the 1996 general elections, India sealed the 739-km border with Nepal following intelligence reports about ISI designs to create disturbances during the elections. Later, the foreign ministers of India and Nepal agreed to set up a joint working group 'to discourage movement of undesirable elements across the border'. Both sides reiterated their resolve not to allow any activities on their soil which were 'prejudicial to the security of the other'. In July 2014, India and Nepal decided to address their border related issues by constituting a Boundary Working Group. It worked out its immediate tasks, namely, the construction and restoration of new and damaged boundary pillars, their GPS observation, and streamlining procedures to prevent encroachments and crossholdings along the border (Das 2014b).

# India's North-East

On India's north-eastern flank, insurgencies of all kinds, arising from the region's ethno-demographic complexion, which is under constant pressure from external migrations, pose serious security problems for Bangladesh and India. In the past, the Chinese presence in the neighbourhood used to be viewed with alarm by India in this context. But with the relative thawing in Sino-Indian relations the problem does not exist any longer, although it is a potential concern. These ethnic insurgencies are difficult to handle because they have cross-border linkages, which are further complicated by cross-border movements of people. At one point of time the Indian government had pressurized the Bangladesh government to stop the land settlements in the CHT as they led to the displacement of local tribals and their eventual flight to India. India could take such a stand because restrictions on trade and river water flows could affect the economy of Bangladesh severely (Weiner 1992–93: 123).

Later, India's relations with Bangladesh improved, as was reflected in the signing of the Farakka agreement, the Chakma accord and the present Sheikh Hasina government's cooperative attitude not to allow anti-India insurgent groups to operate from Bangladesh soil or to have their bases there. As a consequence, Bangladesh has descended heavily upon these insurgents. Earlier the United Liberation Front of Assam (ULFA)used to protect the Bangladeshi migrants in Assam but subsequently it demanded the deportation of 'foreigners', which meant the Bangladeshis.

In the Lunglei district of Mizoram, the Chakma accord prompted a strange reaction. Some of the village council presidents this author spoke to sometime in the mid-1990s at Tlabung had argued that the removal of the Chakma insurgent group, Shanti Bahini, had resulted in lawlessness on the borders. Shanti Bahini's presence used to scare other insurgents from operating in the area, but once that fear was gone these insurgent groups had a field day in the area, worsening the law and order situation and encouraging smuggling. From these discussions, it seemed to be common knowledge that the Shanti Bahini operated from Indian soil and that they were armed and trained by India's BSF. The members of the Shanti Bahini knew the local terrain better and therefore were more effective in patrolling the border on behalf of the BSF. It was a strange situation. On the one hand, the Mizos in that part of Mizoram resented the existence of the Chakma Autonomous District Council in Tlabung as we have noted in Chapter 2 but, on the other hand, they were in favour of the Shanti Bahini operating under the overall guidance of the BSF.

With respect to the tri-junction between Bangladesh, India and Myanmar, it is clear that there is always a close connection between the cross-border movements of people and international security. When, as a result of the Myanmarese policy of settling non-Muslims in Arakan, many Muslims flocked to Bangladesh as refugees, the Bangladesh government threatened to arm them if the settlement policy was not stopped. As we have noted above, the Rohingya is a problem in Bangladesh–Myanmar relations.

Similar linkages are noticeable in Indo-Myanmarese relations, too. By the end of the 1980s, a democracy movement had been unleashed in Myanmar under the leadership of Aung San Suu Kyi, daughter of Burma's great independence hero Marshal Aung San. The state repression followed, resulting either in the formation of rebel armies like the KNU or in escapes to India and Thailand, which were considered safe places. Several thousands of democracy activists arrived in India where they were welcome. There were allegations from the Myanmar government that India was not only supporting Aung San Suu Kyi's NLD it was even funding the government-in-exile called the NCGUB. According to the Indian government and UNHCR reports, between 1988 and 2001, 6,324 had entered India, of which 1,245 were granted UNHCR refugee status. India's pro-democracy policy, however, had started changing towards the end of the 1990s because of two reasons, one, China's close proximity to the Myanmarese military rulers, and two, Myanmar's providing shelters to several insurgent groups operating in India's north-east (Bhaumik 2003: 196–204).

In 1994, India and Myanmar entered into agreements aimed at solving border problems. As a result, the Mizoram government forcibly repatriated about 10,000 Chins to Myanmar. But when India welcomed student activists and pro-democracy members and kept them in refugee camps, the relations between the countries soured, with the result that the joint counter-insurgency operations were suspended. Arrested insurgents told the police that some military officers of the SLORC were extending full support to certain underground organizations of Manipur. Besides, all the outfits in the region had begun to send new recruits to camps in Myanmar for guerrilla training. With the improvement of relations between India and Myanmar, the problem has been contained to the advantage of both the countries. That Myanmar is slowly moving towards democracy is an added positive factor.

Considering the political volatility of the region and the field day all kinds of insurgent groups have there, it was often suspected that some of the groups had established operational links with the LTTE, which was at that time a powerful insurgent group threatening the territorial integrity of Sri Lanka. In 1984, the LTTE had purchased a second-hand cargo vessel named 'Cholan' and obtained permission from the authorities in Myanmar to establish a modest shipping base in the island of Twante located off the Irrawady delta. This helped the LTTE to engage in arms trafficking in the region. In August 1995, an LTTE vessel conveyed 50 tons of TNT and 10 tons of RDX from the Ukrainian port of Nikolayev to speedboats operating off the north-eastern coast of Sri Lanka. In February 1996, a joint operation launched by the naval patrols of India and Sri Lanka destroyed MV Comex-Joux owned by the LTTE. Both these vessels had set sail from Pukhet, carrying large consignments of arms and explosives which were believed to have been purchased in Cambodia.

It was also surmised that the LTTE was also using the 17,000-strong Tamil community in Moreh in Manipur to establish contact with the local insurgents. These Tamils were proficient in Manipuri, Burmese, Nagamese, Hindi, Tamil and English. They had relatives and business contacts in Myanmar, India and other parts of Southeast Asia, which facilitated commerce. Together with Punjabis, Marwaris and Nepalese, they controlled a large portion of both trade and smuggling across Myanmar and beyond. In 1991, when the Government of India launched its 'Operation Rhino' against the ULFA, it came across documentary evidence of the links between the Kachin Independent Army of Myanmar, the National Socialist Council of Nagaland (NSCN) and the LTTE. In one of their press interviews, the NSCN admitted as such (Verghese 1996: 59, 123, 406).

Insurgency in the area has close connection with drug trafficking, in which Moreh plays an important role. Its population of 27,000 consists of ten communities, namely, Kukis, Tamils, Meiteis, Punjabis, Nepalis, Marwaris, Nagas, Bengalis, Assamese and Maliyalees, and, therefore, in true sense it is cosmopolitan. Ever since border trade between India and Myanmar in 22 trade items was legalized in 1995 through Moreh, Champhai in Mizoram and Lungwa in Nagaland, narcotics, such as heroin, number 4, *ganja* (cannabis) and so on were smuggled into Moreh, from where these were sent to various other parts of India as well as the international market. On account of this drug connection, various insurgent groups considered Moreh as a strategic transit point through which they obtained not only money but also arms and ammunition. The India-Myanmar border is as complex as the India-Bangladesh border, and border fencing as a strategy to handle the problem is equally fraught with uncertainties, if not overall short-sightedness, because of historical, social and economic reasons (Bhattacharjya & Daniel 2012, Das 2013, Sharma 2011: 53–64).

## The Kashmir Issue

The Kashmir problem cannot be understood without reference to China. At the time of independence, China was not a factor as it was still in the midst of a civil war. Kashmir was purely an India–Pakistan problem, as for both the nations it was important for their respective nation-building strategies. But as the Cold War engulfed South Asia and India–China relations moved from bonhomie to suspicion to war, Kashmir no longer remained an India–Pakistan affair alone and became crucial for the triangular relationship. Pakistan's cession of some parts of the POK to China, and later giving autonomy to Gilgit and Baltistan (erstwhile Northern Areas), virtually put an end to all possibilities of seeing J&K as an undivided state as it existed in 1947. The following passages from the report of the interlocutors appointed by the Government of India on 13 October 2010 are relevant in the context of our discussion in respect of the migration–security interface (Padgaonkar et al. 2012: 115).

> ...[F]rom 1980 onwards many outsiders, especially from Pakistan's Khyber-Pakhtoonkhwa and Panjab, have been encouraged to settle in Gilgit-Baltistan. This has resulted in a change in the demographic balance, leading to sectarian conflict between armed militias, especially in Gilgit. The issue of the future of these settlers and their rights within Gilgit-Baltistan needs to be discussed, as persons from outside Jammu and Kashmir are not regarded as State citizens.
>
> Similarly, while the property of those who fled Jammu and Kashmir during 1948-49 has been protected by the State government, no such system exists in AJK [Azad Jammu and Kashmir], where the property of those who fled to Jammu and Kashmir has been assigned to migrants and/or displaced persons. Thus, while migrants and/or displaced persons from AJK can claim their original properties in Jammu and Kashmir, migrants and/or displaced persons from Jammu and Kashmir cannot claim their original properties in AJK.

All said, unless two things happen, no lasting peace in Kashmir is possible. These are: one, let India and Pakistan move towards making the LOC the de jure border between India and Pakistan, an argument this author had made earlier (Ghosh 2002), and two, instead of harping on Article 370, Kashmir's political agenda should concentrate on regional autonomy as many other states in India have demanded and gained through bargaining with the centre. Given the evolving texture of Indian politics, this is the most opportune moment. But who would take care of the Afghan factor?

# Notes

1. Derived from Zomi, a term to mean highlander common to several related Tibeto-Burman languages spoken in the India-Bangladesh-Myanmar borders.
2. But rhetoric apart, there is little evidence that the party's foreign policy suffered from this vision (see Ghosh 2000: 319-25). Once in power, the party in its new incarnation, BJP, rather covered the extra mile to make a reconciliation with Pakistan which was epitomized by Prime Minister Atal Behari Bajpayee's dramatic bus ride to Lahore and his signing of the historic Lahore Declaration with his Pakistani counterpart, Nawaz Sharif, on 21 February 1999. The same is true for Narendra Modi's Pakistan policy.

3. It is interesting to read the following statement from Varadarajan (2009): 'There is a story senior journalist A.S. Pannerselvan tells of the experience of the first group of Tamil Tigers who were brought to a remote camp in Uttar Pradesh for arms training by the Indian government in the early 1980s. Every evening the camp's Tibetan cook would look at the group of Sri Lankan Tamils and start laughing. Eventually, one of the Tamils learnt enough Hindi to ask the cook what was so funny. "Thirty years ago," the old man said, "I was in this camp with other Tibetans getting trained and there was somebody else to cook for us. Now you are here and I am cooking for you." "That may be so," the LTTE man said, "but I still don't see what's so funny." Prompt came the reply: "You see, I'm wondering who you will be cooking for 20 years from now—I think it may be the Chakmas!"

4. There was a slight deviation in the 2014 general elections. The BJP did not talk much of *Hindutva*, rather it emphasized on good governance, development and a corruption-free society. The subsequent UP by-elections, however, saw a return to the *Hindutva* rhetoric.

5. This argument draws from a study that analysed Muslim votes in Gujarat in the 2014 Lok Sabha elections. It found that Muslims by and large did not vote for the BJP. Only in those pockets where the community was very small and it was subjected to severe violence during the anti-Muslim riots of 2012, it had given more votes to the BJP than previously, ostensibly out of fear to avoid future riots when their security would be threatened (Susewind & Dhattiwala 2014: 99–110).

6. Now that the Land Border Agreement has been signed between India and Bangladesh, it is to be seen whether the fencing gets completed or not, which is unlikely given the nature of the terrain and other sociopolitical factors.

# 4

# Relief and Rehabilitation

*Unfortunately humanitarianism has been the mark of an inhuman time.*

—G.K. Chesterton

## Introduction

A region that has experienced hosting millions of migrants and refugees that too without a proper legal framework in place (discussed in Chapter 5) must have handled a huge task at hand to provide relief, if not rehabilitation too, to this massive mass of people. How has this task been achieved, through national efforts, or through bilateral efforts, or through regional efforts? As we will see in Chapter 5, regional efforts towards building a regional refugee regime have not made any headway. Some bilateral efforts have been there, but essentially it has been the individual state's effort that is responsible to take care of the refugees to whatever extent possible. In this chapter, we will discuss four national relief efforts as experienced by India, Pakistan, Bangladesh and Nepal. The remaining four states, namely, Afghanistan, Bhutan, Maldives and Sri Lanka, are not relevant in this context as none of them is a refugee-receiving country.[1]

# I
# Indian Experience

## The Partition Refugees

The two regions that mattered most for India in this regard were, one, Delhi and its neighbouring regions, and two, Calcutta and its neighbouring regions. Besides, the refugees had to be settled in many other parts of India as well. Sometimes they themselves chose the places for their resettlement; the Sindhis chose Bombay, for example. A study of the Delhi and Calcutta experiences shows how the two respective state responses differed and why. In the case of Delhi, the Central Government was clear about its mission, but in the case of the West Bengal government the mission was not that clear. The primary reason for this differentiated outlook was that while the migrants from West Pakistan had come to India for good, without any doubts in their minds that they would not return, but in the case of West Bengal the migrants were not sure about that. It was true for the Bengali Muslim migrants as well who had left for East Pakistan. Even Nehru and the West Bengal government used to think that the phenomena in Bengal were temporary and as the situation would normalize the refugees would return to their respective homes. The ground realties tended to suggest that they were not completely off the mark. In early 1950 the Bengali refugee flow peaked at 3.5 million, but following the Nehru–Liaquat Pact on minorities signed on 8 April 1950, 1.2 million Hindu refugees returned to East Pakistan.[2] Before long, however, a large number of them migrated back to India. By any measure it was a fluid situation and no one was sure about the exact numbers. For example, while the West Bengal government said that by 1954, 2.7 million refugees had arrived, the central government put the figure at 2.8 million by 1951, and then at 4 million by 1956 (Bandyopadhyay 2000: 32). Besides, while in the case of Punjabi refugees in Delhi the Central Government was directly involved because Delhi was the capital city under its administrative jurisdiction, for West Bengal it was the state government which was the nodal agency. Compared to Delhi, the latter lacked the necessary resources. Only in the cases of the rehabilitation schemes in Dandakaranya in Madhya Pradesh and those in Andaman and Nicobar Islands the Central Government too was involved, more so in the latter, which was a Union Territory (discussed below).

# Refugees from West Pakistan

There were several kinds of refugees from West Pakistan. Though most of them were Hindus and Sikhs from West Punjab, there were other refugees as well, such as the Sindhis from Sind and Hindus and Sikhs from the NWFP (now called Khyber Pakhtunkhwa). The government decided that the refugees from West Punjab should mostly be resettled in East Punjab only, and their migration to other parts like Delhi or UP should be as less as possible. What ultimately happened was that the agricultural communities from West Punjab were resettled in East Punjab, while the townspeople were sheltered in Delhi and its adjacent areas. Thus, the refugees from the canal colony districts of West Punjab were resettled in their original places from where they had migrated a few decades ago. Similarly, the refugees from Lahore *tehsil* (an administrative division in Pakistan and India) were resettled in Ajnala tehsil, those from Sialkot in Gurdaspur and those from Rawalpindi in Ambala. The Sikhs were generally resettled in the riverine areas of Ferozepur, Fazilka and other places. It was the general policy of both the Indian and Pakistani governments to consider the community factor in resettlement so that in future they could be safeguarded against the devastating effects of breakdown of support systems such as family and tribe.[3]

The task of resettlement of millions of farmers from West Punjab in the vacated lands of East Punjab was a herculean task and that too when the government machinery in Punjab was still not fully in place. Just like it was expected by the Muslim League that Calcutta would go to East Pakistan,[4] it was expected in East Punjab till the last moment that Lahore would be retained by India. As a result, there was complete uncertainty about the new seat of government (Alexander 1951: 17). Still the job of resettlement of the farmers was accomplished with amazing speed and efficiency by the Punjab administration (meaning, the Punjab Provincial Government and PEPSU—Patiala and East Punjab States Union—put together) with commendable efforts by such dedicated officers as Sardar Tarlok Singh, the first Director General of Rural Rehabilitation, and his successor from 1949, M.S. Randhawa, the Rehabilitation Commissioner of Punjab. Of course, there was huge community participation as well. In doing so, as noted above, the consideration of community affinity was taken seriously into account. By the middle of 1950, as many as 3,000,000 farmers were resettled. The strategy was: First, a group allotment was made and then the members of the group divided the land amongst themselves. There was, however, one flip side. A contemporary analysis noted: 'Land has been assigned to all men who held land in West Punjab, but no others. Landless labourers have been overlooked. It was assumed, perhaps, that they would find employment on the land in East Punjab as they had done in the West. But, with the reduction of the size of the holdings, this has not happened' (Alexander 1951: 24). Besides East Punjab, some farming families were resettled in the rather distant foothill (*terai*) region in UP (now Uttarakhand).

The Punjab rural rehabilitation, however, was a challenging job for two reasons. First, the lands vacated by Muslims in East Punjab were much less compared to those vacated by Hindus and Sikhs in West Punjab, and second, the East Punjab lands were less fertile and less irrigated compared to those in West Punjab. Altogether, there was an assessment of 617,401 claims put up by displaced landholders from Pakistan, of which 606,879 were from West Punjab. The total agricultural land was estimated to be 6,729,050 acres, of which 1,464,281 acres were uncultivated. Against this, the total area abandoned by the Muslim evacuees in East Punjab and PEPSU was 5,015,616 acres, of which 894,795 acres were uncultivated. Also, as discussed above, there were marked differences in the relative fertility of land in East and West Punjab. It has been noted:

> For a long time, the resources of the composite province had been devoted largely to the development of waste tracts in the western districts so that, against 4,306,558 acres of irrigated land abandoned by displaced persons, only 1,325,853 acres of irrigated land were now available for them. The proportion of perennial irrigation available was even smaller, being 433,829 acres in East Punjab and PEPSU, compared to 2,555,844 acres in West Punjab. (Singh 1969: 220–21)

This complicated the process of land allocation to the refugees in East Punjab villages. Still with the painstaking efforts of Randhawa, the job was well accomplished. His idea was not to resettle the refugees on the pattern that existed in West Punjab villages but through new innovative ideas, such as the Garden Colonies and the Rural Housing Scheme (Model Villages), in keeping with availability of lands and other realties (details in Randhawa 1954: 127–61).

The non-farming Punjabi families were resettled in various towns in and around Delhi. One problem that had to be encountered was the mismatch in occupations held by Muslims who left for Pakistan and the Hindus and Sikhs who migrated to India. For example, in Delhi most of the mechanics and artisans were Muslims, and as they left for

Pakistan there was a scarcity of such people. Similarly, the number of Hindu and Sikh shopkeepers outnumbered their Muslim counterparts: 51,000 shops against 17,000 shops (Alexander 1951: 30). As a result, the type of rehabilitation that was possible in respect of farming families was not possible for the townspeople. There was limited scope of resettlement in vacated urban properties. Indeed, the refugee camps were not the permanent solution and new housing colonies had to be constructed and soon Delhi was dotted with such colonies. In order to provide the maximum number of plots with a frontage, narrow strips were arranged, packed tightly like sardines. The front-to-depth ratio was sometimes as stark as 1:4, meaning a 15 feet wide plot would extend to 60 feet in depth. The tenements provided by the state were just two rooms covered by corrugated sheets with large openings on either side. Due to the lack of space, most families constructed the entire plot area, resulting in houses that resembled train compartments where access to the rear room was through preceding ones. Richer families incorporated corridors, even if it allowed them smaller rooms and tighter spaces in order to achieve a minimum level of privacy. Because of the lack of funds and the key issues of survival, not many refugee families were able to construct their own houses. Over the years, many families built temporary kitchen and toilet structures in their backyards. During the last few decades, most of the original homes have been converted into multi-storey buildings, often devoid of proper ventilation or light in the inner rooms (based on the author's discussions with Suparna Ghosh, a Delhi-based architect).

In Delhi there was an interesting case of reverse resettlement. The Muslim Meo community who lived in parts of Gurgaon, Alwar and Bharatpur had fallen victims to communal riots, making them flee to Delhi in more than a hundred thousand. While some had migrated to Pakistan, most of them took shelter in Delhi's Jama Masjid area. They wanted to return to their homes which Mahatma Gandhi had promised to facilitate. But his assassination dashed their hopes. But the government honoured the Mahatma's promise. Under the humane guidance of Gandhi's close associate Vinoba Bhave, most of them were resettled in their vacated lands. It was feared that they would not be welcomed by their erstwhile hostile Hindu neighbours. But nothing of that sort happened and the process of resettlement was carried out smoothly (Alexander 1951: 27–28).

Besides Delhi, in several other places refugees were resettled, such as Kurukshetra and Faridabad (both now in Haryana, then in Punjab),

Chandigarh (Punjab), Rajpura (PEPSU), Tripuri (Patiala), Govindpuri (UP), Hastinapur (UP), Pratapnagar (Rajasthan), Gandhidham (Kutch), Ulhasnagar (Bombay) and Sardarnagar (Ahmedabad, then in Bombay Province). Efforts were made to make these refugees self-sustaining through government loans to set up small businesses as well as by training them in various vocations. One such model training centre emerged near Kurukshetra in a small hamlet by the name Nilokheri, which was the brainchild of S.K. Dey, 'an anonymous farmer's son with the training of an engineer'. When Nehru visited the centre in 1948 he was so excited that he said that he wanted to see 'springing up across the expanse of India a thousand townships humming with the music of the muscles as it is this centre'. The refugees from the NWFP were resettled mostly in Faridabad. Though they were in small numbers in the NWFP (not more than 8 per cent of the population), they were a successful trading community that contributed 80 per cent to the province's income tax revenue. Besides being good traders these people were also rough and tough like their Pashtoon counterparts. This helped the construction industry that was encouraged to rehabilitate these refugees (Alexander 1951: 29–58, Vernant 1953: 751–52).

The refugees from Sind preferred to settle primarily in Bombay, partly because they were mostly small traders for which Bombay provided them with better opportunities and partly because it was possible to reach Bombay rather easily by sea. Only a very small percentage of Sindhi refugees were cultivators. As a result, the government schemes that were oriented towards resettling them by agricultural land grants did not excite them much. They did not need state assistance in this regard as they could bring with them their liquid cash to start their businesses. Since they were dispersed in several towns and places in the larger Bombay State and Madhya Pradesh, the most notable being the colony at the neighbouring Bombay township of Ulhasnagar (close to the important railway junction of Kalyan), it was easy for them to get absorbed into the local communities. Of course, there was some amount of nativist ire expressed by the traditionally established small traders of these towns who were replaced by their more wily and business-oriented Sindhi counterparts (Alexander 1951: 59–70).

The Dalit refugees were specifically looked after by the India Harijan Sevak Sangh (Pan-Indian Association for Harijans) under the auspices of the Ministry of Rehabilitation. It had its headquarters in Delhi with branches in Jullundur, Ahmedabad, Calcutta, Ganganagar, Alwar and Rajkot (Vernant 1953: 753).

# Restoration of Abducted Women

During the Partition riots, scores of women had suffered rape, torture and other forms of dishonour in the hands of men belonging to the other community. Many of them had been abducted by the same perpetrators, or, under different circumstances, were forced to live in families belonging to the other religion and in the other country than their so-called own. Subsequently, there were demands from the families of these abducted women as well as by their national leaders to retrieve these women and restore them to their respective families. The Governments of India and Pakistan had responded to such demands, and on 6 December 1947 in an Inter-Dominion Conference held at Lahore it was decided that both the governments would take steps to recover and restore such women. Mridula Sarabhai was appointed as the Chief All India Organizer who chose Kamlaben Patel to assist her by reposing full confidence in her. The recovery operation was in the charge of the Women's Section of the Ministry of Relief and Rehabilitation with Rameshwari Nehru as Honorary Advisor. Necessary police support was built into the system. On 11 November 1948, India and Pakistan set out the terms for recovery in each country which were to remain in effect till May 1949 for Pakistan and January 1950 for India. As the latter date approached, India passed, on 19 December 1949, an act called The Abducted Persons (Recovery and Restoration) Act to be effective till December 1951. Till December 1949, 12,552 recoveries in India and 6,272 in Pakistan had been made. By 1957, in all, about 30,000 Muslim, Hindu and Sikh women were recovered by both countries—Muslim: 20,728; Hindu: 9,032 (Hassan 2006: 57, Menon & Bhasin 1998: 68–73, 99).

But as future studies and oral history sources would show, the scheme had many pitfalls and the efforts were sometimes counterproductive. The first and foremost criticism that was made against the scheme was that it was conceived on male chauvinistic lines and what seemed to be more important was family/male honour and national prestige than what the abducted women really wanted. It was as if given that every woman's chastity was the central component of family honour. And in this regard one finds even Gandhi on the same male-opinionated plank. Here is what he said at one of his prayer meetings:

> I have heard many women did not want to lose their honour and chose to die. Many men killed their own wives. I think that is really great because I know that such things make India brave. After all, life and death is a transitory game. Whoever might have died are dead and gone; but at least they

have gone with courage. They have not sold away their honour. Not that their lives were not dear to them, but they felt it was better to die with courage rather than be forcibly converted to Islam by the Muslims and allow them to assault their bodies. And so those women died. They were not just a handful, but quite a few. When I hear all these things, I dance with joy that there are such brave women in India. ('223 Speech at Prayer Meeting', *Collected Works of Mahatma Gandhi*, Vol. 89, quoted by Didur 2006: 3)

One has reason to argue that what was so sacrosanct about female chastity when men seemed to have no concern for male chastity. Why should women alone be glorified for sacrificing their lives to protect their honour and not men? Did any man find the abduction of a family member so revolting to his family honour that he committed suicide for not being able to bear the psychological pain? On the contrary, as Gandhi glorifies, he killed his wife to prevent her potential abduction.

There were several cases, as Menon and Bhasin (1998: 65–129) have shown, where the abducted women had reconciled themselves to their lives in their abductors' homes and had no desire to return to their original families apprehending that they would be ostracized there. Even Gandhi and Nehru had to advise and admonish such families publicly. Yet both the Indian and Pakistani governments had made it a prestige point to show which nation had retrieved how many abducted women to score a political point.

> The Abducted Persons Act was remarkable for the impunity with which it violated every principle of citizenship, fundamental rights and access to justice, and for contravening all earlier legislation with regard to marriage, divorce, custody and guardianship and, eventually, inheritance, not so much to property but, more critically, to membership of a (religious) community....Free choice, freely exercised, is what neither state nor community could allow abducted women in post-Partition India, so much so that it was legislated out. In its desire to restore normalcy and to assert itself as their protector, the Indian state itself became an abductor by forcibly removing adult women from their homes and transporting them out of their country. It became, in effect and in a supreme irony, its hated Other. (Menon & Bhasin 1998: 125)

## Refugees from East Pakistan

Like any refugee situation anywhere, the question about the refugees from East Bengal was also as to how to deal with the situation humanly and administratively. Since India had decided not to sign the Refugee

Convention of 1951 while the flow of Bengali refugees continued well up to the end of the 1950s and even beyond (unlike the Punjab situation), it was necessary to frame laws keeping in view the local realities. Efforts were on in any case to handle the refugee situation and to take care of the abandoned properties. To find a solution to the problem, India and Pakistan signed a pact in 1949 known as the Karachi Agreement. But it could hardly succeed because of serious conflicts of interest between the countries. India wanted to extend the agreement to include entire India, to which Pakistan did not agree (Hassan 2006: 36–40). The next more serious effort was the Nehru–Liaquat Pact of April 1950. It envisaged policies to secure the return of the displaced minorities and to protect and return their abandoned properties. In pursuance of these policies, Minorities' Boards and Evacuee Property Management Boards were established in both West and East Bengal. Notably the Hindu refugees in Bengal were not to be designated as refugees by the West Bengal government but only as 'displaced persons'. The West Bengal Land Development and Planning Act, 1948, was meant to acquire land wherever possible for 'public purposes' to settle the immigrants. Such acquisitions were largely to be governed by the provisions of the Land Acquisition Act of 1891. But the problem was of finding enough suitable paddy land which was ready for cultivation. The only way out was to convert waste land into arable tracts, which the government tried to do through the passage of The Waste Lands (Requisition and Utilization) Act, 1952. The real problem, however, was how to implement these laws. In most cases, the day-to-day care of the refugees became the responsibility of the district administrations which continued till July 1958 when it was decided to wind up all the relief camps in the state (Sen 2000: 49–56).

Bengali refugees were primarily in West Bengal, but they were also in large numbers in Tripura, Assam, Bihar and Orissa. Many of them were sheltered in refugee camps: 160,000 in West Bengal, 30,000 in Tripura, 14,000 in Assam, 20,000 in Bihar and 13,000 in Orissa. By 1950, 181,000 displaced agriculturist families from East Pakistan were resettled in various parts of eastern India. Other non-agricultural families were allotted homestead plots in West Bengal. Soon in Habra, Baigachi and Fulia new townships were developed to accommodate as many of them as possible (Alexander 1951: 83, 121, 127). Besides doing whatever could be done within West Bengal and the neighbouring states, efforts were also made to shift a portion of the refugees outside the region. It was against this background that the central government decided to treat the East Bengali refugee problem as a national problem. Sucheta Kripalani, an MP, said:

'It was not on West Bengal's decision that this country was partitioned. This country was partitioned by a decision of India .... Therefore, it is a national problem and all the states should pull their weight in rehabilitating them' (*Lok Sabha Debates*, 31 March 1956: 3888). Two locations were chosen to rehabilitate at least a portion of the refugees, one in the Raipur district of Madhya Pradesh known as the Dandakaranya rehabilitation scheme and the other in the Andaman and Nicobar Islands as the Andaman rehabilitation scheme. The two schemes yielded different results, as we would see below.

## The Dandakaranya Project

For teeming millions of land-hungry refugees, there was hardly any land available in West Bengal. Even the 100,000 acres of land that the neighbouring states offered was not good enough. Moreover, by 1956–57 it was almost certain that West Bengal would not be in a position any longer to look after the refugees on its soil. The only possibility of one's continuing to have state support was if he was willing to be shifted outside the state. It was against this background that the Dandakaranya project was conceived in 1957 and approved by the National Development Council. The project started in 1958 and ended in failure in 1970 when refugees re-migrated to West Bengal in massive numbers. In 1980 the Dandakaranya Development Authority was wound up (Alok Ghosh 2000: 106–7).

The reason that the project failed was that the area was not suitable for East Bengali refugees, who were mostly farmers adept in rice cultivation in the wet lands. In contrast, the land in Dandakaranya was dry and arid, particularly unsuitable for rice cultivation. Besides, only a fraction of the real grant for development had reached the refugees in whose name the grants were sanctioned. According to one refugee, who spent years in the Dandakaranya camp and who later became a writer, it was in the name of refugee rehabilitation that massive funds were released that led to road and bridge constructions, but from these infrastructural projects the refugees gained hardly anything. The whole Dandakaranya project area was bigger in size than the state of West Bengal. As such, the real gainer was the state of Madhya Pradesh and not the refugees. Moreover, the refugee settlements were scattered at long distances, making it impossible for them to maintain their cultural and social life. Existential tension with the local tribal communities was yet another problem (Alok Ghosh 2000: 122, Biswas 2011: 205–7).

# The Andaman Project

Compared to the Dandakaranya project the Andaman rehabilitation scheme worked well. The project had three phases, first the refugees were settled in southern Andaman, then in the middle of the island and then in the northern part of the island. Table 4.1 gives the details of these settlements in terms of the number of refugee families brought to the island.

As a result of these colonization schemes, the population of the island increased multi-fold. In 1951 the population of the Andaman and Nicobar Islands was 30,971, in 1961 it became 63,548, in 1971 it became 115,133 and in 1981 it was 188,741 (Basu Ray Chaudhury 2000: 134).

The Andaman project succeeded for three reasons: first, the deforested tracts that were made available to the refugees were highly suitable for rice cultivation; second, the refugees who were brought to the island were real farmers, young and well bodied which was necessary to convert forest lands into arable land; and third, being far away from West Bengal the left agitational politics of the state did not hamper the administrative activities on the island. The lands were particularly fertile for paddy cultivation because there was plenty of rainfall, and being the jungle tracts for millennia the soil was rich in nitrogen content and hence highly fertile. No wonder that the refugee Bengali community there is now a well-to-do people with representatives in several middle-class professions. This success story, however, had its political repercussions. The West Bengal government dreamed of incorporating the islands into the state on the ground that the state was overcrowded, which needed more breathing spaces. The Government of India turned down the request partly under pressure from the already settled people of the islands who were mostly from South India and partly for security reasons. The argument was that the strategic location of the islands required close watch from Delhi which a state government was not in a position to do (Chakrabarty 2012: 47–55).

**Table 4.1**
*Rehabilitation of Bengali refugee families in the Andaman Island*

| Region | Number of Families | Relevant Years |
| --- | --- | --- |
| South Andaman | 350 | 1949–52 |
| Middle Andaman | 1,118 | 1953–59 |
| North Andaman | 1,141 | 1956–59 |

*Source:* Chakrabarty (2012: 24, 37, 52–53).

# Punjabi and Bengali Rehabilitation Schemes Compared

The trickle process of migrations in the east, unlike the one in the west, made things more difficult for the Bengali refugees compared to their Punjabi counterparts. In Bengal there was neither an exchange of populations nor adequate state response. Shyama Prasad Mukherjee and K.C. Niyogee, ministers from West Bengal in the Union Cabinet, were of the view that had the central government not intervened through the expedience of the Nehru–Liaquat Pact of April 1950, both the exchange of populations and properties would have taken place automatically.[5] Already, the statement of the Union Minister for Refugee Rehabilitation, Mohan Lal Saxena, on 2 March 1950, in a meeting at the Writers' Building (the seat of West Bengal government) had irked many West Bengal politicians. Saxena's proposal was to distinguish between the pre- and post-1950 refugees. The pre-1950 refugees were entitled to both relief and rehabilitation, whereas post-1950 refugees were entitled to only relief, not rehabilitation. Saxena's argument was that once the communal hostilities would subside, the refugees would return to their respective places of origin. The ground realities, however, were so different that such hopes were not entertained by anyone in West Bengal. Against this background, the pious commitments contained in the Nehru–Liaquat Pact of safeguarding the lives and properties of the respective minorities in India and Pakistan looked hollow. While the Bengali Muslim evacuees from West Bengal returned to their native places, there was hardly any reverse migration of Hindus from West Bengal to East Bengal (Basu Ray Chaudhury & Dey 2009: 9).

Moreover, the Muslims in India could bank upon the provisions of the Indian Constitution promulgated on 26 January 1950, but there were no corresponding guarantees in the Pakistan's Objectives Resolution.[6] The relevant provisions in the latter were at best vague and contradictory. Shyama Prasad Mukherjee unequivocally opposed the pact on the floor of the Parliament on 19 April 1950 in the following words (quoted from the *Parliament Debates* by Mandal 2011: 164):

> First, we had two such agreements since Partition for solving the Bengal problem and they were violated by Pakistan without any remedy open to us. Any agreement which has no sanction will not offer any solution. Second, the crux of the problem is Pakistan's concept of an Islamic State and the ultra-communal administration based on it. The agreement sidetracks this cardinal issue and we are today exactly where we were previous to the agreement.

Third, India and Pakistan are made to appear equally guilty, while Pakistan was clearly the aggressor. The agreement provides that no propaganda will be permitted against the territorial integrity of the two countries and there will be no incitement to war between them. This almost sounds farcical so long as Pakistan troops occupy a portion of our territory of Kashmir and warlike preparations on its part are in active operation. Fourth, events have proved that Hindus cannot live in East Bengal on the assurances of security given by Pakistan. We should accept this as a basic proposition. The present agreement on the other hand calls upon minorities to look upon the Pakistan government for their safety and honour which is adding insult to injury and is contrary to assurances given by us previously. Fifth, there is neither [any] proposal to compensate those who have suffered nor will the guilty be ever punished, because no one will dare give evidence before a Pakistan Court. This is in accordance with bitter experience in the past. Sixth, Hindus will continue to come away in large numbers and those who have come will not be prepared to go back. On the other hand Muslims who had gone away will now return and in our determination to implement the agreement Muslims will not leave India. Our economy will thus be shattered and possible conflict within our country will be greater.

It was one of the constant refrains for West Bengal that in dealing with the refugee issue the central government was behaving like a stepmother compared to what it did in Punjab. Many of these criticisms were not unfounded.

In March 1955, under the auspices of the Relief and Rehabilitation Ministry of the Government of India, two teams of social workers visited many refugee camps in Delhi and Punjab (it included Haryana and Himachal Pradesh at that time) to present an eyewitness account of the ground reality so as to make a comparison with that of West Bengal. The first team consisted of Bina Das, Sheila Davar and Suniti Pakrashi and the second of Ashoka Gupta and Amar Kumari Varma. Their report, entitled 'East is east, West is west', provided detailed accounts of camp lives and facilities in the two regions and found that the Bengal situation was not comparable to that of the north-west, which was much better. It was felt that since the problem in Bengal was ongoing, the state relief and rehabilitation measures must continue indefinitely, and unlike the Punjab case they should not be considered as closed. The two concluding paragraphs of the report read (Gupta et al. 2003):

> It must not be forgotten that the refugee problem in West Bengal is likely to be [a] recurring phenomenon for many years to come and is not a closed case like that in West Punjab or Sind. It would therefore be extremely unwise to fix a dateline (sic) and to state that future arrivals after that date

would be denied any special consideration. That would not only be untrue historically but would aggravate the situation by accelerating migration at about the prescribed dateline (sic). Facts should be faced and the door should be kept open for treating as refugees any Hindu who permanently come away from East Pakistan on account of political tension whenever such tension may arise.

We have gone through the recent circular issued by the Ministry of Rehabilitation, Government of India—G.O. No 15(7)(1)/54 dated 15 March 1955—meant for the refugees from West Punjab and Sind. We are in general agreement with the suggestions made in the circular and insist of their also being made applicable to the refugees from East Bengal.

An analysis of the first two Five Year Plans (1952–57 and 1957–62) would reveal the pro-West Pakistani refugee bias of the Indian government. Though the larger part of the task of rehabilitating West Pakistani displaced persons was accomplished by the end of the First Plan period, still ₹187 million was allocated for the purpose in the Second Plan. In the same plan ₹668 was allocated for the East Pakistani refugees, which was grossly inadequate (Basu Ray Chaudhury & Dey 2009: 9). One scholar who has studied the Bengali refugee issue carefully has argued that two factors led to this differentiated approach on behalf of the Indian government. First, the proximity of Punjabi refugees to the seat in power and any disturbance in Delhi could destabilize the government, and second, since there were a large number of Punjabis in the Indian army, a mutiny in the army was not ruled out if their relatives were not taken care of (Chakrabarti 1990).

Our conclusion would be that Delhi had several inherent advantages in dealing with its refugee influx besides, of course, the major one that in Delhi the flow was massive but short-lived while in Calcutta it was not so massive and it was staggered. Delhi's advantage was threefold. First, the vacation of a large number of dwellings by migrating Muslims gave the opportunity to the refugees either to forcibly or to legally occupy them; second, the continuous process of acquisition of land by Delhi administration often by violating the Wakf rights to provide shelter to the refugees; and third, the urban or semi-urban character of the Punjabi refugees in Delhi made them take better advantage of the government funds by setting up small businesses which the then Delhi needed badly because of its growing population.

The number of migrating Delhi Muslims was as large as 320,000 (Dupont 2000: 229). Their houses were mostly in Old Delhi and Mehrauli areas, which the refugees soon occupied. Besides, there was a systematic enlargement of Delhi administration's authority over its land use. Already much of Delhi that provided land to set up refugee colonies belonged to the Delhi Municipality as successors to these Mughal landed properties called 'nuzul' (Gupta 2003: 43). After independence, four government bodies competed for control over them, namely, the ASI, the New Delhi Municipal Committee, the Cantonment Board and the Municipal Corporation of Delhi. But with the establishment of the DDA in 1957 there were plans to urbanize the rural areas in, and adjacent to, Delhi by dividing many of these areas into zones. Delhi, therefore, had plenty of land at its disposal to rehabilitate the refugees (Gupta 2000: 158–59). Table 4.2 gives an idea of the man-to-land ratio in Delhi during this period, showing how new lands were acquired by the Delhi government to manage the rehabilitation, of course, that included the housing for the migrants from other parts of India.

Regarding the third advantage of Delhi mentioned above, one must refer to the industriousness of Punjabi refugees, which was immensely facilitated by the other two factors mentioned above. By the end of December 1950, about 300,000 refugees had been rehabilitated: 190,000 in abandoned Muslim houses, 100,000 in new constructions and the rest in 1,100 houses constructed by refugees themselves in state-allotted plots and with government assistance. City-Sadar–Paharganj, Karol Bag–Patel Nagar, Civil Lines–Sabji Mandi areas became the main resettlement locations, which soon served as the nuclei for further expansion. Soon the refugees started dominating the trade of Delhi, and before long the city emerged as India's retail and wholesale capital. The refugee community became so prosperous over time that their standard of living exceeded that of their West Punjab days (Datta 2012: 287–303, Kraft 2003: 105–11). But it must be reiterated here that those Bengali Hindu refugees who could be rehabilitated in areas conducive to their traditional livelihood practices, such as Andaman's rainy climate, too did very well.

**Table 4.2**
*Population, area and density of urban Delhi agglomeration, 1941–61*

| Year | Population | Area (Sq. km) | Density (Pop/ha) |
|------|-----------|---------------|------------------|
| 1941 | 695,686 | 174.31 | 40 |
| 1951 | 1,437,134 | 201.36 | 71 |
| 1961 | 2,359,408 | 326.55 | 72 |

*Source:* Dupont (2000: 230).

## Drawing the Larger Picture

By all accounts, the Bengal refugees were not so well looked after, as was the case with the Punjabi refugees. Academic writings have convincingly shown that the allegations made by contemporary Bengali leaders that their province was given a stepmotherly treatment by the central government were largely true. But the question arises that if it was so, why it was so. When we see the debate from a politico-administrative perspective, we may tend to give the benefit of doubt to the Nehru government. It is necessary to look at the larger national picture which was in ferment in those formative years. It was a mosaic of uncertainties then. The first and foremost uncertainty was about the seats of power of East Punjab and West Bengal. Till the last there were talks that Calcutta might go to Pakistan and Lahore might remain in India, as we noted earlier.

So far as the Interim government of Nehru was concerned, it was bogged down with all kinds of uncertainties—political, administrative, financial and, over and above, federal–state tensions. There were intense political differences between Nehru and Patel and often it had become necessary to seek Gandhi's interventions to sort out matters (details in Khare 2014). It can be legitimately surmised that Gandhi's death probably prevented a total rupture in the relationship from taking place (Kapoor 2014, see excerpts of the book in *Outlook*, 3 February 2014: 62–68). The administrative machinery lacked effective control by Indian officials. A BBC documentary on Mountbatten showed how Nehru frantically searched for his help and advice to deal with the recurrent communal riots. The finances of the new state were in bad shape. Philip Talbot, an American journalist, wrote on 19 August 1947: 'This is the tragedy of India today. It is a sick country. The new government takes over a crippled administration, a blood-stained heritage of the recent past, and only the slimmest resources to establish decent civilized order' (Khare 2014: 3).

The centre–state equation was fragile. The state leaders were equally influential like their central counterparts, which while in one way helped build Indian federalism, and on the other created difficulties in making the views of the central government prevail upon them. The study by Jha and Jha (2012) on Ayodhya tells how the UP government under the leadership of G.B. Pant was knowingly concealing facts pertaining to the controversy over the overnight installation of Ram *Lalla* (idol of Lord Ram as a child) in the Babri Masjid on the night of 22 December 1949. No wonder that Nehru had to take recourse to writing weekly letters to the Chief Ministers to apprise them of the state of the union. There were intrigues of all kinds within the Congress party itself which, to be noted, was in any case not sure of its own popular base. The elections of 1952 did ensure a comfortable Congress majority in the Parliament (364 seats out of 489) but the popular votes cast in favour of the party did not touch the halfway mark. It got only 45 per cent of the votes which meant that 55 per cent voters did not support the Congress. The real challenge for the Congress and more specifically for the Nehruvian concept of a secular India came from Hindu nationalistic forces. If we put this big picture against the controversy whether West Bengal was not given justice by the central government we may have to give the benefit of doubt to the Nehru government.

There was an overall resource crunch, still in the Second Five Year Plan (1957–62) the allocations for the Punjab refugees were much higher compared to those meant for the Bengal refugees. Since by 1957 the problem of Punjab refugees had been virtually solved while the Bengal situation was still bad, West Bengal had reasons to have legitimate grievances against the centre. But there were other factors which must be factored in to draw one's conclusions. For example, there was the question of availability of land for rehabilitation for the two sets of refugees. While the Punjabi farmers could be resettled in the lands in East Punjab vacated by Muslim famers (of course the real gainers were their Muslim counterparts in West Punjab), West Bengal could not provide much in that sense. Besides West Bengal, Assam and Tripura, only two other small refugee settlements were organized outside of the region, one in Dandakaranya in Madhya Pradesh and the other in the Andaman and Nicobar Islands, which was a Union Territory. The Dandakaranya project was a total failure while the Andaman one was a success story particularly because of its wet paddy cultivation potential. But it was a very small comfort. It may be noted here that more Bengali refugees had gone to Assam than West Bengal (see Table 1.2 in Chapter 1) but one did not hear about their problems because they could get enough rain-fed wet paddy cultivation land, which was not available in enough quantity in West Bengal.

In terms of the occupational backgrounds of the refugees the Punjabis were farmers, small traders and shop keepers. Other than the farmers most of them essentially were urban people who had to be resettled outside of East Punjab. In contrast, Bengali refugees were primarily landless farmers who could not be helped in any other way than by providing cultivable rain-fed or irrigated land. Moreover, it may be remembered that

West Punjab had been a prosperous province and hence their people had been much better off than their Bengali counterparts who were mostly landless farmers belonging to lower castes. This caste factor which we have discussed in Chapter 2 must be understood in this context also. The upper caste Bengalis who had already started migrating from the pre-Partition days could not identify their interests with these later immigrants. So far as the Sindhi refugees were concerned they were mostly traders who migrated to Bombay where they had gone by ships and boats from Karachi. There was also the issue of the nature of violence and the probability of its recurrence. Though the violence in Punjab was much more brutal but it was one-time. In Bengal it was sporadic, and seemingly unending, but less brutal. Against this background while it was possible to sign a Nehru–Liaquat Pact type of agreement, it was unthinkable in Punjab. Moreover, Nehru had a nod from B.C. Roy before he had tabled it in the Parliament for approval. This pact became the guiding principle of dealing with the refugee issue in West Bengal.

What kind of comparison one can make of the respective characteristics of political opposition to relief administration in Delhi and West Bengal? In Delhi and its neighbourhood the potential political opposition was much more serious because of the noticeable presence of RSS, Hindu Mahasabha and the Arya Samaj. In contrast, RSS and Arya Samaj were virtually non-existent in West Bengal. The Hindu Mahasabha, though strong earlier, was also on the wane. The only opposition that could have worked, therefore, was from the Left. But even that had a limited possibility. Against the background of the Telangana movement in which the Communist Party of India (CPI) had played an active role and for which it was ruthlessly suppressed by the Indian state the party was constantly exposed to the wrath of the Congress government of West Bengal. The latter virtually hounded the party. In contrast, B.C. Roy as a prominent Congress leader and Chief Minister of the state was in full command of state politics. His proximity to Nehru was an additional source of political strength. Politically speaking, therefore, the real concern for the Nehru government was Delhi and Punjab, and not West Bengal.

Another factor to consider was India–Pakistan administrative coordination in handling the Punjabi refugee situation better. Both were in agreement that the models available to them were to be the Custodian of Enemy Property and the War Damage Commissions of Europe. For the two states their major concerns were three: (a) the property rights of those who migrated, (b) the question of abducted persons meaning women and (c) the rights of those minorities who chose not to migrate. Between December 1947 and June 1949 several India–Pakistan meetings were held to deal with the problem of evacuee properties. It had already been agreed that no illegal requisition of property would be recognized and action would be taken to protect and restore such properties to their lawful owners. In September–October 1947, Pakistan and India appointed officers to serve as custodians of evacuee properties in both the wings of Punjab. Later, on the Indian side the exercise was extended to Delhi, the United Provinces, the Central Provinces and some princely states. Notwithstanding these legal regimes, enforcement of the law had to confront many problems, such as, how to define an evacuee property, how to define a movable property, how to decide the time frame for the beneficiary to take advantage of the act and the jurisdiction of the law (e.g., was it to cover Kashmir and other disputed territories). Some solution to these vexed problems was found in the policy of the Evacuee Property Organisation in both countries by (a) accepting the statements of the refugees at their face value in respect of their losses as it was not expected of them to possess any valid legal documents and (b) by both governments exchanging their land records and title deeds. In 1948, the case of Bengal was dealt with separately through the Evacuee Property Act. Assam, Cooch-Behar, Manipur and Tripura were specifically excluded from the jurisdiction of the act (Menon 2003: 158–59). Still, whatever success was there it was confined to north India. So far as Bengal was concerned nothing really worked. The reason was that in the former there was more or less full exchange of population and assets, in Bengal, because of different circumstances it was not possible.

# The Tibetan Refugees

Tibetan refugees have posed a twofold challenge to India: diplomatic and humanitarian (in Chapter 3 we have discussed the first one). India has steadfastly adhered to its commitment to *non-refoulement* in dealing with these refugees as per international customary norm without endorsing the demand for Tibetan independence to avoid any confrontation with China. There has been some UNHCR assistance but virtually India has borne the entire responsibility of taking care of the refugees. Indeed assistance has arrived from various sources such as the United States, CARE, the International Red Cross, the YMCA, the Catholic Relief, the Church World Service, the International Rescue Committee and the Save the Children Fund. India has made all efforts to make their stay comfortable by sheltering them at places climatically suitable for them. Initially they were put in camps in Assam and West Bengal. Later other camps were also organized in states like Karnataka, Himachal Pradesh, Sikkim, Dehradun (then in UP, now in Uttarakhand), Arunachal Pradesh, Orissa, Madhya Pradesh and Delhi. Considering the fact that there is little possibility of their return to Tibet, Government of India has tried to facilitate their finding gainful employment in sectors conducive to their capabilities. Thus besides providing them with agricultural lands wherever possible they have been employed in road building works, carpet weaving industries, agro-based industries and in the handicrafts sector (Dhavan 2004: 122–23, Kharat 2003: 287–93).Today one finds that the Tibetans are doing good restaurant business in many metropolitan towns.

Tibetans are often said to be the model refugee community in India. Their educational institutions are encouraged and they are allowed to pursue their cultural, social and political goals. In 1961 the Tibetan Schools Society was set up as an autonomous society under the auspices of the Ministry of Education and Youth Service. The existence of a large number of Tibetan schools helps in maintaining their ethnic and cultural identity. According to Section 3 of the Indian Citizenship Act, 1955, Tibetan refugees born in India are entitled to Indian citizenship (Dhavan 2004: 122–23). This was reaffirmed in 2010 through a Delhi High Court ruling in the case of Nmgyal Dolkar, born in 1986, whose passport application had been rejected on the ground that she was not an Indian. The Tibetan Government-in-Exile, however, discouraged the practice as it would dilute their demand for independence. Most Tibetans in India have what they call the 'green book' and the 'yellow book'. The first is an identity document issued by the Tibetan Government-in-Exile while the second is an identity certificate issued by the Indian government 'in lieu of a national passport'. In the wake of the 2014 parliamentary elections the Election Commission of India, by taking into consideration some recent High Court rulings, issued a directive that all Tibetans born in India between 1950 and 1987 would be eligible to vote in the elections. The Tibetan Government-in-Exile was not happy with the situation yet it relented and agreed that whoever wanted to vote was free to do so (*Hindustan Times*, 30 March 2014).

## Bangladesh Liberation Refugees

It was a challenging task for India to deal with 10,000,000 strong refugees that arrived in India in the span of a few months in 1970–71. They went to all the neighbouring states of India, namely, Assam, Meghalaya, Tripura and West Bengal, as well as in other states like Bihar, Madhya Pradesh and Uttar Pradesh where some refugee camps were set up. Quickly India did two things, one, it sanctioned a grant of ₹2,000,000,000 for relief, and two, it set up a special Branch Secretariat in Calcutta under the leadership of P.N. Luthra, an Additional Secretary in the Department of Labour and Rehabilitation. Reserve food stocks were created and makeshift shelters were put up overnight. Foreign assistance at this stage was non-existent; it started coming only later. Till August 1971 it was US$146.85 million against the total cost of US$576 million. This was 25 per cent, which later rose to 40 per cent. Visiting foreign officials were impressed by India's efforts. Dr. S. Komar, an ambassador from Yugoslavia, wondered 'how it was possible to have taken care of such an unprecedented influx in such a short time' (Bandyopadhyay 2000: 42). The UNHCR also played some role in relief and repatriation though there was a controversy when India alleged that the organization had failed to maintain its non-political role as its High Commissioner Sadruddin Aga Khan who happened to be a Pakistani travelled extensively in East Pakistan in June 1971 on the invitation from President General Yahya Khan. India's charge against the High Commissioner was that when the refugee flow was still in full swing (3,000,000 refugees arrived after June 1971) he was already talking about their repatriation which gave the impression that he was trying to help the Pakistan government by overlooking the ongoing gross violations of Human Rights in East Pakistan (Saha 2003: 240–42).

# Indian Tamil and Sri Lankan Tamil Refugees

In both cases of Indian Tamil resettlement and Sri Lankan Tamil refugee relief India's humanitarian measures and related polices have registered limited success. So far as the Indian Tamils are concerned India has failed to fulfil its commitment to grant them Indian citizenship as per the Shastri–Sirimavo Pact of 1964. The issue has been festering for half a century with no satisfactory solution to the problem though Sri Lanka has fulfilled its part of the responsibility as enshrined in the said pact. Earlier, on 9 November 1988 the Sri Lankan Parliament had unanimously passed the bill entitled 'Grant of Citizenship to Stateless Persons (Special Provisions) Act', which conferred Sri Lankan citizenship on all stateless persons lawfully residing in the country and those who had not applied for Indian citizenship (Sabaratnam 1990: 205). Later, in 2003, the Government of Sri Lanka enacted 'Grant of Citizenship to Persons of

Indian Origin', which said that a person of Indian origin who had been a permanent resident of Sri Lanka since 30 October 1964 or a descendent of such a person would be granted Sri Lankan citizenship. In spite of all these efforts, however, the problem has not been fully solved so far as Sri Lanka was concerned, because many people could not provide the proof of their residence as provided by law. Many remained stateless (Basu Ray Chaudhury 2013: 99–100). The general state of poverty among the plantation workers has been forcing many of them to look for alternative vocations in cities like Colombo and Kandy (see Meera Srinivasan's report in *The Hindu*, 21 November 2014).

So far as the Indian component of the Shastri–Sirimavo Pact is concerned, it largely remains unimplemented. By 31 January 1989, 116,000 families had been repatriated to India, but neither the problem of their statelessness nor that of their rehabilitation had been resolved (Vedavalli 1994: 38–39, 46–49, 154–55). S. Thondaman, the Sri Lankan Minister for Animal Husbandry and Rural Industries, and the president of the Ceylon Workers' Congress, in a press conference in April 1997 alleged that while, through his efforts, Sri Lanka had granted citizenship in 1988 to all stateless Indian Tamils who had opted for Sri Lankan nationality, India had not done its part. According to him, many repatriates to India had been denied citizenship rights. He further informed that of about 200,000 Indian Tamils who had applied for Indian citizenship, most had since died but their children still remained stateless. Due to discontinuation of the ferry service between Sri Lanka and India in the late 1990s on account of the war in Sri Lanka's Northern Province, the process of repatriation of Indian Tamils to India had come to a halt. Indeed not many Indian Tamils were really keen to migrate to India. According to a contemporary estimate, there were 250,000 such stateless people in Sri Lanka then. A sample survey revealed that the majority of them had to opt for Indian citizenship because they had no option (Vedavalli 1994: 46–47, 154–55). It was estimated later that of the total number of Tamil refugees in India 30 per cent belonged to the Indian Tamil community. The problem was that often these Indian Tamils were taken for Sri Lankan Tamils, as a result of which they had to suffer both in Sri Lanka and India (Suryanarayan 2003: 343–45).

In respect of Sri Lankan Tamil refugees also, much more needs to be done by India both at the local administrative level and in relation to Sri Lanka for after all the latter would have to take them back someday. There are four categories of Sri Lankan Tamil refugees in Tamil Nadu: (a) refugees in the camps, (b) recognized refugees outside the camps, (c) Sri Lankan nationals and (d) Tamil militants detained in special camps. In 2010, 115 refugee camps in Tamil Nadu (113 ordinary camps and 2 special camps) sheltered 73,251 refugees belonging to 19,916 families. Besides, there were 11,478 families with 32,242 refugees who did not live in the camps (GOTN 2010). According to a recent report, there are now 113 camps that shelter 80,000 Tamil refugees (Priyamvatha 2013: 20). Reportedly, 17,000 refugee children neither have been issued birth certificates by the Indian authorities nor simultaneously registered with the Sri Lankan Deputy High Commission in Chennai, both of which being important for their repatriation to Sri Lanka whenever the situation improves (*The Hindu*, 7 June 2014). India has neither succeeded in putting enough pressure on Sri Lanka to take back the Sri Lankan Tamil refugees living in India nor been able to rehabilitate them appropriately. India's pledge to Sri Lanka to maintain its territorial integrity together with its constricted intervention in Sri Lanka's ethnic strife has come in the way of India finding a political solution to the Sinhala–Tamil political conflict, allowing the problem to persist (Guha 2014).

While there can never ever be complete satisfaction from the refugees' perspective in terms of food supply or health care delivery, still it may be said that the relief machinery run by the Tamil Nadu government is handling the task well. According to a document prepared by its Department of Rehabilitation, by 2010, 52,373 identity cards had been issued to every adult refugee above 12 in order to ensure their welfare and security. The remaining refugees were going to get the same, the document said. The health care needs of the refugees were also taken care of by regular vaccinations against polio and other diseases. Expectant mothers were particularly looked after. For their recreation even colour TV sets were supplied to the camps. Under the scheme each family was to get one such set free and 19,438 sets had already been distributed (GOTN 2010).

# The Chakma Refugees

Ever since the Chakma refugee arrivals started, India has been handling the issue at several levels. Besides its policy of sheltering them in some of the north-eastern states, India has taken the cooperation of Bangladesh to solve the problem of their repatriation to the extent possible. Their stay in Arunachal Pradesh and Mizoram, particularly in the former, has been massively protested by the locals, which even the Supreme Court intervention has not been able to overcome. Since we have discussed the question in Chapter 2 and would further discuss it in Chapter 5, we are not repeating it here. At the diplomatic level, however, India has extended its good offices to help Bangladesh resolve the issue by talking to the Chakma refugee leaders in India. As a result on 9 March 1997, the Government of Bangladesh and the Chakma refugee leaders signed an agreement for the repatriation of the 50,000 refugees sheltered for the last 11 years in six camps in Tripura. The repatriation commenced on 28 March 1997 and by April 1997, 6,701 refugees had been repatriated. India continued its good offices, which later led to a more lasting agreement between the Bangladesh government and the Chakmas, which is discussed later in this chapter in the Bangladesh subsection.

## The Afghan Refugees

India has a tradition of welcoming Afghans. In India's popular imagination, Pashtoons are friendly people (recall Gandhi's association with Khan Abdul Gaffar Khan of the NWFP, who was known as Frontier Gandhi). It was as late as 1965 when, prior to the war with Pakistan, India–Pakistan border controls were not strictly enforced, it was a common sight to routinely spot Afghans/Pashtoons in India's big and small towns as bicycle-riding vendors of dry fruits, used clothes and petty loans. Popularly known as *kabuliwala*,[7] his simplicity was immortalized by Rabindranath Tagore in his short story *Kabuliwala*. Through the character of Rahmat Ali, the author portrayed the innocence of the Pashtoons which coexisted with their ruggedness that did not stomach any nonsense when their honour was in question. Rahmat's penchant to return to his motherland to reunite with his little daughter exemplified the pathos of any lonely father in a forlorn land. *Kabuliwala* became the theme of several Indian movies, the most famous being the one in Hindi produced by Bimal Roy in 1961. In one of its songs, one can feel the reverberation of that passion filled with sadness of the *kabuliwalas* to return to their *watan* (motherland). No wonder that the movie was a hit in Kabul.[8] These three things, namely, the inherent simplicity, physical ruggedness and the uncompromising sense of honour, are what Pashtoons are made of and this is what the global actors have failed to appreciate over the centuries. Seemingly, India too could not appreciate this ethnic attribute either when it decided to support the Soviets after they intervened in Afghanistan in 1979. Probably the Americans did the same mistake post-9/11.

Following the Soviet intervention, there was a massive flow of Afghan refugees to neighbouring Pakistan. A good number of them also went to Iran. Only a small group of refugees came to India. By 2011 their total number was 11,400, of which 2,400 had applied for Indian asylum. As Mandate Refugees, all Afghan refugees are registered with the UNHCR. But because of India's complicated relationship with Pakistan, coupled with the evidence of cross-border terrorist threats to India in which Afghan Taliban were both actual and potential conduits, the UNHCR had to face problems in dealing with the Afghan refugees. Funds constraints were additional handicaps. Afghan refugees suffered primarily from two problems, one, education of their children, and two, finding employment. Unless the children could be sent to English medium schools, they could not find jobs if and when they got any chance to be repatriated outside India. English medium schools were privately run and they were expensive. Government schools imparted education only in Hindi and the madrassas only in Urdu, neither of which was good for further education or employment abroad. Afghan refugees could not do jobs in India either as they were Mandate Refugees on UNHCR doles, which, however inadequate, was the only source of their income. There were also reports of police harassments and even imprisonment (Hans 2003: 373–76). In 2012 India granted work permits and long-term visas to all Mandate Refugees which included the Afghan refugees as well but the process has been slow and because of their lack of skill many Afghans cannot take advantage of the situation (*Indian Express*, 14 July 2013, also see the interview of Antonio Guterres, the UNHCR in Delhi, in *The Hindu*, 4 January 2013).

# The Myanmarese Refugees

After 1948 when Myanmar became independent, India had to deal with two waves of refugees from the country. The first wave was related to the nationalization drive in Myanmar, resulting in the forced return of Indian traders and bankers, mostly consisting of Chettiars from Tamil Nadu. The second wave was when by the end of the 1980s the pro-democracy movement resulted in state repression causing exodus of Myanmarese refugees to India. In Chapter 2, we have discussed the political dimensions of both of these phenomena. Since many in the second category of refugees are Mandate Refugees, who are taken care of by the UNHCR, let us see how the Indian state has handled those belonging to the first category. It is estimated that between 1966 and the 1980s, about 250,000 Indians settled in Myanmar left the country mainly for three destinations, namely, one, their respective states of origin in India which primarily was Tamil Nadu, but also were West Bengal, Punjab and Bihar, two, the north-eastern states of India (mostly in Moreh in Manipur), and three, other countries in Asia or in some of the British Commonwealth countries. It was, however, Tamil Nadu which had to bear the biggest responsibility for their rehabilitation because the number of Myanmarese refugees there was the largest. While the richer Chettiars gradually re-established themselves through business enterprises others were pro-vided relief and rehabilitation assistance by the Tamil Nadu government under its various schemes. By March 2001, 144,445 refugees were rehabilitated either through land grants or through loan-based house-building schemes. Besides Tamil Nadu, other states like West Bengal and Andhra Pradesh too provided similar help to the Myanmarese refugees, although their activities were limited as the number to be looked after was few. In the north-east of India, the resettlement of the Myanmarese refugees was not always without conflict as they got entangled into the region's complicated inter-ethnic squabbles. Still, Moreh became the hub of Chettiar business interests in the region as they managed to revive their old contacts in Myanmar (Bhaumik 2003: 191–96).

Besides the above two categories, there is yet another set of refugees from Myanmar. They are the Rohingyas. Since they speak Bengali and look like Bangladeshis they often get mixed up with Bangladeshi illegal migrants. According to the UNHCR, in 2014, there were 9,000 registered Rohingya refugees in Delhi. There were many more who were unreg-istered and who lived, besides Delhi, in Jammu and Hyderabad. Quite often the Government of India does not recognize the identity cards issued to them by the UNHCR. It recognizes only those cards that have been issued by the state. But in any case, India is 'a functioning protec-tion regime', as Dominik Bartsch, UNHCR Chief of Mission in India, acknowledged.[9]

# II
# Pakistan Experience

## The Partition Refugees

Pakistan had to deal with its Partition refugees in both East and West wings. It was, however, in West Pakistan that the challenge was much larger as of all the refugees that came to Pakistan, 91 per cent arrived in West Pakistan (73 per cent in Punjab alone) while merely 9per cent arrived in East Pakistan. It may be noted that the refugees who came from the Indian part of Punjab to the Pakistani part came largely en masse and within a short span of time. But those from other parts of India came in relatively smaller numbers and over a longer period of time, almost till 1965. The latter category settled mostly in Sind, particularly Karachi. As a result, while the refugees in Punjab spoke the same Punjabi language as the locals did, those settling in Sind spoke mostly Urdu, while the locals spoke Sindhi. This resulted in two different kinds of responses from the Punjab and Sind governments to their respective refugee communities. The Government of Punjab was more sympathetic to the refugees there compared to the Sind government to the refugees in Sind. The Central and Punjab governments jointly established the Pakistan Punjab Refugee Council for the purpose of refugee rehabilitation. The Punjab government was allocated a grant of Rs. 12,500,000 and a development loan of Rs. 80,000,000. Besides, 42 satellite towns were built to accommodate 80,000 families. A rehabilitation tax was instituted, and credit agencies were created to fund new businesses. At the village level, a *guzara* (managing daily affairs with limited resources) scheme was introduced for temporary allotments of agricultural lands. In spite of delays and other controversies, by and large the schemes worked well. For example, by the end of January 1959, of the total of 1,390,362 pending cases 1,315,544 had been settled (Waseem 1994: 109–10).

As noted earlier, the Punjabi refugees from India were rehabilitated mostly in the Punjab. Those rehabilitated in the erstwhile Sikh-dominated great canal colonies of Montgomery, Lyallpur and Shahpur were granted five to eight acres of land per family, while in other areas they were given more, even up to 12 acres. However, provincial interests often clashed with the policies of the central government in this regard. The same problem arose in respect of Sind as well. Still, since Prime Minister Liaquat Ali Khan had virtually permanently stationed himself in Lahore, he could exert his influence more on the Punjab government, which was not the case with Sind (Sayeed 1960: 288–90). This situation was similar to that what happened in India. Nehru was more effective in dealing with the Punjabi refugees in Delhi and its neighbourhood than those in West Bengal.

In respect of settlement of evacuee properties, there was cooperation between India and Pakistan, although it was not all that hunky-dory. There were claims and counterclaims put by India and Pakistan in respect of immovable properties. Even in respect of such matters as shares and debentures, which were otherwise easier to verify, there were many difficulties. A contemporary study noted:

The Agreement of 27 June 1950 has enabled a large number of refugees in either country to recover the personal effects they left behind when they fled and to transfer them to their new place of residence. Certain difficulties were, however, encountered in carrying out the Agreement, generally in connexion with problems having to do with shares, insurance policies, bonds, debentures, safe deposits and other banking accounts. The Government of Pakistan does not regard them as insurmountable, but it considers that the Government of India has shown little alacrity in unfreezing shares and debentures belonging to Moslems.... [A]ccording to Pakistani estimates, the value of the property left behind by Moslems in the whole of India, except West Bengal and Assam, far exceeds that abandoned by non-Moslems in Western Pakistan alone. (Conversely, according to Indian estimates, the final account, immovable property included, is alleged to be in favour of Pakistan.) (Vernant 1953: 761–62)

Insofar as property exchange was concerned, it worked very well in the Punjab province. Within a short span of time, 6.6 million hectares of evacuee land was allotted to incoming refugees in the Punjab province (Waseem 1994: 107). In contrast, in Sind land was allotted on a temporary basis and, that too, on a much smaller scale. Unlike Punjab, the process of refugee rehabilitation in Sind remained grossly dissatisfactory. Even in 1954, seven years after Partition, there were as many as 240,000 refugees out of a total of 750,000 who were yet to be rehabilitated. Since the process of refugee flow continued, the problem multiplied. In Punjab, by 1948 the immigration had stopped (Table 4.3).

In the overall politico-economic context, the Muslim Punjabis were the biggest gainers from the Partition, notwithstanding the general loss of life and honour to which all communities were subjected to. They acquired agricultural lands and other immoveable properties in West Punjab disproportionate to their losses in India. This new prosperity

**Table 4.3**
*Patterns of refugee rehabilitation in Pakistan*

| Punjab Situation | Sind Situation |
| --- | --- |
| Settlement: Smooth and quick (90% by July 1948) | Settlement: Problematic and delayed (30% unsettled by 1954) |
| No returnees | Refugees returning to India |
| Refugees spread over Punjab | Refugees concentrated in Karachi |
| Permanent allotment | Temporary allotment |

*Source:* Waseem (1999).

coupled with their swelled demographic advantage eventually led to the Punjabi domination of Pakistan politics at the cost of all other communities, although in the initial phase the Urdu-speaking Muhajirin were politically ascendant.

# The Afghan Refugees

There was a massive flow of Afghan refugees to Pakistan after the Soviet intervention in Afghanistan in 1979, which we have discussed in Chapter 1. In Chapters 2 and 3 we have discussed their registration-related issues as well as the implications of their presence in Pakistan for the latter's domestic and international politics. In this section, we would see how Pakistan has coordinated its efforts with UNHCR and other international agencies to repatriate them or to rehabilitate them. Legally speaking there is no case for their rehabilitation in Pakistan, for after all they are foreign refugees who are to be handled under Pakistan's Foreigners Act of 1946. But since the refugees are mostly Pashtoon and since the provinces of Khyber Pakhtunkhwa and Balochistan, where they have migrated, are populated by their co-ethnics in large numbers, there have been moves for their permanent settlement there, at least for some. Indeed, many law-and-order-related issues exist as there are incidences of refugees illegally occupying private lands for their permanent settlement, particularly in Khyber Pakhtunkhwa.

Efforts aimed at addressing the needs of the refugees, together with those of Pakistan on a durable basis, have been undertaken within the framework of the regional Solutions Strategy for Afghan Refugees (SSAR). The three major players in this are the UNHCR, the Government of Pakistan and the Government of Afghanistan. There are primarily three segments in the strategy: (a) voluntary repatriation to the country of origin, (b) integration in the host country and (c) resettlement in a third country. Although the UNHCR has been very active still to complement its efforts, the Pakistan government has extended Afghan refugees' POR cards until the end of 2015. Under the scheme it has issued birth certificates to 800,000 Afghan refugee children, has provided land for several refugee villages and has given refugees access to government schools and health centres.[10]

The plan of action for 2015 includes UNHCR's support for Pakistan in implementing the regional SSAR through Pakistan-specific portfolio of projects developed in 2014, in advancing efforts to mobilize resources for prioritized activities and in helping Pakistan implement its national policy on Afghan refugees so as to find durable solutions (voluntary repatriation and resettlement). UNHCR would also enhance asylum space and support to both host communities and refugees through its Refugee Affected and Housing Areas (RAHA) initiative, which is an integral component of the in-country implementation of the SSAR. As per UNHCR's estimate, its Pakistan budget for 2015 would be in the tune of US$137,100,000, of which US$58,800,000 would be allocated specifically for the Afghan refugees. Besides UNHCR and other international agencies, many Pakistan-based and international NGOs would also be involved in the activities.[11]

So far as resettlement in a third country is concerned the EU has taken active interest in the plan. It has conducted field surveys in the refugee camps, tried to familiarize the refugees about the idea, registered the support of many NGOs for its plan of action and made efforts to identify the potential repatriates to specific EU countries. One of the data gaps that the field workers had to encounter was the scarcity of information from 'women at risk' because of social and cultural factors (Chattha 2013).

# III
# Bangladesh Experience

The Bangladesh experience has been threefold, as the victim of Partition, as a refugee-generating country and, then, also as a refugee-receiving country. The first is with regard to the Biharis, the community of Muslim refugees who arrived in East Pakistan from the Urdu-speaking areas of India such as Bihar, UP, Hyderabad and other places. The second concerns its efforts to get back the Chakma refugees who had fled to India to avoid prospective starvation on account of their loss of lands to plains area Muslims as well as to avoid state repression that was unleashed to quell their protests. The third is in respect of Rohingya refugees from adjoining Myanmar. We have discussed the Bihari question in Chapter 2 in political terms, which includes references to their camp lives and overall miseries. State intervention to improve their lot has limited efficacy, partly because of their split loyalty (ultimate goal of many Biharis is to go and settle in Pakistan) and partly because of the general apathy of Bangladeshis to their uplift, though since 2008 there is a blanket allowance to them to opt for Bangladeshi nationality if they are born in Bangladesh, which means a fairly large section of them. In this section, therefore, we would not repeat that discussion and concentrate on the remaining two issues, Chakmas and Rohingyas.

# Agreement with Chakmas

On 9 March 1997, the Bangladesh government and the Chakma refugee leaders located in India signed their first agreement aimed at finding ways to repatriate the refugees. As a follow-up, a memorandum of understanding (MOU) was signed on 2 December 1997 between the Government of Bangladesh and the Parbatya Chattagram Jana Sanghati Samiti (PCJSS; CHT People's Coordination Committee) to make the solution to the problem enduring. The 72-point agreement that was worked out was divided into four parts: (a) General, (b) Parbatya Chattagram Regional Council, (c) Parbatya Zila Parishad and (d) Rehabilitation, General Amnesty and Miscellaneous Affairs. Declaring the CHT as a region inhabited by tribes people, both the parties accepted the need to work for the overall development of the area and to protect the special characteristics of the region. The agreement called for establishing a Parbatya Zila Parishad for each of the Hill Tracts districts. It also conceded that a regional council named Parbatya Chattagram Anchalik Parishad comprising the three Hill Tracts districts would also be created. This council would have sweeping powers to govern these districts. A hill people's representative, with the rank and status of a state minister, would head the council, and he would be consulted whenever the government wanted to legislate on the CHT. There would also be a separate ministry dealing with affairs of the region and the minister heading it would be chosen from the hill people. The accord granted the Regional Council the power to impose various kinds of taxes, collect tolls and revenue, give or withhold permission to set up industrial units, levy commissions on profits from minerals, as well as assume responsibility for the police, land administration and legal system.

In October 1998, the MOU was deadlocked when the PCJSS formally 'rejected' the formation of the Regional Council alleging that the Sheikh Hasina government had not kept its promise to nominate three Bengali settlers selected by the Samity to the Council. The PCJSS communicated its decision to the President, Justice Shahabuddin Ahmed, and the Prime Minister, Sheikh Hasina. The three Bengali settlers nominated by the government were reportedly from among the ruling party leaders from the hills. The PCJSS wanted its own sympathizers from among the settlers for strategic reasons. There were problems from other quarters as well. For example, the *Pahari Gana Parishad* (Hill People's Council), the *Pahari Chhatra Parishad* (Hill Students' Council) and the Hill Women's Federation were up in arms against the accord because according to them it amounted to a total sell-out of the interests of the CHT people. One of the major grievances of these groups was that the accord did not provide any possibility of driving the Bengali Muslim settlers out from their traditional homeland, which was at the core of the conflict. They also pointed out that while the accord provided for the rehabilitation of members of Shanti Bahini and Jana Sanghati Samiti and condoned their past activities, it did not guarantee the same for their members. Moreover, there was no provision for the trial of the military personnel and settlers who were involved in the killings and massacre of the CHT people.

The opposition BNP criticized the accord on exactly opposite grounds. It said that the accord had compromised the sovereignty of the nation for the sake of one-tenth of its territory. It had also tarnished the unitary character of the state and had thereby 'sown seeds of dissension and separatist tendencies' in other parts of the country as well. The party also pointed out that Article 36 of the Constitution of Bangladesh, which guaranteed freedom of movement and settlement in any part of the country, was sacrificed by Clause 26(B) of the accord. BNP claimed that the accord had reduced the Bengalis to second class citizens in the CHT. The overall result of these bickering was the slow implementation of the accord in terms of rehabilitation and development. Even after more than a decade the situation in the CHT did not show much promise. The provisions of the accord largely remained unimplemented, and dominance of the locals by Muslim setters from other parts of Bangladesh continued unabated, which often had the tacit approval of the law enforcement authorities. The problem was that there was lack of firm political commitment on behalf of the ruling elites, the spillover effect of which was gradual erosion of group harmony, the hallmark of tribal communities. Intra-group rivalries and conflicts marked the political landscape of region (Jamil & Panday 2008: 482–87).

## The Rohingya Refugees

While India faced the problem of refugees from Myanmar more in terms of political refugees and, in a limited sense, from that of the Rohingyas, Bangladesh has faced a much greater challenge in respect of Rohingyas, who have been seeking refuge there for many years now. These people, who belong to the adjacent Rakhine province of Myanmar, consider Bangladesh as their natural refuge whenever in trouble. We have discussed in Chapter 1 how in the 1970s certain ethnic policies of Myanmar led to their flight to Bangladesh in large numbers. By 2009 there were between 200,000 and 400,000 Rohingyas in the country (Rahman 2010: 235). From time to time there were negotiations between Bangladeshi and Myanmarese authorities with the good offices of the UNHCR to repatriate them to Myanmar, which yielded limited success. For example, in April 1992 they signed an agreement allowing the 'safe and voluntary' return of the refugees. The two governments also 'agreed to cooperate for the prevention of illegal border crossings' after they had successfully completed the repatriation. They had also agreed to enhance security on the borders to prevent their territories from being used by terrorists, insurgents, smugglers, gun runners and drug traffickers. The real importance of the accord, however, was in the fact that it made Myanmar acknowledge the existence of Rohingyas as an integral part of the Myanmarese society (Saeed 1993: 30–44). Even repatriations had begun on 22 September 1992.

Subsequently, two MOUs were signed to facilitate the return of the refugees, one between the Government of Bangladesh and the UNHCR on 12 May 1993, and the other between the SLORC of Myanmar and the UNHCR on 5 November 1993. The plan was to repatriate approximately 190,000 refugees at the rate of 15,000 to 18,000 per month. The process, however, got bogged down in the controversy over whether the repatriation was voluntary or compulsory. A survey conducted in March 1995 reported that 65 per cent of the interviewees claimed that they were not aware that they had the choice to refuse repatriation. UNHCR statistics found that out of 55,000 refugees, 19,000 had chosen not to return. Both the RSO and the *Jamaat-i-Islami* incited the refugees to refuse repatriation by selling them the dream of an independent Arakan/Rakhine state. They also hoped that if these refugees could be settled in the CHT region then they would automatically solve the Chakma problem to the advantage of Muslim Bengalis. The problem of repatriation was also compounded by the fact that 18,000 new babies had been born in the camps. A report in *The Asian Age* of 27 June 1995 said that 3,000 refugee mothers were expecting babies. Given the fact that Myanmar, though heading towards democracy, and yet is not in a mood to recognize the Rohingyas as one of its indigenous ethnic communities, the problem of Rohingya refugees in Bangladesh is not likely to die soon. Moreover, because of the terrorist connection of some of the Rohingya refugees in Bangladesh there is lukewarm sympathy for them from the government side. The latter recognizes the presence of only 30,000 of them who are eligible for food, housing and other basis assistance provided by the UN. Even there are restrictions on their marriages with locals as they would legitimize their stay (Blumberg 2014).

# IV
# Nepal Experience

## Lhotshampa Refugees from Bhutan

According to a 2008 fact sheet prepared by the International Organization for Migration (IOM) there were seven camps in Nepal which housed 111,232 Lhotshampa refugees from Bhutan as follows: Beldongi 1, 2 and Extension (52,756), Sanischare (21,320), Goldhap (9,632), Khudunabari (13,180) and Timai (10,344). The inmates belonged to various Hindu caste groups, as was natural to the Nepalese society at large. The male-to-female ratio was by and large balanced. Children under 18 constituted 35.5 per cent of the camp population. Interestingly, family planning seemed to be widely practiced, as was evident from the fact that the age 0–2 population was just the same as the age 65+ population. In terms of health care and education, the camps were relatively in good stead compared to the refugee camp experience in many other parts of the world. Education was free till the 10th grade. From the 10th to 12th grades there was a nominal fee as Caritus, a donor-supported implementing partner of UNHCR, funded those grades partially. The camps were primarily managed by democratically elected bodies and functionaries (http://www.hrdi.in/?p=2849, accessed on 30 December 2014).

So far as the repatriation of the refugees to Bhutan is concerned, in spite of several rounds of parleys between Nepal and Bhutan it has virtually reached a dead end. The only thing that has been achieved through these discussions is that there is a categorization of the refugees into four groups, namely,

1.   Bona fide Bhutanese who have been forcibly evicted,
2.   Bhutanese who have voluntarily emigrated,
3.   Non-Bhutanese people and
4.   Bhutanese who have committed criminal acts.

The UNHCR, which is at the centre of refugee relief and rehabilitation in Nepal, follows its general three-pronged mandate, namely, (a) facilitate voluntary repatriation of refugees to home country, (b) facilitate local integration in the country of refuge and (c) facilitate voluntary resettlement in a third country. Of the three options, the second and the third have the potential to succeed. The United States have offered to resettle 60,000 of them but there is scepticism among many camp dwellers that they might face the same kind of discrimination in America. Moreover, once they migrate to America the hope of their return to Bhutan is permanently gone. T.B. Subba, the director of the Human Rights Organisation of Bhutan, is one such opinion maker (http://infochangeindia.org/agenda/migration-a-displacement/lhotshampas-evicted-from-bhutan. html, accessed on 8 January 2016). Still, according to IOM, the resettlement project has been working since October 2007 and by February 2013, 76,179 Lhotshampa refugees had departed to eight Resettlement Countries, namely, America, Australia, Canada, Denmark, Holland, New Zealand, Norway and the UK.[12]

# Notes

1. There are some stray cases of refuge-seeking Pakistanis and Afghans in Sri Lanka. According to a UNHCR briefing note, until September 2014, there were 38 such Pakistanis and 64 Afghans in detention camps in the country. http://www.unhcr.org/5412e24a6.html (accessed on 8 January 2016).
2. Officially called the Delhi Pact, it was signed between Indian and Pakistani prime ministers, Jawaharlal Nehru and Liaquat Ali Khan, respectively, on 8 April 1950, following the escalation of tension between India and Pakistan in East Pakistan after economic relations between the two countries had been severed in December 1949. The idea was that let the refugees be allowed to return unmolested to dispose of their properties, allow abducted women and looted properties to be returned, to derecognize forced conversions and to reconfirm minority rights. Minority commissions were established to implement these terms, and confidence was, in fact, restored for some time. However, in the months following the pact, more than a million additional refugees migrated to West Bengal. The continuing struggle over Kashmir also strained relations between the two countries.
3. It may be mentioned here that the Partition had two social consequences, both, arguably, positive. On the one hand, it tore apart the parochial kinship networks and, on the other, it unleashed women's energy to educate them and to enter into the job market, which was not the case in pre-Partition Punjab. One can find a glimpse of this in the inspiring biography of a mother by her sociologist daughter. See Singh (2013).

4. When it became almost certain that Bengal would be divided on religious lines, the Bengal provincial Muslim League leader Huseyn Shaheed Suhrawardy floated the idea of an independent Bengal in April 1947. Suspecting that he was eyeing Kolkata, then the largest Indian city and also an industrial and commercial hub, and eventually entire Bengal as part of Pakistan, the dominant section of the Congress party as well as the Hindu Mahasabha vehemently opposed the idea. In the partitioned Bengal, Kolkata remained in West Bengal. For more on this point, see Partha Ghosh (2000: 77–79).

5. One many surmise, did they mean that had there been more anti-Muslim violence in West Bengal, it would have made them flee to East Pakistan in panic. This would have resulted in abandoning their lands and other properties as it happened in Punjab. Those abandoned lands could then be occupied by the incoming Hindu refugees from East Pakistan.

6. Passed by the Constituent Assembly of Pakistan on 12 March 1949, the Objectives Resolution was the foundational stone of the constitutional development in Pakistan. It contained the basic principles of both Islamic political system and Western democracy. It served as a preamble for the constitution of 1956, 1962 and 1973 and ultimately became the part of the Constitution when the Eighth Amendment to the Constitution of 1973 was passed in 1985. Its Islamic thrust cannot be overemphasized as it ordained that Muslims shall live their lives according to the teaching of Quran and Sunnah.

7. A popular Bengali/north Indian expression to mean those Afghans who used to come to India routinely to sell small items like dry fruits or second-hand clothes before and after India's Partition. The 1965 India-Pakistan War brought an end to the phenomenon.

8. In Bollywood flicks, Pashtoons are almost always portrayed as highly masculine yet warm-hearted and friendly people who can be trusted for their commitments. In *Zanjeer*, the character of Sher Khan, as portrayed by the quintessential actor Pran (1920–2013), is one of many such examples.

9. http://www.unhcr.org.in/index.php?option=com_news&view=detail&id=47&Itemid=117 (accessed on 27 December 2014).

10. http://www.unhcr.org/cgi-bin/texts/vtx/page?=49e487016&subm (accessed on 4 January 2015).

11. See Note 10.

12. http://nepal.iom.int/jupgrade/index.php/en/aboutus/18-topic-details/52-about-us-2, accessed on 30 December 2014.

# 5

# The Legal Dynamics

*The greater the number of laws and enactments, the more thieves and robbers there will be.*

—Lao Tzu, the Chinese philosopher

## Introduction

Do the refugees, migrants and the stateless persons have legal rights? Since the refugees are a legal category, at least in those countries which have signed the international refugee convention, the answer is yes. But in South Asia, barring Afghanistan, none has signed the convention. Even otherwise when it comes to migrants, both documented and undocumented, leave alone the stateless persons, the answer does not seem to be so straightforward in those countries also which have signed the convention. In South Asia, where the refugee, migrant and stateless categories are often not clearly distinguishable, and where the humanitarian records of the governments across the board have by and large been satisfactory in dealing with their refugee/migrant/stateless issues, the legal dimensions alone do not tell the whole story.[1] Alongside, one must look into the societal, humanitarian and political considerations as well.

Over the years, many concerned individuals in South Asia have highlighted the human dimensions of these problems to plead for a law-based approach to the question. They argue that South Asia's reluctance to join the international community in signing the 1951 Convention or its 1967 Protocol cannot be dissociated from the anthropological discourse over human rights. At the core of the debate is the conflict between the concept of universality of human rights and the cultural relativity of the same. While the former is generally grounded in the Western notion of human rights, the latter is imbedded in the approaches of the decolonized countries after the end of the Second World War. Though the gap is increasingly narrowing, differences between the two approaches persist. These differences are not always interstate or inter-cultural, they sometimes can as well be intrastate or intra-cultural (Subba 2004: 468–71). Given these complexities, it is not unlikely that individual states have different notions of human rights and thereby different approaches to refugee/migrant/stateless protection. Although, as noted above, seven out of eight South Asian countries have not signed the international refugee covenants yet, partly because of their respective constitutions or partly because of their overall societal make-up, they do not show outright hostility to these people, and, in spite of the resource shortages of the concerned governments they are generally willing to recognize and address their plight from humanistic angles.

## Some Basic Questions

In this chapter, we will raise the following questions and try to find their answers:

1. Even though the South Asian states, except Afghanistan, have not signed the international refugee covenants of 1951 and 1967 and some other relevant international covenants, what legal bases they have to deal with their refugee/migrant/stateless issues? Is there anything like a definition of a refugee/migrant/stateless in any South Asian state?

2. What could be their reservations or apprehensions in not signing the 1951, 1967 and some other relevant international covenants?

3. What kind of discourse is there in South Asia, most notably in India, about the rights of the refugee/migrant/stateless?

4. Is there a case for a South Asian regional convention as the problems are often not strictly state-centric? Would it not be more appropriate to find a regional solution instead of a national or bilateral?

5. Is the legal discourse, both nationally and regionally, out of steam as doubts are being expressed even in the West about the efficacy of their own legal regimes?

Our answers to the above questions are drawn primarily from the Indian experience, but wherever relevant other experiences too have been taken into account.

# Origin of Refugee Rights in South Asia

It may be argued that the concept of refugee *rights* in its South Asian context had its origin in the post-Partition East Bengali refugee experience. The Refugee Central Rehabilitation Council (RCRC), the refugee wing of the RSP in West Bengal, and the East Bengal Minority Welfare Association (EBMWA) underlined the fact that Bengali refugees were not asking for compassion or benevolence from either the West Bengal or the Central Government, but they were demanding their legitimate rights as Indians. In one of its pamphlets, the RCRC said:

> The East Bengalis expelled from Pakistan, can demand to build their homes on every inch of Indian soil on the strength of their *adhikar* (own right). They are not *sharanarthi* (supplicants) but *kshatipuraner dabidar* (claimants to compensation for losses). (RCRC n.d.: 1, quoted by Chatterjee. n.d.: 7)

The EBMWA was equally emphatic with its demand for *rights*. One of its pamphlets said:

> The partition left us homeless, bereft of everything. We did not fight for independence in order to lead the lives of beggars. Those of us who cannot remain in East Pakistan are not doing anything wrong by seeking shelter in India. Why should the police push us back? Why should we live in hovels next to rail-tracks? Why should we be the object of people's mercy? ... [I]t is only right that those who struggled and sacrificed for independence be repaid. (EBMWA n.d.: 8–9, Chatterjee. n.d.: 7–8)

Horace Alexander, a close associate of Mahatma Gandhi and the one who wrote a book on the post-Partition refugees as early as in 1951, had the following to say on the question: How India should define its refugees?

> A word on the word 'refugee'. I have used it throughout. Some people have a violent antipathy to the word. They say: 'These people are not refugees. They are displaced persons.' According to the dictionary definition they certainly are refugees; that is, they are people who have fled from a place where they felt unsafe to find *refuge* in a place where they expected to be safe, and to be cared for. That they should not be treated as alien is, however, quite another matter. When they declare to their neighbours in India: 'We

are flesh of your flesh, we are blood of your blood. Please do not treat us as aliens and foreigners', then surely they are right. It is true, perhaps, that in Europe the term 'refugee' is commonly used of aliens seeking refuge, whilst a 'displaced person' tends to mean one who has been driven out owing to changes of frontier. But the term 'displaced person' has in Europe almost superseded the term 'refugee'. It is long and ungainly, and is therefore readily contracted to 'D.P.s'. I do not think it is easy any nicer to be a 'D.P.' than to be a 'refugee'. I assure my refugee friends that no discourtesy is intended. (Alexander 1951: 5–6)

In the context of framing a refugee law the most important problem that South Asian countries, India in particular, faced was in respect of defining a migrant and a refugee. Because of historical and social circumstances most of the time they get mixed. Probably that is so with many other regions unless the refugees arrive from distant regions or from other cultural backgrounds. Jacques Vernant in his 1953 book *The Refugee in the Post-War World* defined a refugee as 'someone who has been compelled to abandon his home'. If so, all kinds of victims of natural or man-made calamities, or those who find it difficult to make a living in the country of their origin because of all kinds of reasons and decide to move out to another country, would be refugees. From the same logic 'voluntary economic = migrants' and 'involuntary political = refugees' does not make sense. For example, a purely economic decision on the part of Bangladesh government to encourage shrimp cultivation in Satkhira had resulted in outmigration of local peasants to the neighbouring districts of West Bengal just like the Irish migrations of the mid-19th century, although the latter was much larger (Samaddar 1997: 102–3). That leads to the question whether Bangladeshi undocumented migrants in India are refugees or migrants. If not, what particular purpose is going to be served even if India enacts a refugee law. Millions would still be out of the ambit of this law. Would finding a definition of stateless persons help in this regard? We have discussed this question later in this chapter.

So far as Pakistan was concerned, according to Section 17 of the Pakistani Nationality Act of 1951, any refugee from India who arrived in Pakistan before 13 April 1951 was recognized ipso facto as a Pakistani citizen. Under Section 6 of the same Act, refugees who emigrated permanently after the above date but before 1 January 1952 might be accepted as Pakistani citizens by migration, provided they obtained a certificate of domicile in accordance with the provisions of the Act. It was not deemed important to keep records of the refugee movements as all refugees were considered to be on equal footing with other nationals and were, therefore, authorized to settle anywhere they chose to. But this was not so in respect of refugees from Kashmir. They were treated as displaced persons whose proper domiciles were in the state of Jammu and Kashmir and, therefore, refugees. Their stay in Pakistan was understood to be temporary, and as and when normalcy would return to Kashmir they would return to their homes (Vernant 1953: 759, 767).

In Bengal, where the refugee flow was a lingering phenomenon, the definitional problem was more complex. There, the preferred term for the Government of India was 'displaced' rather than 'refugee'. Since there was no passport system at that time between India and Pakistan, the migrants had citizenship rights in both the states. The issue was complex, as one can see in the following quote:

> Those Hindus, who had left East Pakistan before 15 October 1947 due to the communal frenzy, were excluded from the previously mentioned official definition. At that time, the 'passport system' was yet to be launched, and it was regarded as a special case since the refugees had citizenship rights in both the states. Therefore, the Government of India officials probably thought the term 'displaced' more suitable than 'refugee'. Moreover, although India became independent on 15 August 1947, the extended period of two months was given to the people for settling themselves in the country of their choice. However, in the later phase these 'displaced' people were referred to as 'migrants' and were divided into two broad categories – the 'old migrants' [those who migrated between October 1946 and 31 March 1958] and 'new migrants' [those who migrated between 1 January 1964 and 25 March 1971]. One should not forget that, many people crossing over to West Bengal between 1958 and 1964 were excluded from the definition of 'migrants'. Moreover, although many people came from East Pakistan to India with 'migration certificates' [introduced by India in 1956 to allow entry in 'certain special circumstances such as split families and girls coming into India for marriage'] they were treated like refugees and in many cases they were sent to the camps because they needed relief and rehabilitation for their survival. (Basu Ray Chaudhury & Dey 2009: 6)

# Refugee Laws in South Asia: The Framework

Even without any refugee-specific legal regime, India and Pakistan have handled millions of refugees starting with the arrival of massive numbers of refugees during and after the Partition. The processes were on for several years after Partition, as we have discussed in Chapter 1. Even now there are refugee arrivals from Afghanistan and Myanmar to India, although they are not many in number. But in the case of Pakistan, the refugees from Afghanistan are large in number and the flow is unabated with varying degree of intensity. Besides, there are Bangladeshis in fairly large numbers in India, but they cannot be called refugees unless we make the definition flexible, as we have discussed in the previous section. In any case, they are economic migrants who illegally arrive in India and settle in various parts of the country; in other words, they fall within the category of undocumented migrants. How have India and Pakistan managed their problems without a refugee law? Are there other laws and rules that help India, Pakistan and other South Asian states guide their refugee protection regimes?

Rajiv Dhavan, a senior Supreme Court lawyer of India and human rights activist, has provided seven frameworks under which India's refugee protection regime can be studied (Dhavan: 2004). These frameworks can be valid for other South Asian countries as well. The frameworks are as follows:

1.  The citizenship regime
2.  The fundamental rights regime
3.  The statutory framework
4.  India's obligations arising out of its international treaty obligations
5.  The judicial interventions
6.  The SAARC framework (or the regional framework)
7.  The Model Law of Refugee Protection

Given South Asia's experience one may as well add two other frameworks, namely, the bilateral framework and the informal framework. Many refugee issues in the region have been tackled either through bilateral cooperation without invoking state or international laws or simply by informal mechanisms without taking recourse to legal processes at all.

## The Issue of Citizenship

The question of citizenship is at the core of a modern state system. Just as international borders form the most critical geographical expression to delineate the physical limits of a state, the notion of citizenship determines who the legitimate residents within that defined space are. The existence of aliens, denizens (aliens admitted to rights of citizenship), refugees and unauthorized settlers or migrants reinforces the concept of citizenship. It is the same kind of dialectic—the unauthorized border crossing proves that there is something called border. Likewise, an average individual is not conscious of the fact as to how much valuable this routine certification by the state is critical for him until when he loses it or tries to acquire the citizenship of another state. Scholars who have tried to understand the issue holistically have viewed the theme from theoretical, political, feminist and humanistic perspectives.

To provide an immediate historical backdrop to the above, it may be mentioned that besides millions of Hindu, Muslim and Sikh refugees whose nationality question was virtually settled automatically by the fact that the respective Governments of India and Pakistan both legally and emotionally/socially accepted them as their own people, rightly characterized by Horace Alexander as the 'new citizens' (Alexander 1951), there were some small groups for whom the nationality question was not so easily resolved. One such category consisted of Hindus and Sikhs who fled the POK (Azad Kashmir, according to Pakistan) and the Muslims who left the Indian part of Kashmir to settle either in POK or in other parts of Pakistan. There was also the issue of long-settled Kazakh-speaking migrants from Xinjiang in Lahore, Karachi and Kashmir (both parts). Even there was a small group of Czechs (mostly in the Bata shoe factories) who had turned stateless because of the European circumstances. Their nationality question remained unresolved. Also included in this uncertain category were a small number of people who belonged to the French and Portuguese possessions in India but who were settled in places that formed India and Pakistan. They too had difficulties in respect of their status in the new states of India and Pakistan (Vernant 1953: 741–45).

In India one may identify three landmark developments to trace the evolutionary terrain of the citizenship discourse.[2] The first concerned the Partition of India and the resultant movement of millions of people across the borders, a process that continued for several years thereafter, as we have discussed in Chapter 1. No wonder that the Government of India took as many as eight years after independence to pass its first Citizenship Act, 1955, which is still in force with certain amendments. The second milestone in the evolution was the 1986 amendment to the 1955 Act initiated against the background of a serious turmoil in Assam politics that fomented a separatist tendency in the state as never before. The third development was yet another amendment to the same citizenship act. Through this 2003 amendment, persons of Indian origin living in select foreign countries were granted virtual Indian citizenship.[3] This raised a fundamental question as to what constituted the core of the citizenship criterion. If one critically analyses this history of citizenship in India, one would see how the Indian state has systematically compromised on its earlier premises to respond to political expediencies. Probably there is nothing wrong in doing so for after all citizenship in itself is a political contraption and it is natural, therefore, that the state would have to respond to changing political realities to suitably adapt its given premises.

A fourth amendment to India's Citizenship Act, 1955, seems to be in the offing now. Recently there have been moves by the government to grant Indian citizenship to all those Hindus, Buddhists, Christians, Sikhs, Jains and Zoroastrians who have fled from Pakistan and Bangladesh in the teeth of religious persecution and arrived in India. These categories also include those whose visas have expired and who do not want to get them renewed. To effectuate its policy the government is reportedly proceeding to appropriately amend the Citizenship Act, 1955, as well as the Foreigners Act, 1946, the Passport (Entry into India) Act, 1920, and the Passport (Entry into India) Rules, 1950. The Ministry of Home Affairs is reportedly drafting a bill to this effect. If amended, the Citizenship Act would exempt these illegal migrants from that status. The Ministry of External Affairs, however, is not cherishing the move. It argues that it would affect India's relations with its neighbours.[4] That it would ruffle political feathers in Assam is inevitable. The state has the record of a long-lasting agitation against illegal Bangladeshis that include Hindus as well, though it has been largely directed against Muslim immigrants (discussed in Chapter 2 and further in this chapter as well). Given the *Hindutva* orientation of BJP it is not difficult to explicate the motivation behind the government's penchant to pass the amendment. It is, however, relevant here to recall what the Bengali Hindu refugees had argued in the aftermath of Partition that we have discussed above. Is not it, once again, the question of refugees' rights, and not state doing a favour to them? Minorities in Pakistan or Bangladesh were not responsible for the Partition of India. The same logic, of course, should apply to Biharis in Bangladesh also, but one knows that politics does not necessarily listen to logic.

# Evolution of Citizenship Debate

The independence of India in 1947 had to make the country respond to its citizenship question. But since Partition of the subcontinent was part and parcel of independence it galvanized the thinking process with regard to conceptualizing the notion of citizenship. Those who came to India from the newly carved state of Pakistan were British subjects prior to Partition, just like those Indians who were not dislocated. As such there was no issue in calling all as Indian nationals. But the problem arose with respect to abducted women who were later restored to their families, or those Indian Muslims who returned to India after having left for Pakistan. Writing on these matters six decades after the events is one thing, but to deal with the massive human tragedy and framing just and equitable policies to deal with the situation at that point in history was quite different. Both legally and humanly, therefore, the challenge for the Indian state was massive. The same was true for the new state of Pakistan.

The Constituent Assembly of India was in session when the Partition came. It spent considerable time to address the question, the result of which was that when the constitution was introduced on 26 January 1950 it had to answer the question: 'Who is a citizen of India?' This was done in its Part II (Articles 5–11), titled 'Citizenship'. Since the Constitution had actually been *adopted* by the Constituent Assembly two months ago, on 26 November 1949, this became the operative date to distinguish between citizens and aliens. The constitutional provisions suggested that Indian citizens could fall under two broad categories: (a) those who were 'found' to be residing in India at the time of independence automatically 'became' Indian citizens and (2) those who, unlike the earlier category, moved in from across the borders. But problems arose with the latter category because they fell in different patterns of movement, namely,

1. those who migrated from Pakistan to India after Partition and before 19 July 1948;
2. those who migrated from Pakistan to India *after* 19 July 1948 but *before the commencement* of the Constitution and registered themselves as citizens of India before the concerned authority; and
3. [sic] those who went to Pakistan after 1 March 1947 and returned to India under a permit for resettlement or permanent return issued by the competent authority (Roy 2010: 36–37).[5]

The constitutional provisions were clear, yet the enormity of the human tragedy that the Partition brought in its train was such that the problem of citizenship seemed resistant to easy solution. One odious issue that the state had to grapple with was about the abducted women and their restoration to their respective families. In achieving the task, the state exposed itself to the feminist critique for its male bias. It was on 15 December 1949 that the Constituent Assembly had passed The Abducted Persons (Recovery and Restoration) Act, which remained in force till 1957, two years after the Citizenship Act, 1955. In the implementation of the Act the masculine chauvinism of the Indian society came to the fore (for a detailed discussion on the subject, see Roy 2010: 42–55). The following passage from Roy's study would give some idea of this bias:

> The Hindu and Sikh women who were recovered from Pakistan to be restored to the 'nation' and to their 'homes' were differently positioned from Muslim women who, as 'recovered abducted women', were 'taken into custody' and placed in detention camps in India under what may be called a 'state of exception' till the time their own government [that is Pakistan] claimed them. For the purpose of the Abducted Persons (Recovery and Restoration) Act, 'Muslim abducted persons' constituted a distinct class, and the Act extended only to some states—United Provinces, Provinces of East Punjab and Delhi, Patiala and East Punjab States Union (PEPSU), and the United States of Rajasthan. It was through what constituted an exception—the *suspension* of the writ of habeas corpus—in these detention camps, as Pratibha Baxi has put it, that notions of 'national honour' were instituted through law: 'Muslim women who had been "recovered" and sent to camps were constituted as *impure* body populations who had no claims to Indian citizenship, and no man or his family could claim that these women had been unlawfully detained in the camps, unlike routine law'. (Roy 2010: 42–43)

In 1955, the Parliament of India enacted The Citizenship Act as provided in Article 11 of the Constitution, which said, that nothing 'shall derogate from the power of Parliament to make any provision with respect to the acquisition and termination of citizenship and all other matters relating to citizenship'. The act specified five conditions to acquire Indian citizenship: birth, descent, registration, naturalization and incorporation of territory. To effect the 1955 act, Citizenship Rules were introduced in 1956. In the early 1960s when the Portuguese and French colonies in India were incorporated into the Indian Union there was the possibility of some confusion about granting Indian citizenship to people who lived in these colonies. To avoid any such problem, the Dadra and Nagar Haveli Citizenship Order, 1962, the Goa, Daman and Diu (Citizenship) Order, 1962 and the Citizenship (Pondicherry) Order, 1962 were promulgated (Dhavan 2004: 36).

# The Citizenship Issue and the Assam Agitation

The issue of citizenship got complicated as the Indian state was called upon to deal with the agitation against foreigners that rocked Assam politics in the late 1970s and the early 1980s. To deal with the situation a new dimension was added to the citizenship debate: Whether citizenship should have a universal pan-Indian application or it could be region specific as well.[6] To the five criteria that were set for citizenship rights in the Citizenship Act, 1955, that is, birth, descent, registration, naturalization and incorporation of territory, yet another criterion was added, which was meant only for the state of Assam. Accordingly, in 1986, the Citizenship Act, 1955, was amended by adding Section 6A to the act. According to the amendment, every person born in India after the commencement of the 1986 Act had to prove that one of his/her parents was a citizen of India before his or her claim to Indian citizenship was accepted. Thus, if a person was born in India after 1 July 1987 to non-Indian parents, that person would not be entitled to Indian citizenship. It is ironical that in the course of the discourse the Assamese protesters who were actually upholding the cause of India as a nation against the Bangladeshi foreigners came to be seen as anti-nationals while sympathy seemed to pour for those who were the so-called 'foreigners'. The politics of citizenship was on display as never before.

The transformation of Assam's anti-foreigners agitation to an anti-Indian state movement followed the same pattern as it happens in other similar situations. To teach the rest of India a lesson for its indifference to the Assamese concerns, they tried to raise barriers against the exploitation of Assam's natural resources, such as oil, tea, coal, plywood and water, by non-Assamese. To safeguard the Assamese identity from the numerical assault of undocumented Bangladeshi immigrants, the Assam movement launched an agitation against them by alleging that they were grabbing the land of the autochthonous farmers and settling down in the Assamese homeland, and in the process they were coming in the way of the autochthonous people's means of livelihood. It was also alleged that because of their large presence, they were poaching into the political space of the Assamese. Soon the movement degenerated from an anti-foreigner agitation to an anti-non-Assamese agitation by turning its wrath against even the domestic migrants from other parts of India, mostly Bihar. The latter were seen as representatives of a 'stepmotherly' Indian state. To draw the attention of the Indian state, economic blockades were set up, which threatened the outflow of Assam's resources to the rest of India. *Tej Dim, Tel Nidiu* (we will shed our blood, but not give our oil) thundered the supporters of the Assam movement (Goswami 2014: 173–74).

Because of historical and geographical reasons, the Assam scene was complex. On the one hand, the flow of unauthorized Bangladeshi migration to the state was virtually unpreventable, then, on the other, the mix of Bengali language of these migrants with the Bengali-speaking people of Assam and that of their religion with Assamese Muslims made the problem extremely intricate. As a result, neither the Assamese Bengalis nor the Assamese Muslims could fully identify themselves with the Assam agitation. The potentiality of turning the unauthorized Bangladeshis into Indian voters made the political game even more complex. The massacre of about 3,000 Bengali Muslims at Nellie, the assembly elections that brought the Hiteshwar Saikia-led Congress to power and the passage of the IMDT Act by the Indian Parliament when all the MPs from Assam were on a boycott, all in 1983, clearly indicated that the matter of Bangladeshi migration was much beyond the simple logic of Indians versus the foreigners (Bangladeshis). The political polarization between the Congress and the AASU/AGP was complete (see details in Kimura 2013). No wonder that the IMDT Act, which departed from the basic premise of the Foreigners Act of 1946, by transferring the burden of proof to prove one's Indian nationality from the person identified as a foreigner to the one accusing him to be so was a total departure from the earlier practice when it was the other way round. Partly because of this structural anomaly and partly because of the indifference of the Congress-led government of Assam, as well as the helplessness of the Central Government, the act was hardly implemented as the records showed (discussed in Chapter 2). The leaders of the Assam movement understood from the beginning how they had been taken for a ride by this clever political move of the government.

That the act would flop was a foregone conclusion. Still it took more than two decades to scrap it. In 2005, in its judgment to the writ petition filed by Sarbananda Sonowal, the Supreme Court summarily scrapped the act. The Supreme Court judgment equated illegal migration as *aggression* against India by referring to Article 355 of the Constitution, which said: 'It shall be the duty of the Union to protect every State against external aggression and internal disturbance and to ensure that the Government of every State is carried on in accordance with the provisions of this Constitution'. It further clarified:

> To preserve its independence, and give security against foreign aggression and encroachment, is the highest duty of every nation, and to attain these ends nearly all other considerations are to be subordinated. It matters not in what form such aggression and encroachment come, whether from the foreign nation acting in its national character or from vast hordes of its people crowding in upon us.[7]

The judgment has been critiqued for its evident political tone. One such criticism noted, inter alia:

> It is significant that while declaring the IMDT Act unconstitutional, the court described immigration not merely as 'illegal' entry into foreign territory, *but as an act of aggression,* arguing within a discursive framework that makes for a bounded notion of citizenship, with the policing of boundaries and the determination of citizenship construed as a significant manifestation of state sovereignty. Moreover, the arguments that the judges made before identifying migration as an act of aggression placed their articulation of citizenship squarely within the framework of an ethnically determined membership of the nation-state. In this exposition, the constituent outsider was marked out not only on account of being a foreigner, but also on account of being a Muslim, the latter inevitably associated with Islamic fundamentalism, as well as a threat to the nation (*read* Hindu) and its security. (Roy 2010: 116)

It is interesting to note that in spite of such questionable assumptions in the judgment, the Indian state did not mind it to go uncontested either through a review petition or even through political means. By 2005 Assam agitation had exhausted all its steam and, although the problem of unauthorized entry of Bangladeshis remained, it was not a hot political potato except during the elections.

# Citizenship of the Third Kind

One way of becoming a citizen is by the process of naturalization. Is it possible for the illegal Bangladeshis to become naturalized citizens of India to evade their potential eviction? The South Asian experience, or for that matter the experience of the entire developing world, suggests that it is probably easier to circumvent this route and get the citizenship by all kinds of illegal means. A large number of Bangladeshis in

India and Pakistan, and, similarly, Afghans in Pakistan, have managed to acquire legal documents which facilitate their obtaining citizenship in due course. What has made this possible is corruption and indifference at the administrative levels besides ethnic and communal sympathy at the local level. In Pakistan, data entry operators working for NADRA have been apprehended preparing computerized IDs based on duplicate finger prints (Sadiq 2009: 213). If it can happen in Pakistan there is no reason for complacency that the same would not happen in India or Bangladesh for after all they all are Siamese twins.[8] The fact that the illegal immigrants provide cheap labour serves as yet another facilitating factor. The neighbourhood middle class residents would often cry hoarse against these illegal immigrants but would seldom mind employing them as domestic helps or using their rickshaws for local transport.

Like the question of illegal Bangladeshis in India, Pakistan too has its problem of illegal Bangladeshis and illegal Afghans. At the time of the creation of Bangladesh in 1971, there were 40,000 East Bengalis in West Pakistan. They were supposed to be legal Pakistani nationals. But, as much more than that number migrated to Pakistan illegally after 1971, mostly in the 1980s, first by illegally entering into India and then by illegally crossing the India–Pakistan border, the situation got complicated. Pakistan's Citizenship Act of 1978 made it compulsory for all, both pre- and post-1971 immigrants, to apply for Pakistani citizenship. The same law applied to Afghans as well. This was protested by both the Bangladeshis and Afghans, most of whom had managed to acquire the Pakistani national identity cards (NICs). By 2003, only 18,500 Bangladeshis and 6,500 Afghans had adhered to the act. The fact, however, is that there are millions of illegal Bangladeshis and Afghans, and even some Mynamarese are in Karachi who form a formidable vote bank for several political parties, including the Pakistan Muslim League–Nawaz, making the issue of their foreignness extremely complex for an administrative and political response (Sadiq 2009: 161–62). According to a recent investigation carried out to unearth the fake ID cards scam, during the last 10 years tens of thousands of computerized identity cards (CNICs)were issued to foreign nationals, a majority of whom were unregistered Afghan refugees, in which allegedly more than 372 NADRA officials were involved. A senior investigating official was quoted saying: 'We've already blocked 22,349 CNICs issued to Afghan citizens since 2005. After expanding the scope of investigation, we have also put 50,110 CNICs on our radar in Balochistan, Punjab, Sindh and Khyber-Pakhtunkhwa (K P)' (Asad and Gishkori 2015).

Sadiq in his study has shown that large illegal immigrant flows into India and Pakistan have been possible through the existence of a strong web of networks that traverse the international borders in South Asia which existed even during the British rule. Mostly these illegal residents are silently absorbed into the host states. Given the 15 to 20 million of Bangladeshis who have settled in India, 'it is clear that immigrant communities possess efficient and complex networks to ensure ease of settlement and access to membership. Ethnic networks override the exclusionary power of modern states to resist illegal immigrants from their territories and political membership' (Sadiq 2009: 56).[9] Following the ratification of the India–Bangladesh land border agreement, which resulted in the summary exchange of enclaves between the two countries (discussed in Chapter 1), it became common knowledge how many people in Bangladeshi enclaves used to routinely come to various parts of India in search of small jobs (see one such report in *The Hindu*, 9 August 2015). In terms of the legality of the whole exercise of enclave exchange, some problems might arise with regard to transferring the land rights. According to one suggestion, they can be sorted out if the policy is modelled after what was done in the aftermath of Partition to solve similar problems in East Punjab, while allocating lands to refugee farmers from West Punjab (Bhadada & Mittal 2015: 15–18, Kumar 2015).

## Fundamental Rights and the Refugees

Part III of the Constitution of India (Articles 12–35) incorporates the Bill of Rights that guarantees a series of fundamental rights drawn essentially from the international human rights discourse. There are two categories of rights enshrined in Part III: one, those meant only for Indian *citizens* and two, those meant for all *persons*. It is this second category read with the Preamble of the Constitution which talks of liberty, equality and justice that provide the potential framework for protecting the rights of refugees/migrants/stateless persons. For example, rights to life and personal liberty are as much the privilege of Indian citizens as they are for the refugees or undocumented migrants. Article 21 of the Constitution states: 'No *person* shall be deprived of his life or personal liberty except according to procedure established by law'. So far as the question of equality is concerned, Article 14 states: 'The state shall not deny to any *person* equality before the law or the equal protection of the laws within the territory of India'. Besides these two articles, there are other articles too that guarantee many rights to all *persons*, meaning refugees or undocumented migrants as well. They are: the right against prosecution under retrospective penal law, the right against double jeopardy, the right to silence (Article 20), the rights of an arrestee or detainee (Article 22), the right to freedom of religion (Articles 25–28), freedom from payment of taxes for promotion of any religion (Article 27) and freedom from attendance in religious worship in state educational institutions (Article 28, Clause 3[Dhavan 2004: 60]).

It may be underlined that refugees were not entitled, which Indian citizens were, to freedoms enshrined in Article 19, which included the following:

1. To freedom of speech and expression;
2. To assemble peacefully and without arms;
3. To form associations or unions;
4. To move freely throughout the territory of India;
5. To reside and settle in any part of the territory of India; and
6. To practise any profession or to carry on any occupation, trade or business.

It was, however, not so simple that Article 21 was written in the Constitution and it was all hunky-dory for refugees as they were guaranteed protection of the Indian state as *persons*. The article had to undergo a series of court cases, such as *A.K. Gopalan v. State of Madras* (1950), *Hans Muller v. Superintendent, Presidency Jail, Calcutta* (1955), *Maneka Gandhi v. Union of India* (1978), *Unnikrishnan v. Union of India* (1993), *P. Rathinam v. Union of India* (1994) and many others (see details in Dhavan 2004: 61–63) till it was finally clarified by the Supreme Court in its verdict in the case of *National Human Rights Commission v. State of Arunachal Pradesh* (1996) in the following words:

> We are a country governed by Rule of Law. Our Constitution confers certain rights on every human being and certain other rights on citizens. Every person is entitled to equality before the law and equal protection of the laws. So also, no person can be deprived of his life or personal liberty except according to procedure established by law. Thus the State is bound to protect the life and liberty of every human being, be he a citizen or otherwise.... The State Government [of Arunachal Pradesh] must act impartially and carry out its legal obligations to safeguard the life, health and well-being of Chakmas residing in the State without being inhibited by local politics. (quoted in Dhavan 2004: 62)

Similar was the fate of Article 14, which talked about *equality before law* for all *persons*. In the case of *P. Mohammad Khan v. State of Andhra Pradesh* (1978), while dealing with an Afghan national who had been ordered to leave India under certain provisions of the Foreigners Act, the High Court of Andhra Pradesh ruled:

> There is a duty cast upon the authorities to decide whether the petitioner should not be permitted to stay in India because of the fact that he happened to be a foreigner. *That duty to decide carries with it the duty to act fairly.* The concept of fairness dictates that the authorities can proceed against the person concerned only after giving him notice and opportunity to being heard, as regards the statutory grounds on which the action contemplated by the statute is proposed to be taken. (quoted in Dhavan 2004: 63)

In the absence of dedicated refugee laws, court cases in India have in many instances gone in favour of the asylum seekers on humanitarian grounds. As Justice Markandeya Katju, the former Chief Justice of India, said:

> While the Executive branch of the Indian state does not recognize refugees and refugee law, the judicial wing of our state does recognize refugees and refugee law to a certain extent.... It is not subordinate to our government, and it often censures the government.... In particular, *the Indian judiciary has introduced refugee law into our legal system through the back door.* (Katju 2001, emphasis added)

The Supreme Court of India has, in several instances, applied Article 14 (right to equality) and Article 21 (right to life and dignity) to all, including migrants and refugees living in India, as well as conferred the refugees the basic human rights as defined by the UN (Nair 2007: 5). Here are some pieces of evidence of High Courts upholding the basic human rights of the refugees.

In the cases of *Gurunathan and Others* v. *Government of India and Others* and *A.C. Mohd. Siddique* v. *Government of India and Others*, the Madras High Court ruled that no Sri Lankan refugee should be sent back to Sri Lanka against his or her will. In the case of *Nedumaran* v. *Government of Tamil Nadu* before the Madras High Court, Sri Lankan refugees had prayed for a writ of mandamus directing the Governments of India and Tamil Nadu to allow the UNHCR to certify whether the Sri Lankan refugees were willing to go back to Sri Lanka voluntarily, and if they did not so desire they should not be sent back. They should not be even forced to return to the refugee camps. The High Court ruled that 'since the UNHCR was involved in ascertaining the voluntariness of the refugees' return to Sri Lanka, hence being a World Agency, it is not for the Court to consider whether the consent is voluntary or not'. The court acknowledged the competence and impartiality of the UNHCR officials.

Likewise, the Bombay High Court in the case of *Syed Ata Mohammadi* v. *Union of India* ruled that 'there is no question of deporting the Iranian refugee to Iran, since he has been recognized as a refugee by the UNHCR'. There are many other similar cases (Ananthachari 2001: 7–8).

In addition, certain other provisions of the Indian Constitution entitle at least the migrants for employment on the basis of non-discrimination. Articles 23(1), 39, 42 and 43 are applicable for all workers, including migrant workers from outside the country. Besides, there are other legislative frameworks under which migrants' rights are protected. These laws include the Workmen's Compensation Act, 1923; the Payment of Wages Act, 1936; the Minimum Wages Act, 1948; the Employees State Insurance Act, 1952; the Maternity Benefit Act, 1961; the Contract Labour (Regulation and Abolition) Act, 1970; the Equal Remuneration Act, 1976; the Bonded Labour Act, 1976; the Child Labour (Prohibition and Regulation) Act, 1986 and the Building and Other Construction Workers (Regulation of Employment and Conditions of Service) Act, 1996 (Chatterjee 2006: 23–25).

# The Statutory Framework

Barring a few notable judicial exceptions, the Indian statutory framework does not recognize refugees as a separate category of people who deserve separate treatment (Dhavan 2004: 37). But although the refugees are treated in an ad hoc basis and usually on par with *foreigners* and *illegal migrants or entrants*, certain laws and procedures are in place which govern the Indian state's response to the refugee question. These laws are as follows:

1. Extradition laws as a precursor to refugee protection;
2. Laws regulating foreigners and illegal migrants;
3. Laws governing legal entry procedures;
4. Laws dealing specifically with refugees.

## Extradition Laws

Extradition law by nature is a prelude to refugee protection. In the Indian subcontinent the idea has evolved from the British days. While some of the provisions of the then practices were retained in India after independence, some amendments were made in the Extradition Act in 1993. As it stands, extradition law is significant for the following reasons:

1. The receiving country has the prerogative to refuse the request for extradition.
2. The receiving country through due process of law can consider giving justice in the instant case.
3. In cases of 'political offence', the return could be injuncted by the receiving state.
4. If the country requesting the extradition is not considered just and politically mature, extradition request can be rejected because in that case the person may be victimized for his political views.

But where the extradition regime falls short of a refugee protection regime, the situation is the following:

5. 'Whilst the extradition law proceeds on the basis of the *right* of the receiving state *not to extradite*, refugee law imposes on a state a *duty not to return* under conditions where a person has reason to fear persecution' (Dhavan 2004: 22).

## Laws Regulating Foreigners and Illegal Migrants

In the 'Fundamental Rights and the Refugees' section, we have noted how refugees are protected in India through the expedience of Articles 14 and 21 of the Indian Constitution and how they are not entitled to the provisions of Article 19. Those protection mechanisms are, by and large, valid in the case of foreigners as well. Foreigners in India are governed by the Foreigners Act, 1946, together with the following regulations: the Foreigners Order, 1948, the Foreigners (Restriction on Movements) Order, 1960, the Foreigners (Restriction on Activities) Order, 1962, the Foreigners (Restrictions on Residence) Order, 1968, the Foreigners (Proof of Identity) Order, 1986, the Foreigners (Report to Police) Order, 1971, and other regulations. Through various court cases, it has been upheld that for the security of the nation and other considerations the executive has the power to prevent foreigners, in individual cases, from pursuing various kinds of activities. Over the years, such restrictions have become more stringent and broad-based under the various national security-related laws and ordinances. These developments do not augur well for advocacy in favour of refugee and migrants' rights.

## Laws Governing Legal Entry Procedures

The issue of illegal migrations to India from neighbouring countries, particularly from Bangladesh, has concerned policy makers for decades. This concern found political expression in 1998 when it was proposed to amend the Foreigners Act, 1946. The proposed amendment was referred to the Parliamentary Standing Committee and then to the Law Commission for consideration. The latter, in its *One Hundred and Seventy-fifth Report on the Foreigners (Amendment) Bill (2000)* (http:// lawcommissionofindia.nic.in/reports/175thReport.pdf, accessed on 8 January 2016), recommended the inclusion of a definition of 'illegal migrant' (who may well be a refugee) in the Act to mean a foreigner who entered India without valid papers or overstayed the legally pre-scribed duration. The report recommended stringent measures to nab illegal entrants and judicial action against them. During the next couple of years, the matter was discussed in both the houses of the Parliament and eventually passed (details in Dhavan 2004: 50–57). Since this was the time when the Hindu chauvinistic BJP was in power leading the NDA coalition, the subject got entangled in communal rhetoric with primary target being the Muslim Bangladeshi migrants and terrorists. Writing in 2004, Rajiv Dhavan noted:

> In recent years, the legal discourse on foreigners in India has been dictated by the influx of economic migrants from Bangladesh. The numerous legal measures that have been taken to curb such migration make no distinction between genuine refugees in need of protection and economic migrants. There is no due process mechanism in place either, which can make such differentiation. Hence, the assumption is that all entrants into India in that area are either economic migrants or terrorists. In the context of growing presentiments about terrorism and increasing communal trends in India's polity, the fact that most of these migrants are Muslims is not without sig-nificance. Alleged security threats posed by them then become the unques-tionable justification for any entry barrier that is sought to be created. (Dhavan 2004: 57, also see Ghosh 1999)[10]

Dhavan seemed to have pre-empted the Supreme Court verdict of 2005, which squashed the IMDT Act on the ground that the Bangladeshi (Muslim) migrations to Assam amounted to an act of aggression against the Indian state.

## The Refugee-Specific Laws

India's experience in this regard started with the Partition refugees, and most of the laws were either compensatory or rehabilitative. They were, however, not confined to Partition refugees only, and later as other prob-lems arose several new laws were enacted. The following list provides the titles of these laws:

1. East Punjab Evacuees (Administration of Property) Act, 1947
2. UP Land Acquisition (Rehabilitation of Refugees) Act, 1948
3. East Punjab Refugees (Registration of Land Claims) Act, 1948
4. Patiala Refugees (Registration of Land Claims) Ordinance, 1948
5. Mysore Administration of Evacuee Property (Emergency) Act, 1949

All the above laws were pre-Indian Constitution laws. Once the Constitution became operational on 26 January 1950, many more acts were added as follows:

1. Displaced Persons (Claims) Act, 1950
2. Immigrants (Expulsion from Assam) Act, 1950
3. Administration of Evacuee Property Act, 1950
4. Evacuee Interest (Separation) Act, 1951
5. Displaced Persons (Debts Adjustment) Act, 1951
6. Influx from Pakistan (Control) Repealing Act, 1952
7. Displaced Persons (Claims) Supplementary Act, 1954
8. Displaced Persons (Compensation and Rehabilitation) Act, 1954
9. Transfer of Evacuee Deposits Act, 1954
10. Registration of Foreigners (Exemption) Order, 1957
11. Foreigners Law (Application and Amendment) Act, 1962
12. Goa, Daman and Diu Administration of Evacuee Property Act, 1969
13. Refugee Relief Taxes Act, 1971 (another Act abolished it in 1973)
14. Registration of Foreigners (Bangladesh) Rules, 1973
15. The Illegal Migrants (Determination by Tribunals) Act, 1983 (quashed by the Supreme Court in 2005)

It may be noted that many of the laws passed in the 1950s and 1960s were relevant only for the Punjab refugees. It was the constant refrain of the Bengali refugees that the central government showed stepmotherly attitude towards them, as a result of which their woes were multiplied, which lingered on unlike those of the Punjabi refugees. Though the latter had been subjected to a much bigger tragedy compared to the Bengalis in terms of loss of life and property, yet they were rehabilitated well and in a shorter time (discussed in Chapter 4).

# Refugee Rights: Some Practical Dimensions

The enactment of a law is one thing but the enforcement of that law is often quite another. In the case of refugee rights or the rights of stateless persons, if any, the question of enforcement often becomes problematic because both security and political considerations come in the way. And, depending upon the political attitudes of the people in power such considerations may as well vary. Then there is also the federal question of power sharing between the central government and the state governments. As a former Director General of the BSF noted:

> While law and order is a State subject under the Indian Constitution, international relations and international borders are under the exclusive purview of the Indian government. This has resulted in a variety of agencies, both of the Central as well as the State governments, having to deal with refugee matters connected with law enforcement. Also, all policies governing refugees are laid down by the Union government though the impact of the refugee problem as such has to be borne by the State administration to a greater degree if not wholly. (Ananthachari 2001: 1)

It would be instructive to understand how the security agencies are expected to deal with the issue of entry of foreigners either as refugees or otherwise. The BSF, which guards the India–Pakistan and India–Bangladesh borders, the ITBPF, which is deployed along the India–Tibet (China) border, the Assam Rifles, which is deployed along the India–Myanmar border, are usually the first functionaries of the Indian state that the refugees or other unauthorized entrants into India may encounter unless they manage to dodge them, which is not uncommon. Because of the difficult terrain as well as ethnic and cultural bonds, border enforcement is extremely difficult in South Asia. Insofar as enforcement of law is concerned, there are potential turf wars between central security agencies and the state police forces.

The above situation exists so far as land borders are concerned. In the case of human entries through sea routes or by air, the concerned agencies are the Coast Guards, the Immigration Department and the Customs Department. If a person is accosted with illegal, invalid or no travel documents, the immigration authorities, after ensuring that it is a prima facie case of unauthorized entry, are supposed to deport him to the country from where he has come. But the matter is not that simple. Though it violates the principle of *non-refoulement*, the latter is not always applicable as the entrant may not have any danger to his life in the place of his origin. It may be noted that India has not yet incorporated the principle of *non-refoulement* in its legal statutes. An unauthorized entrant is lodged in confinement in the airport itself, where he is expected to pay for his food and other consumables as well as to buy his return ticket.

There are several technicalities involved when a person enters India without valid documents and he is caught. His detention, unless the authorities are able to send him back, is just the initial problem. But it gets complicated in several possible situations, such as medical aid to the detainee during his confinement, if the detainee is a female or a child, how to ensure that the detainee does not become untraceable once he is out of detention, how to ensure that, if need be, he would be arrested once out of detention and timely filing of charge sheets by the prosecution to enable pleading guilty. Generally in the case of illegal entrants nabbed by the concerned authorities, cases are registered against them under the provisions of the Indian Penal Code or the Foreigners Act. In case the accused seeks legal assistance, he can be allowed to contact the local 'legal-aid cell', failing which the court may be requested to notify the UNHCR to provide the necessary legal aid. Even an NGO may be contacted for help. It is possible that during his detention the refugee requires some medical attention. In such cases the concerned authorities or the court concerned can also seek assistance from the UNHCR or some NGOs. More or less the same situation prevails in the case of women detainees, who are to be treated more sympathetically. Refugee children have the specific problem of getting separated from their refugee parents. Often with the help of the UNHCR and NGOs such possibilities are prevented (Ananthachari 2001: 13–14).

The release of a refugee from detention involves several legalities. Pending the disposal of a case, the court wants to ensure the appearance of the refugee in the court when wanted again. Efforts are first made to make the UNHCR responsible for their assured appearance in the court, but if the UNHCR fails to take that responsibility then the state has no other option than putting the person in jail. There is a possibility that after serving the jail term following the disposal of the court case, the refugee still fails to provide any necessary travel documents and is not in a position to leave the country, in which case he is again arrested and put in jail (Ananthachari 2001: 14). We often read in the newspapers of so many Pakistanis and Indians languishing in Indian and Pakistani jails, respectively. Besides being suspected as spies, they are often people without valid travel documents and not necessarily looking for refugee status. In any case, all this discussion is about a relatively small number of people. When large numbers of unauthorized entrants are in question, like the Bangladeshis in India, Afghans in Pakistan, or Rohingyas in Bangladesh, these legal procedures hold little meaning as India's IMDT experience or Pakistan's NADRA experience suggests. Do these so-called stateless people too have rights, a theme that we would address next?

## Rights Issue of Stateless Persons

We have discussed above how the Indian constitution and the legal system take care of the rights of refugees, or, for that matter all others in similar categories, just by dint of the fact that they are humans (constitution does not distinguish between 'citizens' and 'persons' insofar as basic legal rights are concerned). But when such a group is large and whose basic concern is mere survival they do not entertain the luxury of spending their time asking for their civil and legal rights. They would rather prefer to remain faceless for in any case it is the society at large that takes care of them by proving them with small economic opportunities. As such, the more state is indifferent thereby allowing them to lead their routine lives they consider themselves blessed. They fear that as soon as they would ask for their rights as stateless persons or as undocumented migrants, a contradiction in terms in any case, they would become pawns in the political chessboard particularly during the elections. The way the issue of Bangladeshis in India figures in every Indian election in specific electoral pockets underscores the point (Delhi's electoral politics surrounding Bangladeshis is discussed in Chapter 2). The ideal situation for this category people indeed is to, without asking for their rights, take maximum advantage of the loopholes in the public utility delivery systems to better their daily lives.

In India, there is no clear definition of statelessness (see the Introductory chapter, 'Introduction: Definitional and Theoretical Issues', about how the concept developed in India), though the Indian Parliament, during the last two decades, has discussed the matter time and again in a discursive format in respect of Chakmas in Arunachal Pradesh, Pakistanis in Gujarat and Rajasthan who would like to become Indian citizens, undocumented Bangladeshis and other foreigners overstaying in the country. That there is some amount of additional sympathy for Hindu refugees from Pakistan cannot be overstated. Here is an example. On 17 August 2012, the Parliament passed a resolution which read, inter alia:

> The powers to grant Indian Citizenship to nationals of Pakistan belonging to minority Hindu community were delegated to the Collectors of Kutch, Patan, Banaskantha, Ahmedabad of Gujarat and Barmer and Jaisalmer of Rajasthan in 2004 for one year to grant citizenship to Pak nationals of minority community staying in the border districts of Rajasthan and Gujarat as a special case. This delegation was extended up to 2007 on year to year basis. *Such powers were not delegated to any other State.* Sufficient time was given to these two States to decide such pending cases.... The Government of India is very sensitive to the issue related to the welfare of all foreign nationals in India including Hindu Pak nationals who deserve support and attention subject to the laws of the land and policies of the Indian Government. (Emphasis added)[11]

It must, however, be underlined that behind the sympathy for Hindu refugees from Pakistan, there was an element of insecurity to life faced by the minority Hindu community there, but in the case of Bangladeshi undocumented migrants in India there was no such element as fear of life and loss of dignity if they returned to Bangladesh.

# International Treaty Obligations

Since cross-border movements of people without travel documents involve two or more countries, they have ramifications at various diplomatic levels, both bilateral and multilateral. As such it becomes imperative to explore international rights-based mechanism and their reflections in domestic laws and policies for safeguarding the rights of different categories of migrants. International human rights standards serve as a level-playing field for safeguarding the fundamental rights of refugees and migrants, though these standards differ in nature of protection they offer to migrants.

There is no dearth of international literature on the rights of refugees, migrants and stateless persons or are there any dearth of human rights guarantees enshrined in international statutes and conventions. India is a party to many international covenants, such as the Universal Declaration of Human Rights (1948), the International Convention on Civil and Political Rights (ICCPR; 1966, ratified on 10 April 1979), the International Convention on Economic, Social and Cultural Rights (1966, ratified on 10 April 1979), the Convention on the Elimination of All Forms of Discrimination Against Women (1979, ratified on 9 July 1993), the Convention on the Rights of the Child (1989, ratified on 11 December 1992), the International Convention on the Elimination of All Forms of Racial Discrimination (1965, ratified on 3 December 1968) and the Convention Against Torture (CAT; 1984, yet to be ratified). But even as a party to these covenants, India has made certain modifications in their clauses through optional protocols to suit its specific requirements.

India's basic commitment starts with its virtual endorsement of the principle of *non-refoulement*, which is part of customary international law. Besides, as a signatory to the 1984 CAT, it has formalized its commitment to the principle of *non-refoulement*. Article 3 of the CAT states: 'No State shall expel, return (refouler), or extradite a person to another State where there are substantial grounds for believing that he would be in danger of being subjected to torture' (Chimni 2003: 448). If Indian security forces prevent the entry of Bangladeshis at the border, India cannot be blamed for violating the principle as there is no such situation as the entrant 'would be in danger of being subjected to torture' in his own country. India's record, however, has proved both ways. Here are two examples. One, on 25 October 1988, India's External Affairs Minister, P.V. Narasimha Rao, told a parliamentary panel that 'strict instructions have been issued not to turn back any genuine Burmese refugee seeking shelter in India' (Dhavan 2004: 132). Two, in 2001, 34 families fleeing communal violence in Bangladesh were allegedly forcibly sent back to Bangladesh by Indian border guards within 24 hours of their arrival (Dhavan 2004: 124). The problem in South Asia is that it is extremely difficult to exactly ascertain whether the entrants would be subjected to torture if they are forced back even if there is no turmoil in the country of their origin or if there is turmoil.

Insofar as the role of the UNHCR in India is concerned, India's attitude towards the organization is by and large cooperative, but there are some tensions in the relationship. These tensions have their origin in the early years of India's independence. In 1953, the Indian government told the UNHCR that the global refugee policy was essentially a part of the Cold War. The then Foreign Secretary R.K. Nehru bluntly told the UNHCR representative Amir Ali that 'you help refugees from the so-called non-free world into the free world. We do not recognize such a distinction'. In India's perception the 1951 Convention was more political and less humanitarian (Dhavan 2004: 26–27). It was only after the arrival of Tibetan refugees in late 1950s and early 1960s that the ice started melting, although India's suspicion of the UNHCR continued till the late 1960s. Still it was only through the League of Red Cross Societies that India allowed some UNHCR assistance to the Tibetan refugees. In 1969, after intense negotiations a UNHCR office was finally established in India (Dhavan 2004: 27). Though India joined the Executive Committee of the UNHCR in 1995, still it is not seen to be enough, given the fact that it is yet to be a signatory to the 1951 Convention. The UNHCR is not allowed to visit refugee camps, to take up the welfare questions of the refugees or to involve with refugees from the region with some small exceptions as in the case of Sri Lankan Tamil refugees. After Afghanistan became a member of the SAARC, this does not mean much because UNHCR does take care of Afghan refugees in India, and indeed in Pakistan in a big way.

In one important respect the UNHCR does something on behalf of India, that is, refugee status determination, since there is no government mechanism for this exercise. For example, a refugee from Myanmar in India has first to make an application to the UNHCR in person, then, once recognized, the UNHCR would issue a Refugee Status Certificate (RSC) which is renewable every 18 months, and then after obtaining an RSC he becomes entitled to Residence Permit issued by the Ministry of Home Affairs, Government of India (The Other Media 2010: 19–33). The recognized refugees have access to government health and educational facilities, and since 2013 they are allowed to work in the formal sector. Everything, however, is not excellent as the above tends to suggest, but with some improvements in the mechanism the system can function better.

While the authority of the Indian state to deport unwanted foreigners is absolute, it is also fettered by certain international covenants to which India is a party or by judgements passed by Indian law courts. Sometimes India agrees to be a party to a covenant but makes certain exceptions to its provisions depending upon its needs. For example, in 1979 India became a party to the ICCPR but not fully. ICCPR codifies the rights of both citizens and aliens, and its Article 13 reads:

> An alien lawfully in the territory of a State party to the present Covenant may be expelled from there only in pursuance of a decision reached in accordance with law and shall, except where compelling reasons of national security otherwise require, be allowed to submit the reasons against his expulsion and to have his case reviewed by, and be represented for the purpose before, the competent authority or a person or persons specifically designated by the competent authority.

India's reservation is as follows:

> With respect to Article 13 of the International Covenants on Civil and Political Rights, the Government of the Republic of India reserves its right to apply its law relating to foreigners. (see Chimni 2003: 452)

There are studies which have discussed the challenges faced by the contemporary international protection regime, with a particular reference to the human rights issues of those displaced (see McAdam 2008). They begin by assessing the impact of anti-terrorism laws on refugee status, both at the international and domestic levels, before turning to examine the effects which offshore immigration control mechanisms and extraterritorial processing have on asylum seekers' access to territory and entitlements both in procedural and substantive terms.

# Institutional Mechanisms to Protect Migrants' Rights

The existing human rights regimes that include organizations, conventions and recommendations accord several rights, such as right to equal pay for equal work, right to be free from discrimination, right to organize and join associations and unions, right to collective bargaining and so on. These international human rights mechanisms play a moral role in ensuring equal opportunity and fundamental rights to the migrants. We are presenting here the respective roles that some of the important international organizations play.

## Human Rights Council

The Human Rights Council (HRC) is an intergovernmental body within the UN system. It was established in 2006 by replacing its predecessor, the Commission of Human Rights. The HRC is responsible for strengthening the promotion and protection of human rights around the world and for addressing situations of human rights violations and making recommendations on them, including the rights of migrants. Among the Charter-based bodies, the HRC holds an important position because most of these bodies receive secretariat support from the HRC and the Treaties Division of the Office of the High Commissioner for Human Rights (OHCHR). HRC also works with the UN Special Procedures established by the former Commission on Human Rights. One such procedure is the mandate of Special Rapporteur on Human Rights of Migrants, which was established in 1999 for an independent assessment of situations of migrants across the globe. Prior to this, the Commission established the working group on intergovernmental experts on human rights of migrants.

As part of the UN Secretariat, the OHCHR also provides expertise and support to different human rights monitoring mechanisms in the UN system created under the international human rights treaties and made up of independent experts mandated to monitor State parties' compliance with their treaty obligations. The Council seeks to promote, along with other thematic issues, the human rights of migrants with a migrant-centric approach. Through its various committees, such as the Human Rights Committee, Committee on Economic, Social and Cultural Rights, Committee on the Elimination of Racial Discrimination, Committee on the Elimination of Discrimination Against Women, Committee Against Torture, Subcommittee on Prevention of Torture, Committee on the Rights of the Child, Committee on Migrant Workers, Committee on the Rights of Persons with Disabilities and Committee on Enforced Disappearances that uphold certain inalienable human rights to every individual, including International Convention on the Protection of the Rights of All Migrant Workers and Members of Their Families (18 December 1990, popularly known as the Convention on Migrant Workers). The Committee on Migrant Workers and the Special Rapporteur on the Human Rights of Migrants make it clear that, although nations have a sovereign right to determine conditions of entry and stay in their territories, they also have an obligation to respect, protect and fulfil the human rights of all individuals under their jurisdiction, regardless of their nationality or origin and regardless of their immigration status. There are also other UN instruments which are indirectly applicable for migrant workers: the UN Convention against Transnational Organised Crime and two accompanying protocols—the Protocol to Prevent, Suppress and Punish Trafficking in Persons, especially Women and Children and the Protocol against the Smuggling of Migrants by land, sea and air.

In addition to the above conventions or covenants, the following declarations and resolutions can also be regarded as steps in the development of the notion of migrants' rights. These are as follows: World Conference Against Racism, Durban, South Africa (2001), Follow-up and Declaration of the Conference (including the Programme of Action); Bangkok Declaration on Irregular Migration—International Symposium on Irregular/Undocumented Migration, Bangkok, Thailand,

1999; Declaración de Buenos Aires; South American Migration Dialogue Meeting, Buenos Aires, Argentina, 2000; Lima Declaration on Migration, Integration and Development, Meeting in Lima, Peru, 1999; Declaration on the Elimination of All Forms of Intolerance and of Discrimination Based on Religion or Belief; Best Practices Concerning Migrant Workers and Their Families, in Compliance with the Plan of Action of the Summit of the Americas, Santiago Workshop on Best Practices Related to Migrant Workers, Santiago de Chile, Chile, 2000; South American Migration Dialogue; Brussels Declaration, Third UN Conference on the Least Developed Countries—Brussels, Belgium, 2001; Declaration on the Human Rights of Individuals Who Are Not Nationals of the Country in Which They Live; Vienna Declaration and Programme of Action (1993); Declaration on Race and Racial Prejudice (1978) and UN General Assembly Resolution 56/145 on the International Convention on the Protection of the Rights of All Migrant Workers and Members of Their Families. Besides, various allied agencies of the UN continue to engage with varied aspects of the human migrations. In this regard, the UNHCR, the World Trade Organization and the World Bank also try to accord many rights to migrants and refugees.

## Role of International Labour Organization

While discussing migrants' rights, the role of the International Labour Organization (ILO) must be highlighted. Since, like many other notions, emigration law has also undergone a long evolutionary process, the central element of which was international cooperation, the role played by ILO, which came into being as a part of the League of Nations, was very valuable. The International Emigration Commission which the ILO created in 1921 produced voluminous data on national labour statistics and laws that made the ground for organizing an International Conference on Migration Statisticians in 1932. This resulted in a 1936 volume on immigrants in countries around the world that served to reinforce nationalized understandings of migration. International cooperation and conflicts continued, giving shape to our clearer understanding of the phenomenon in both national and international contexts that shaped relevant internal laws. The simplest definition of an immigrant as provided in *Black's Law Dictionary* (2004) is 'a person who arrives in a country with the intention of settling there permanently (McKeown 2008: 336–37, 22–28).

Through its various conventions and recommendations, the ILO sets the guidelines for the concerned states to treat migrant labourers and their families at par with national migrants and to provide them with equal opportunity and protection of law. All the instruments adopted by the ILO that concern issues of migration for employment have been governed by its twofold aims: to achieve a regulation of the condition in which migration takes place and to protect migrant workers from exploitation. The ILO Recommendation No. 86 (1949) contains a set of detailed guidelines for providing migrants with access to information, access to education, and access to medical assistance for them and their families. Guided by changed circumstances and trends of irregular migration and unemployment, the 1975 ILO Convention and Recommendation focused on controlling illegal migration, though the term 'illegal' was not used and in its place the term clandestine was used.

Besides the ILO, another relevant body in this regard is the IOM. As envisaged in its constitution, the primary aim of the IOM is to act as a facilitator of migration and a promoter of cooperation among states and also among international, government and non-governmental organizations. The IOM has covered a long distance from being an organization whose primary role was repatriating refugees and securing their admission in host countries to being an organization whose principal goal is management of migration. The activities of the IOM help to protect human rights of migrants, but the right to protect migrants has not been bestowed on the organization legally. Further, while there is no comprehensive framework that can regulate the movement of migrant workers, ensuring a better system by which those who are migrating are accounted for, and reduce illegal migration and guarantee better safeguards for them.

In conclusion to this section, it may be mentioned that is spite of all the pious commitments contained in the human rights and rights of migrants of all types, the fact remains that unless these commitments are incorporated in the national legal systems their efficacy, at best, would remain limited. The battles will, therefore, have to be fought at the domestic political levels to see to it that the states modify their legal systems appropriately at both the statutory and implementation levels to guarantee the refugee rights. Here the role of NGOs assumes significance. Throughout the world, particularly in the democratic societies, judicial activism has been able to translate many of the international norms and conventions into effective domestic law. This trend can be traced to the 1988 Bangalore colloquium for which the ideas came to be called the Bangalore Principles. Organized by the Commonwealth Secretariat on the Domestic Application of International Human Rights Norms, the colloquium was held under the chairmanship of P.N. Bhagwati, the then Chief Justice of India. The other participants included such eminent names as Ruth Bader Ginsburg of the US Supreme Court, Anthony Lester, a leading British human rights lawyer, and Michael Kirby, an Australian judge. The communiqué underlined the huge impact of judicial activism worldwide and the 'growing tendency for national courts to have regard to [evolving] international norms for the purpose of deciding cases where the domestic law—whether constitutional, statute or common law—is uncertain or incomplete'. It defined principles that should guide the judiciary, including a warning that 'this process must fully take into account local laws, traditions, circumstances and needs' (Bhagwati 2004: 251–52).

## The Regional Framework

No South Asian country, with the lone exception of Afghanistan, is a party to the 1951 Convention and the 1967 Protocol. When the refugee convention was being prepared in the late 1940s and early 1950s, India and Pakistan were facing a massive refugee problem. Because of historical and social reasons, such strict legal frames that Europe was contemplating were of no use, a point the Government of India had clarified, as discussed earlier. In the context of East Bengali refugees in West Bengal, it has been noted that the unenviable task of rehabilitation of the refugees in the post-Partition Bengal had to be carried out within and by the impoverished economies that were left for this region. Given the very inadequate state assistance, community networks and support systems often became important tools of sustenance (Basu Ray Chaudhury and Dey 2009: 4–5). The same was true for Pakistan.

As years passed and the Partition-related refugee issues became less critical, a demand crystallized in intellectual circles that since the South Asian region faced the refugee and migrants' problem almost across the board, they should work out a regional refugee convention. In a meeting organized by the South Asian Forum for Human Rights held in Kathmandu on 18–22 November 1996 it was decided to have a South Asian protocol/charter on refugees, migrants, internally displaced and stateless persons. The forum took note of all the earlier charters and protocols aimed at defining a refugee and pleaded for an expansion of the definition so as to include 'victims of forced eviction, man-made and natural disasters and environmental refugees'. The forum believed that 'the states have an obligation to protect the rights of its citizens to remain in their habitat' but 'when such displaced persons seek refuge in another state, the host state should respect the principle of *non-refoulement*'.

This kind of NGO efforts continued, and in April 1999 following a Round Table Workshop on Refugees held in New Delhi, under the auspices of the Colombo-based South Asian Association for Regional Cooperation in Law (SAARCLAW)[12] and the UNHCR, a model national law on refugees was suggested. The model law drew primarily from the earlier international conventions in this regard, but its basic purpose was to legally address the problem arising out of 'the absence of refugee-specific national and regional frameworks in South Asia coupled with the history and scale of refugee movements within the region'. It was further proposed that the law 'should be harmonized with country-specific legislative and judicial requirements with a view to formally proposing it to the respective governments of the region'.

It was argued that since South Asia was a refugee-prone area where India, Bangladesh, Nepal and Pakistan had faced the problem from time to time, they should work out a common regional protocol. India, being the most experienced country in this regard, should take the lead. Several Supreme Court and High Court judgments reinforced the need for a humane due process for the refugees that arrived from Bangladesh like the Chakmas, the Sri Lankan Tamil refugees, or the Afghan Hindu and Sikh refugees but, unfortunately, this pro-refugee jurisprudence was handicapped by the normal law of the land relating to foreigners, which, following the Law Commission's 175th Report of 2000, was even more strict. Read with India's subscription to the SAARC Terrorism Protocol (2004), which allowed SAARC members not to extradite but protect those being persecuted on account of their race, religion, nationality, ethnic origin or political opinion, this made the situation complex. According to human rights lawyer Rajeev Dhavan, the fear of terrorism which was behind India's ambivalence was addressed by Justice P.N. Bhagwati's model code, but the problem was that India did not seem to be interested to look into the issue with an open mind. Notably, China had joined the 1951 Convention and enacted refugee protection laws (Dhavan 2004).

Over the years, the phenomena of migration and refugee movements in South Asia have evoked two sets of responses: nation-centric and region-centric. So far as the first is concerned, the states that have faced the refugee problem have tried to handle the issue within their own legal and political frameworks and have tried to provide relief and rehabilitation to the best of their abilities. It is expected of the state to formulate policies first to control the inflow of people from beyond its borders, through creating barriers both physical and diplomatic, failing which reconcile itself to the problem and provide humanitarian assistance within the political and economic means of the state. Depending upon specific requirements, as was the case when refugees in millions arrived in India and Pakistan after Partition, both the states had to devise schemes for their relief and rehabilitation either permanently or on a temporary basis. Such efforts have not been confined to India and Pakistan and that too not merely to the Partition days. Out of eight South Asian states, five—namely, Bangladesh, India, Nepal and Pakistan—have provided similar help to their refugees from time to time in big or small measure or tried to get rid of them by one means or the other. But once the state has decided to grant the permanent residential status to these refugees, the question of their citizenship has become an issue, as had been the case for India and Pakistan in respect of their Partition refugees, which we have discussed above and will further discuss below. So far as the regional level response is concerned, given the fact that most of the South Asian states have more or less identical questions in respect of refugee relief and refugee rights, and since none of them have signed the 1951 Refugee Convention (except Afghanistan), they have made efforts at the non-governmental level to find out if some coordinated refugee regime at the regional level could be worked out.

Considering the fact that refugees, migrants and stateless persons cause considerable strain on regional politics and security, it would be instructive to find out how concerned states have tried to deal with the challenge. Little has been achieved at the SAARC level, notwithstanding regular meetings of the organization and its various standing committees. Since there is a perceptual hiatus between India and its regional neighbours on matters of regional security, SAARC's political agenda is limited. India finds it easier to deal with its neighbours bilaterally, although many would like to dilute its pre-eminence to the extent possible through multilateral understanding (Partha Ghosh 2013). There has been some talk of sub-regionalism under the umbrella of the so-called Gujral doctrine, but insofar as the refugee issue is concerned, it is not on the agenda at all. The subject has received attention only indirectly. The lack of official enthusiasm, however, has been compensated to some extent by non-official attempts to prepare a blueprint of a regional convention which we will discuss below.

# Search for a Model Regional Convention

By September 2008, there were nine international human rights treaties. Monitored by the human rights treaty bodies, they have created legal obligations for participating states to promote and protect human rights. When a state accepts a human rights treaty through ratification or accession, it becomes a state party to that treaty and assumes the legal obligation to implement the rights set out in it. The treaties provide for the creation of international committees of independent experts to monitor the implementation of their provisions in those countries that have ratified or acceded to them. The UN treaty body system plays a pivotal role in strengthening the protection of human rights nationally. The primary mandate, common to all human rights treaty bodies, is to monitor the implementation of the relevant treaty by reviewing the reports submitted periodically by the states. The most relevant among the nine human rights treaty bodies so far as refugee rights are concerned is the 1990 Committee on Migrant Workers. It monitors the implementation of the International Convention on the Protection of the Rights of All Migrant Workers and Members of Their Families.

To think of a South Asian refugee regime, the first step should be the enactment of national laws dealing with refugee rights. Let us take the example of India. Has it fared well in dealing with its refugees without a refugee law? India has three kinds of refugees: (a) refugees who receive full protection according to standards set by the Government of India—Tibetan refugees, Sri Lankan Tamil refugees and Jumma (CHT) refugees from Bangladesh; (b) refugees whose presence in Indian territory is acknowledged only by the UNHCR and protected under the principle of *non-refoulement* (Mandate Refugees)—Afghan, Iranian, Somali, Sudanese and Myanmarese and (c) refugees who have entered India and have assimilated into the local communities; their presence is acknowledged by neither the Indian government nor the UNHCR—Chins, Rakhain refugees (in Mizoram) and Naga refugees (in Nagaland), all from Myanmar, and ethnic Nepalis from Bhutan (in Sikkim and in the Dargeeling, Jalpaiguri and Karseong districts of West Bengal).

It is, however, argued that the humanitarian and judicial approach, though helpful for the refugees and which must be appreciated, is not enough. It should be buttressed by legal commitments aimed at specifically recognizing and protecting the rights of the refugees. In the Indian context, it has been argued:

[I]t has to be understood that the call for humane treatment of refugees does not mean that the special existential or security concerns of the Indian people have to be ignored. The case for a humane and rights-based treatment of refugees will sit well with a democratic and responsible order. A rights-based approach means that these concerns are given weight within a framework that recognises *the distinctive essence of humanitarian problems* and gives legal recognition to the fact that every person, alien or national, is of equal moral worth, and worthy of treatment that does not violate his or her dignity. (Chimni 2003: 466–67, emphasis in the original).

Simultaneously with pleading for national refugee laws, activists across the region have been pleading for a regional refugee regime, for most of the refugees in the region are intra-regional. This is considered particularly important because it has been seen that, although many countries have signed the 1951 Convention and the 1967 Protocol, there is a lack of coordination between these instruments on the one hand and the respective national laws on the other. This results in hardships for refugees and migrants. In South Asia a number of seminars and conferences have been organized under the auspices of SAARCLAW and the Indian Centre for Humanitarian Law and Research to discuss the subject. By 1994, efforts were underway to draft a legal framework for the protection of refugees in South Asia. An Eminent Persons Group (EPG) was established on the initiative of Sadako Ogata, a former UN High Commissioner for Refugees. The India EPG led by Justice P.N. Bhagwati, former Chief Justice of India, presented a draft model national law in 2000, which was shared with all the relevant ministries of the Government of India. According to this model draft, a refugee was defined as follows:

Any person who is outside his/her Country of Origin and is unable or unwilling to return to, and is unable or unwilling to avail himself/herself of the protection of that country because of a well-founded fear of persecution on account of race, religion, sex, ethnic identity, membership of a particular social group or political opinion... owing to external aggression, occupation, foreign domination, serious violation of human rights or events seriously disrupting public order in either part or whole of his/her country. (Nair 2007: 2)

The NHRC discussed the draft and proposed several amendments. In January and October 2009, the Indian NGO Public Interest Legal Support and Research Centre presented another model draft on refugee protection to a group of concerned individuals for consideration. But not much progress has been registered in actual terms. The reasons are, one, the political class is indifferent to the demand as it feels that India's track record in refugee protection is satisfactory, which does not warrant any drastic change, and two, there is fear from the security establishment that in the name of refugees all sorts of unwanted elements would enter India, making its already difficult task more complex. In late 2009 when the Ministry of Home Affairs was preparing the draft of the Refugees and Asylum Seekers (Protection) Bill, there was strong misgivings expressed by the security agencies. Interestingly, the 46-page draft did not mention anything about the illegal Bangladeshi settlers in India. The security set-up was apprehensive that in the absence of citizenship cards in India, unlike Europe and America, coupled with the fact that India has vast and porous borders with poorer nations, the refugee entries would be unmanageable. In any case, the draft was careful not to accept all the recommendations contained in the Model Code prepared by Bhagwati. For example, it dropped the refugee and/or asylumseeker's right to choose the place of residence and move freely within India, right to adequate housing facilities, right to employment, right to health care, right to free primary education and right to move courts for enforcement of rights conferred under the Indian Constitution.[13]

# The Informal Arrangements

South Asia is a strange region where informal arrangements often have more popular acceptability than formal arrangements. This is quite evident in the regional experience in respect of introducing a uniform civil code, in India the pattern is uniformization through court cases (on this point, see Ghosh 2009). The same is true with regard to dealing with migrants and refugees. The most glaring evidence of this is that while the Indian government has not formally recognized the UNHCR, yet it allows it to function and sometimes even solicits its help to deal with particular refugee situation. In 1995, India even joined the Executive Committee of the UNHCR. As per the arrangement, it is the UNHCR which is supposed to determine the refugee status and not the Government of India, yet the latter has flouted its own norms by using two different yardsticks to determine the exact status of Tibetan and Sri Lankan refugees, and this is done by the ministries of Home and External Affairs. Even residence permits have been selectively issued in respect of Afghan and Myanmarese refugees. In mass influx situations such as the massive flow of East Bengalis in 1971, India dealt with the situation as an emergency keeping in mind its political and diplomatic interests. The problem is that in most of the cases of informal arrangements, the actual practice is not known because, as Dhavan writes, 'apart from the more obvious arrangements, much of the practice is handled confidentially on the basis of records and official notations that are not publicly available for scrutiny' (Dhavan 2004: 83).

## Rethinking in the West

Leave aside illegal migrants, even in the case of legal migrants with or without work permits, the answer is complex. At the core of the dilemma is the issue of multiculturalism. Increasingly a voice is being heard in some European countries, which host large numbers of migrants from Africa and Asia, particularly in the context of growing Islamist terror incidents, about whether their governments' commitment to multiculturalism has served any purpose. German Chancellor Angela Merkel raised a controversy in 2010 when she lamented that in her country multiculturalism as a policy had 'utterly failed'. The British Prime Minister David Cameron and French President Nicholas Sarkozy were soon to endorse her in respect of their own countries. Sarkozy told the French: 'We have been too concerned about the identity of the person who was arriving and not enough about the identity of the country that was receiving him'.[14] Such concerns are making the discourse on refugee and migrants' right more and more convoluted. In South Asia, where both refugees and migrants constitute a huge political question, the discourse assumes serious proportions, particularly during the elections. More generally, the quarrel is primarily between those who see it from a national interest and security perspective and those who see it from a compassionate angle. While the second group is more or less homogenous with only nuanced differences, the first group has several shades. Because of the region's inherent religious, ethnic and linguistic diversity and over and above its political–strategic dissonance, the issue gets mixed with its domestic and international linkages, making it almost impossible to find a coherent policy response.

## Notes

1. One does occasionally come across newspaper reports about the plight of refugees or undocumented migrants in South Asia but it may be just a part of the overall destitution of large masses of people as most regional states are poor and large sections of the populations live in poverty and deprivation.

2. For a brief historical background until the passage of the Foreigners Act, 1946 (see Dhavan 2004: 32–34).

3. During his high-profile visit to the United States in the last week of September 2014, Prime Minister Narendra Modi enthused his Indian–American audience that those holding PIO cards would be granted Indian visa for life. Even before his return to India, the Ministry of Home Affairs issued a notification on 30 September 2014 that stated that the PIO card 'shall be valid for life and the PIO card holder shall be exempt from police reporting/registration'. It further clarified that all the cards issued prior to 30 September 2014 shall be automatically deemed to have lifetime validity. Earlier these cards had a 15-year validity for visa-free entry (*Times of India*, New Delhi, 2 October 2014). Subsequently, on the eve of the *Pravasi Bharatiya* (Indians settled abroad) meet in Ahmedabad in early January 2015, the government through an ordinance merged both the PIO and Overseas Citizen of India (OCI) schemes into one PIO. This proposed amendment to the Citizenship Act of 1955 meant to relax the stipulation of one year continuous stay in India by certain categories of applicants—including a PIO, a foreign national married to an Indian citizen and an OCI of five years—before they could seek Indian citizenship. The PIOs would thus enjoy a life-long Indian visa, besides exemption from registering themselves with the Foreigner Registration Office or the Foreigner Regional Registration Office(*Times of India*, 7 January 2015). In this connection, please refer to Note 18 of Chapter 1.

4. *The Hindu*, 5 August 2015.

5. The choice of the dates, 19 July 1948 and 1 March 1947, can be explained by going through the debates of the Constituent Assembly.

6. Or, religion specific, as the proposed amendments to the Citizenship Act, 1955, envisage. See our discussion on the subject above at pages 220–21.

7. Contrast the tenor of this judgment with what Myron Weiner had said in respect of East German exodus to West Germany and the resultant collapse of the East German state. He said it was peaceful migration and not war that led to this collapse. We have discussed this in Chapter 2.

8. In Bangladesh, fake passports are referred to as *galakata* passports, meaning the faces have been changed in already issued passports. The literal meaning of *galakata* is a head that is severed.

9. Given the Indian and Pakistani experiences it is conceivable that such things are happening in Bangladesh as well in respect of Rohingya refugees from Myanmar.

10. In this context, we may once again read the criticism of the 2005 Supreme Court judgment that scrapped the IMDT Act, on pages 224–25.

11. Against the background of a surge of *Hindutva* ideology post-2014 general election, which brought Narendra Modi of the BJP to power, there is an added sympathy for the oppressed Hindus in Pakistan. A U.P. village even boasted of having a list of 130 Hindu men willing to marry Hindu women from Pakistan, including those sheltered in Delhi's camps (*The Hindustan Times*, New Delhi, 18 January 2015). We have discussed above how the

Narendra Modi government is contemplating granting citizenship rights to minorities fleeing religious persecution in Bangladesh and Pakistan.

12. Established in Colombo on 24 October 1991, and now registered with the SAARC Secretariat at Kathmandu, SAARCLAW is an association of legal communities of SAARC countries comprising judges, lawyers, academicians, law teachers, public officers and a host of other law-related persons. It disseminates information about the developmental concerns of the region. It has affiliate Country Chapters in Bangladesh, Bhutan, India, Nepal, Pakistan and Sri Lanka and activities of the organization have also taken place in the Republic of Maldives.

13. http://news.rediff.com/report/2009/oct/19/home-ministrys-refugee-bill-worries-security-agencies.htm (accessed on 28 March 2011).

14. http://www.dailymail.co.uk/news/article-1355961/Nicolas-Sarkozy-joins-David-Cameron-Angela-Merkel-view-multiculturalism-failed.html#ixzz30c3Ff5DN (accessed on 3 May 2014).

# 6

# Cultural and Psychological Dimensions

*Confusion is the most fertile state for creativity! It's where ideas are born.*

—Prasoon Joshi, adman and lyricist, *Sunday Times of India*, 31 March 2013

## Introduction

It works both ways. Migrants and refugees influence the society and culture of the places they move in. Likewise, the host societies too both influence the migrants and get influenced by them. This two-way interaction is not always benign. Sometimes social tensions develop which may not always take violent turns, but their presence is felt psychologically at both individual and collective levels. These aspects of migration research are as important as other more palpable mundane ones, and in South Asia they are increasingly drawing scholarly attention.

Migration of culture and ideas and their transformation or adaptation in the new land is always there. Though it may not be noticeable in a short span of time, but in a long-term perspective it is not difficult to locate. For example, Buddhism migrated from India first to China, where it got intermingled with Confucianism and Taoism, and then from there it went to Japan, where it got mixed up with traditional Shintoism. In this long journey, Buddha, who was known in India as Avalokiteshwara, transformed into Omida in China and then to Kannon in Japan. Not many people know that the famous Cannon camera owes its name to this deity.[1] In Japan there is a harmonious blending of Shintoism and Buddhism in Japanese shrines. In this kind of blending experience no country can match the United States. Until the 1820s a large number of European migrants arrived there as contract workers, which further mixed the American population which was already a huge crucible. The later Chinese and Japanese migrations made the society even more diverse. All of them have left their imprints on American culture. So much so that the common phrase for America is not 'the melting pot' but 'a salad bowl' (for more on the point, see Ghosh 2012).

There are two types of migrants, one those who migrate to unfamiliar lands and the other who migrate to familiar lands. The first is culturally unfamiliar, the second culturally familiar. In the first category we have, for example, African slaves in America, Indian indentured labourers in West Indies, Fiji and Mauritius, and Indian traders and job seekers in such British colonies as Burma (till 1937 a part of the British India), South Africa, Kenya, Tanzania and Uganda. Indian traders in Burma were mostly Tamil Chettiyars and in Africa mostly Gujaratis, Punjabis and Sindhis. An interesting case of cultural amalgamation in Mauritius and West Indies is that many Hindu temples there resemble Catholic churches and where an entrant is not necessarily expected of taking off one's shoes. In the second category, which is more valid for South Asia, we have the cases of Hindu and Sikh Partition refugees in India and similarly Muslim Partition refugees in Pakistan. We have also the case of Sri Lankan Tamil refugees in India, Bangladeshi illegal migrants in India, Indian Tamils in Sri Lanka, Lhotshampa (Nepalis from southern Bhutan) refugees in Nepal and Rohingyas in Bangladesh.

International literature on migration–culture interface talks primarily of Asian, African and East/Central European migrations to the Western countries. A recent Oxford study on the subject is conspicuously silent on similar processes in South Asia as if it is a non-issue in this regard. The study concentrates only upon how the migrants from the aforesaid regions in Europe, America and even Israel as a nation of immigrants have innovated their new cultural moorings in their places of habitation and what kind of acculturation has taken place in the process (Werbner 2012). One explanation for this absence of intra-South Asian migrations in international scholarship could be that these scholars thought that since these migrations were to culturally familiar lands only, there was no situation for any cultural clash, coexistence or integration. Though apparently it is true, the fact is that South Asia is a continent-sized region whose cultural and ethnic pluralism is no less than that of Europe. Not only did Punjabis settling in Delhi or Muhajirin settling in Sind find themselves placed in culturally alien places, even East Bengali Hindus found themselves so much different from their co-religionist and co-lingual Bengalis in West Bengal. As we will see in this chapter, this story of migration–culture interface in South Asia can be as fascinating as the European or American stories.

## Recalling the Partition

Even after almost seven decades of Partition, the event is recalled in the Indian subcontinent almost every day. Not only literary writings keep pouring in, even new doctoral dissertations are written on the subject. There is no dearth of Bollywood flicks on the event. But was Partition all about death, destruction and displacement? Did it not push human creativity as well? Also, what happened to those who were neither refugees nor hosts, like the Muslims of Delhi? They suffered as both refugees and migrants. How did Partition influence South Asian literature, music, plays, painting, architecture and cinema? What role collective memory played in these art forms? What has been the connection between culture and memory? The list of queries is unending. But some answers will have to be attempted.

Culture and memory have umbilical connection. Culture encompasses both everyday life and the psychic realm which is largely intangible. It requires anthropological perspectives to grapple with. There is also another dimension of it, that is, cultural expression, which is tangible and is expressed through human creativity. Likewise, memory, in this case the memory of violence, is also a complex phenomenon. How does that memory influence cultural creativity? The focus of memory discourse all over the world is on collective memory: Who remembers what? What part of the memory is selected, highlighted, amplified, modified, or, just not mentioned? Since history and mythmaking go side by side, collective memory is seldom authentic. It is often the case that history is invented to suit the requirements of the power elites. Martha Minow in her book *Between Vengeance and Forgiveness* (1998) writes: 'To seek a path between vengeance and forgiveness is also to seek a route between too much memory and too much forgetting. Too much memory is a disease' (Minow 1998: 118). Ariel Dorfman, the playwright of the famous British–French drama film of 1994, called *Death and the Maiden,* that dealt with post-terror revenge and justice, wrote: 'How do we keep the past alive without becoming its prisoner? How do we forget it without risking its repetition in the future?' (quoted by Minow 1998: 119).

## Impact on Culture

It is intellectually challenging to relate the impact of Partition on culture for culture is a complex phenomenon which largely falls in the domain of ethnography and anthropology. An ethnographer's or an anthropologist's trade encompasses both everyday life and the psychic realm.[2] Reflecting on his research on Delhi's Muslim life, a scholar of the field stated this author that one should 'consider these more "intangible" yet palpable aspects of culture—a good example would be the aggression and rudeness of Delhi Punjabis, which seems to me to be a continuing manifestation of the post-traumatic stress of Partition violence, which has never adequately been addressed'.[3] To make ends meet, many Punjabi women had to come out of the confines of their kitchens and join the workforce, leading to women's emancipation in general, which had a lasting impact on Delhi culture. Sociologist Supriya Singh tells this story through the life of her mother, which was a profile in courage and determination (Singh 2013). But there were some retrograde impacts too, like the introduction of dowry system and unethical trade practices (Mehra 1991: 82–84). The Muslims of Delhi were not used to such life. They found it difficult to adapt themselves to these rapid changes in the city which the marginalized existence of the refugees had resulted in.

According to Taneja, the growing veneration of *jinn*[4] among the Muslims could be linked to the trauma of Partition and the nature of the post-colonial project to remember as little as possible of Delhi Muslim culture and archaeology, while at the same time the larger project was aimed at making India a secular nation. The fear was that it could come in the way of rehabilitating millions of Punjabi refugees whose problem was more immediate and visible. The demand for refugee rehabilitation was so strident and for which so much land was required that the government followed a policy of 'authorized forgetting' (Taneja 2013: 147). The Archaeological Survey of India (ASI) was reluctant to check its own archives or to allow scholars to look into them lest some uncomfortable facts might be unearthed to the advantage of the Waqf Boards and corresponding detriment to the refugee relief and rehabilitation schemes. 'It seemed that the ASI's archive was not an archive of authorized memory, but of authorized forgetting, where what was once consigned to dust and darkness was never meant to reappear in public, not even as diminutive flickers from academic footnotes' (Taneja 2013: 147).

Even Nehru, who was no doubt secular in his orientation and was concerned about the welfare of Muslims as reflected in his policy perspectives, was not sufficiently appreciative of the cultural heritage of Delhi Muslims. Taneja writes:

> The violence of Partition as it played out in India wished to remove all signs of Muslim sovereignty and belonging from India. This was a Hindu-majoritarian violence that the state could not (or did not) control, despite its avowed secularism. The specter of uncontrollable violence, foundational to the beginning of the new state, now haunted all government actions and social relations. The history of state and society in postcolonial India could well be the story of trying to accommodate the law-making violence that the state recognized it could not monopolize. This is reflected not only in the denial of Muslim claims to worship in monuments rendered 'dead' by postcolonial policy but also in the erasure of Muslim graves and mosques and shrines, spaces of living Muslim memory, from the landscapes of the new nation-state.... The graves disappear, Delhi becomes primeval: 'virgin' territory for development. Qasimi [Ata-ur-Rahman Qasimi is the author of Dilli ki tarikhi masajid (2001)—The historic mosques of Delhi] tells us the anecdote of Maulana Azad (who was the Education Minister at the time and the only Muslim member of the central cabinet) trying to intervene with Prime Minister Nehru against the destruction of tombs and graveyards going on in Delhi, to which Nehru is said to have replied, 'Maulana, half of Delhi is graveyards and mosques. Our schemes will fail if we don't have room to build'. (Taneja 2013: 148–49)[5]

There were also visible impacts on cultural gatherings, dress habits and food. Not only Urdu lost its pre-eminence in Delhi life but such retrograde customs like dowry, which was not known to Delhi Muslims, also entered their social fabric that the growing commercialization resulted in (Mehra 1991: 82–84). With the replacement of Urdu by Hindi and colloquial Punjabi, Urdu *mushairas* were replaced by *Kabi sammelans* (poetry recitation gatherings). Similarly, *mujras* (music and dance patronized by rich and powerful) also died down. In their place Punjbai bhangra and loud music during marriage ceremonies in which the grooms arrived in white mares became fashionable. Fabric arts like *zari* (gold or silver thread work woven into cotton fabric) and embroidery were no longer patronized as much and in their place fashion cut clothes became popular (Kumari 2013: 66–67). In the following section, we would concentrate on the impact of migrations on cultural productions such as literature, music, cinema, paintings and architecture.

One cannot draw a comparable picture in this regard with the Bengal scene. East Bengali migrations to West Bengal and other places in eastern India were not like the Muslim migrations from these places to East Pakistan as we have seen in Chapter 1. East Bengali refugees neither implanted new cultural values of any vast magnitude on their new neighbours nor the vice versa because both had more or less the same cultural patterns. Whatever was there it was in terms of food, which we would discuss below. But at another plane, there was unhappiness amongst the West Bengalis. As one scholar has noted, that the way Delhi Muslims were economically and culturally suffocated by the sudden massive presence of Punjabi refugees in their midst, likewise West Bengalis of Kolkata too, though they were all Hindus, faced similar predicament. Coupled with a sense of being neglected by the central government in dealing with their refugee-related difficulties, they had a sense that their state was suffering from the disease called 'refugee-itis'. The doctor, that is Chief Minister B.C. Roy, attending to the patient, that is West Bengal, was anxiously asked by all there whether the case was 'hopeless' (Nilanjana Chatterjee. n.d.: 6).

## Impact on Cultural Productions

One of the most fascinating aspects of the migration saga is the movement of cultural forms. The movements of people across the border left their lasting imprints on literature, music, lyrics, painting, drama and even architecture. Since the places involved primarily were northern undivided India and eastern undivided India, these impacts were largely noticeable among those communities there who spoke Punjabi, Urdu, Hindi, Bengali and Sindhi. As English increasingly became popular among the educated masses across the communities, much of the literature influenced by migration started appearing in English as well. So far as Tamil literature and cinema were concerned, they too were influenced by the existence of Sri Lankan Tamil refugees on Tamil Nadu soil, but since they were mostly confined to refugee camps such impacts were limited.

## Literature

While there is abundance of political history of Partition, there is hardly any social and cultural history of the time which witnessed so much of violence and human suffering. As one social worker, Gulab Pandit, noted: *Itihas mein sirf naam aur tarikh sahi hoti hai, baaqi nahin* (in history books, only the names and dates are correct, not the rest). This vast gap between political history and human reality of the Partition of Punjab was largely filled by Hindi, Urdu and Punjabi literature. As Menon and Bhasin write:

> The futility and tragedy of demarcating boundaries, and the impossibility of dividing homes and hearts are the theme of story after story, as is the terrible violence that accompanied forced migration. Nowhere in the thousands of pages of fiction and poetry do we find even a glimmer of endorsement for the price paid for freedom, or admission that this 'qurbani' (sacrifice) was necessary for the birth of two nations. Rather, a requiem for lost humanity, for the love between communities, for shared joys and sorrows, a shared past. In the annals of Indian history, Partition is unique for the literary outpouring that it occasioned; Jason Francisco, reviewing recent anthologies of Partition writing—fiction, memoirs, poetry, testimonies, diaries, fragments—identifies three thematic concerns in these texts: rupture, protest and repair. These three motifs, he says, 'form a natural response to Partition, a continuum from pain to healing' and, via stories of repair, to the 'healing power of memory'. (Menon & Bhasin 1998: 7)

In Bengali, Hindi, Punjabi, Urdu and English literature, however, the impact of Hindu and Sikh refugee movements from Pakistan or, in general, Partition, is palpable. Partition and the resultant woes became a big theme for Hindi and Urdu literature and they continue to be so. Alok Bhalla's four edited volumes containing stories about the Partition of India is just one example (2012a, 2012b).[6] The stories written by Saadat Hasan Manto during the days of Partition riots are still referred to as among the best representations of that human tragedy.[7] To escape the wrath of Hindu rioters in Bombay, this Amritsar-born Muslim had left for Pakistan where he was accused of obscenity in five of his short stories. He did not live long and died an alcoholic in 1955, fighting court cases, although he was ultimately found not guilty. In a very thoughtful essay on Manto's writings, Priyamvada Gopal writes:

> Read typically as 'exclamations of horror' or 'documents of barbarism' ..., stories like 'Cold Meat' [*Thanda Gosht*] and 'Open it' [*Khol Do*] are brief and intense in their representation of the violence of Partition. While many of Manto's Partition stories, including his aphoristic sketches in Black Marginalia ['Siyah Hashiye'], are undoubtedly powerful evocations of the sheer horror and human brutality that marked the nation-formation in 1947, these narratives also tell us something about the changes that historical processes effected in Manto's thinking about human and social existence in general and violence in particular. (Gopal 2001: 247)[8]

On Bengali literature the impact of the Partition and refugee inflow was not immediate, although the deteriorating Hindu–Muslim relations and the communal riots had formed the themes of many writings. But as the problem of the refugees started sinking into the collective psyche of West Bengal, many authors addressed the issue in their literary creations. Though the list here is not exhaustive, the following writings may fall in this genre: Jeebananda's *Jalpaihati* and *Basmatir Upakhyan* (1948), Abinash Saha's *Prangana* (1949), Amarendra Ghosh's *Bhangchhe shudhu Bhangchhe* (1950), *Manthon* (1954) and *Thikkan Badol* (1957), Narendranath Mitra's *Durobhasini* (1951), Prabodh Kumar Sanyal's *Hasbanu* (1952), Manik Bandyaopadhyay's *Sarbaojonin* (1952), Bonophool's *Pancha Parba* (1954), and *Treeborna* (1963), Ramesh Chandra Sen's *Pub Theke Poschime* (1956), Amiya Bhushan Majumdar's *God Shrikhanda* (1957), Narayan Gangopadhyay's *Bidisha* (1954), Achuyat Goswami's *Kanagolir Kahini* (1954), Tarashankar Bandyopadhyay's *Bipasa* (1958), Narayan Sanyal's *Bokultola P.L. Camp* (1955) and *Bolmik* (1958), Amiya Bhushan Majumdar's *Nirbaas* (1959), Pratibha Basu's *Samudra Hriday* (1959), Shaktipada Rajguru's *Tabu Bihanga* (1960), Narendra Mitra's *Upanagar* (1963) and *Mahanagar* (1963), Saroj Kumar Roy Choudhury's *Neel Aagun* (1963), Samaresh Basu's *Suchander Swadeshjatra* (1969) and *Saudagar* (1971), Prafulla Rai's *Keyapatar Nouko* (1970), Atin Baandyopadhyay's *Neelkantha Paakhir Khoje* (1971) and *Maanusher Gorbari* (1978), Sunil Gangopadhyay's *Arjun* (1971) and Sonkho Ghosh's *Supuriboner Saari* (1990).

Among the poets to be militant about what all happened because of the Partition displacements were Sunil Gangopadhyay, Tarapada Roy, Bishnu De, Dinesh Das and Jyotirmoyee Devi. According to Sunil Gangopadhyay, Partition 'was a subject to be militant about, a subject to feel anger and distress, a subject to romanticize, a subject to cry for, a subject to make a statement'. Among the novels that were published in East Pakistan/ Bangladesh on the same theme, mention may be made of the following: Golam Kuddus's *Mariyam* (1956), Shahidullah Kaiser's *Songshoptak* (The Indomitable Soldiers, 1965), Abu Rushad's *Nongor* (1967), Sardar Jayeuddin's *Onek Surjer Aasha* (1967), Taslima Nasreen's *Lajja* (1993) and *Phera* (1993), Selina Hossain's *Gayatri Sandhya* (1994), and Akharuddin Iliyas's *Khoabnama* (1996) (Mandal 2011: 168–72, Sinha 2010).[9]

Strangely, such an eminent Bengali writer like Tarashankar Bandyopadhyay, who otherwise handled so many social themes, including the tragedy of the 1943 Bengal Famine in his novel *Ashani Sanket* (The Distant Thunder), did not write anything on the Partition refugees barring *Bipasa* that we have mentioned above, but it too was about Punjabi refugees. One reason could be, as one author writes by referring to Ashis Nandy's argument in this regard:

> [I]t is a national trauma that had to be forgotten, because memory could not relive the traumatic experience and still remain focused on the national issues of governance and security both external and internal. Tormented voices mourning for the dead, for the lost, had to be swept out of hearing, denied their histories, just so that the task of nation building could be carried on uninterrupted.... The year 1984 [infamous for the anti-Sikh riots] had opened the floodgates of memory, with all the bitterness of coming full circle for many.... [W]ithout this trigger, these memories might have remained buried. Literature had allowed itself to forget them. (Mukhopadhyay 2002: 209)

There are many literary works representing this memory in both India and Pakistan, a glimpse of which can be found in several contributions in the volume edited by S. Settar and Indira Gupta (2002).

The impact of Partition and migration on the literature has over the years spread to English language in a massive way, and the process seems unending. It is impossible to even try to make a summary of these writings in this short subsection, but a fairly long bibliography can be created by just going into the references of such authors, such as Anup Beniwal (2005), Jill Didur (2006) and Tarun Saint (2010). Beniwal is right when he says that 'however hard we may try to wish it away, the very notion of India's freedom is inextricably enmeshed with the reality of Partition. The sociopolitical and psychological culture that this entangled inheritance has spawned, has impacted almost every domain of Indian life—public or private. Instead of exhausting itself with the passage of time, the atavistic in the phenomenon of Partition has continued to implode/explode Indian sensibility/reality in myriad ways' (Beniwal 2005: v). Here is a passage from his concluding remarks:

> The creative responses to Partition in Indian novel in English, when analyzed as a whole from the point of view of their emotional content, slot themselves along a two-fold classification: the pre-Rushdie cathartic expression and post-Rushdie parodic metafiction. Within this classificatory schema *Train to Pakistan, The Rape, Ashes and Petals, Sunlight on a Broken Column, Azadi* belong to the first category; *Midnight's Children, The Great Indian Novel* and *Looking Through Glass* belong to the second one. The former expresses itself in realistic-naturalistic terms, the latter in parodic-surrealistic terms. Whereas the trauma of the lived experience tends to make the former responses melodramatic, but didactic, this

element is palpably missing in the latter responses. However, in both the responses, violence is viewed as unnatural. In pre-Rushdie Partition novels, the historical revisiting of Partition, being a conscious enterprise, is frozen in time. These authors do not seem to outgrow this time warp. But in post-Rushdie novels, the revisiting of Partition history is both incidental and its repercussions spread over time. Both the responses in their historical analyses of Partition, nevertheless, strike a pronounced anti-colonial stance. Yet Partition history per se, when seen from the perspective of its victims, in both the categories is conceived of as an impersonal force beyond human agency. (Beniwal 2005: 184–85)

# Cinema

Among all art forms probably cinema has the biggest popular appeal, for it can be viewed and watched by all for which no particular training or appreciative faculty is needed. As Ingmar Bergman said: 'No art passes our consciousness in the way film does and goes directly to our feelings, deep down into the dark rooms of our souls' (quoted by Sharmila Tagore 2013). There is no dearth of literature on Hindi, Bengali, Tamil and other Indian regional cinema. Even such segments as music, direction, photography and art in them have also been dissected by scholars and other writers. Themes such as family, romance, nationalism, societal violence, and terrorism too have been studied. But the impact of cross-border migrations on cinema has either been not so much there or it has not been studied in depth. Whatever one can cull from the scattered literature on the subject informs us that this connection between migration and cinema is largely indirect. Both in terms of the themes of the movies as well as the influence of the directors and producers of those movies, the interconnected events of Partition violence and displacement had their imprint which was not necessarily confined to movies produced immediately after the events but also in movies produced much later. Let us try to find this connection first in the Bombay movies and then those produced in Calcutta and Dhaka.

# The Film Industry

In pre-Partition India, film studios existed in Bombay (now Mumbai), Calcutta (now Kolkata) and Madras (now Chennai) to which Lahore was added later. Although Lahore was a late entrant, compared to Calcutta and

Madras it had an advantage.[10] Unlike Calcutta and Madras, which generally catered to regional languages cinema, because of the general acceptance of Urdu in Punjab, the Lahore film industry could cater to the Hindi–Urdu–Hindustani audience of the entire north-central region of India. It may be noted that after the British annexation of the Punjab in 1849, Urdu was introduced as the official language of the province (Kamran 2012: 174). As a result of these, a close connection was established between the Bombay and Lahore film industries during the pre-Partition days. Such eminent names in the Bombay film world were actor-singer K.L. Saigal, actors Prithviraj Kapur, Dilip Kumar (Yusuf Khan), Shyam, Khurshid, Suraiya, Shyama (Khurshid Akhtar) and Manorama (a Christian from Lahore). Among the music directors were Vinod (real name Eric Roberts), Shyam Sunder, Ghulam Haider, Jhandey Khan, Feroze Nizami and Khurshid Anwar. The lyricists in the same category were Qamar Jalalabadi and Tanveer Naqvi. Renowned singers like Mohammad Rafi, Noorjahan and Shamshad Begum had all moved from Lahore to Bombay in the 1940s. Even the famous producer A.R. Kardar, who was one of the pioneers of the Lahore film industry, had shifted to Bombay in the early 1940s. No one had anticipated that Bombay and Lahore would soon belong to two different countries (Ahmed 2012: 60–61).

Following the Partition, which marked the culminating point in the process of deterioration in the inter-communal relationship, many Hindu and Sikh artistes belonging to the Lahore film industry left for Bombay. That is why many prominent actors, producers, directors and technicians who ruled the Bombay film industry for decades after Partition were either directly from Pakistan or were their descendants. The predominance of ethnic Punjabis in the industry is a consequence of this history (Ganti 2004: 22). With the rise of the Bombay film industry, many Calcutta-based Bengali producers and directors also started migrating to Bombay. Among the Punjabi actors, one may mention the names of Pran, Om Prakash, Jeevan, Hiralal, Meena Shori, Balraj Sahni, Geeta Bali, Kamini Kaushal, Rajendra Kumar, Manmohan Krishan, Gulshan Rai, Chetan Anand, Dev Anand and Vijay Anand; film producers Ramanand Sagar, B.R. Chopra and I.S. Johar; and music directors Husnlal, Bhagatram, Hanslal Behl and O.P. Nayyar. The Lahore connection of Bombay continued much later when Lahore-born Kabir Bedi, Prem Chopra, Simi Garewal and Shekhar Kapur made themselves famous in Bombay (Ahmed 2012: 60–61). Bombay movies also gained in terms of production quality as after the Partition many technicians from the Lahore film industry migrated to the city.

Bombay's gain was Lahore's loss, which had the noted Pancholi and Shorey production units. The Hindus and Sikhs were prominently placed in the city. The 40 per cent strong Hindu–Sikh community owned 80 per cent of the modern buildings of Lahore and all its cinema theatres and studios. Even outsiders like D.M. Pancholi, a Gujarati, and Himanshu Roy, a Bengali, had started their careers in Lahore as producer and director, respectively. The exodus of the Hindus and Sikhs coupled with the general stifling atmosphere generated by the Islam-centric politics of the country encouraged even Muslim artists who were progressive minded to leave Pakistan and settle in Nehruvian India that promoted secular temper. One such ideological refugee was Sahir Ludhianvi (Abdul Hayee 'Saahir') for whom it was actually a second migration. He and his family had fled from Ludhiana in India to Lahore to escape the wrath of the Hindu–Sikh terrorism. But soon he realized that Islamism would come in the way of his left-oriented poetry. He migrated to India in either 1948 or 1949. Some of his lyrics in Bombay films are legendary.[11] But Lahore was not totally a loser. There were some prominent returnees also. For example, music director Ghulam Haider, singer Noorjehan and a few others resettled in Lahore. For some time Lahore regained its activity but it did not last long (Ahmed 2012: 64–65).

Financially, both Calcutta and Bombay film industries suffered severely. Bengali films lost their East Bengal market, which provided about 40 per cent of their revenue and subsequently the overall Pakistani ban on Indian films affected both Bombay and Calcutta film industries. In 1952, Pakistan imposed taxes on imported Indian films and then in 1962 it banned all imports of Indian films (Ganti 2004: 22). There was no impact of Partition on the Madras film industry. It rather gained to some extent by taking advantage of the difficulties of the Bombay industry. Already it had a market in the rest of South India, Sri Lanka and Malaysia, to which was now added portions of the Hindi film market. The production houses that made this possible were those of S.S. Vasan, A.V. Meiyappan (of the AVM fame), and L.V. Prasad from the Telugu film industry (Vasudevan 2010: 207–9).

## Thematic Impact on Bombay Cinema

In terms of productions, while Bombay alone gained from the arrival of new artistes and technicians from Lahore, both Bombay and Calcutta gained in terms of some outstanding productions which were inspired, directly or indirectly, by the displacements that accompanied Partition. The question of the impact of Partition migrations, or more broadly, the Partition trauma, on Indian cinema, however, is a complex subject and has much to do with the memory discourse. Interestingly, neither the Partition nor the trauma associated with it got directly reflected in the cinema produced immediately after the events. Bhaskar Sarkar in his study *Mourning the Nation* (2009) has tried to find the impact in many movies that were not otherwise connected with the Partition trauma. Though out of a total of about 1,800 movies produced between 1947 and 1962, the events of Partition figured directly in fewer than a dozen Hindu–Urdu movies—for example in *Lahore* (M.L. Anand, 1949), *Nastik* (I.S. Johar, 1954), *Chhalia* (Manmohan Desai, 1960) or *Dharamputra* (Yash Chopra, 1961)—there were several other movies in which the trauma found an indirect presence in terms of physical injury resulting in bodily scars and wounds, reunion of separated families, the loss of near and dear ones due to accidents or natural disasters, and the dishonoured woman, the illegitimate child and suspicions of paternity. One may mention in this category such movies as Bibhuti Mitra's *Shabnam* (1948), Raj Kapoor's *Aag* (1948), and Yash Raj Chopra's *Dhool ka Phool* (1959) and *Waqt* (1965). About *Aag*, Raj Kapoor's first film, Sarkar writes that it

> cannot ignore the deep wound inflicted by the national amputation and the accompanying violence; the tone of the film, which casts a shadow over its youthful idealism, intimates the shock more eloquently than the narrative's single direct reference to Partition. *Aag* cues us to the cryptic ways in which Indian popular cinema engaged with a portentous historical horizon inescapably constituted by the trauma of Partition. An array of indirect, tacit figurations come into play: conscious displacements; subconscious, even unintended allusions; indexical citations; accidental traces; evocations of broad, analogous sentiments. (Sarkar 2009: 92)

This indirect connection that Sarkar has talked about is to be found if one compares it with a similar connection between wars or the Holocaust on the one hand and art and literature on the other in the West. Sarkar borrows from Dominick La Capra's reference to collective trauma when people's art rendition 'departs from ordinary reality to produce surrealistic situations or radically playful openings that seem to be sublimely irrelevant to ordinary reality but may uncannily provide … insight into that reality'. People suffering from trauma cannot remember the source of the trauma, yet they remember it through other means.

In this connection, he quotes from Joshua Hirsch's insightful book on Holocaust films:

> As trauma is less a particular experiential content than a form of experience, so posttraumatic cinema is defined less by a particular image content—a documentary image of atrocity, a fictional image of atrocity, or the absence of an image of atrocity—than by *the attempt to discover a form for presenting* that content that mimics some aspects of posttraumatic consciousness itself, *the attempt to formally reproduce* for the spectator an experience of suddenly seeing the unthinkable. (Sarkar 2009: 23, emphasis in the original)

Thus, 'Hirsch is essentially arguing for a mode of representation that is more adequate to the charge of conveying a traumatic experience; in a sense, his is a hyperrealist quest for appropriate forms, given the task at hand' (Sarkar 2009: 23).

Psychoanalysis recognizes trauma through this non-remembering the source. Any description connected to the original event may get transformed into other events. The traumatized persons tend to feel secure only when they are able to bring back the past events into the realm of their transforming capacity. Indian cinema, therefore, may not have dealt with Partition directly, but it has done so in transformed narratives, which often has taken the form of melodrama (Biswas 2008: 210–11, Panjwani 2010: 271–75, Vasudevan: 2010: 152–55, Virdi 2010: 1–2). In this context, the Raj Kapoor persona on the screen is of importance.

> The Raj Kapoor character immediately alerts the film public to a certain populist, even agitprop view of the street personality as the vehicle of meditations on issues of social injustice and community bigotry. The figure is at a crucial level produced through a desire to distance the public from investments in a social field shot through with the claims of lineage. This was particularly important not only for an imagination of a more egalitarian society, but one also unencumbered by the anxiety arising from a scrutiny of blood ties which could compromise the 'purity' of ethnic religious communities in the wake of the Partition. (Vasudevan 2010: 71)[12]

Against the background of Nehruvian secularism and the continued existence of Hindu–Muslim psychological trauma over the pains of broken families in north India, the necessity was ever felt by producers to somehow highlight the coexistence of the communities. Amongst the leading characters in successful movies at the box office, there has to be a Muslim character, if a Christian is added to it, it is even better. Manmohan Desai, who produced several blockbusters, had once said in an interview that if a movie was rejected by India's Muslims, it was a commercial failure. It goes to the credit of Bombay film industry that it has not allowed itself to be touched by the fire of Hindu–Muslim communalism, and for this, the credit should go to both the Hindu and Muslim film fraternities that belonged to Bombay and Lahore film industries. One of the best examples of this secular ethos was a song sequence in the 1954 flick, *Amar* (the immortal), an otherwise box office flop. The song, *Insaaf ka mandir hai ye, bhagwan ka ghar hai*, was an all-Muslim affair against a Hindu backdrop. The temple scene of the song was directed by Mehboob Khan, enacted by Dilip Kumar and Madhubala (both Muslim), the lyric was by Shakeel Badayuni, sung by Mohammad Rafi on the tune of Naushad Ali.[13]

Several years later, *Garam Hawa* (1973) was released. Based on Ishmat Chugtai's story and adapted for the screen by Kaifi Azmi, the movie was directed by M.S. Sathyu. It dealt with the tensions within an Agra-based Muslim family squeezed between two pressures, one arguing for migrating to Pakistan and the other for staying put in India whatever the difficulties. The movie forcefully depicted the tensions that Partition generated both within families and among communities. Here is a crisp description of the theme:

Misfortunes start piling up on the stoical [Salim] Mirza[owner of a shoe factory in Agra]: orders to deliver shoes are canceled; his employees refuse to work for him or banks to loan him money for fear that he will escape to Pakistan; his ancestral home, in the name of the now-absent elder brother, is declared evacuee property and allotted to a Sindhi businessman; Mirza is forced to move to cramped rented quarters; Mirza's eldest son also leaves for Pakistan when the shoe business is on the verge of collapse. But worst of all is the pain that Amina suffers as a result of the political changes. Her lover, Kazim, secretly returns to India to marry her, but before the ceremony can take place, the police arrest him for having entered India illegally. Mirza watches helplessly as his beloved daughter sinks into despondency. Shamsad takes advantage of her situation and woos her; a lonely and vulnerable Amina succumbs to his blandishments. But Samshad too escapes across the border with his opportunistic parents. Still, Amina hopes for his return, only to have her dreams shattered once more, and this situation culminates in her suicide. Mirza's family has now shrunk to three, a progressive decrease that is signified by the number of plates set during mealtimes, once shared by by the whole family. Unable to avoid the move he had resisted so far, Mirza too sadly prepares to leave. On the way to the station, their *tonga* is stopped by a procession of people out to protest injustice. Sikander [Mirza'a younger son], drawn to the cause, jumps off the carriage and joins the rally, as, after a few moments, does Mirza. They decide to stay on and struggle for communal harmony and social change. (Chakravarty 1996: 250)

In 1987 against the background of the Babri Masjid controversy, a six-part TV serial called *Tamas* was telecast. It was a slightly changed version of the novel by Bhisham Sahni of the same name published in 1974. Sahni was a Sikh refugee from Rawalpindi in West Punjab, and the serial was directed by Govind Nihalani, a Sindhi refugee from Karachi. It was a very powerful statement against communalism and showed how communal riots could be manufactured by vested interests if the circumstances were conducive (for a detailed interview with the author, see Bhalla 2002).[14]

Even in recent times the trauma of Partition has been revisited in Hindi/Urdu films in South Asia against the background of the nationalist, secularist and feminist discourses. Referring to movies, such as John Mathew Matthan's *Sarfarosh* (Fervour, 1999), Anil Sharma's *Gadar: Ek Prem Kahani* (Revolt: A Love Story, 2001), Sabiha Sumar's *Khamosh Pani* (Silent Waters, 2003) and Kunal Kohli's *Fanaa* (Destroyed in Love, 2006), Kavita Daiya has discussed the representation of romantic intimacy (she calls it 'inter-ethnic coupledom'), secular citizenship and intricate phenomenon of subjugation of feminine independence. We have discussed this last element in the section 'Pakistani Cinema', where we have referred to *Khamosh Pani*. About the rest of the films, Daiya writes:

> [B]oth *Gadar* and *Fanaa* fetishize the Muslim female as icon towards the project of inventing a legitimate space for Muslims' secular citizenship in India. *Sarfarosh* in contrast, pays little attention to the figure in its narrative about ideal citizenship and the nation-state. Instead, it fetishizes the heteronormative, Hindu male body, such that both the disabled and able Hindu male citizens become critical to the production and preservation of the masculinized nation-state. *Sarfarosh* and *Fanaa* connect Partition to contemporary terrorism in India, even as they write 1947 as relevant to the contemporary experience of Indian citizenship for minoritized Muslims. (Daiya 2011: 590)

# Ambivalence about Progress and Harmony

One author has drawn our attention to the post-Partition contrast between the cultural representation in Indian cinema on the one hand and state's representation of the national project on the other. He has analysed the contemporary Bombay films in contrast to 1,742 documentaries that the Films Division of India produced during the first twenty years of Partition.[15] Those days the cinema theatres were required to screen these documentaries before the start of the movie. It is another matter how serious was the audience to watch them. These documentaries were conspicuous by the absence of the theme of Muslim culture, which was prominent in several contemporary movies, particularly with their emphasis on *tehzib*, '*sharafat*' and '*nazaqat*' (gentlemanly/womanly ways of life rooted in the cultural ethos and the use of sophisticated language) as exemplified in the life of nostalgically remembered Lucknow as portrayed in those movies. They underlined how Hindus and Muslims appreciated each other's culture.[16] The emphasis of the documentaries was on the symbols of modernism as tools of nation-building, massive developmental projects and public services that the state was committed to provide in the fields of education, health and social welfare (Teneja 2009: 1–4). Drawing from the theories of memory research, one may argue that probably the memory of Partition was too cruel to recall without any purpose being served and hence forgetting them and emphasizing the tasks ahead in building the nation on a modernist mode were considered more appropriate.

Guru Dutt's *Pyaasa* (The Thirsty, 1957) reflects the nostalgia about the Hindu–Muslim coexistence on the one hand and the frustration with the ways things were in contemporary India on the other. In a significant sense, the poet-hero in the movie, Vijay, was representing the ambivalence of Sahir, the lyricist of the movie to whom we have referred to above. Sahir represented the eternal ambivalence about progress and modernity. Guru Dutt, however, made Sahir to modify his original poetry for the movie to make it more emphatic for contemporary times. Taneja writes:

> *'Jinhe naaaz hai Hind par who kahaan hain?'* asks Vijay in an iconic song from *Pyaasa*, as he drunkenly wanders through the red light district. Where are those who are proud of India? This song has a telling history. Saahir had already published the poem (*Chakle*/Brothels); the song is based on his collection *Talkhiyaan* (Bitterness), before he was hired to write the songs for *Pyaasa*. When the poem was brought to Guru Dutt's notice by his assistant, he said, 'Raj! This is it! This is *Pyaasa*!' The song as it appears in the film is a slight but significant modification of the poem. The earlier refrain of the poem was *'Sanakhwan-e tasdeeq-e mashriq kahan hain?'* Where are those who extol the holiness of the East? The story goes that Nehru had given a speech in which he had remarked, 'I am proud of India'. Guru Dutt asked Saahir to work this line into the refrain of the song. (Taneja 2009: 7)

Reflecting the nostalgia part at the end of the movie, only three characters, all Muslim, stood by the side of the failed but celebrated hero. Taneja questions: 'Are they merely representatives of their community, which it is imperative to portray sympathetically in the new secular nation-state, trying to forget histories of Partition violence? Or is their 'Muslimness' a sign of something else, images and markers of another way of being, not quite comfortable with the dispensation and demands of modern nationalism as shown in the Films Division documentaries, where there are no Muslims at all?' (Taneja 2009: 8).

It must, however, be mentioned that it is probably much more difficult to explain this disproportionate influence of Muslim culture and Muslim presence on Bombay cinema. While many eminent lyricists, singers, actors and directors were Muslim, and Dilip Kumar and Nargis (Fatima Rasheed) were adjudged as most popular actors in a 1952 magazine poll, Hindu–Muslim romance or marriage on the screen was unthinkable (it was as late as 1995 that the movie *Bombay* showed such a possibility for the first time). Cinema as such was looked down upon by the political class that included Gandhi, Nehru or Patel. Even such a movie like *Achhut Kanya* (Untouchable Maiden, 1936) that showed a Brahmin man's love for an untouchable girl could not evoke any interest in that great crusader against untouchability, Mahatma Gandhi. He did not watch it in spite of its producer Himanshu Rai's efforts (Guha 2007: 721–38).

The importance of Urdu and Lucknow in Hindi movies is better explained by Mukul Kesavan who by drawing from the definition provided by Marshall Hodgson prefers to call it the 'Islamicate' impact. He quotes Hodgson:

> It [Isalmicate] has a double adjectival ending on the analogy of 'Italianate', in the Italian style, which refers not to Italy itself directly, not to just whatever is to be called properly Italian, but to something associated typically with Italian style and with the Italian manner. One speaks of 'Italianate architecture' even in England and Turkey.... *Isalmicate would refer not directly to the religion, Islam, but to the social and cultural complex historically associated with Islam and the Muslims, both among Muslims themselves and even when found among non-Muslims.* (Hodgson quoted by Kesavan 1994: 246, emphasis in the original)[17]

In any case, as Kesavan explains, Urdu had a pedigree in the Parsi theatre of Bombay and then, as the cinema started becoming popular, as the lingua of the Bombay cinema. Rather, this 'unpartitioned homeland of the people of al-Hind' (Kesavan 1994: 256) successfully withstood the divisive impact of the Partition.

# Bengali Cinema

So far as the impact of Partition and the Calcutta refugee scene on Bengali cinema was concerned, the most notable name to be mentioned is that of Ritwik Ghatak. In his films, he narrated how the Partition of Bengal struck at the roots of Bengali culture. Of the eight films that he directed, six dealt with Partition and displacement. Through them he sought to express the nostalgia that many Bengalis felt for their pre-Partition life. Reproducing the last part of the screenplay of his movie *Meghe Dhaka Tara* (The Star Veiled by Clouds, 1960, based on Shaktipada Rajguru's story *Chenamookh*, meaning, familiar face), it has been said:

> If you are asked to choose a single film which captures the trauma and tragedy of the Bengal Partition with unmatched power and sensitivity, you choose, without a question, Ritwik Ghatak's *Meghe Dhaka Tara* (The Star Veiled by Clouds, 1960). This classic is built on a simple story line: how the eldest daughter of an uprooted family, in a stifling, desperate environment, turns into the breadwinner and ultimately sacrifices her life. In fact, Nita, the protagonist in the film, has become a deathless symbol of Partition itself and the uprooted woman's tragic struggle against it. Here we present a translation of the last part of the screenplay where Nita after fulfilling her mission succumbs to tuberculosis. Her piercing cry 'I wanted to live' sums up the essence of all displacements, exodus and partitions. (Bagchi and Dasgupta 2003: 219)

According to Erin O'Donnel: 'In his [Ghatak's] films, he tries to convey how Partition struck at the roots of Bengali culture. He seeks to express the nostalgia and yearning that many Bengalis have for their pre-Partition way of life' (quoted by Chattopadhyay 2007: 266). In response to a question as to what inspired his films, Ghatak said: 'Being a Bengali from East Bengal, I have seen the untold miseries inflicted on my people in the name of independence—which is a fake and a sham. I have reacted violently towards this and I have tried to portray different aspects of this in my films' (Mandal 2011: 178). He was the quintessential Bengali of the undivided Bengal. On hearing about his death on 6 February 1976, Satyajit Ray said: 'Ritwik was out and out a Bengali director, a Bengali artist. He was much more Bengali than what I am' (as told to Chakrabarty 2014: 7).

Some of Ghatak's outstanding films, besides *Meghe Dhaka Tara,* were *Nagarik* (Citizen, 1951—the movie was released in 1977, a year after his death), *Bari Theke Paliye* (The Runaway, 1958), *Komal Gandhar* (a soft note on a sharp scale, 1961), *Subarnarekha* ('The Golden Line', 1962) and his penultimate film made in Bangladesh in 1972 called *Titas Ekti Nadir Naam* (A River Called Titas). It has been said about *Titas Ekti Nadir Naam* that it 'does not deal with the Partition, but it tackles the moral, ethical and political problems connected with displacement' (Chatterjee 2002: 67). Another notable film in this genre was Nemai Ghosh's *Chhinnamool* ('The Uprooted', 1950). *Chhinnamool* tried to portray as realistically as possible the havoc that Partition resulted, which could be seen on the streets of Calcutta and all over the city. To capture the temper of the time, much of the movie was shot on location at Sealdah railway station that swarmed with refugees under temporary sheds. This sort of emotively charged documentation of the refugee exodus is rare, however extensive is the catalogue of relevant Indian cinema. Compared to *Chhinnamool*, Ghatak's *Nagarik*, which was ready for release a year later, 'had extensive faults due to Ghatak's initial lack of command over filmic language and his overtly Marxist pedagogy' (Chattopadhyay 2007: 266).

The question, however, remains as to why Ghatak, who was a self-professed Marxist and who was in a way obsessed with the trauma of Partition and as such was in a position to directly connect his experience to his creations, took recourse to melodrama like the Bombay films which we have discussed above. Probably the answer may be given this way: 'A key difference between realism and melodrama is that realism posits a material universe while melodrama includes a metaphysical/occult component—often a moral order which rewards and punishes—driving the narrative and manifesting itself in devices like coincidences' (Raghavendra 2014: 86). Ghatak, who has been called 'the troubled signature of epic melodrama in Calcutta' (Sengupta 2005: 121), took recourse to melodrama in both his *Meghe Dhaka Tara* and *Subarnarekha*, particularly the latter. In this movie, through the characters of Ishwar and Sita, the director combines two tragedies, one of family dislocation and the other of millions of displaced people groping in the dark as refugees on Calcutta streets. It was not easy to narrate this complex interconnection for it would inevitably remain incomplete. It was, therefore, necessary for him to find the solution in some melodramatic sequences like Ishwar visiting a prostitute only to find that she was none other than his lost sister, Sita (Biswas 2008: 213–14, Chattopadyay 2007: 266, Vasudevan 2010: 30). Vasudevan writes: 'The event [Partition] marked his work deeply, generating a highly innovative inquiry into the ramifications of this violent rupture. Using mythic and epic resonances in his delineation of characters and settings, his work documented how displacement had blighted attempts to put a world together again, whether on the basis of the household, the radical collective, or the ground of a realist and rationalist ontology' (Vasudevan 2010: 306).

There were other popular melodramatic movies too in this genre, such as *Agneepariksha* (1954), *Harano Sur* (1957), *Bipasha* (1962) and many others, most of which were acted by the legendary romantic duo Uttam Kumar and Suchitra Sen. The duo 'lent its name to the era (1950s and 1960s) and can be used as a sign for a large number of films that did not actually feature the stars together'. Several of these movies fell in the category of the 'Comedy of Remarriage' talked about by Stanley Cavell in the context of Hollywood films—by meeting just once is not the complete story, the couple must re-meet to complete the story. In many of the Uttam–Suchitra movies, the hero and heroine were without parents or at least their presence was negligible. Compared to the present-day TV serials where families are shown so prominently, this parental absence is easily noticeable (Biswas 2000: 122, Biswas 2008: 215–16). This was same like many Bollywood movies as we have discussed above.

# Pakistani Cinema

Prior to its decline after Partition, the Lahore film industry was rated highly in terms of production. It was one of the world's top 10 film industries. While the first Bollywood movie, *Harishchandra*, was released in 1913, the first movie from Lahore to be released was *Daughter of Today* in 1924, produced by G.K. Mehta. Against the background of the Islamic drive after the creation of Pakistan, coupled with the exodus of Hindu and Sikh artistes, the Lahore film industry suffered a lot. Film-making as a general rule was looked down upon as un-Islamic. The Minister of Industries Sardar Abdur Rab Nishtar announced: 'In principle Muslims should not get involved in filmmaking. Being the work of lust and lure, it should be left to the infidels'. But the left-oriented artists, patronised by people like Faiz, continued to have their presence in the industry to the chagrin of the vigilant authorities who came in action to identify this so-called Red threat. In 1954, W.Z. Ahmed's *Roohi*, a socialist kitsch, was banned. For decades, films on poverty-related themes were censored. During General Ayub Khan's rule (1958–69), two shrewd bureaucrats, Qudratullah Shahab and Altaf Gauhar, were mandated to see to it that Pakistani films projected the ideology of Pakistan. These two bureaucrats vitalized the Department of Film and Publications at the Ministry of Information, the first major attempt of which was *Nai*

*Kiran*, a feature-length documentary. It exposed the greedy politics of the country probably to make a pro-military political statement. Shahab who wrote the story was paid Rs. 20,000 in 1959 (remember that Sadat Hasan Manto was paid barely Rs. 200 for a story). Fearing that prominent artistes would avoid associating themselves with such undertakings, the state empowered the producers of *Nai Kiran* to book any artiste for their film. Those who refused to comply were coerced by the police. For instance, Noor Jehan had originally refused to act in the film, but when harassed she had to relent (Sulehria 2013).

Still, the impact of Partition on Pakistani movies though limited was not non-existent. In 1959, the talented producer, director, poet and writer Saifuddin Saif made a Punjabi film, *Kartar Singh*, which depicted a true story of the atrocities and violence perpetrated by various communities during the Partition. The theme song of the movie was Amrita Pritam's classic poem *Ajj Aakhan Waris Shah Nuu*.[18] Many years later, in 2003, in another context and against another background, Sabiha Sumar's *Khamosh Pani* (Silent Waters) was released. It depicted the trauma of a Sikh woman who had converted to Islam during the Partition tragedy and had become a practicing Muslim only to face wrath of her militant Islamist son for whom she was a non-believer who could not be trusted. According to an analyst:

> *Khamosh Pani* structurally connects this demonization and entrapment of femininity under the religious, state-sponsored orthodoxy in Zia's Pakistan to its traumatic prehistory: the ethnicized rape and abduction of women during the 1947 Partition.... [It] showcases how hard-line Islamist ideology used the fact of the Partition and the creation of Pakistan for Muslims, to justify the turn away from secular democracy and into an Islamic state. Simultaneously, the constant parallel between the scenes of Partition violence and the contemporary fundamentalist violence structurally and ideologically links the revival of ethnic politics in the seventies, and its destruction of pluralism, to the gendered ethnic violence during Partition. (Daiya 2011: 598–99)

## East Bengali/East Pakistani Cinema

The refugees in East Bengal consisted of Bengali Muslims from West Bengal and Urdu-speaking Muslims mostly from Bihar and UP but also from some other parts of India, such as Hyderabad. There is little evidence of either their participation in the East Bengal film industry or their being the subject matter of contemporary cinema. In any case at the time of Partition, the cinema industry of East Bengal was in its rudimentary stage. Otherwise, devoid of competition from Calcutta, it could have gained substantially. Partly because of its underdevelopment and partly because of discouragement of such an art form by the Pakistani authorities, East Bengali cinema took almost a decade to show some signs of action.

In spite of their underdevelopment, Dhaka cinema studios, however, had a tradition of producing movies. It was as early as in 1927–28 that *Sukumari* (The Beautiful Lass) and in 1931 *The Last Kiss* were produced, both directed by Ambuj Gupta. In the post-Partition phase, a few short movies and documentaries were released, namely, *In Our Midst* (1948), *Salamat* (Remaining Safe, 1954), *Bonya* (The Flood, 1954) and *Aappayan* (The Reception, 1954) (Hussain 2013: 40). East Bengal those days had 92 cinema theatres, most of which showed foreign movies, including Indian. This situation must change, that is how the director of the statistical department of the East Bengal government, Abdus Sadeq, said in January 1953. Although the department encouraged the local movie makers, it did not enthuse the non-Bengali producers who had a disdain for Dhaka as a place conducive for movie-making because of its damp and wet climate. For example, Fazle Dossani virtually debunked the idea of making movies in Dhaka for the same reason. This annoyed the local producers, and one of them, Abdus Jabbar Khan, picked up the gauntlet to declare that he would produce a movie in less than two to three years. He started the shooting for his *Mookh O Mukhosh* (The Face and the Mask) in 1954 and released the same in 1956. It was a great boost for the East Bengali movie makers. Abdul Kalam Shamsuddin, editor of *Azad* magazine, said emotionally that 'it was not merely a challenge for Jabbar but it was the challenge for the entire Bengali nation'. The movie ran full house for four weeks in Dhaka. Within nine months after the release of the movie, on 3 April 1957, the then industry and commerce minister of the Provincial Council, Sheikh Mujibur Rahman, passed the East Pakistan Film Development Corporation to further encourage the local film industry. The Film Development Corporation, however, encountered severe roadblocks after the military takeover of Pakistan in 1958 (Dastidar 2013: 71–72, Rafiq 2013: 56–57).

In the development of the film industry in East Bengal, the role played by the film magazines and journals was significant. Some of the notable ones were *Cinema* (Bogura, 1950), *Udayan* (Chattogram, 1950), *Chitrakash* (Dhaka, 1959), *Roopchhaya* (Dhaka, 1951), *Chhayabani* (Dhaka, 1951), *Jhhinook* (Dhaka, 1966) and *Sachitra Sandhani* (Dhaka, 1966). Some of them continued to exist for a long time (Hussain 2013: 42).

It must be confessed that in the above discussion, we could hardly identify the impact of Partition or the arrivals of Muslim refugees in East Pakistan. One may to some extent conclude by the experience of Kalim Sarafi that the Partition had certainly cast its shadow on this art form. In the life of Sarafi, we can find some similarities with Saadat Hasan Manto and Sahir Ludhianvi (discussed above) who could not adjust in the suffocating cultural atmosphere of Pakistan. Sahir Ludhianvi even had to return to India to escape the claustrophobia. But, unlike Sahir, who made his presence felt in Hindu/Urdu cinema of Bombay through his glorious lyrics that continue to be popular, Sarafi's career in East Bengal was one of frustration and dejection. In Kolkata, he felt the heat of communalism that made him migrate to East Bengal, but there he was looked down upon for his love for Rabaindra Sangeet and general disapproval of religious conservatism (Basu Ray 2013: 133–36).

## Drama

Compared to cinema, the impact of Partition on drama was less visible. Barring Mumbai, where the Sindhi refugees had generally settled, in other places where most of the West Punjab refugees were rehabilitated, notably Delhi, there was not much of a tradition of drama in any case. Let us, therefore, see what kind of influence the East Bengal refugees had on the Bengali theatre, which had a long tradition of staging drama in various formats. Given the fact that millions of Bengali refugees took shelter in Calcutta itself, which hugely dislocated the civic life of the city, one would imagine that the refugee phenomenon would be the subject matter of a large number of plays. But it was not so. It has been said that whether it was in painting or other forms of art, 'nowhere was this paralytic lack of response more in evidence than in the theatre' (Raha 2001: 153). Since just a few years ago (in 1943), there was the great Bengal famine, and since there was a leftist response to that event in the form of popular plays, the presence of refugees got mixed up with that event and the phenomenon was viewed in terms of class conflict and the oppression of the poor and dispossessed in the hands of the privileged sections of people. In this context, the role of the Indian People's Theatre Association (IPTA) is to be particularly recognized.

Bengal had a tradition of political plays. In the early decades of the 20th century, patriotic plays of Girish Ghosh, Jyotirindranath Tagore, Dwijendra Lal Roy and K.P. Vidyabinode had started the tradition. In the form of *jatra* (a conventional Bengali theatre form where the audience sat on three sides of the stage, which itself was without sets and props), Mukunda Das preached nationalism. In the 1930s, Manmatha Ray made use of mythological legends as allegories to make political statements on contemporary events (Raha 2001: 162). Against this background, it is rather surprising that the theatre community of Bengal would not adequately respond to the massive post-Partition displacement of people and the huge refugee influx in Calcutta in particular. There can be four possible explanations.

One, the refugee issue got mixed up within the overall leftist diatribe of the IPTA, which we have referred to above. Two, IPTA, which was in the forefront of political theatre, did not find the post-independence situation conducive to promote its leftist ideology, as the Indian state had identified it as one of its enemies as reflected in the suppression of the Telengana movement in the south. The CPI to which the IPTA belonged, which was able to popularize itself after the Soviet entry into the Second World War in support of the Allied Powers, found an altogether new situation 'where the common imperialist enemy had left the scene and the recently empowered bourgeois leadership [had] engaged itself in crushing the various mass upsurges and the influence of the Communists' (Bhattacharya 2009: 172–73). The IPTA found itself unprepared to deal with the situation.

> The vanguard position which organizations like IPTA had achieved over a broad congregation of intellectuals and artists in the earlier period was being lost in this critical situation, and the problems of growth which it had been facing even in 1945–46 became paralyzing after 1947. At least from early 1948, official and unofficial attacks were also concentrated against IPTA programmes and activists. The theatre movement still went on sporadically, but the character of purposive intercommunication which the organization had given to it was severely hampered. (Bhattacharya 2009: 172–73)

The third reason was that the IPTA had become so ideologically committed that it became suffocating for many who had supported its cause but were not willing to sacrifice their professional theatrical standards just for the sake of an ideology. For example, Sombhu Mitra, who had pioneered the successful IPTA production *Nabanna* (1944), drifted away from the organization and started his own troupe called Bohurupee, without, of course, compromising on his leftist ideology as was reflected in its first production, a remake of *Nabanna* in 1948 (Raha 2001: 166). And fourthly, plays had become more expensive to watch compared to cinema, and unlike the latter, they dealt with depressing themes which the escapist audience in general had no stomach for, particularly in those gloomy days (Chattopadhyay 2002: 302).[19]

Besides the above-mentioned plays, one may refer to a few other plays as well that represented the Partition and its attendant tragedy. It may be noted that Ritwik Ghatak, who is generally known for his films, was a playwright to start with. In the preface of his 1947 play, *Dalil* (The Property Deed), he said the Partition tragedy was too pervasive and intense to be captured in anything but an epic (Chattopadhyay 2002: 301). His other plays were *Saanko* (The Boat), *Sei Meye* (That Girl) and *Jwalonto* (Burning). In all his plays, the underlying theme was the tragedy of displacement (Chakrabarty 2014: 7–8). Two other plays that directly dealt with the theme were Salil Sen's *Natun Ihudi* (The New Jews, 1950) and Tulsidas Lahiri's *Banglar Maati* (The Earth of Bengal, 1953). While both the plays depicted the contemporary socio-economic tragedy, there was an undercurrent of nostalgia in both the plays of an undivided Bengal, the division of which had started with Lord Curzon's effort to divide it into two parts in 1905, though it had not succeeded then. There was indeed a *bhadralok* connection in this outlook. Jayanti Chattopadhyay, who has analysed these two plays, writes: 'The nationalist elites of Bengal, predominantly the *bhadralok,* remained comfortably ensconced in their position as leaders of the society as well as the nation that they had imagined into existence till the 1940s. Then came the war, the Famine and lastly the Partition—events that shook the very existence of this class' (Chattopadhyay 2002: 311). Besides, one may also mention Digindrachandra Bandyopadhay's play *Bastuvita* and Bijon Bhattacharya's *Gotrantar* (Gangopadhyay 2014: 49).

## Bhojpuri Drama

It is interesting to note that Partition had an impact on Bhojpuri folk drama also, and this impact seems to be persistent. In many popular plays that continue to be enacted in the Bhojpur region of UP and Bihar, there are indirect but clear references to the Partition of the country often represented through the jealousy factor of the younger brother in a joint family (by implication the demand for Pakistan by the Muslims) or by the scheming tactics of an outsider meaning the British or the caprices of leaders like Jinnah and Nehru. To be underlined is the fact that religion is considered the villain in these plays, which not only leads to the division of the country but continue to divide the society (Tiwari 2002: 70–73).

# Painting and Photography

Like other art forms, in the field of painting and photography also, the refugee phenomenon (which included the famine refugees in Calcutta) did not leave much visible mark in Bengal barring the sketches and paintings of Zainul Abedin (1914–76), Chittaprosad (1915–78) and Ganesh Haloi and the photographs of Sunil Janah (1918–2012). 'But the scanty number of such exceptions underlined the atrophy of sensibility' (Raha 2001: 153). In the sketches of Haloi, who was born in Mymensingh in East Bengal and migrated to Calcutta in 1950 as a refugee, one gets the traces of his psyche formed through his childhood experience as a refugee. 'Everything begins in pain', said Haloi. He also said: 'I try to fit the irregular movements of life into the artificial boundaries of paintings'.[20] Haloi's works concentrated mostly on abstract renderings of landscapes in which the nostalgia for a lost world pervaded.

So far as photography is concerned, the 1998 feature story on Janah in the *Frontline* magazine was conspicuous by the absence of any reference to Janah's paintings on Bengal refugees, though he very much belonged to that time and photographed on other contemporary events (Ramachandran 1998). However, in the 2013 OUP compilation of Janah's photographs in *Photographing India,* there is at least 'one shot from the aftermath of the Partition of a child with a parrot and dog in a refugee hut. It is a powerful image that marries innocence and destruction, hope and futility, all soaked in familial longing' (Sen 2013: 58–59). Still, the explanation for this scanty representation of the refugee issue in contemporary paintings and photographs can be the same as given above in the context of Bengali drama.

In Punjab, the impact of Partition was reflected in the paintings of Satish Gujral. His works reflected the tragedy of the time by expressing his uncontrollable emotions on the contemporary events. Among his notable paintings in this regard were Mourning En-Masse (1947–48), Mourning En-Masse II (1948), Dance of Destruction (1950), The Pilgrim (1952), Sermon on the Mount (1952) and Snare of Memory (1954). He was probably 'the only one who has tackled a difficult and painful subject with conviction' … 'without any artistic guile, since he had by the early 1950s acquired a good grounding in his craft' (Malik 2002: 81).[21]

# Music and Lyrics

So far as music and lyrics are concerned, there is no visible impact of Hindu–Muslim migrations, though IPTA, which we have discussed above in the context of drama, included many notable names like Pandit Ravi Shankar, Sahir Ludhianvi (also mentioned in the section above on cinema) and Kaifi Azmi (Kalidas 2013: 9). What is, however, most fascinating is the impact of Goan (a Portuguese colony reclaimed by India in 1961) musicians on Hindi film music, which is largely unsung and unnoticed. If the 1940s through 1960s period is known to be the golden age of Hindi film melodies,[22] it was equally the golden age of fusion music, long before Ravi Shankar brought it to the world stage—the fusion of Indian ragas and western instruments and jazz. It was possible only because there was a huge migration of Goan musicians to Bombay. Here is what a researcher in the field writes:

> The arc of their [the Goan Catholic musicians] stories—determined by the intersection of passion and pragmatism, of empire and exigency—originated in church-run schools in Portuguese Goa and darted through royal courts in Rajasthan, jazz clubs in Calcutta and army cantonments in Muree. Those lines eventually converged on Bombay's film studios, where the Goan Catholic arrangers worked with Hindu music composers and Muslim lyricists in an era of intense creativity that would soon come to be recognised as the golden age of Hindi film song. (Fernandes 2004: 1)

The journey of the Goan musicians did not always end at Bombay, but it often served as 'a stepping stone to other territories held by the British', such as East Africa as well as other parts of the subcontinent, mostly in the princely courts (Fernandes 2004: 3–5).

In the realm of Hindi film music, the Partition had a significant impact, though it is not always recognized. In the 1930s and early 1940s, film music was a mix of Indian classical music as well as folk music. In this, the Bengal music industry had a significant impact because of two things, one that the Calcutta-based studio, the New Theatres, was a leading film studio in India those days which produced mostly Hindi films, which invariably had many songs, and two, these songs derived considerably from the folk music tradition of Bengal as well as from Rabindra Sangeet. But the sentimental and melodious appeal of these songs was seriously challenged by

> the sudden and robust calls of the Punjab in a film from Lahore (*Khazanchi*, 1945) which shocked the nation by its appealing vulgarity. A new conception was born. Rhythm, which had hitherto been dormant shot up

in glaring prominence while melody which had been so far following set semi-classic formulae suddenly welded itself into catching, almost folk-like, and haunting shapes. (Bhatia 1961: 25)

Following the Partition and the resultant migration of many important artistes and technicians from Lahore film industry to Bombay, which we have discussed above, this new trend took the shape of a 'Bhangra-inspired music: a whole-scale importation from the West. The more vulgar the "find" the better. The famous champion of this Western "oompism" [sic] was Naushad and later O.P. Nayyar…. Naushad adopted the West without ever fully understanding it' (Bhatia 1961: 25).

# Migration of Bhojpuri Music

One of the most fascinating migration stories is the migration of Bhojpuri music beyond the South Asian region along with the indentured Indian workers in the British plantations in several parts of the British empire. Bhojpuri folk music's influence on Caribbean pop music, which Surabhi Sharma's documentary, *Jahaji Music*, brilliantly presents, is one such example. The idea of the film came from Tejaswini Niranjana's work (2006). After having heard Goan musician Remo Fernandes, Niranjana observed that his music contained strains of the Trinidadian Calypso. Intrigued, she contacted Fernandes who responded with enthusiasm. Sharma notes:

> This was the journey Tejaswini asked me to document: Remo's encounter with the music and musicians of Jamaica and Trinidad. But this journey had to resonate, I felt, with other journeys—of African slaves and Indian indentured labourers being shipped to Jamaica and Trinidad to work on the colonial sugar plantations in the mid nineteenth century. The world was on the move.[23]

According to ethnomusicologist, Manuel (2012: 115):

> Indo-Caribbean music culture is a rich and heterogeneous entity, comprising syncretic commercial popular hybrids like chutney-soca, unique neo-traditional forms like tassa drumming and local-classical singing, and traditional genres like *chowtal* which are essentially identical to their South Asian forebears.

The Bhojpuri connection of the Indian Bhojpuri-speaking Indian diasporas, particularly through Bhojpuri movies, has been noted by many.

The noted Hindi film song singer Udit Narayan's recent Bhojpuri flick *Kab Hoi Gavna Hamar* (English: When would I go to my husband) shot in Mauritius, which depicted the plight of these migrant workers brought there 150 years ago, was successful not only in Mauritius but also in several parts of India, encouraging Narayan to produce more movies in Bhojpuri (Abbi 2013: 56–57). The songs in these movies are runaway hits.

## Migration of Food

In his essay: 'Food and the Making of the Nation', the popular food and culinary columnist, Pushpent Pant, writes:

> Through millennia, imperial armies and caravans of traders have marched through ancient routes, criss-crossing Bharat, transporting goods and ideas—including the culinary—in an almost ceaseless flow. From India, as a land of diverse nations, to a unified nation-state has been a long journey, and the contribution of Indian cuisines in this evolutionary process is usually overlooked. (Pant 2013: 2)

By reading his essay, one realizes how food as well can have a nation-building function. As man migrates from one place to another, he not only carries with him his culinary preferences but also comes in contact with other tastes preferred by his neighbours. In the process, a two-way communication takes place, resulting in exposures to all kinds of cuisines that in due course lead to many culinary innovations.

The Punjabi refugee arrivals in Delhi during the Partition led to new dishes that the Muslim-dominated Delhi was hardly familiar with. A new kind of restaurants called dhabas became popular, which served such typical Punjabi dishes as *chhole bhature* (a typical Punjabi gram/chickpea curry served with fried Indian bread), *kulfi faluda* (an Indian version of ice cream served with boiled noodles), *makke di roti* (bread made out of corn flour), *sarso da saag* (a curry made of mustard leaves), *gajar ka halwa* (a sweetmeat prepared with milk and carrot), *Karachi da halwa* (a sweetmeat supposed to have originated in Karachi), tandoori chicken and so on. In every way, there was an effort to recreate Lahore in Delhi. So much was this nostalgia that the famous Volga restaurant of Lahore was reproduced in Delhi with the same name (Kumari 2013: 66–67). As the Punjabi refugees moved to other parts of India in search of better opportunities

> [T]hey carried with them the *tandoor*, the clay oven, that had served in happier times as the *sanjha chulha*—community stove—around which

women gathered to gossip, sharing their joys and sorrows as they waited their turn to bake bread. In these sadly changed circumstances, the *tandoor* was pressed into service by intrepid and enterprising refugees to provide hot, nourishing meals tasting like home-cooked food at an affordable price. *Dal-roti* was the staple; *bhartha* [a particular north Indian delicacy made from burnt eggplants] a treat, all of which could be cooked in the *tandoor*. The rest of the country was introduced to the magic of the *tandoor* without suffering the trauma of bloodshed and arson. (Pant 2013: 21)

In Bengal, which had a huge culinary tradition (Basu 2012: 137–62, Ray 2012: 703–29), still it is not easy to come across any dedicated research on the subject. One can, however, draw certain broad perspectives about post-colonial Bengali food habits from the following passage which discusses the impact of the 1943 famine. Since we have tried to draw some common impacts of the famine and the trauma of Partition refugees in the context of our discussion on Bengali drama, the same justification is here.

> The 'purity' of food or caste remained in texts, but the materiality of the situation made the fluidity of caste much more palpable. The famine almost did away with caste rules regarding interdining. In Calcutta, Hindus received cooked food from the Muslims and vice versa. In Bibhutibhushan Bandyapadhyay's novel *Ashani Sanket* (Sign of Thunder), also about the Bengal Famine of 1943, even the priestly class was ready to eat snails (eaten by the lower castes) when the famine struck them. These violent images left indelible marks on the discourse of taste that the Bengali Hindu middle class had constructed as an epitome of aesthetic and refined gastronomic practices. (Ray 2012: 728)

Similarly, the East Bengali (Baangal) refugees, who mostly belonged to the lower castes, introduced new ways of cooking fish and vegetables to the West Bengali (Ghoti) upper castes. Prior to the refugee movement, West Bengali food was relatively bland. East Bengalis introduced spicy and hot cuisines. Since the refugees provided cheap maids and cooks to serve at West Bengali homes, this culinary passage occurred without being noticed. In the food columns of Bengali newspapers, one keeps reading about such impacts mainly on fish preparations. Some such dishes are prawn fingers with coconut and steamed hilsa (illish) with green goad (Sengupta 2013).

Even the small Afghan refugee community in Delhi's Lajpat Nagar area is slowly entering into the capital's thriving restaurant industry through its specialized Afghan dishes like *Kabuli pulao* (a special rice preparation supposed to have originated in Kabul/Afghanistan), *chopan kebab* (special kind of cutlet made of minced meat) and *Afghani naan* (a special kind of naan/wheat flour flat bread). No surprise that the street that hosts these restaurants is called Afghan Street. As the political situation in Afghanistan remains murky, it is likely that most of these Afghans, particularly the younger generation, would refuse to make efforts to go back to their country. Afghan food, therefore, has a future for Delhi's food lovers, which over time might spread to other parts of India.[24]

## Indian Festivals Abroad

Of the Indian festivals, Diwali has become popular wherever the Indian diaspora has a visible presence. Since it is a festival of lights and fireworks accompanied by dining and much joy, it has a popular appeal with the local population. Even in far-flung New Zealand, which has a small population with a not-too-insignificant Indian minority—100,000 in a population of 4.4 million—mostly of Gujarati, Punjabi and Fijian–Indian descent, Diwali is celebrated in public places in Auckland and Wellington with great gusto. Even city councils, besides community groups and semi-government organizations, have come forward to financially support these events, which have been characterized as cultural supermarkets where one feasts on a range of social and cultural identities (Johnson 2005: 19).

## Impact on Architecture

The Partition was a turning point in Delhi's housing history, though it had no impact on Calcutta because its circumstances were different. This impact was not so much felt in Old Delhi (Shahjahanabad, the Walled City), as it was already crowded and there was not much room for refugee settlements. Still, since many Muslims had left for Pakistan and many more Hindus and Sikhs had arrived, pressure on existing houses was visibly felt, as many residents felt that earlier they used to live in *kothis* (large houses), but now they had to reconcile themselves to staying in *kothris* (small rooms). The town was essentially a residential space, but post-Partition, it became so much commercialized with small workshops coming up in large numbers that the town saw massive vertical expansion to the extent the walls could bear. The 1,240-acre Walled City was meant to accommodate 60,000 people, but within a couple of decades, it had to accommodate about 360,000 people (Mehra 1991: 8 85).

Unlike Old Delhi, New Delhi could provide the space for refugee rehabilitation. To provide maximum number of plots with a frontage, narrow strips were arranged, packed tightly like sardines. The front-to-depth ratio was sometimes as stark as 1:4. Due to the lack of funds and the key issues of survival, not many refugee families were able to construct their own houses. In the small rooms provided, however, the interior arrangements were made in distinct ways. In elite families, a living space (traditionally *baithak*) became necessary to greet guests. Residential construction in Delhi, eventually, as a result of the social potpourri of varied groups of people, became a palette of confused styles. Architect Gautam Bhatia satirically characterizes them as Punjabi Baroque, Bania Gothic, Chandni Chowk Chippendale, Marwari Mannerism, Anglo-Indian Rococo and Bengali Ascetism. His choice of grouping based on ethnic backgrounds and their misplaced means of architectural expression only goes to show the impact of migrations on the city's urban scape. 'If the view of the street in the city is strikingly discordant today, it is only because the sociological view of the urban home is in direct contrast to the collective life of the traditional house. Over the years, the single plot and individual villa became the dream of the independent Indian' (Bhatia 2002: 92).

What was this traditional house? Historically, the architecture of a house tends to be a cultural beacon, as it is built by the people, for their own use and in so being is often devoid of any superseding agenda. The house type is as a result a personal expression of its resident, historically of its designer. This could be seen, till a few decades ago, in Delhi's urban villages. Rapid urbanization has led to the sad demise of the earlier proliferant *havelis,* another noticeable result of the increase in densities caused by various migrations. These *havelis* were typically designed around a courtyard, often on a single axis with centred doors. With the growing affluence of the families, the fenestrations ameliorated. Design of doors, niches, staircases and railings all had an idiosyncratic connection with its resident. The ubiquitous courtyards helped naturally ventilate and cool the rooms in the hot, arid climate of the city. Today, in a typical street in an urban village, not more than 10 per cent of the *haveli* type remains (based on discussions with Suparna Ghosh, a Delhi-based architect).[25]

# A Research Note

The scope of the subject matter of this chapter is unending. All kinds of micro studies are possible that can look into various dimensions of migrations of cultures in South Asia. Even some macro studies can as well be attempted which the present study could not do justice to. For example, it is conceivable that the eviction of Tamils (of course, along with other Indians) from Myanmar in the early 1950s or the massive flow of Sri Lankan Tamil refugees to Tamil Nadu in the aftermath of 1983 anti-Tamil Colombo riots has left their imprints on Tamil literature and cinema, if not on other cultural productions. Likewise, the arrival of Rohingya refugees in Bangladesh in massive numbers must have left some marks on the country's literature, cinema and other art forms. Another area where huge research possibility exists is the mutual impact of Indian and Nepali migrations on respective countries' cultural productions and expressions. This limited study has not been able to address them, but their importance is recognized nonetheless.

# Notes

1. In Japan, although religion plays little role in society and politics, yet there is a temple of computer god in Tokyo known as Kanda-myojin shrine (Yamaguchi 2006: 59–60).
2. Let me reproduce here the concluding portion of a study on migration and culture: '[The argument is] that the translocation of culture is a process of dislocation, transplantation, and relocation, both painful and joyous, as immigrants invent and re-create a local culture and viable community, while they struggle to sustain local and transnational commitments. In this process of translocation, culture cannot be conceived of simply as an instrumental badge of identity; it is … a compelling moral and symbolic reality, conferring role and agency, to be struggled over by cultural actors, even when it is hybrid, contested, permeate, and open to change. If culture and traditions are often felt to be axiomatic, eternal, and hence compelling, they are nevertheless subject to challenge, transgression, or rejection by fellow migrants. In a world of transnational migrations and blurred borders, immigrant cultures cannot therefore be neatly packaged in fixed multicultural policies or subjected to loyalty tests devised by politicians in a futile attempt to create order out of ambiguity and flux. Rather, immigrant cultures are constantly evolving, historical social formations, as new arrivals and their children work to put down roots in and transform their newly adopted homes' (Werbner 2012: 14).
3. Dr. Anand Taneja, Assistant Professor, Vanderbilt University, Nashville, TN, USA. Correspondence with the author, 16 August 2013. See also Taneja (2012).
4. 'In Islamic cosmology, the jinn are a separate species of being, different from and older than humans. "He [Allah] has created man from dry clay and created the jinn from smokeless fire and made them invisible to the eyes of

men" .... Formed of a completely different substance than humans, they are also said to be physically stronger and to have the ability to shape-shift and to travel vast distances very quickly. Like humans, and unlike angels, they exercise free will and can choose between good and evil. The jinn are mortal, like human beings, but live far longer lives; some of the jinn alive today are counted among the *sahaba*, the companions of the Prophet Muhammad, having seen him personally, and heard his recitation of the Qur'an' (Taneja 2013: 140–41).

5. In post-Partition West Bengal too, Muslim graveyards and small mosques were occupied by East Bengali refugees but the difference was that unlike in Delhi they were forcibly occupied without state support. These actions, however, were not aggressively communal because of the influence of the CPI among them.

6. Bhlla is now actively engaged in enriching the digital memory library called www.1947partitionarchive.org, which by now has collected 1,100 recordings. The project showcases some of its works on YouTube and Facebook. Similarly, Guneeta Singh Bhalla's The 1947 Partition Archive is digitally storing Partition memories. Her team of 500 people from 20 countries has collected 1,200 statements since 2011 and the efforts are on as it is 'a race against time, since more witnesses are lost every day' (*Outlook,* New Delhi, 13 October 2014: 66). Recently some important documentaries have been produced to recall the Partition. Some of them are as follows: *A Season Outside* (English, 1997), *Stories My Country Told Me* (English, 2000), *Abar Ashibo Phire* (Bengali, 2004), *Anhad Baja Baajey* (Punjabi, 2004), *Partition: The Day India Burned* (English, 2007), *Crossing the Line* (English, 2007), *Rabba Hun Kee Kariya* (Punjabi, 2007), *The Sky Below* (English, 2008), *Three Women of Three Times and the Border* (English, 2011) and *Khayal Darpan* (Urdu, 2014). See Amandeep Sandhu, 'Digitising Memories', *The Hindu*, 3 August 2014.

7. In the short span of his 43-year-old life, Manto produced 22 collections of short stories, one novel, five collections of radio plays, three collection of essays, two collections of personal sketches and many movie scripts (Sharma 2014).

8. According to Ayesha Jalal, 'Combining facts collected from forays into refugee camps with elements of realistic fiction, Manto documented the multi-faceted partition miseries that have eluded professional historians due to methodological limitations of their craft' (Jalal 2012). Besides Manto, there were other writers in the same genre, for example, M. Aslam ('Raks-e-Iblis ['The Devil's Dance]), Rasheed Akhtar Nadvi ('The Fifteenth of August') and Qudratullah Shahab ('Ya Khuda' ['Oh God']). See Dutt (2010).

9. A short description and analysis of several of the books mentioned here are given in Sinha (2010). It may be noted that the backdrop of Tarashankar Bandyopadhyay's *Bipasa* was not the refugee situation in Bengal but that of Punjab. Since Bandyopadhyay was a Congress member, he had to spend a lot of time in Delhi and probably that can explain his choice of the background. Between 1960 and 1966, he was a member of the Rajya Sabha (see Sinha 2010: 75–84).

10. It may be noted that the New Theatres studio of Calcutta produced both Hindi and Tamil movies. Many of the Bengali movies had Hindi and Urdu versions. Between 1931 and 1955, it made 150 movies, after which it became defunct following court cases. In 2011, it was revived with the release of *Ami Aadu* (English: I am Aadu) (*The Hindu*, New Delhi, 26 February 2011).

11. Here is a small sample: '*Jinhe naaz hai Hind par wo kahan hai*' (all those who are proud of India, where are they) (*Pyasa*, 1957), '*Chin-o-Arab Hamara, Hindustan hamara/Rahne ko ghar nahi hai, sara hahan hamara*' (China and Arabia are ours, Hindustan is ours/there is no home to stay, yet the whole world is ours) (*Phir Subah Hogi*, 1958), '*Tu Hindu banega na Musalman banega, Insan kee aulad hai insan banega*' (You would neither become a Hindu nor a Muslim, you are the child of a human being, you would become only a human being) (*Dhool ka Phool*, 1959). Certainly this last song would not have been possible in a Pakistani movie of 1959.

12. About the importance of melodrama in our lives, Panjwani writes: 'That is the name of the game: losing yourself so as to journey into a world of fictional representations. This is what the experience of art is—whether it is a song, a tune, a novel or a film' (Panjwani 2010: 275).

13. On a lighter note, a humorous similarity is a recent Bollywood flick, *Quick Gun Murugun* (2009). It was a movie with a Telugu comedian, Rajendra Prasad, as its hero, who portrayed a Tamil character, was directed by a Bengali director, Shashank Ghosh, the makeup man was a Marathi, and the ethos and stiffness of the hero were that of a Britisher.

14. Three other major novels on Partition were Yashpal's *Jhootha Sach* (False Truth, Part I published in 1958, Part II in 1960), Rahi Masoom Raza's *Aadha Gaon* (Half-a-Village, 1966) and Abdullah Hussain's (real name Mohammad Khan) *Udaas Naslein* (The Weary Generations, 1963). According to Kuldeep Kumar, a noted literary critic, *Udaas Naslein* 'is by far the best novel ever written on the Partition' (*The Hindu*, 25 July 2015).

15. These documentaries probably had their beginning during the Second World War when the British government established the Information Films of India and the Indian News Parade to promote its war efforts (Shah 1950: 276).

16. After the decline of the Mughals it was Awadh (Lucknow) which became the centre of Muslim power and aristocracy. Notably, Lucknow was the only city in north India which did not see any Hindu–Muslim riot.

17. See also the interview of poet Gulzar in the *Frontline* (Chennai, 18 October 2013: 19).

18. It is a famous requiem about the horrors of the Partition. The poem is addressed to the historic Punjabi poet Waris Shah (1722–98), who had written the most popular version of the Punjabi love tragedy, *Heer Ranjha*. It appeals to Waris Shah to arise from his grave, record the Punjab's tragedy and turn over a new page in Punjab's history.

19. Alongside, the traditional folk culture of pantomime called *swang*, which had already entered into a phase of decline towards the end of the colonial rule, further lost its appeal. For more on the tradition of *swang*, see Sur (2013, 2014).

20. http://www.saffronart.com/auctions/PostWork.aspx?l=6859 (accessed on 4 January 2014).

21. One can get a glimpse of the painter's mind in an autobiographical article that he wrote in 2002 (see Gujral 2002).

22. It may be noted that this was the time when playback singing was gaining respectability, which was no longer ghost-singing. About the evolution of playback singing, see Indraganti (2012).

23. http://li261-173.members.linode.com/films/2007/jahaji-music (accessed on 3 March 2013).

24. Report in *Times of India*, 25 July 2015.

25. More than six decades later, in July 2014, the Land and Development Office of the Delhi government allowed the conversion of the leasehold refugee apartments in Ramesh Nagar, Patel Nagar, Tilak Nagar, Lajpat Nagar and Jungpura into freehold properties. It was also agreed to sanction their upward rise up to five floors if the ground-floor owners so agreed. The scheme was to benefit 15,000 such flat owners. *The Hindu* (New Delhi), 11 July 2014.

# 7

# Conclusion: Making Sense

*Because the human being is the connecting creature who must always separate and cannot connect without separating—that is why we must first conceive intellectually of the merely indifferent existence of two river banks as something separated in order to connect them by means of a bridge. And the human being is likewise the bordering creature who has no border. The enclosure of his or her domestic being by the door means, to be sure, that they have separated out a piece from the uninterrupted unity of natural being. But just as the formless limitation takes on a shape, its limitedness finds its significance and dignity only in that which the mobility of the door illustrates: in the possibility at any moment of stepping out of this limitation into freedom.*

—Georg Simmel, German sociologist and philosopher[1]

Everybody, including this author, is a migrant. Before he came to Delhi almost five decades ago, he lived in Bhagalpur (Bihar), where his great-grandfather had migrated from present West Bengal sometime after the 1857 revolt. Where the latter's family had originally come from, this author has no clue. His DNA may reveal that as it did in the case of *New York Times* columnist Nicholas Kristof. An 'unadulterated' Caucasian that he was, Kristof suddenly discovered that he was a Black American (Kristof 2003). On reading this author in *IIC Quarterly* (2012), where he had mentioned this story, his US-based Sri Lankan friend, Professor Sam Samarasinghe, emailed:

A couple of years ago I tested my DNA. The mythology and fact broadly match on my father's side. His origins (150,000 years) can be traced back to the lower Nile region in South Sudan. His ancestor had moved north to Egypt, then moved towards Iraq, then probably took the Silk Route crossing

Turkmenistan and Afghanistan to northern India/Nepal. The arrow stops there. I should claim that my father was related to Buddha but that may not go down well with the Sinhala Buddhists whose belief about the conception of Buddha is similar to the view of Christian fundamentalists' view of Christ's conception.

Human beings are perpetual wanderers. Just as birds, animals, winds and rivers know no borders, humans too once used to move freely across boundaries. The rise of nation-states restricted their movements. The introduction of passports during the First World War made them even more difficult.[2] Since borders are now strictly enforced, migration as a regular phenomenon has come to an end. Exceptions are the routine small-scale immigrations to the United States under their immigration quota system and other migrations to erstwhile colonial nations or to economically successful nations in general such as America, Australia, Germany or some EU countries. According to the World Migration Report 2013, there were 232,000,000 international migrants. Contrary to common perception, migrations from developing to developed countries accounted for only 37 per cent while those from one developing country to another accounted for more than 60 per cent. For instance, 35 per cent of Asian migrants migrate within the region. This is because of their weak border control mechanisms and ethno-religious and economic reasons. During the past few decades, the number of people living outside the country of their birth has more than doubled, from 80,000,000 to 180,000,000. One out of every 35 persons is a migrant. It is estimated that if the migrants could form their own state, it would be the fifth largest in the world (Human Development Report 2009, International Labour Organization 2010, International Organisation of Migration (IOM) 2013).[3]

Interestingly, however, the World Migration Report mentioned above only marginally referred to the South Asia. Since migration-related academic literature is mostly produced in the West, South Asia largely remains unrepresented barring such matters which are relevant for global security or economy. Thus, the Afghans in Pakistan and South Asian migrants to the West or Gulf regions, who send large remittances back home, matter much. About past experiences too, most Western studies mention the migrations of 50 million Britons and Europeans between 1846 and 1930 to the Americas, Australia, New Zealand and South Africa. They also refer to the 12 million refugees that West Germany hosted between 1945 and 1959, raising its labour force from 21 million to 25 million. But they seldom discuss Indian migrations to various parts of the world as indentured labour or as trading communities barring a few studies (for example, see Oonk 2007, 2013). The fact that South Asia witnessed massive movements of people in the wake of India's Partition remained under-researched till recently. It is estimated that by now about 50 million South Asians have crossed borders intra-regionally for either permanent or semi-permanent settlement in their new abodes. For ethnic, political or practical reasons, the host communities generally tolerate them if not actually welcome them. Of course, depending on circumstances, they sometimes invite the ire of certain political forces, once again for the same ethnic, political or practical reasons. It is this paradox that the present book has tried to unravel. The region not only has created millions of refugees but has also taken care of them in spite of all odds.

This benign outlook is embedded in South Asia's shared history. Notwithstanding, so much of animosity between India and Pakistan displayed through their public posturing (they have fought three wars and also the Kargil war), Indians and Pakistanis feel at home in each other's country. Anand Patwardhan's anti-nuke documentary/film 'War and Peace' produced right after the back-to-back nuclear tests by India and Pakistan in May 1998 was hugely appreciated in both countries at the popular level in spite of all hurdles that the dominant political forces in the countries tried to put up (Patwardhan 2010: 95–102). The runaway success of Kabir Khan's Bollywood flick *Bajrangi Bhaijan* (2015), which portrays India-Pakistan relationship in positive terms yet again proves the point. The entertainment industry of the region wants to see a borderless South Asia.

Everything, however, is not Bollywood. There are deep-seated intercommunal suspicions which serve as both the cause and consequence of interstate migrations. These collective memories often play havoc. In South Asia riots victims have experienced both good and bad people from the attacking community, but during the post-traumatic stress they tend to mostly recall their bad experiences. This was evident among East Bengali refugees in Kolkata, even though not all had directly experienced Muslim violence (Chatterjee. n.d.: 2). Psychology of fear often matters. For example, the fear psychosis that had gripped Kashmiri Hindus of the valley in the early 1990s, which led to their flight to Jammu and Delhi, was the result of militant propaganda either through mosque loudspeakers or through threatening leaflets distributed overnight. The terrorized Pandit community was left with no option other than leaving the valley. It was not material how many Pandits were actually killed, indeed not many. In the Pakistan–Bangladesh context, it worked differently in Pakistan. Its memories about the way it treated the Bengalis remain shrouded in 'a fog of confusion' or lost in 'collective amnesia'. Many textbooks used in Pakistani schools tend to whitewash the anti-Bengali atrocities and falsely claim that America wanted to divide Pakistan (Bass 2013: 330).

Beyond memory recall, migrations are relevant for contemporary politics. As soon as the initial sympathy for the refugees dries up, political conflicts arise over power sharing. Even a homogenous Jew-welcoming state of Israel has experienced that Jews who arrived later faced hostility of the earlier immigrants. Likewise, the later European settlers in America encountered the hostility of earlier settlers. The later Chinese and Japanese immigrants in America had the same experience, although they all were subjected to racial discrimination. In South Asia too, similar patterns have been noticed. There were social and political tensions between West Bengalis and East Bengali refugees in post-Partition Bengal. Even the caste variable associated with East Bengali migrant groups, which remained dormant for a long time, has emerged as a factor in recent elections. In North India, the establishment of the BJS (1951), precursor of the BJP, was the direct outcome of the arrival of Hindu/Sikh refugees from West Punjab in droves. In Pakistan, the Muhajir and Afghan refugees' experiences tell the same story. Once the most valued component of Pakistan politics Muhajirin are now the bête noire of almost every other ethnic group, namely, Punjabi, Pashtoon and Sindhi, although they themselves may have their own inter-ethnic contradictions.

Closely connected to politics is the issue of national security. Although the connection between migration and security was always recognized, after 9/11 it has assumed greater salience. A 2004 Nixon Center document noted: 'Immigration and terrorism are linked—not because all immigrants are terrorists but because all, or nearly all, terrorists in the West have been immigrants'. The report cited Rohan Gunaratna's claim that 'all major terrorist attacks conducted in the last decade in North America and Western Europe, with the exception of Oklahoma City, have utilized migrants' (Adamson 2006: 195). In South Asia, terrorists do not have to depend on migrants as the region's social base is even otherwise conducive, in which migrations play a contributory role. It works in two ways. Terrorists in South Asia operate either through their diaspora networks or through covert assistance from their co-ethnics in the target country. In India, insurgents in Kashmir, North East or Punjab (in the 1980s) are known for their co-ethnic, cross-border and diaspora links. The assassination of Rajiv Gandhi in 1991 was carried out by Sri Lankan Tamil refugees in Tamil Nadu. Prime Minister Sheikh Hasina Wajed of Bangladesh suspects that threats to her regime, if not life, emanate also from pro-Islamic elements within the illegal Bangladeshi community in India.

All states are duty-bound to control the migrant flows, and South Asian states are not exceptions. But in these days of Human Rights awareness, no state is able to assert its sovereign rights without fetters. Even their authority to put up border fences is questioned. In any case, fences have limited efficacy to prevent illegal migrations if the US–Mexico border fence experience is any guide. There are about 11,400,000 unauthorized persons in the United States, a majority of whom are Mexicans, strict US immigration control notwithstanding. Even there are unauthorized Indians. It is estimated that out of 3,000,000 Indians in America, 450,000 are unauthorized residents (*The Hindustan Times,* 21 November 2014). When such things can happen in America with its best possible border surveillance and immigration control systems, one may imagine what could be the situation in South Asia. The India–Bangladesh border fence has hardly controlled the flow of illegal Bangladeshi migrations to India. The case of Afghan refugees in Pakistan is particularly challenging because Afghanistan does not even recognize the Durand Line, which separates it from Pakistan. In a situation like this, Pakistan cannot even dream of fencing its Afghan border.

Is forcible repatriation a viable strategy which has been touted so often, say, in the case of unauthorized Bangladeshis in India? Can the experience of Sri Lankan Tamil refugees in Europe teach us any lesson in this regard? Between 1990 and 1998 there were 138,000 Sri Lankan Tamil asylum seekers in Europe. Of this, only a small fraction were granted asylum, a slightly larger number granted Temporary Right to Stay (TRS), but the majority neither. Of the 13,100 asylum applicants in 1998, only 350 got asylum and 820 TRS. For the remaining refugees, the Sri Lankan government and that of the individual European country worked out some legal repatriation frameworks. But, they hardly succeeded in terms of both actual repatriation and eventual resettlement back home. According to a 1994 Sri Lanka–Switzerland agreement, it was decided to send 350 refugees back to Sri Lanka every year. But between 1994 and 1999 only 696 refugees were repatriated. Similar was the experience with agreements signed between Sri Lanka and other European countries. Even those refugees who were repatriated had difficulties back home as they had to undergo all kinds of questioning in an atmosphere of general distrust of local Sinhalese neighbours. They often remained unemployed. All this made the returnees suffer from psychological depression (Bertrand 2004: 271–81, also see Velamati 2009).

In view of the above, one can gauge the situation in respect of any repatriation scheme if at all it is put in place for Bangladeshis or Tibetans in India. From the repatriation experience of Sri Lankan Tamils, it is clear that everything has to start with a bilateral agreement. In the case of repatriation of Bangladeshis or Tibetans from India, can there ever be agreements between India and Bangladesh or between India and China, both seemingly impossible? Bangladesh does not even acknowledge the presence of Bangladeshis on Indian soil. There is a vast difference between Sri Lankan Tamil migrations to Europe and those of Bangladeshis to India. In the first case, it is not because of economic hardships at home but because of insecurity at home. But in the case of Bangladesh, it is economic hardship, not security to life. As such, while in the Sri Lankan case, even if repatriated according to a legal framework, there is no guarantee that the returnees would be happy and safe. In the Bangladesh case, if and when the Bangladeshis are sent back, the Bangladesh government is duty bound to see to it that they do not go back to India. How and why should any Bangladesh government guarantee that? The situation would, therefore, be back to square one, once again forcing them to migrate to India, and once again, illegally. In respect of Tibetan refugees, an India–China agreement is virtually impossible. China would love to take the Tibetans back, but would the Tibetans go? They fear massive repression back home in the Tibetan Autonomous Region of China and also know that it would mean the total destruction of their culture. Indeed, neither the Tibetan refugees nor the Indian government is even thinking on those lines partly because of the human rights situation in Tibet and partly because of the inherent complexity involved with regard to India–China relations, which at the best of times are not free from tensions. In any case, repatriation as a refugee relief strategy has not succeeded much in any part of the world. In South Asia, efforts at repatriation of India-based Chakmas to Bangladesh and Nepal-based Lhotshampas to Bhutan have massively failed (Subba 2004: 475).

In South Asia, two ideas have been floated to address the issue of cross-border movements of people: one, to work for a region-centric refugee regime, and two, to deal with the situation politically through the only regional mechanism that is available, namely, SAARC. Efforts aimed at achieving the first are still at the drawing board stage, though many years have lapsed from its inception (discussed in Chapter 5). Most of the regional states are seemingly happy with their existing legal arrangements to address the problem, and therefore have little interest in a regional refugee regime. Domestic laws offer them enough scope for political manoeuvring on a case-by-case basis without getting embroiled into international legal hassles. Mercifully, the domestic judicial systems are by and large helpful in addressing the migrant/refugee issues from humanitarian angles. With regard to the second possible mechanism, that is SAARC, less said the better. First, the grouping has the statutory handicap of not taking up any bilateral and political question, and second, because of India–Pakistan congenital rivalry nothing effectively moves forward (Partha Ghosh 2013a, 2013b). Against this background, an innocuous subject like a regional refugee convention under the auspices of SAARC does not make any real sense.

Finding a solution to the region's migrant/refugee problem through the SAARC system has other difficulties too. Regionalism itself is getting messier every day in conceptual terms. One is not sure whether globalization is promoting regionalism or actually destroying it. The most interesting feature of the present phase of globalization is its emphasis on multilateralism but it is of a different kind. It is unlike the earlier variety—UN, Group of 77 or Non-Aligned Movement. The present one is something that criss-crosses regional groupings like the Chinese checkers. On the one hand, it is potentially detrimental to regional systems and on the other supportive of members embarking upon strategies to bolster their regional systems through other regional systems. In essence, most nations operate at multiple forums without giving up their regional hats. India is a member of G-20, Brazil, Russia, India, China, and South Africa (BRICS), The Bay of Bengal Initiative for Multi-Sectoral Technical and Economic Cooperation (BIMSTEC), India–Brazil–South Africa (IBSA), and Brazil, South Africa, India and China (BASIC), at the same time it is a member of SAARC. These interlocking networks have totally distorted the concept of regionalism. The following rather incomplete list of regional and cross-regional groupings, with the number of their members in brackets, would drive the point home: Agadir (4), African Union (53), Arab League (22), ASEAN (10), ASEAN Regional Forum (27), BASIC (4), BIMSTEC (7), BRICS (5), Central American Common Market (20), Caribbean Community (20), Cooperation Council for the Arab States of the Gulf (Gulf Cooperation Council) (8), Central European Free Trade Agreement (16), Commonwealth of Independent States (11), Economic Community of West African States (15), EU (28), EurAsian

Economic Community (5), European Free Trade Association (4), G-8, G-20, IBSA (3), The North American Free Trade Agreement (3), SAARC (8), Shanghai Cooperation Organization (8) and UNASUR (12).

The essential question, however, is not how to find solutions to South Asia's problems in respect of its refugees, migrants and stateless persons. It is whether to treat it at all as a problem and whether laws alone can do the magic. Lao Tzu, the great Chinese philosopher, said: 'The greater the number of laws and enactments, the more thieves and robbers there will be'. Global history is replete with evidence of how humans have changed their habitats and in the process have enriched themselves as well as their host communities. Both have gained. Ram Mohun Roy spent the last three years of his life in England (effectively he had migrated) before his death in 1833. Since at that time cremation was not allowed in England, his body had to be buried, which was not be done to the Hindus or Brahmans. England allowed cremation 50 years later, as Hindus in England had grown in number.[4] Was England a loser by hosting more Hindus? In the light of the massacre of about a dozen French cartoonists in Paris in January 2015 by some disgruntled immigrant Muslim terrorists, several such questions were raised both in France and elsewhere: Whether at the root of such troubles was the failure of the West to integrate the disparate mix of its immigrant communities, particularly when they were racially different. France, which does not recognize any category other than 'French' for the purposes of its law and social justice interventions,[5] would probably be forced to reconsider its premises before long. The liberal view is that the more we coexist harmoniously the more we gain collectively. Is it not for the migrations of people across the regions that now most Singapore Indians are bilingual or multilingual? They are adept in mixing Malay and Hokkien words in their speech. In India, one comes across such expressions as Hinglish, a mixture of Hindi and English, and in China, Chinglish, a mixture of Chinese and English. America has now a Black president who had a Muslim father. The present US ambassador to India is an Indian American and so are America's two state governors.

Migrations have hugely enriched literary, musical and artistic traditions and productions. But for the arrival of African slaves in America, we would not have had the Jazz or the Blues. Arthur Flowers, a professor of literature at Syracuse University in New York, and author of novels *Another Good Loving Blues* and *De Moji Blues* writes that 'the reason the oral tradition became so powerful in African American culture is because when Africans were brought to the United States they

were systematically stripped of their culture to make them better slaves'
(workers shipped from India to the West Indies in the 19th century were
not allowed to take their musical instruments with them). All that the
slaves could carry with them was their oral tradition, which was used to
keep their culture alive. Though the circumstances were extremely hostile in many parts of the then colonies/states (it was even against the law
for the Black folks to read and write) still the essence of their culture survived through oral tradition. In the cotton plantations in the antebellum
South, these Negro slaves used to use the field hollers to communicate
with one another, without words, how they were feeling. Another slave
from across the field would respond with his own holler. This call-and-
response style is part of African music, which evolved into rock 'n' roll.
Later, 'at the time of the great migration, at the turn of the 20th century,
when Black folks moved out of the farms and into the cities of the South,
and moved from being a rural people to an urban people that the oral
traditions became art forms.... Their folk tales became literature and
their blues music became jazz' (Keyslong 2009: 48–49).

Similarly, the Chinese workers who had settled in India in the late
19th and early 20th centuries tried to maintain their cultural traditions,
though their circumstances were not as hostile as those of the Black
slaves. Over time, their interactions with the local folks influenced both
the communities culturally. Some of these Chinese learned the local
Bengali or Assamese languages and started worshipping Indian deities.
One of the Hindu Kali temples in Kolkata was frequented by so many
Chinese that people started calling it the Cheena (the Chinese) Kali. On
the other end, their unique temples, schools and restaurants enriched the
local communities (Xing 2009–10: 405–12). Drawing from these experiences, we have tried to discuss the migration of music back and forth
between India and the West Indies through the experience of indentured
labour in those islands, as well as the experiences of South Asian inter-
border migrants post-Partition (Chapter 6). This is a field where there is
enormous scope for further research.

Another dimension of the migration saga, which, unlike the above, is
negative, and which has not been discussed in the book, is in respect of
migration of the diseases. Cross-border disease transmission has been
a constant curse in human history. Historically, it has been seen that
many forms of communicable diseases have spread along with human
movements from one place to another. For example, the plague which
originated in China in 1331 reached Crimea in 1345, and soon it reached
Constantinople, Pisa and Genoa. Once the germs reached the European
ports, they spread fast to major cities. *The famous trading route that*

*had once brought prosperity to European cities was transformed into a highway of death that travelled in the shape of furry black rats.* Historian Ole Benedictow concludes that 'about 60 per cent of the population, or some fifty millions of Europe's estimated eighty million, perished from the plague and related ailments' (Chanda 2007: 229, emphasis added).

Similarly, along with the Black slaves came to America the yellow fever, hookworm and African versions of Malaria. In the early 19th century, cholera went from India's northeast to Sri Lanka, Afghanistan and Nepal and soon it reached the Arabian Peninsula, East Africa, Myanmar, China, Japan, Java, Poland, Russia, Thailand and Turkey and then Austria, Germany, Poland and Sweden and ultimately the British Isles, Canada and the United States. In the beginning of the modern times, the Spanish conquistadors devastated the Mexico City by bringing with them many European diseases. In his book *Guns, Germs and Steel* (1997: 77–78), Jared Diamond wrote:

> Small pox, measles, influenza, typhus, bubonic plague, and other infectious diseases endemic in Europe played a decisive role in European conquests, by decimating many peoples on other continents. For example, a smallpox epidemic devastated the Aztecs after the failure of the first Spanish attack in 1520.... Throughout the Americas, diseases introduced with Europeans spread from tribe to tribe far in advance of the Europeans themselves, killing an estimated 95 percent of the pre-Columbian native American population. (quoted by Bhagwati 2004: 225)

There was, however, at least one positive impact of these disease migrations. Large sums of money were allocated to do research on tropical and other diseases by the colonial rulers since mosquitoes and tsetse flies would not distinguish between the colonizers and the colonized. This is how the famous Institute for Tropical Medicine in London and the Royal Tropical Institute in Amsterdam came into being (Bhagwati 2004: 225). This line of argument, however, has been challenged on the ground that there was nothing like tropical disease and it was more an imperial project to justify the positive side of the European expansionism. Still, our argument here is that with human arrivals in a new land, there is always the possibility of new diseases entering into those areas. That is why there are so many restrictions on the import of livestock and so much paraphernalia about health checks at every point of entry in Australia and New Zealand.

In this book, we have not discussed this impact of migrations. But in the South Asian context, its relevance cannot be overemphasized, particularly because of the region's poverty and overpopulation. There is an awareness about the problem and several NGO reports and magazine/

newspaper articles on the subject, still we need more interdisciplinary research. The way severe acute respiratory syndrome (SARS), swine flu, HIV and AIDS, and drug addictions are threatening humanity in the region, their cross-border dimensions cannot be overlooked. A Background Note issued in November 2011 by the London-based think tank, the Overseas Development Institute (ODI), based on interviews of cross-border migrants between India, Nepal and Bangladesh, found that there was considerable amount of awareness among the migrants about the danger of HIV and AIDS, but because of their poverty, common sharing of living spaces and loneliness they often fell victims to these scourges. Within the rubric of non-traditional security, which includes such matters as environmental degradation, ecological imbalance, poverty and so on, it is important that we study the cross-border disease spread and their prevention/treatment. Mere national efforts would not do. In this regard, the role of SAARC becomes important in spite of its handicaps that we have mentioned. Through its technical committees and sponsored studies, it must at least create a body of literature in this regard.

Let this book conclude by saying that it has been one of the most critical experiences of South Asia to manage massive cross-national movements of people, primarily driven by fear for life. Historically, and even in present times, such migrations have been both ways—to India, and, from India, to Pakistan and from Pakistan, and similarly with many other nations. Over the past two millennia, hundreds of thousands of people have either come and settled in South Asia or left the region for good in search of better life prospects. The massive forced migration that occurred in the wake of Partition still haunts the concerned nations. Mercifully the phenomenon also unleashed human creativity in the form of literature and all other art forms. Along with humans, their cultures and habits too migrated, resulting in a wonderful mix of inventiveness ranging from music to culinary practices—all human stories in different formats. South Asia's experience, thus, stands out as an example of one of the most fascinating human sagas.

# Notes

1. This quotation is from his famous 1903 essay 'Bridge and Door' (reproduced in *Rethinking Architecture: A. Reader in Cultural Theory*, London: Routledge, 1997, page 69), cited in Patrizio n.d.: 1.

2. Introduction of the system of passport and visa has a long history, and no particular date can be assigned to this institution. Even in ancient and medieval times, important merchants were sometime made to obtain permission by the border authorities before entering into another kingdom. This indicated that some kind of documentation like modern-day passport and visa existed. In 1689 and 1727, Russia and the Chinese Qing rulers in Central Asia entered into detailed border arrangements, which made the Russian merchants present a passport to the Chinese officials at the border, who in turn provided them with Chinese documents that allowed them to travel to Beijing through a particular sanctioned route (McKeown 2008: 34). Indian and Pakistani visa holders experience the same restrictions in each other's country even today.

3. For more information refer to International Organisation of Migration (IOM; 2013)

4. Documentary *Bristol Pilgrimage: In Search of Raja by Ram Mohun Roy* by Aniruddho Sanyal (*The Times of India*, 11 January 2010).

5. Across religions, races or colours, all are French; the census does not disaggregate the information on these lines.

# References

Abbi, Kumool. 2013. 'Politics of Linguistic, Cultural Recovery and Reassertion: Bhojpuri Migrant Population and Its Films'. *Economic and Political Weekly* (Mumbai), 48 (33), August 17: 54–62.

Adamson, Fiona B. 2006. 'Crossing Borders: International Migration and National Security'. *International Security* (Cambridge, MA), 31 (1): 165–99.

Ahmed, Haroon. 1997. 'Bangladeshi Immigrants in Sindh'. In *States, Citizens and Outsiders: The Uprooted Peoples of South Asia*, edited by T. Bose and R. Manchanda. Kathmandu: South Asia Forum for Human Rights.

Ahmed, Imtiaz. 1996. 'Refugees and Security: The Experience of Bangladesh'. In *Refugees and Regional Security in South Asia*, edited by S.D. Muni and Lok Raj Baral. New Delhi: Konark.

Ahmed, Ishtiaq. 2011. *The Punjab Bloodied, Partitioned and Cleansed: Unraveling the 1947 Tragedy through Secret British Reports and First Person Interviews.* New Delhi: Rupa Publications.

Ahmed, Ishtiaq. 2012. The Lahore Film Industry: A Historical Approach. In *Travels of Bollywood Cinema: From Bombay to LA,* edited by A.G. Roy and C. Beng Huat, 55–77. New Delhi: Oxford University Press.

Aiyar, Swaminathan A. 2012. 'Declassify Report on the 1948 Hyderabad Massacre'. *Sunday Times of India* (New Delhi), 25 November.

Alexander, Horace. 1951. *New Citizens of India.* Oxford: Oxford University Press.

Ananthachari, T. 2001. 'Refugees in India: Legal Framework, Law para_bold Enforcement and Security'. Available at: http://www.worldlii.org/int/journals/ISILYBIHRL/2001/7.html- (accessed on 7 September 2014).

Andreas, Peter. 2003. 'Redrawing the Line: Borders and Security in the Twenty-first Century'. *International Security* (Cambridge, MA), 28(2), Fall: 78–111.

Anisuzzaman. 2011. 'Aamra Pakistane Elam' [in Bengali] (We Arrived in Pakistan). In *Deshbhag: Binash O Binirman* [in Bengali] (Country's Partition: Destruction and Deconstruction), edited by M. Pal, 39–55. Kolkata: Gangchil.

Asad, Zia and Zahid Gishkori. 2015. "Dual Nationality": NADRA Workers Figure in Citizenship for Sale Scandal. *The Express Tribune* (Karachi), 27 February. Available at http://tribune.com.pk/story/845010/dual-nationality-nadra-workers-figure-in-citizenship-for-sale-scandal/ (accessed on 14 August 2015).

Bagchi, Jasodhara and Subhoranjan Dasgupta (eds). 2003. *The Trauma and the Triumph: Gender and Partition in Eastern India*. Kolkata: Stree.

Bagchi, Romit. 2012. *Gorkhaland: Crisis of Statehood*. New Delhi: SAGE Publications.

Bandyopadhyay, Sandip. 1997. 'The Riddles of Partition: Memories of the Bengali Hindus'. In *Reflections on Partition in the East*, edited by R. Samaddar, 59–72. Calcutta: Calcutta Research Group.

Bandyopadhyay, Sandip. 2000. 'Millions Seeking Refuge: The Refugee Question in West Bengal: 1971'. In *Refugees in West Bengal: Institutional Practices and Contested Identities*, edited by P.K. Bose, 32–48. Calcutta: Calcutta Research Group.

Bandyopadhayay, Sekhar and Anasua Basu Ray Chaudhury. 2014. *In Search of Space: The Scheduled Caste Movement in West Bengal after Partition* as Issue No. 59 of *Policies and Practices*. Kolkata: Calcutta Research Group.

Banerjee, Paula. 1998. 'Borders as Unsettled Markers in South Asia: A Case Study of the Sino-Indian Border'. *International Studies* (New Delhi), 35 (2), 179–91.

Baral, Lok Raj. 1975. 'The Press in Nepal'. *Contributions to Nepalese Studies* (Kathmandu), 2 (1): 169–86.

Baral, Lok Raj. 1990. *Regional Migrations, Ethnicity and Security: The South Asian Case*. New Delhi: Sterling.

Baral, Lok Raj. 1994. *Nepal: Problems of Governance*. New Delhi: Konark.

Baruah, Sanjib. 1986. 'Immigration, Ethnic Conflict and Political Turmoil— Assam 1979–1985'. *Asian Survey* (Berkeley), 26 (11): 184–206.

Bass, Gary J. 2013. *The Blood Telegram: Nixon, Kissinger and a Forgotten Genocide*. New York: Alfred A. Knopf.

Bastiampillai, Bertram. 1996. 'The Changing Fortunes of an Immigrant Community, 1931–1948: The Indians in Ceylon (Sri Lanka)'. *South Asia* (Armidale) 19, Special Issue: 221–31.

Basu, Pradip. 2012. *Paribarik Probondha: Bangali Poribarer Sondorbha Bichar* [in Bengali: *An Essay on Family: Analysis of the Bengali Family Context*]. Kolkata: Gangchil.

Basu Ray, Iraban. 2013. 'Thatyachitra O Nishaat Jahan Rana' [in Bengali] (Documentaries and Nishat Jahan Rana). In *Bangladesher Anya Cinema* [in Bengali] (The Other Cinema of Bangladesh), edited by S. Saha, Vol. 4, 129–38. Kolkata: Abhijan.

Basu Raychaudhury, Anasua. 2013. 'Nationality Matters: From Statelessness to Citizenship of the Up-county Tamils in Sri Lanka'. *Purba Darshan: A Journal of Asian Studies* (Kolkata), 1, September: 79–106.

Basu Raychaudhury, Anasua and Ishita Dey. 2009. *Citizens, Non-Citizens and in the Camps Lives*. Kolkata: Mahanirban Calcutta Research Group.

Batabyal, Rakesh. 2005. *Communalism in Bengal: From Famine to Noakhali, 1943–47*. New Delhi: SAGE Publications.

Baud, Michiel and Willem van Schendel. 1997. 'Toward a Comparative History of Borderlands'. *Journal of World History*, 8 (2): 211–42.

Beniwal, Anup. 2005. *Representing Partition: History, Violence and Narration*. Delhi: Shakti Book House.

Bertrand, Didier. 2004. 'The Forced Repatriation of Tamil Asylum Seekers from European Countries to Sri Lanka and their Reintegration Process'. In O. Mishra (ed.), *Forced Migration in the South Asian Region: Displacement, Human Rights and Conflict Resolution*, 264–88. Delhi: Manak.

Bhadada, Shubhangi and Yashaswini Mittal. 2015. 'In Pursuit of Happiness: Towards Resolving the Land Rights Dilemma of Chit-Dwellers'. *Economic and Political Weekly* (Mumbai), 50 (26&27), June 27: 15–18.

Bhagwati, Jagdish. 2004. *In Defense of Globalization*. New York: Oxford University Press.

Bhalla, Alok. 2002. 'The Landscape of Memories and Writing of *Tamas*: An Interview with Bhisham Sahni'. In *Pangs of Partition: The Parting Ways*, edited by S. Settar and B. Gupta, 83–116. New Delhi: Manohar Publications.

Bhatia, Gautam. 2002. *A Moment in Architecture*. New Delhi: Tulika.

Bhatia, Rajiv. 2014. 'Hope and Angst'. *Frontline* (Chennai), May 30: 64–66.

Bhatia, Vanraj. 1961. 'Film Music'. *Seminar* (New Delhi), December: 23–26.

Bhattacharjya, Satarupa and Frank Jack Daniel. 2012. 'India Unprepared for New Myanmar'. Available at http://in.reuters.com/article/2012/02/26/india-myanmar-idINDEE81P00820120226 (accessed on 21 November 2014).

Bhattarcharya, Gayatri. 1978. 'Refugee Rehabilitation and Its Impact on Tripura's Economy'. PhD dissertation, University of Calcutta, Calcutta.

Bhattacharya, Malini. 2009. 'Indian People's Theatre Association: A Preliminary Sketch of the Movement and the Organization 1942–1947'. In *Modern Indian Theatre: A Reader*, edited by N. Bhatia, 158–81. New Delhi:Oxford University Press.

Bhattacharya, Budhaditya. 2013. 'Reimagining Kashmir'. *The Hindu*, 1 March.

Bhattacharya (Chakraborti), Swapna. 1995. 'Bangladesh–Myanmar Relations: A Study of the Problem of Refugees in Bangladesh'. In *Integration, Disintegration and World Order: Some Perspectives on the Process of Change*, edited by A.K. Banerji. Calcutta: Allied.

Bhattacharya, Swapna. 2001. 'The Refugee-generating Chittagong Hill Tracts: Past, Present and Future'. In *Refugees and Human Rights: Social and Political Dynamics of Refugee Problem in Eastern and North-Eastern India*, edited by S.K. Roy, 317–44. Jaipur: Rawat.

Bhaumik, Subir. 2003. 'The Returnees and the Refugees: Migration from Burma'. In *Refugees and the State: Practices of Asylum and Care in India, 1947–2000*, edited by R. Samaddar, 182–210. New Delhi: SAGE Publications.

———. 2014. 'Raising the Bogey of Illegal Immigration'. *The Hindu*, 10 May.

Biswas, Moinak. 2000. 'The Couple and Their Spaces: Harano Sur *as Melodrama Now*'. In *the Making of Indian Cinema*, edited by R. Vasudevan, 121–42. New Delhi: Oxford University Press.

Biswas, Moinak. 2008. 'Ek asahaniya itihas o cinemar smriti' [in Bengali] ('An unbearable history and the memory of cinema'). In *Desh Bhag: Smriti Ar Stabdhata* [in Bengali] (Country's Partition: Memory and Silence), edited by S. Ghosh, 209–19. Kolkata: Gangchil.

Biswas, Radhikaranjan. 2011. 'Dandakaranya ja dekhechhi, ja payechhi' [in Bengali] ('what I saw and what I found in Dandakaranya'). In *Deshbhag: Binash O Binirman*, edited by Modhumoy Pal, 195–206. Kolkata: Gangchil.

Blumberg, Antonia. 2014. 'Rohingya Muslim Refugees Can No Longer Wed in Bangladesh under New Marriage Ban: Report'. *The Huffington Post*, 10 July.

Borooah, Vani Kant. 2013. 'The Killing Fields of Assam: Myth and Reality of its Muslim Immigration'. *Economic and Political Weekly* (Mumbai), 48 (4): 43–52.

Bose, Ashish. 1988. *From Population to People*, Vol. 2. New Delhi: B.R. Publishing.

Bose, Nayana. 2004. 'Mohajirs: Refugees by Choice'. In *Forced Migration in the South Asian Region: Displacement, Human Rights and Conflict Resolution*, edited by O. Mishra, 143–59. Delhi: Manak.

Bose, Pradip Kumar (ed.). 2000. *Refugees in West Bengal: Institutional Practices and Contested Identities*. Calcutta: Calcutta Research Group.

Bose, Sumantra. 2003. *Kashmir: Roots of Conflict, Paths to Peace*. New Delhi: Vistaar.

Burgess, J. Peter. 2007. 'Non-military Security Challenges'. In *Contemporary Security and Strategy* (2nd ed., pp. 60–78), edited by C.A. Snyder. London: Palgrave.

Burki, Shahid Javed. 1973. 'Migration, Urbanisation and Politics in Pakistan'. In *Population, Politics and the Future of Southern Asia*, edited by W.H. Wriggins and J.F. Guyot. New York: Columbia University Press.

Butalia, Urvashi. 2003. 'The Nowhere People'. In *The Trauma and the Triumph: Gender and Partition in Eastern India*, edited by Jasodhara Bagchi and Subhoranjan Dasgupta, 113–22. Calcutta: Stree.

Census of India. 1991. Rajasthan, Series 21, Part IV-B (ii). Table C-9.

Chakrabarti, Prafulla K. 1990. *The Marginal Men: The Refugees and the Left Political Syndrome in West Bengal*. Kalyani, West Bengal: Lumiere Books.

Chakrabarty, Bikash. 2012. *Andamaney Punarbashan: Ek Baangal Officacer Diary* [in Bengali] (The Rehabilitations in Andaman: The Diary of a Bengali of East Bengali Origin). Kolkata: Gangchil.

Chakrabarty, Bivash. 2014. 'Ritwik Srijane Asthir: Prokrita Arthe Ek Bastuhara' (meaning, Ritwik, in real sense Restless: A Refugee in the Real Sense), *Ei Samay* (Kolkata), 9 February: 7–8.

Chakrabarty, Dipesh. 1996. 'Remembered Villages: Representation of Hindu-Bengali Memories in the Aftermath of the Partition', *Economic and Political Weekly* (Mumbai), 10 August: 2143–52.

Chakravarty, Sumita S. 1996. *National Identity in Indian Popular Cinema, 1947–1987*. New Delhi: Oxford University Press.

Chand, Raghuvir and Mahavir Chand Thakur. 1991. 'Changing Population Profile', *Seminar* (New Delhi), February, no. 378.

Chanda, Nayan. 2007. *Bound Together: How Traders, Preachers, Adventurers, and Warriors Shaped Globalization*. New Delhi: Penguin/Viking.

Chandra, Uday and Kenneth Bo Nielsen. 2012. 'The Importance of Caste in Bengal'. *Economic and Political Weekly* (Mumbai), 47 (44): 19 April: 59–61.

Chandrasekhar, S. 1954. *Hungry People and Empty Lands: An Essay on Population Problems and International Tensions.* London: George Allen and Unwin.

Chatterjee, Chandrima B. 2006. *Identities in Motion: Migration and Health in India.* Mumbai: The Centre for Enquiry into Health and Allied Themes (CEHAT).

Chatterjee, Nilanjana. n.d. 'Interrogating Victimhood: East Bengali Refugee Narratives of Communal Violence'. Available at www.swadhinata.org.uk/document/chatterjeeEastBengal%20Refugee.pdf (accessed on 20 December 2012).

Chatterjee, Partha. 1997. 'The Second Partition of Bengal'. In *Reflections on Partition in the East,* edited by R. Samaddar, 35–58. New Delhi: Vikas Publications.

Chatterjee, Partha. 2002. 'The Films of Ritwik Ghatakand the Partition'. In *Pangs of Partition, The Human Dimension,* edited by S. Settar and I.B. Gupta, Vol. 2, 59–68. New Delhi: Manohar Publications.

Chatterjee, Partha. 2012. 'Historicising Caste in Bengal Politics'. *Economic and Political Weekly* (Mumbai), 47 (50), December 15.

Chatterji, Joya. 2007. *The Spoils of Partition: Bengal and India, 1947–1967.* Cambridge: Cambridge University Press.

Chattha, Ilyas. 2013. *Refugee Settlement from Pakistan: Findings from Afghan Refugee Camps in the North-West Frontier Province (NWFP).* Brussels: European Council on Refugees and Exiles.

Chattopadhyay, Jayanti. 2002. 'Representing the Holocaust: The Partition in Two Bengali Plays'. In *Pangs of Partition: The Parting of Ways* (Vols I & II, pp. 301–12), edited by S. Settar and I. B. Gupta. New Delhi: Manohar Publishers.

Chattopadhyay, Saayan. 2007. 'Framing Frontiers: The Suspended Step towards Visual Construction of Geopolitical Borders'. *Frontiers: Sarai Reader 07,* 264–72. New Delhi: CSDS.

Chester, Lucy P. 2009. *Borders and Conflict in South Asia: The Radcliffe Boundary Commission and the Partition of Punjab.* Manchester: Manchester University Press.

Chimni, B.S. 2003. 'Status of Refugees in India: Strategic Ambiguity'. In *Refugee and the State: Practices of Asylum and Care in India, 1947–2000,* edited by Ranabir Samaddar, 443–71. New Delhi: SAGE Publications.

Choucri, Nazli. 1974. *Population Dynamics and Violence: Propositions, Insights and Evidence.* Lexington: D.C. Heath.

Choucri, Nazli. 1978. 'The Pervasiveness of Politics'. *Populi* (New York), 5 (3): 30–44.

Cohen, Stephen Philip. 2004. *The Idea of Pakistan.* New Delhi: Oxford University Press.

Cox, Wendell. 2012. 'Pakistan: Where the Population Bomb Is Exploding'. Available at http://www.newgeography.com/content/002940-pakistan-where-population-bomb-exploding (accessed on 17 December 2014).

Daiya, Kavita. 2011. 'Visual Culture and Violence: Inventing Intimacy and Citizenship in Recent South Asian Cinema'. *South Asian History and Culture* (London), 2 (4): 589–604.

Das, Pushpita. 2013. 'India-Myanmar Border Problems: Fencing Not the Only Solution'. Available at http://www.idsa.in/idsacomments/IndiaMyanmar-BorderProblems_pdf (accessed on 21 December 2014).

Das, Pushpita. 2014. 'Issues in the Management of the India–Pakistan International Border'. *Strategic Analysis* (New Delhi), 38 (3): 307–324.

Das, Samir. 2000. 'Refugee Crisis: Responses of the Government of West Bengal'. In *Refugee in West Bengal: Institutional Practices and Contested Identities*, edited by P.K. Bose, 7–31. Calcutta: Calcutta Research Group.

Das, Suranjan. 1990. *Communal Riots in Bengal, 1905–1947*. Delhi: Oxford University Press.

Dastidar, Soumitra. 2013. 'Bangladesher Cinema' [in Bengali] (The Cinema of Bangladesh). In *Bangladesher Anya Cinema* [in Bengali] (The Other Cinema of Bangladesh), edited by S. Saha, Vol.1, 70–75. Kolkata: Abhijan.

Datta, Pranati. 2004. 'Push-Pull Factors of Undocumented Migration from Bangladesh to West Bengal: A Perception Study'. *The Qualitative Report* (Kolkata), 9 (2), June: 335–58.

Datta, V.N. 2012. 'Panjabi Refugees and the Urban Development of Greater Delhi'. *The Delhi Omnibus*, Vol. 4. New Delhi: OUP. Originally published in 1986 in R.E. Frykenberg (ed.). *Delhi Through the Ages*. [The latter forms one of the volumes in the four-volume *The Delhi Omnibus*.]

Davis, Kingsley. 1949. 'India and Pakistan: The Demography of Partition'. *Pacific Affairs* (Vancouver), 22.

De, Barun. 1997. 'Moving Beyond Boundaries: Contradictions between People and Territory'. In *States, Citizens and Outsiders: The Uprooted Peoples of South Asia*, edited by T. Bose and R. Manchanda, 14–39. Kathmandu: South Asia Forum for Human Rights.

de Silva, K.M. 1995. *Regional Powers and Small State Security: India and Sri Lanka, 1971–90*. Washington, D.C.: Woodrow Wilson Center Press/ Baltimore, MD: Johns Hopkins University Press.

de Silva, K.M. 2012. *Sri Lanka and the Defeat of the LTTE*. New Delhi: Penguin.

de Silva, K.M. and Howard Wriggins. 1994. *J.R. Jayewardene of Sri Lanka—A Political Biography from 1956 to his Retirement (1989)*, Vol. 2. London: Leo Cooper.

Dhavan, Rajeev. 2004. *Refugee Law and Policy in India*. New Delhi: PILSARC— The Public Interest and Legal Support and Research Centre.

Diamond, Jared. 1997. *Guns, Germs and Steel*. New York: W.W. Norton.

Didur, Jill. 2006. *Unsettling Partition: Literature, Gender, Memory*. Toronto: University of Toronto Press.

Diener, Alexander C. and Joshua Hagen (eds). 2010. *Borderlines and Borderlands: Political Oddities at the Edge of the Nation-State*. Lanham: Rowman & Littlefield.

Dupont, Veronique. 2000. 'Spatial and Demographic Growth of Delhi since 1947 and the Main Migration Flows'. In *Delhi Urban Space and Human Destinies*, edited by V. Dupont, E. Tarlo and D. Vidal, 229–39. New Delhi: Manohar Publishers.

Dutt, Nirupama. 2010. 'Jottings by an Original Lahoran'. In *Bridging Partition: People's Initiatives for Peace between India and Pakistan*, edited by S. Kothari and Z. Mian (with Kamla Bhasin, A.H. Nayyar and Mohammad Tahseen), 253–67. Hyderabad: Orient Blackswan.

Eaton, R. M. 1994. *The Rise of Islam and the Bengal Frontier, 1204–1760*. Delhi: Oxford University Press.

Evans, Rosalind. 2013. 'The Perils of Being a Borderland People: On the Lhotshampas of Bhutan'. In *Borderland Lives in Northern South Asia*, edited by D. Gellner, 117–40. Durham: Duke University Press.

Fernandes, Naresh. 2004. 'Remembering Anthony Gonsalves'. *Seminar* (New Delhi), (343): 1–9. Available at www.india-seminar.com/2004/543 (accessed on 24 September 2013).

Franda, Marcus. 1971. *Radical Politics in West Bengal*. Cambridge, MA: MIT Press.

Frank, Andre Gunder. 1967. *Capitalism and Underdevelopment in Latin America: Historical Studies of Chile and Brazil*. New York: Monthly Review Press.

Frank, Andre Gunder. 1998. *ReOrient: Global Economy in the Asian Age*. Berkeley, CA: University of California Press.

Frank, Andre Gunder and Barry K. Gills (eds). 1993. *The World System: Five Hundred Years or Five Thousand*. London: Routledge.

Fuchs, Lawrence H. 1993, November. 'An Agenda for Tomorrow: Immigration Policy and Ethnic Policies'. *Annals* (Philadelphia), 530, November: 171–86.

Gandhi, Ramachandra. 2007. 'Two Cheers for Tolerance'. *IIC Quarterly* (New Delhi), 34 (1), Summer: 146–51.

Gangopadhyay, Ashis. 2014. 'Khandida Bongo O Dui Banglar Sahitya' [in Bengali] (The Divided Bengal and the Literature of the Two Bengals). *Saptahik Bortoman* (Kolkata), 22 November: 48–9.

Ganti, Tejaswini. 2004. *Bollywood: A Guidebook to Popular Hindi Cinema*. London: Routledge.

Gayer, Laurent. 2012. 'Political Turmoil in Karachi: Production and Reproduction of Ordered Disorder'. *Economic and Political Weekly*, 47 (31), 4 August: 76–84.

Ghosh, Alok. 2000. 'Bengali Refugees at Dandakaranya: A Tragedy of Rehabilitation'. In *Refugees in West Bengal*, edited by P.K. Bose, 106–29. Calcutta: Calcutta Research Group.

Ghosh, Atik. 2013. 'The Inhabitants of Bangladeshi Chhitmahals in India'. Available at http://refugeewatchonline.blogpost.in/?view=flipcard (accessed on 15 December 2013).

Ghosh, Bimal. 2000. *Managing Migration: Time for a New International Regime*. Oxford: Oxford University Press.

Ghosh, Bimal. 2012. 'Global Economic Crisis and Governance of Human Mobility'. In *India Migration Report 2012: Global Financial Crisis, Migration and Remittance*, edited by S. Irudaya Rajan, 1–13. New Delhi: Routledge.

Ghosh, Papiya. 2004. 'Partition and the South Asian Diaspora'. In *Forced Migration in the South Asian Region: Displacement, Human Rights and Conflict Resolution*, edited by Omprakash Mishra, 111–42. New Delhi: Manak Publications.

Ghosh, Papiya. 2007. *Partition and the South Asian Diaspora: Extending the Subcontinent*. London: Routledge.

Ghosh, Partha S. 1982. 'On Drawing a Red Herring'. *Alternatives* (New Delhi/New York), 8 (1): 131–38.

Ghosh, Partha S. 1989. *Cooperation and Conflict in South Asia*. New Delhi: Manohar Publishers. Reprinted in 1995.

Ghosh, Partha S. 1998. 'Bhutan: Ethnicity, Democracy and Nation-Building'. In *Democratisation in South Asia: The First Fifty Years,* edited by J.M. Richardson Jr and S.W.R. de A. Samarasinghe, 213–37. Kandy: International Centre for Ethnic Studies.

Ghosh, Partha S. 1999. *BJP and the Evolution of Hindu Nationalism: From Periphery to Centre.* New Delhi: Manohar Publishers. Reprinted in 2000.

———. 2002. 'From Legalism to Realism in Kashmir: Internationalising the Line of Control'. *Heidelberg Papers in South Asian and Comparative Politics* (Heidelberg University). Available at, http://www.sai.uni-heidelberg.de/SAPOL/HPSACP.htmWorking Paper No. 7 (accessed in September 2002.)

——— 2003. *Ethnicity versus Nationalism: The Devolution Discourse in Sri Lanka.* New Delhi: SAGE Publications.

Ghosh, Partha S. 2004. *Unwanted and Uprooted: A Political Study of Migrants, Refugees, Stateless and Displaced of South Asia.* New Delhi: Sanskriti.

——— 2009. 'Politics of Personal Law in India: The Hindu-Muslim Dichotomy'. *South Asia Research* (New Delhi), 29 (1): 1–17.

———. 2010. 'Foreign Policy and Indian Politics: Issues before the Fifteenth General Election'. In *Emerging Trends in Indian Politics: The Fifteenth General Election,* edited by A.K. Mehra, 304–26. New Delhi: Routledge.

———. 2011. 'Changing Frontiers: Making Deeper Sense of India-Bangladesh Relations'. *South Asia Research* (New Delhi), 31 (3): 195–211.

———. 2012. 'To and Fro India with Love,' *IIC Quarterly* (New Delhi), 39 (2), Autumn: 54–66.

———. 2013a. 'Mapping the Mixed and Massive Human Flows in South Asia: Impact of Women, the Stateless and Other Disadvantaged Groups'. In *Unstable Populations, Anxious States: Mixed and Massive Human Flows in South Asia,* edited by Paula Banerjee,18–49. Kolkata: Samya.

———. 2013b. 'An Enigma that is South Asia: India versus the Region'. *Asia Pacific Review* (Tokyo), 20 (1), May: 100–20.

———. 2014. 'India-Bangladesh Border Fence: The Financial, Political and Diplomatic Costs'. ICSSR-funded project report, NASSDOC, New Delhi.

Ghosh, Partha S., Deepak K. Mishra and Vandana Upadhyay. 2005. *Electoral Politics in Arunachal Pradesh: An Analysis of the 14th Loksabha Election.* Guwahati: Omeo Kumar Das Institute of Social Change and Development (project report).

Ghosh, S.K. 1993. *Unquiet Border.* New Delhi: Ashish Publishing House.

Ghosh, Subhasri and Debjani Dutta. 2003. 'Forgotten Voices from the P.L. Camps'. In *The Trauma and the Triumph: Gender and Partition in Eastern India,* edited by J. Bagchi and S. Dasgupta, Vol. 2, 199–221. Kolkata: Stree.

Ghoshal, Baladas. 2013. 'Democratic Transition in Myanmar: Challenges Ahead'. *India Quarterly* (New Delhi), 69 (2), June: 117–31.

Ghufran, Nasreen. 2011. 'The Role of UNHCR and Afghan Refugees in Pakistan'. *Strategic Analysis* (New Delhi), 35 (6), November: 945–54.

Gopal, Priyamvada. 2001. 'Bodies Inflicting Pain: Masculinity, Morality and Cultural Identity in Manto's "Cold Meat"'. In *The Partitions of Memory: The Afterlife of the Division of India,* edited by S. Kaul. Delhi: Permanent Black.

Goswami, Uddipana. 2014. *Conflict and Reconciliation: The Politics of Ethnicity in Assam*. New Delhi and London: Routledge.

GOTN. 2010. *Information Handbook under Right to Information Act 2005*. Chennai: Director of Rehabilitation, Department of Rehabilitation, Government of Tamil Nadu.

Graham, Bruce D. 1990. *Hindu Nationalism and Indian Politics: The Origins and Development of the Bharatiya Jana Sangh*. Cambridge: Cambridge University Press.

Grant, Madison. 1916. *The Passing of the Great Race: Or, the Racial Basis of European History*. New York: Charles Scribner's Sons.

Guha, Amalendu. 2006. *Planter Raj to Swaraj: Freedom Struggle and Electoral Politics in Assam 1826-1947*. New Delhi: Tulika (revised edition, first published in 1977 by ICHR).

Guha, Maitrayee. 2014. 'Forced Migration of the Tamils: India versus Sri Lanka'. *India Quarterly* (New Delhi), 71 (1), January–March: 1–15.

Guha, Ramachandra. 2007. *India After Gandhi: The History of the World's Largest Democracy*. New Delhi: Picador.

Guhathakurta, Meghna. 2002. 'Communal Politics in South Asia and the Hindus of Bangladesh'. In *Religious Minorities in South Asia: Selected Essays on Post-Colonial Situations,* edited by M. Hussain and L. Ghosh, Vol. 1. New Delhi: Manak Publications.

Gujral, Satish. 2002. 'Crossing the Jhelum'. In *Pangs of Partition: The Parting of Ways* edited by S. Settar and I.B. Gupta, Vols I & II, pp. 47–58. New Delhi: Manohar Publications.

Gupta, Ashoka, Bina Das, Amar Kumar Varma, Sudha Sen and Sheila Davar. 2003. Report 'East is east, West is west'. In *The Trauma and the Triumph: Gender and Partition in Eastern India*, edited by J. Bagchi and S. Dasgupta, 235–52. Kolkata: Stree.

Gupta, Narayani. 2000. 'Concern, Indifference, Controversy: Reflections on Fifty Years of "Conservation" in Delhi'. In *Delhi Urban Space and Human Destinies,* edited by V. Dupont, E. Tarlo and D. Vidal, 157–71. New Delhi: Manohar Publishers.

———. 2003. 'The Indomitable City'. In *Shahjahanabad/Old Delhi: Tradition and Colonial Change,* edited by E. Ehlers and T. Kraft, 29–44. New Delhi: Manohar Publishers.

Gurung Report.1983. *Internal and International Migration in Nepal: Summary and Recommendations*. Kathmandu: Nepal, National Commission on Population, Task Force on Migration.

Gurung, Harka. 1997. 'Ethnicity and Regionalism in the Nepal Elections'. *South Asian Survey* (New Delhi), 4 (1): 109–28.

Haidar, Suhasini. 2014. 'Moving the Discourse to Ground Zero'. *The Hindu* (New Delhi), 27 October.

Haley, Alex. 1976. *Roots: The Saga of an American Family*. Garden City, NY: Doubleday & Company.

Handlin, Oscar. 1951. *The Uprooted: The Epic Story of the Great Migrations That Made the American People*, 2nd ed. Philadelphia: University of Pennsylvania Press, 2002.

Hans, Asha. 2003. 'Refugee Women and Children: Need for Protection and Care'. In *Refugees and the State: Practices of Asylum and Care in India, 1947–2000*, edited by Ranabir Samaddar, 355–95. New Delhi: SAGE.

Harzig, Christiane and Dirk Hoerder (with Donna Gabaccia). 2009. *What Is Migration History?* Cambridge: Polity Press.

Hasan, Mushirul. 1997. *Legacy of a Divided Nation: India's Muslims since Independence.* Delhi: Oxford University Press.

Hashmi, Taj-ul Islam. 1998. 'The "Bihari" Minorities in Bangladesh: Victims of Nationalism'. In *Islam, Communities and the Nation: Muslim Identities in South Asia*, edited by M. Hasan. New Delhi: Manohar Publishers.

Hassan, Amtul. 2006. *Impact of Partition: Refugees in Pakistan: Struggle of Empowerment and State's Response.* New Delhi: Manohar Publishers.

Hataley, Todd. 2014. 'Canada-United States Border Security: Horizontal, Vertical and Cross-Border Integration'. In *Public Security in Federal Systems*, edited by A.K. Mehra, 135–57. New Delhi: Lancer.

Hausner, Sondra L. and Jeevan R. Sharma. 2013. 'On the Way to India: Nepali Rituals of Border Crossing'. In *Borderland Lives in Northern South Asia*, edited by D. Gellner, 94–116. Durham: Duke University Press.

Heine, Jorge and Partha S. Ghosh. 2011. 'The Elephant in the War: India and the Afghan-Pakistan Link'. *Canadian Foreign Policy Journal* (Ottawa), 17(1), March: 50–61.

Hellmann-Rajanayagam, Dagmar. 2013. 'Indians in Myanmar/Burma, assimilation and integration'. In *The Encyclopedia of Global Human Migration*, edited by I. Ness. Oxford: Blackwell Publishing.

Hovil, L. 2007. 'Self-Settled Refugees in Uganda: An Alternative Approach to Displacement'. *Journal of Refugee Studies*, 20 (4): 599–620.

Human Development Report. 2009. *Overcoming Barriers: Human Mobility and Development.* New York: United Nations Development Programme.

Hussain, Mohammad Jehangir. 2013. 'Bangladesher Chalachchitrashilpa Bikasher Patobhumi O Aagami Diner Pratyasha [in Bengali] (The Background of the Development of the Film Industry of Bangladesh and the Expectations for the Future). In *Bangladesher Anya Cinema* (in Bengali: The Other Cinema of Bangladesh), edited by S. Saha, Vol.1, 39–55. Kolkata: Abhijan.

Hussain, Monirul. 1995. 'Refugees in the Face of Emerging Ethnicity in North-East India: An Overview'. *Studies in Humanities and Social Sciences* (Shimla), 2 (1): 123–30.

Hutt, Michael. 2003. *Unbecoming Citizens: Culture, Nationhood, and the Flight of Refugees from Bhutan.* New Delhi: Oxford University Press.

Indraganti, Kiranmayi. 2012. 'Of "Ghosts" and Singers: Debates around Singing Practices of 1940s Indian Cinema'. *South Asian Popular Culture* (London), 10 (3): 295–306.

International Labour Organization. 2010. *International Labour Migration: A Right Based Approach.* Geneva: ILO Publications.

International Organisation of Migration (IOM). 2013. *World Migration Report 2013.* Switzerland.

Jacobson, Karen. 1996. 'Factors Influencing the Policy Responses of Host Governments to Mass Refugee Influxes'. *International Migration Review* (Staten Island, NY), 30 (3), Fall, 655–78.

Jaffrelot, Christophe. 2000. 'The Hindu Nationalist Movement in Delhi: From "Locals" to Refugees—and towards Peripheral Groups'? In *Delhi Urban Space and Human Destinies*, edited by V. Dupont, E. Tarlo and D. Vidal, 181–203. New Delhi: Manohar Publishers.

Jalal, Ayesha. 1998. 'Nation, Reason and Religion: Punjab's Role in the Partition of India'. *Economic and Political Weekly* (Mumbai), 8 August: 2183–90.

———. 2012. Curator of a Hollowed Conscience. *The Hindu*, 11 May.

———. 2014. *The Struggle for Pakistan: A Muslim Homeland and Global Politics*. Cambridge, MA: The Belknap Press of Harvard University Press.

Jamil, Ishtiaq and Pranab Kumar Panday. 2008. 'The Elusive Peace Accord in the Chittagong Hill Tracts of Bangladesh and the Plight of the Indigenous People'. *Journal of Commonwealth & Comparative Politics* (London), 46 (4), November: 464–89.

Janah, Sunil. 2013. *Photographing India*. New Delhi: Oxford University Press.

Jha, Krishna and Dhirendra K. Jha. 2012. *Ayodhya: The Dark Night: The Secret History of Rama's Appearance in Babri Masjid*. New Delhi: Harper Collins.

Jha, N.N. 1994. 'Minorities, Immigrants and Refugee Issues both in the Context of India and India-Nepal Relations', paper presented at the India-Nepal Colloquium, New Delhi, 26–28 September: 1–15.

Johnson Henry (with Guil Figgins). 2005. 'Diwali Downunder'. *New Zealand Journal of Media Studies* (Wellington), 9 (1). Available at http://nzetc.victoria.ac.nz/tm/scholarly/tei-Sch091JMS-t1-g1-t5.html (accessed on 11 August 2014.)

Kalidas, S. 2013. 'Pandit Ravi Shankar—Tansen of Our Times'. IIC Occasional Paper No. 47. New Delhi: India International Centre.

Kamran, Tahir. 2012. 'Urdu Migrant Literati and Lahore's Culture'. *Journal of Punjab Studies* (Santa Barbara, CA), 19 (2), September: 173–92.

Kansakar, Vidya Bir Singh. 2005. 'Nepal-India Border: Prospects, Problems and Challenges'. Available at http://www.fes.de/aktuell/focus_interkulturelles/focus_1/documents/19.pdf (accessed on 13 July 2014).

Kapoor, Pramod. 2014. *My Experiment with Gandhi*. New Delhi: Roli Books.

Kar, Biman. 1986. 'Socio-Economic Implication of the Migration-Dominated High Population Growth Rates of North Eastern India'. In *The Pattern and Problems of Population in North East*, edited by B. Datta Roy, 285–96. New Delhi: Uppal Publishers.

Kar, M. 1997. *Muslims in Assam Politics*. New Delhi: Vikas Publishing House.

Bhasin, Avtar Singh. 1996. *India-Bangladesh Relations: Documents, 1971–1996: Bangladesh*, Volu. I, New Delhi: Siba Exim Pvt Ltd.

Katju, Markandeya. 2001. 'India's Perception of Refugee Law'. Available at http:www.worldlii.org/int/journals/ISILYBIHRI/2001/14.rtf (accessed on 5 October 2009).

Kennedy, Edward M. 1971. *Crisis in South Asia: A Report by Senator Edward M. Kennedy to the Subcommittee to Investigate Problems Connected with*

*Refugees and Escapees of the Committee on the Judiciary, United States Senate.* Washington, D.C.: Government Printing Office.

Kesaven, Mukul. 1994. 'Urdu, Awadh and Tawaif: The Islamicate Roots of Hindi Cinema'. In *Forging identities: Gender, Communities and the State,* edited by Z. Hasan, 244–57. New Delhi: Kali for Women.

Keyslong, Laurinda. 2009. 'That's Why They Call the Blues'. *Span* (New Delhi), April: 48–9.

Khadria, Binod, ed. 2009. *India Migration Report 2009: Past, Present and Future Outlook.* Jawaharlal Nehru University, New Delhi: International Migration and Diaspora Studies Project.

Khan, Akbar, Ex. Maj. Gen. 1975. *Raiders in Kashmir,* 2nd ed. Islamabad: National Book Foundation.

Khan, Md. Nur. 1997. 'Biharis in Bangladesh: Forgotten Pakistani Citizens'. In *States, Citizens and Outsiders: The Uprooted Peoples of South Asia,* edited by T.K. Bose and R. Manchanda, 138–51. Kathmandu: South Asia Forum for Human Rights.

Kharat, Rajesh. 2003. 'Gainers of a Stalemate: The Tibetans in India'. In *Refugee and the State: Practices of Asylum and Care in India, 1947–2000,* edited by R. Samaddar, 281–320. New Delhi: SAGE Publications.

Khare, Harish. 2014. 'Jawaharlal Nehru in the Age of Twitter: Reflections on the Founding of the Office of Prime Minister (1947–1952)'. The 4th Ravinder Kumar Memorial Lecture, India International Centre, 31 January (organised by Deshkal Society, New Delhi).

Kharkongor, Naphisha B. 2014. 'Legal Disputes in Bangladesh-Meghalaya Border'. In *Public Security in Federal Systems,* edited by A.K. Mehra, 182–94. New Delhi: Lancer.

Khilnani, Sunil. 2004. *The Idea of India.* New Delhi: Penguin.

Khilnani, Sunil, Vikram Raghavan and Arun K. Thiruvengadam (eds). 2013. *Comparative Constitutionalism in South Asia.* New Delhi: Oxford University Press.

Khondker, Habibul Haque. 1995. 'Politics, Disaster and Refugees: The Bangladesh Case'. In *Crossing Borders: Transmigration in Asia Pacific,* edited by O.J. Hui, C.K. Bun and C.S. Beng, 173–84. New York: Prentice Hall.

Kimura, Makiko. 2013. *The Nellie Massacre of 1983: Agency of Rioters.* New Delhi: SAGE Publications.

Kollmair, Michael, Siddhi Manandhar, Bhim Subedi and Susan Thieme. 2006. 'New Figures for Old Stories: Migration and Remittances in Nepal'. *Migration Letters* (London), 3 (2), October: 151–60.

Kraft, Thomas. 2003. 'Contemporary Old Delhi: Transformation of an Historical Place'. In *Shahjahanabad/Old Delhi: Tradition and Colonial Change,* edited by E. Ehlers and T. Kraft, 93–119. New Delhi: Manohar.

Krishna, Gopal. 1974. 'Communalism Revisited' (in two parts). *Times of India* (New Delhi), 23–24 July.

Kudaisya, Gyanesh. 1996. 'Divided Landscapes, Fragmented Identities: East Bengal Refugees and Their Rehabilitation in India, 1947–79'. *Singapore Journal of Tropical Geography,* 17 (1): 24–39.

Kulke, Hermann and Dietmar Rothermund. 2004. *A History of India*, 4th ed. London: Routledge.

Kumar, Arvind and Ayan Guha. 2014. 'Political Future of Caste in West Bengal'. *Economic and Political Weekly* (Mumbai), 49 (32), 9 August: 73–4.

Kumar, Dhruva. 1994. 'Reconsidering Nepal-India Bilateral Relations'. *Contributions to Nepalese Studies* (Kathmandu), 21 (1), January.

Kumar, Sanjay. 2013. *Changing Electoral Politics in Delhi: From Caste to Class*. New Delhi: SAGE publications.

Kumar, Vikash. 2015. 'Modi's Visit to Bangladesh: A Paradigm Shift in India-Bangladesh Relations'. Available at http://udayindia.in/2015/06/26/modis-visit-to-bangladesh-a-paradigm (accessed on 10 July 2015).

Kumari, Amita. 2013. 'Delhi as Refuge: Resettlement and Assimilation of Partition Refugees'. *Economic and Political Weekly* (Mumbai), 48 (44), November 2: 60–7.

Kristof, Nicholas. 2003. 'Is Race Real? I am a Black American'. *New York Times*, 11 July.

Labanca, Nicola. 2015. 'Post-Colonial Italy: The Case of a Small and Belated Empire: From Strong Emotions to Bigger Problems', in *Memories of Post Imperial Nations: The Aftermath of Decolonization, 1945-2013*, edited by Dietmar Rothermund, 120–49. New Delhi: Cambridge University Press.

Lama-Rewal, Stephanie Tawa. 2009. 'The Resilient *Bhadralok*: A Profile of the West Bengal MLAs', in *Rise of the Plebeians? The Changing Face of Indian Legislative Assemblies*, edited by Christophe Jaffrelot and Sanjay Kumar, 361–92. New Delhi: Routledge.

Lawson, Edward. 1996. *Encyclopedia of Human Rights*. New York: Taylor and Francis.

Leider, Jacques. 2013. 'Rohingya: The Name, the Movement and the Quest for Identity'. In *Nation Building in Myanmar*, 204–55. Yangon: Myanmar Egres/ Myanmar Peace Center.

Lin, Sharat G. and Madan C. Paul. 1995. 'Bangladeshi Migrants in Delhi: Social Insecurity, State Power, and Captive Vote Banks'. *Bulletin of Concerned Asian Scholars*, 27(1), January–March: 3–20.

Mahadevan, Raman. 1978. 'Immigrant Entrepreneurs in Colonial Burma— An Exploratory Study of the Role of Nattukottai Chettiars on Tamil Nadu, 1880-1930'. *The Indian Economic and Social History Review* (New Delhi), 15 (3): 329–58.

Mahajan, Sucheta. 2012. 'Why Gandhi accepted the Decision to Partition India'. In *Partition of India: Why 1947?* edited by K. Roy, 242–60. New Delhi: Oxford University Press.

Malik, Keshav. 2002. 'The Unsettling—Satish Gujral and his Paintings of Partition'. In *Pangs of Partition: The Parting of Ways* (Vols I & II), edited by S. Settar and I.B. Gupta, 75–82. New Delhi: Manohar Publications.

Manchanda, Rita. 1997. 'Nowhere Peoples: Burmese Refugees in India'. In *States, Citizens and Outsiders: The Uprooted Peoples of South Asia*, edited by T. Bose and R. Manchanda. Kathmandu: South Asia Forum for Human Rights.

Mandal, Monika. 2011. *Settling the Unsettled: A Study of Partition Refugees in West Bengal.* New Delhi: Manohar.

Mandel, Robert. 1980. 'Roots of the Modern Inter-State Border Dispute'. *Journal of Conflict Resolution* (London), 24 (3), September: 427–54.

Manuel, Peter. 2012. 'The Trajectories of Transplants: Singing Alhā, Birhā, and the Rāmāyan in the Indic Caribbean'. *Asian Music* (Austin, TX), 43(2), Summer/Fall: 115–54.

Martinez, Oscar. 1994. *Border People: Life and Society in the U.S.–Mexico Borderlands.* Tucson: University of Arizona Press.

Maung, Shwe Lu. 1989. *Burma: Nationalism and Ideology: An Analysis of Society, Culture and Politics.* Dhaka: University Press.

McAdam, Jane. ed. 2008. *Forced Migration, Human Rights and Security.* Portland: Hart Publishing.

McKeown, Adam M. 2008. *Melancholy Order: Asian Migration and the Globalization of Borders.* New York: Columbia University Press.

Mehra, Ajay K. 1991. *The Politics of Urban Redevelopment: A Study of Old Delhi.* New Delhi: SAGE Publications.

Mehra, Ajay K. 2008. 'India's Experiment with Revolution'. *Heidelberg Papers in South Asian and Comparative Politics,* Working Paper No. 40, September.

Menon, A.G. Krishna. 2000. 'The Contemporary Architecture of Delhi: The Role of the State as Middleman'. In *Delhi Urban Space and Human Destinies,* edited by V. Dupont, E. Tarlo and D. Vidal, 143–56. New Delhi: Manohar.

Menon, Meena. 2014. 'Bleak House: Mud Huts and No School'. *The Hindu* (New Delhi), 15 June.

Menon, Ritu. 2003. 'Birth of Social Security Commitments: What Happened in the West'. In *Refugee and the State: Practices of Asylum and Care in India, 1947–2000,* edited by R. Samaddar, 152–81. New Delhi: SAGE Publications.

Menon, Ritu and Kamla Bhasin. 1998. *Borders and Boundaries: Women in India's Partition.* New Delhi: Kali for Women.

Merritt, Richard L. 1995. 'Political Imbalance and Political Destabilization'. *International Political Science Review* (London), 16(4), October: 405–25.

Milner, James. 2004. 'Refugees and Security in South Asia: Responding to the Security Burden'. In *Forced Migration in the South Asian Region: Displacement, Human Rights and Conflict Resolution,* edited by Mishra, 205–23. New Delhi: Manak Publications.

Minow, Martha. 1998. *Between Vengeance and Forgiveness: Facing History after Genocide and Mass Violence.* Boston, MA: Beacon Press.

Mir, Hamid. 2010. 'Apology Day for Pakistanis,' *Point Counterpoint,* March 30. Available at https://www.google.co.in/?gws_rd=ssl#q=Hamid+Mir,+'Apolog y+Day+for+Pakistan,'+Point+Counterpoint,+March+30,+2010 (accessed on 22 November 2012).

Mir, Hamid. 2014. 'The Truth will Set us Free'. *The Hindustan Times,* New Delhi, 10 May.

Mukherjee, Rudrangshu (ed.). 2007. *Great Speeches of Modern India.* New Delhi: Random House.

Mukherji, Saradindu. 2000. *Subjects, Citizens and Refugees: Tragedy in the Chittagong Hill Tracts (1974–1998)*. New Delhi: Indian Centre for the Study of Forced Migration.

Mukhopadhyay, Anindita. 2002. 'Partition Relived Literature'. In *Pangs of Partition: The Parting of Ways* (Vols I & II), edited by S. Settar and I.B. Gupta, 209–26. New Delhi: Manohar Publications.

Murshid, Navine. 2012. 'Refugee-Camp Militarisation in Bangladesh and Thailand'. *Economic and Political Weekly* (Mumbai), 47 (47–48): 103–8.

Murshid, Navine. 1994. *Muslim India* (New Delhi), no. 141, September: 406.

Nabi, A.K.M. Nurun and P. Krishnan. 1993. 'Some Approaches to the Study of Human Migration'. In *Methodologies for Population Studies and Development*, edited by K. Mahadevan and P. Krishnan, 82–121. New Delhi: SAGE Publications.

Nair, Arjun. 2007. 'National Refugee Law for India: Benefits and Roadblocks'. *IPCS Research Papers*. New Delhi: Institute of Peace and Conflict Studies.

Namboodiri, N. Krishnan. 1992. 'Ecological Demography: Its Place in Sociology'. In *Readings in Population Research: Policy, Methodology, Perspectives*, edited by P. Krishnan, C.-H. Tuan and K. Mahadevan. Delhi: B.R. Publishing.

Narayan Swamy, M.R. 2008. *Tigers of Lanka: From Boys to Guerrillas*. New Delhi: Konarak.

Nath, Abhishek. 2013. 'Migration and Identity: A Study of Post 1971Bangladeshi Migrants in Delhi'. PhD Dissertation. Department of Political Science, Delhi University, New Delhi.

Nauman. 2012. 'A Secret South Asian Meta-Utopia'. *Seminar* (New Delhi), No. 632. Available at http://www.india-seminar.com/2012/632/632_nauman_naqvi.htm (accessed on 15 October 2013).

Mukherjee, Saradindu. 1996. 'Migration: Generous or Hapless Hosts?' *Hindustan Times* (New Delhi), 13 October.

Nawaz, Shuja. 2009. *Crossed Swords: Pakistan, Its Army, and the Wars Within*. Karachi: Oxford Pakistan Paperbacks.

Newland, Kathleen. 1979. 'International Migration: The Search for Work'. *Worldwatch Paper* (Washington, DC) no. 33, November.

Nye, J.S. and S.M. Lynn-Jones. 1988. 'International Security Studies: A Report of the Conference on the State of the Field'. *International Security* (Cambridge, MA), 12 (4): 5–27.

Oli, K.P. Sharma. 2007. 'Different Dimensions of Bhutanese Refugee Problem: Its Implications and Lasting Solutions'. In *Different Dimensions of Bhutanese Refugee Problem: Its Implications and Lasting Solutions*, edited by G. Pokharel, A. Sakya and B. Dahal, 37–48. Kathmandu: Institute of Foreign Affairs.

Oonk, Gijsbert. 2007. 'Global Indian Diasporas: Exploring Trajectories of Migration and Theory'. In *Global Indian Diasporas. Exploring Trajectories of Migration and Theory*, edited by G. Oonk, 9–31. Amsterdam: Amsterdam University Press.

Oonk, Gijsbert. 2013. *Settled Strangers: Asian Business Elites in East Africa (1800–2000)*. New Delhi: SAGE Publications.

Padgaonkar, Dileep, Radha Kumar and M.M. Ansari. 2012. *A New Compact with the People of Jammu and Kashmir: Final Report*, Ministry of Home Affairs, Government of India.

Pandey, Gyanendra. 1997. 'Partition and Independence in Delhi: 1947–48'. *Economic and Political Weekly* (Mumbai), 32(36), 6–12 September: 2261–72.

Panjwani, Narendra. 2010.'India-Pakistan Relations in the Context of Cinema's Hindustan'. In *Bridging Partition: People's Initiatives for Peace between India and Pakistan*, edited by S. Kothari and Z. Mian (with Kamla Bhasin, A.H. Nayyar and Mohammad Tahseen), 268–76. Hyderabad: Orient Blackswan.

Pant, Pushpesh. 2013. 'India: Food and the Making of the Nation'. *India International Centre Quarterly* (New Delhi), 40 (2), Autumn: 1–34.

Pathak, Lalit K. 1986. 'East Bengal Immigrants in Assam Valley: An Analysis of the Census Data'. In *the Pattern and Problems of Population in North East*, edited by B. Datta Roy. New Delhi: Uppal.

Patwardhan, Anand. 2010. 'Reflecting Peace'. In *Bridging Partition: People's Initiatives for Peace between India and Pakistan*, edited by S. Kothari and Z. Mian (with Kamla Bhasin, A.H. Nayyar and Mohammad Tahseen), 95–102. Hyderabad: Orient Blackswan.

Paul, Madan C. and Sharat G. Lin. 1995. 'Social Insecurity, Vote Banks and Communalism: A Study of Bangladeshi Migrants in Delhi'. *Social Action* (New Delhi), 45 (4), October–December: 468–77.

Peiris, G.H. 2009. *Twilight of the Tigers: Peace Efforts and Power Struggles in Sri Lanka*. New Delhi: Oxford University Press.

Piliavsky, Anastasia. 2013. 'Borders without Borderlands: On the Social Reproduction of State Demarcation in Rajasthan'. In *Borderland Lives in Northern South Asia*, edited by D. Gellner, 24–46. Durham: Duke University Press.

Prakash, Anoop and Shailaja Menon. 2011. 'Fenced Indians Pay for Security'. *Economic and Political Weekly* (Mumbai), 46 (12): 33–37.

Prasad, Bimal. 2009. *Pathway to India's Partition, The March to Pakistan, 1937–1947*, Vol. 3. New Delhi: Manohar.

Priyamvatha, P. 2013. 'Ignominy of Homelessness'. *India Today* (New Delhi), 8 April: 20–21.

POT (Public Opinion Trends). 1999. *Nepal Series*, 5 (31): 316–17.

Qasimi, Ata-ur-Rahman. 2001. *Dilli ki Tarikhi Masjid* [The historic mosques of Delhi]. Delhi: Maulana Azad Academy.

Qureshi, Saleem M.M. 1972–73. 'Pakistan Nationalism Reconsidered'. *Pacific Affairs* (Vancouver), 45 (4): 556–72.

Rafiq, Manish. 2013. 'Bangladesher Chalchchitra: Khader Kinar theke Poonaruthanner Sambhabana' [in Bengali] (The Bangladeshi Films: The Hope of their Return from the Brink). In *Bangladesher Anya Cinema* [in Bengali] (The Other Cinema of Bangladesh), edited by S. Saha, Vol. 1, 56–64. Kolkata: Abhijan.

Raghavan, Srinath. 2013. *1971: A Global History of the Creation of Bangladesh*. Ranikhet: Permanent Black.

Raghavendra, M.K. 2014. 'Failure of Realism'. *Frontline* (Chennai), 4 April: 83–7.

Raha, Kironmoy. 2001. *Bengali Theatre*, 3rd ed. New Delhi: National Book Trust.

Rahman, Utpala. 2010. 'The Rohingya Refugee: A Security Dilemma for Bangladesh'. *Journal of Immigrant and Refugee Studies*, 8: 233–39.

Rahman, Tariq. 1995a. 'Refugees in the Face of Emerging Ethnicity in North-East India: An Overview', *Studies in Humanities and Social Sciences* (Shimla), 2 (1).

Rahman, Tariq. 1995b. 'Understanding Barpeta Massacre 1994: Ethnicity, Communalism and State,' *Towards Secular India: TSI A journal for the Study of Society and Secularism* (Bombay): 42–45.

Rahman, Tariq. 2002. 'Language, Power and Ideology'. *Economic and Political Weekly* (Mumbai), 37 (44–45), 2 and 9 November: 4556–60.

Rahul, Ram. 1983. *Royal Bhutan*. New Delhi: ABC Publishing House.

Rai, Satya M. 1965. *Partition of the Punjab: A Study of its Effects on the Politics and Administration of the Punjab, I, 1947–56*. Bombay: Asia.

Raja Mohan, C. 2006. *Crossing the Rubicon: The Shaping of India's Foreign Policy*. New York: Palgrave Macmillan.

Ramachandran, V.K. 1998. 'Photography: Documenting Society and Politics: A Frontline Feature on the Photography of Sunil Jana'. *Frontline* (Chennai), 15(19), September, 12–25. Available at http://www.frontline.in/static/html/fl1519/15190690.htm (accessed on 12 July 2014.)

Randhawa, M.S. 1954. *Out of the Ashes: An Account of the Rehabilitation of Refugees from West Pakistan in Rural Areas of East Punjab*. Chandigarh: Punjab Public Relations Department.

Rao, P.R. 1972. *India and Sikkim, 1814–1970*. New Delhi: Sterling.

Ray, Utsa. 2012. 'Eating "Modernity": Changing Dietary Practices in Colonial Bengal'. *Modern Asian Studies*, 46 (3): 703–29.

Rose, Leo E. 1974. 'Bhutan's External Relations'. *Pacific Affairs* (Vancouver), 47 (2), Summer: 103–20.

Rose, Leo E. 1994. 'The Nepali Ethnic Community in the Northeast of the Subcontinent'. *Ethnic Studies Report* (Kandy), 12 (1), January.

Roy, Anjali Gera. 2010. *Bhangra Moves: From Ludhiana to London and Beyond*. London: Asahgate.

Roy, Anupama. 2010. *Mapping Citizenship in India*. New Delhi: Oxford University Press.

Roy, Beth. 1996. *Some Trouble with Cows: Making Sense of Social Conflict*. New Delhi: SAGE Publications.

Rudolph, Lloyd and Susanne Hoeber Rudolph. 1987. *In Pursuit of Lakshmi: The Political Economy of the Indian State*. Chicago, IL: Chicago University Press.

Sabaratnam, T. 1990. *Out of Bondage: A Biography*. Colombo: The Sri Lanka Indian Community Council.

SARRC. 2006. *Violence, Memories and Peace-Building: A Citizen Report on Minorities in India and Pakistan*. Islamabad: South Asian Research and Resource Centre.

Sadiq, Kamal. 2009. *Paper Citizens: How Illegal Immigrants Acquire Citizenship in Developing Countries*. New Delhi: Oxford University Press.

Saha, K.C. 2003. 'The Genocide of 1971 and the Refugee Influx in the East'. In *Refugee and the State: Practices of Asylum and Care in India, 1947–2000*, edited by Ranabir Samaddar, 211–48. New Delhi: SAGE Publications.

Saikia, Sayeeda Yasmin. 2004. 'Beyond the Archive of Silence: Narratives of Violence of the 1971 Liberation War of Bangladesh'. *History Workshop Journal* (London), 58 (Autumn): 274–86.

Sainath, P. 1999. 'The Borderline of Caste'. *The Hindu*, 4 July.

Saint, Tarun K. 2010. *Witnessing Partition: Memory, History, Fiction*. New Delhi: Routledge.

Samaddar, Ranabir. 1995. 'A Twilight Zone that Divides a Road, a Village and a People'. *Asian Age* (New Delhi), 21 November.

———. 1997. 'Still they come—Migrants in the Post-Partition Bengal'. In *Reflections on Partition in the East*, edited by R. Samaddar, 87–139. New Delhi: Vikas Publishing House.

———. 1999a. *The Marginal Nation: Transborder Migration from Bangladesh to West Bengal*. New Delhi: SAGE Publications.

———. 1999b. 'Borders, Anxieties about Borders and All That'. Paper presented at the International Conference on Cooperation in South Asia: Resolution of Inter-State Conflicts, Jawaharlal Nehru University, New Delhi, 29–30 March.

———. 2013. 'Whatever Has Happened to Caste in West Bengal'. *Economic and Political Weekly* (Mumbai), 48 (36), September 7: 77–9.

Sarkar, Bhaskar. 2009. *Mourning the Nation: Indian Cinema in the Wake of Partition*. Durham, NC: Duke University Press.

Sayeed, Khalid Bin. 1960. *Pakistan: The Formative Phase*. Karachi: Pakistan Publishing House.

Scott, James C. 2009. *The Art of Not Being Governed: An Anarchist History of Upland Southeast Asia*. New Haven, CT: Yale University Press.

Sen, Meenakshi. 2003. 'Tripura: The Aftermath'. In *The Trauma and the Triumph: Gender and Partition in Eastern India*, edited by Jasodhara Bagchi and Subhoranjan Dasgupta, 123–34. Calcutta: Stree.

Sen, Sarbani. 2000. 'The Legal Regime for Refugee Relief and Rehabilitation in West Bengal, 1946–1958'. In *Refugees in West Bengal*, edited by P.K. Bose, 49–64. Calcutta: Calcutta Research Group.

Sen, Sudeep. 2013. Dream Whirligig, and Com Joshi's Lensman'. *Outlook* (New Delhi), 20 May: 58–59.

Sengupta, Shuddhabrata. 2005. 'Reflected Readings in Available Light: Cameraman in the Shadows of Hindi Cinema'. In *Bollywood: Popular Indian Cinema through a Transnational Lens*, edited by R. Kaur and A.J. Sinha, 118–40. New Delhi: SAGE Publications.

Sengupta, Sushanta. 2013. 'Epar Oparer Bondhan' [in Bengali] (The Bond between This Side and That Side). *Ei Samay* (Kolkata), 29 November.

Settar, S. and Indira B. Gupta (eds). 2002. *Pangs of Partition, The Human Dimension*, Vol. 2. New Delhi: Manohar.

Shah, Panna. 1950. *The Indian Film*. Bombay: The Motion Picture Society of India.

Sharma, Sukanya. 2011. 'Negotiating Transnational Identities on Indo-Myanmar Border: The Trade Factor'. *India Quarterly* (New Delhi), 67 (1), January–March: 53–64.

Shreshtha, Devendra Prasad and Hanumantha Rayappa. 1992. 'Levels of Agricultural Development and Pattern of Population Growth in Nepal'. In *Population Transition in South Asia*, edited by Ashish Bose and M.K. Premi. Delhi: B.R. Publishing.

Singh, Deepak K. 2010. *Stateless in South Asia: The Chakmas between Bangladesh and India*. New Delhi: SAGE Publications.

Singh, Supriya. 2013. *The Girls Ate Last*. Eltham, Australia: Angsana Publications.

Sinha, A.C. 1982. 'Immigrants from Nepal'. *The Statesman* (Calcutta), 17 April.

———. 2006. 'Search for Kirat Identity: Trends of De-Sanskritization among the Nepamul Sikkimese'. *Peace and Democracy in South Asia*, 2 (1 and 2). Available at http://himalaya.socanth.cam.ac.uk/collections/journals/pdsa/pdf/pdsa_02_01_01.pdf (accessed on 10 August 2014.)

Sinha, Hena. 2010. *Bangla Upanyashe Deshbhag: Bhagnaneerer Bedana* [in Bengali] (The Partition in the Bengali Literature: The Pain of the Broken Nest). Kolkata: Bangiya Sahitya Sansad.

Singh, Tarlok. 1969. *Towards an Integrated Society: Reflections on Planning, Social Policy and Rural Institutions*. Delhi: Orient Longman.

Sinharay, Praskanva. 2014. 'West Bengal's Election Story: The Caste Question'. *Economic and Political Weekly* (Mumbai), 49 (17), 26 April: 10–12.

Snedden, Christopher. 2001. 'What Happened to Muslims in Jammu? Local Identity, "the massacre" of 1947 and the roots of the "Kashmir Problem"'. *South Asia: Journal of Asian Studies* (Armidale), 24 (2): 111–34.

———. 2013. *Kashmir: The Unwritten History*. New Delhi: HarperCollins.

Spate, O.H.K. 1957. *India and Pakistan: A General and Regional Geography*. London: Methuen.

Sharma, Aasheesh. 2014. 'Why It's Trendy to Read Manto Again'. *Hindustan Times* (New Delhi), 27 July.

Subba, T.B. 2004. 'Anthropology, Human Rights and Tibetans in India'. In *Forced Migration in the South Asian Region: Displacement, Human Rights and Conflict Resolution*, edited by O. Mishra, 468–76. New Delhi: Manak Publications.

Sud, K.N. 1975. 'Nepalese in India'. *Hindustan Times* (New Delhi), 9 September.

Sulehria, Farooq. 2013. 'Lollywood: An Obituary'. *The News International*, 27 March. Available at http://www.thenews.com.pk/Todays-News-9-167643-Lollywood-an-obituary (accessed on 7 July 2014).

Sundaram, Ravi. 2010. *Pirate Modernity: Delhi's Media Urbanism*. New Delhi: Routledge.

Sur, Rajat Kumar. 2013. 'A Forgotten Street Culture'. *Purba Darshan: A Journal of Asian Studies* (Kolkata), 1(1), September: 153–61.

———. 2014. 'Kolkatar Swang: Ekti Swatantra Sanskritik Parichay Nirmaner Itibritta' [in Bengali] (The Swang of Kolkata: The History of the Origin of an Independent Cultural Identity). *Itikatha* (Kolkata), 2(2), December: 1–18.

Suryanarayan, V. 1996. 'Sri Lanka Tamil Refugees in Tamil Nadu'. *The Hindu*, 10 July.

———. 2003. 'Sheltering Civilians and Warriors: Entanglements in the South'. In *Refugee and the State: Practices of Asylum and Care in India, 1947–2000*, edited by Ranabir Samaddar, 321–54. New Delhi: SAGE Publications.

Susewind, Raphael and Raheel Dhattiwala. 2014. 'Spatial Variation in the "Muslim Vote" in Gujarat and Uttar Pradesh, 2014'. *Economic and Political Weekly* (Mumbai), 49 (39), 27 September: 99–110.

Swamy, Praveen. 2014. 'India's New Language of Killing'. *The Hindu* (New Delhi), 1 May.

Tagore, Sharmila. 2013. 'Ray's Magic Lantern'. *The Telegraph* (Kolkata), 2 December.

Talbot, Ian and Gurharpal Singh. 2009. *The Partition of India*. New Delhi: Cambridge University Press.

Taneja, Anand Vivek. 2009. 'Muslimness in Indian Cinema'. *Seminar* (New Delhi). Available at: http:www.india-seminar.com2009/598/598_anand_vivek_taneja.htm (accessed on 10 August 2014).

———. 2012. 'Saintly Visions: Other Histories and History's others in the Medieval Ruins of Delhi'. *The Indian Economic and Social History Review* (New Delhi), 49(4): 557–90.

———. 2013. 'Jinnealogy: Everyday Life and Islamic Theology in Post-Partition Delhi'. *HAU: Journal of Ethnographic Theory*, 3(3), Winter: 139–65.

TARU. 2010. 'Survey of Migrant Households—Cross Border Labor Mobility, Remittances and Economic Development in South Asia: Rapid Review Report'. New Delhi, November.

Taylor, S.P.G. 2003. 'Communal Tension in Bengal and the Riots of 1946'. In *The Trauma and the Triumph: Gender and Partition in Eastern India*, edited by J. Bagchi and S. Dasgupta, Vol. 2, 247–49. Kolkata: Stree.

Thapa, Rudraman. 1995. 'Nepali Migration into Assam: In Retrospect'. *Journal of Politics* (Dibrugarh), 2 (March): 80–92.

Thapan, Meenakshi and Navnita Chadha-Behera (eds). 2006. *Women and Migration in Asia*. New Delhi: SAGE Publications.

The Other Media. 2010. *Battling to Survive: A Study of Burmese Asylum Seekers and Refugees in Delhi*. New Delhi: The Other Media.

Turner, Frederick Jackson. 1893. 'The Significance of the Frontier in American History'. A paper read at the meeting of the American Historical Association in Chicago on 12 July 1893, during the World Columbian Exposition. Available at http://nationalhumanitiescenter.org/pds/gilded/empire/text1/turner.pdf

———. 1920. *The Frontier in American History*. New York: Henry Holt and Company.

———. 1932. *The Significance of Sections in American History*. New York: Henry Holt and Company.

Thieme, Susan and Simone Wyss. 2005. 'Migration Patterns and Remittance Transfer in Nepal: A Case Study of Sainik Basti in Western Nepal'. *International Migration* (Oxford), 43 (5): 59–06.

Timm, Fr. R.W. 2002. 'Christian Community in Bangladesh'. In *Religious Minorities in South Asia: Selected Essays on Post- Colonial Situations* (*Vol. I, Bangladesh, Pakistan, Nepal, Sri Lanka*, edited by M. Hussain and L. Ghosh, 53–69. Delhi: Manak Publications.

Tiwari, Badri Narayan. 2002. 'Partition Memory and Popular Culture'. In *Pangs of Partition: The Parting Ways*, edited by S. Settar and I.B. Gupta, 83–116. New Delhi: Manohar Publishers.

Ullman, Richard H. 1983. 'Redefining Security'. *International Security* (Cambridge, MA), 8 (1) Summer: 129–53.

UNHCR. 2009. *Note on the Nationality Status of the Urdu-speaking Community in Bangladesh*. Geneva: UNHCR. Available at www.unhcr.org/refworld/pdfid/4b2b90c32.pdf (accessed on 11 August 2014.)

Vakil, C.N. 1950. *Economic Consequences of Divided India: A Study of the Economy of India and Pakistan*. Bombay: Vora and Co.

van Schendel, Willem. 2001. 'Working Through Partition: Making a Living in the Bengal Borderlands'. *International Review of Social History* (Cambridge, UK), 46 (3), December: 393–421.

———. 2002. 'Stateless in South Asia: The Making of the India-Bangladesh Enclaves'. *The Journal of Asian Studies* (Ann Arbor), 61 (1), February: 115–47.

———. 2005. *The Bengal Borderland: Beyond State and Nation in South Asia*. London: Anthem Press.

Varadarajan, Siddharth. 2009. 'The Road Ahead for India and Pakistan'. *The Hindu*, 5 October.

Vasudevan, Ravi S. (ed.). 2000. *The Making Meaning in Indian Cinema*. New Delhi: Oxford University Press.

Vasudevan, Ravi S. 2010. *The Melodramatic Public: Film Form and Spectatorship in Indian Cinema*. Ranikhet: Permanent Black.

Vedavalli, L. 1994. *Socio-Economic Profile of Sri Lankan Repatriates in Kotagiri*. New Delhi: Konark.

Velamati, Manohari. 2009. Sri Lankan Tamil Migration and Settlement: Time for Reconsideration'. *India Quarterly* (New Delhi), 65 (3), July–September: 271–94.

Verghese, B.G. 1994. *Winning the Future: From Bhakra to Narmada, Tehri, Rajasthan Canal*. New Delhi: Konark.

———. 1996. *India's Northeast Resurgent*. New Delhi: Konark.

Vernant, Jacques. 1953. *The Refugee in the Post-War World*. London: George Allen and Unwin.

Virdi, Jyotika. 2010. 'Indian Cinema and Partition'. *Jump Cut: A Review of Contemporary Media*. Available at http://www.ejumpcut.org/archive/jc52.2010/VirdiSarkarRev/index.html (accessed on 23 March 2013).

Wallerstein, Immanuel. 1976. *The Modern World System: Capitalist Agriculture and Origins of the European World Economy in the Sixteenth Century*. New York: Academic Press.

Waseem, Mohammad. 1994. *Politics and the State of Pakistan*. Islamabad: National Institute of Historical and Cultural Research.

Waseem, Mohammad. 1998. 'Pakistan Country Paper,' in *Causes of Conflict in Developing Countries: South Asia—Regional Report*, edited by Kingsley de Silva (mimeo), 270–88. Kandy: ICES

———. 1999. 'Partition, Migration and Assimilation: A Comparative Study of Pakistani Punjab'. In *Partition and Region: Punjab and Bengal*, edited by I. Talbot and G. Singh. Karachi: Oxford University Press.

———. 2002. 'Causes of Democratic Downslide'. *Economic and Political Weekly* (Mumbai), 37 (44–45), 2 and 9 November: 4536–40.

Weiner, Myron. 1978. *Sons of the Soil: Migration and Ethnic Conflict in India*. Princeton, NJ: Princeton University Press.

———. 1990. 'Immigration: Perspectives from Receiving Countries'. *Third World Quarterly* (London), 12 (1), January: 140–65.

———.1992–93. 'Security, Stability, and International Migration'. *International Security* (Cambridge, MA), 17 (3), Winter: 103–120.

Weiner, Myron. 1993. 'Rejected Peoples and Unwanted Migrants in South Asia'. *Economic and Political Weekly* (Mumbai), August 21.

Werbner, Prina. 2012. 'Migration and Culture'. In *Oxford Handbook of the Politics of International Migration*, edited by M.R. Rosenblum and D.J. Tichenor. Oxford Handbooks Online.

Whitaker, Ben, Ian Guest and A Doctor. 1977. *The Biharis in Bangladesh*. London: Minority Rights Group.

Woodrow-Lafield, Karen A. 1998. 'Undocumented Residents in the United States in 1990: Issues of Uncertainty in Quantification'. *International Migration Review* (Staten Island, NY), 32 (1), Spring: 145–73.

Wright Jr., Theodore P. 1975. 'Indian Muslim Refugees in the Politics of Pakistan'. *Journal of Commonwealth and Comparative Politics* (London), 12: 189–205.

Xing, Zhang. 2009–10. 'The Bowbazar Chinatown'. In *India China: Neighbours Strangers*, edited by I. Pande, 396–413. New Delhi: India International Centre.

Yamaguchi, Hiroichi. 2006. *Japan*. New Delhi: National Book Trust.

Zagoria, D.S. 1969. 'The Social Bases of Indian Communism'. In *Issues in the Future of Asia: Communist and Non-Communist Alternatives*, edited by R. Lowenthal. New York: Praeger.

Zamindar, Vazira Fazila-Yacoobali. 2008. *The Long Partition and the Making of Modern South Asia: Refugees, Boundaries, Histories*. New Delhi: Penguin.

Zutshi, Ragini Trakroo, Jayshree Satpute and Md. Saood Tahir. 2011. *Refugees and the Law*, 2nd ed. New Delhi: Human Rights Law Network.

# Author Index

# Subject Index

# About the Author

**Partha S. Ghosh** is an Indian Council of Social Science Research (ICSSR) National Fellow at the Institute for Defence Studies and Analyses, New Delhi. Till recently he was a Senior Fellow at the Nehru Memorial Museum & Library, New Delhi. Earlier he was a Professor of South Asian Studies at the School of International Studies, Jawaharlal Nehru University, New Delhi. His previous academic positions are: Visiting Professor, Omeo Kumar Das Institute of Social Change and Development (OKDISCD), Guwahati; Humboldt Fellow, Heidelberg University; Ford Visiting Scholar, University of Illinois at Urbana-Champaign; and Visiting Fellow, Centre for Policy Research, New Delhi. He has also served as a Visiting Professor for short durations at the Maison des Sciences de l'Homme (MSH), Paris; University of Bordeaux; Indian Council for Cultural Relations (ICCR) Chair in Indian Studies at the Victoria University of Wellington, New Zealand; and University of Heidelberg. For many years Professor Ghosh served as the Research Director at the ICSSR, New Delhi. His areas of interest are South Asian politics, migrations, ethnicity and domestic politics-foreign policy interface. For several years Professor Ghosh was the Editor of *India Quarterly*, the flagship journal of the Indian Council of World Affairs, New Delhi.

Professor Ghosh has a long list of publications. His books include *Politics of Personal Law in South Asia* (2007), *Unwanted and Uprooted: A Political Study of Refugees, Migrants, Stateless and Displaced in South Asia* (2004), *Ethnicity versus Nationalism: The Devolution Discourse in Sri Lanka* (New Delhi: SAGE, 2003), *BJP and the Evolution of Hindu Nationalism* (1999, 2000), *Pluralism and Equality: Values in Indian Society and*

*Politics* (New Delhi: SAGE, 2000, co-edited), *Rivalry and Revolution in South and East Asia* (1997, edited), *Cooperation and Conflict in South Asia* (1989, 1995) and *Sino-Soviet Relations: US Perceptions and Policy Responses: 1849–1959* (1981). He has written many research articles in eminent professional journals, and also many newspaper articles.